THE PORTABLE CANADIAN HANDBOOK

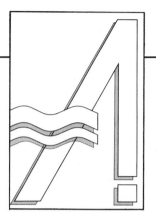

AN INDEX TO GRAMMAR, USAGE, AND THE RESEARCH PAPER

KEITH GILLEY
Langara Campus of
Vancouver Community College

WILLIAM HERMAN
The City College of
The City University of New York

D1057407

Holt, Rinehart and Winston of Canada, Limited
Toronto

Canadian Cataloguing in Publication Data

Herman, William, 1926-
    The portable Canadian handbook

Includes bibliographical references and index.
ISBN 0-03-922563-1

1. English language – Rhetoric. 2. English language –
Grammar – 1950-   . 3. English language – Usage.
4. Report writing. I. Gilley, Keith, 1939-
II. Title.

PE1408.H47   1989   808'.042   C88-094065-4

Publisher: David Dimmel
Editor: Donna Adams
Publishing Services Manager: Karen Eakin
Editorial Co-ordinator: Liz Radojkovic
Editorial Assistant: Graeme Whitley
Copy Editor: Barbara E. Turner
Cover and Interior Design: Falcom Design & Com-
    munications Inc.
Typesetting and Assembly: Q Composition Inc.
Printing and Binding: Webcom Limited

Printed in Canada

1 2 3 4 5   93 92 91 90 89

Preface

The Portable Canadian Handbook has been produced in response to requests from Canadian readers who found William Herman's original, *The Portable English Handbook*, a useful tool but who prefer a book that reflects our country's culture, including our distinctive ways of using the English language. In the process of giving the book a Canadian flavour, I have made contemporary much that, even in the 1986 American edition, was dated. Such changes are revealed especially in the extensive revision made to Part 3, "The Research Paper." As well as emphasizing Canadian research materials, Part 3 now includes a list of computer information retrieval services (databases), instructions on using the microfiche catalogue (which has replaced the card catalogue in most Canadian institutional libraries), and a section on documentation that has also been brought entirely up-to-date according to the style described in the 1984 edition of the *MLA Handbook for Writers of Research Papers*. (The only places in which correct MLA style has not been used are in the acknowledgements of sample paragraphs that have been transferred unchanged from the American edition.) Also entirely new are the two sample research papers, both of which focus on the effects of the computer on writing.

In keeping with William Herman's original intention, the chief purpose guiding the organization of this edition has been to make it useful not only to students and teachers in the classroom but also to students working on their own. Thus I have taken care to retain or enhance its five original key features, to wit: (1) its index organization makes it *easy* to use; (2) it is complete; (3) it contains many exercises; (4) its coverage of the research paper is thorough, including two models of different lengths; (5) it opens with a review of grammar that is thorough but concise.

1. Students find this book easy to use. For one thing, they do not have to waste time deciphering a complicated letter-and-number coding system. Instead, the principal reference section, Part 2 on usage and effective writing, is arranged alphabetically. Parts 1 and 3 on grammar and the research paper consist of units that progress in logical teaching and learning order. Also, there are cross-references throughout the book, and the index and list of correction symbols in the inside front and back covers offer further aids to easy access.

2. The book is complete without dwelling unnecessarily on detail. The alphabetically organized Part 2, ''An Index to Usage and the Principles of Effective Writing,'' contains entries ranging from Abbreviations to Verbs, the latter including a new explanation of the subjunctive mood. Part 2 concentrates on errors in usage and such important rhetorical matters as Unity, Diction, Coherence, and Paragraph Development. This section is conveniently thumb-indexed.

3. The book offers many exercises, ''Test Yourself'' sections that students can use to consolidate the gains they have made through studying the text. Exercises are available for most entries in Part 2 and at critical points in Parts 1 and 3. To provide immediate feedback, answers to the first five questions in objective exercises appear in an ''Answer Key'' preceding the book's index.

4. The book is comprehensive in its treatment of the research paper in Part 3. This section takes the student through a step-by-step approach to writing a research paper, including suggestions on how to use the library. Sample reference materials and bibliographic note cards are reproduced at appropriate stages. While the standard of bibliographic style is derived from the *MLA Handbook*, other styles are referred to, such as the various modes of documenting scientific papers. The section concludes with two complete sample research papers accompanied by instructive commentary. The short paper may serve best as a model for the novice researcher; the long paper is designed as a model for more advanced students.

5. Part 1, ''A Basic Grammar,'' gives students a basic grounding in the fundamentals they need to know before they begin serious writing. This opening section is intended both for use in the classroom and for independent study and review. It clearly explains

words, sentences, clauses, and phrases, in that order, with many examples and exercises along the way. Adding to the earlier editions' remarks on modifiers, the Canadian edition includes an explanation of *verbals*.

The book is, as its title denotes, *portable*. It is easy to carry around and keep handy—an especially important feature. Further, the basic approach to grammar, usage, and rhetoric lays before students only what they need in order to grasp their own writing problems. William Herman's original intention—with which I concur—was to avoid burdening students with excessive detail that might confuse them and take their attention away from their own writing. And it is our joint hope that we have written the book in a style that appeals to students, with plain diction and a lively tone, a middle tone, neither too formal nor too informal.

I want to thank the people who provided me with valuable support and useful criticism, in particular Robert J. Gregg, one of the authors of the *Gage Canadian Dictionary*, for his help regarding Canadian usage and spelling, and Judith Neamtan, Librarian at the Langara Campus of Vancouver Community College, for her help in identifying the latest in databases. I also wish to thank those of my colleagues in Canadian post-secondary institutions who reviewed the manuscript and made constructive comments, in particular, Bob Bennett, of the Centre for Continuing Education at McGill University, Reid Gilbert, of Capilano College, Karen Jakob, of Humber College, Birk Sproxton, of Red Deer College, and James Streeter, of Seneca College. My editors, Donna Adams and Tessa McWatt, earned my gratitude for doing well what all good editors do: gently but persistently massaging the book into shape, ever remembering that a writer is only human.

Finally, I want to thank my family: my children, Jason, Susannah, and Cameron, for respecting my need for peace and quiet in which to concentrate; and especially my wife, Margaret, for her constant reassurance and inexhaustible patience.

K.G.

Publisher's Note to Instructors and Students

This text book is a key component of your course. If you are the instructor of this course, you undoubtedly considered a number of texts carefully before choosing this as the one that will work best for your students and you. The authors and publishers of this book spent considerable time and money to ensure its high quality, and we appreciate your recognition of this effort and accomplishment.

If you are a student, we are confident that this text will help you to meet the objectives of your course. You will also find it helpful after the course is finished, as a valuable addition to your personal library. So hold on to it.

As well, please don't forget that photocopying copyright work means the authors lose royalties that are rightfully theirs. This loss will discourage them from writing another edition of this text or other books, because doing so will simply not be worth their time and effort. If this happens, we all lose—students, instructors, authors, and publishers.

And since we want to hear what you think about this book, please be sure to send us the stamped reply card at the end of the text. This will help us to continue publishing high-quality books for your courses.

Contents

PART 3 ▪ *The Research Paper*

Part 1
A Basic Grammar

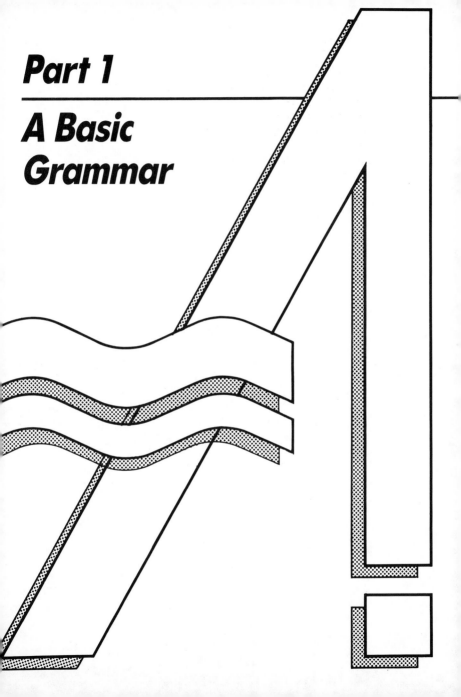

Why Study Grammar?

Grammar need not frighten you.

Grammar is simply a set of rules that describes how we all speak and write. The frightening word here is *rules*, because it makes us think of penalties for doing something wrong. But it need not. There are all kinds of rules, some of which we don't know are operating, and most of which we fall easily into obeying. For example, you understand what these words you are now reading are saying. The reason for this is that you are obeying the grammatical rules *you* already know.

For all of us, this understanding of some grammatical rules is unconscious, long ago learned and incorporated into our mental processes. The purpose of studying grammar here is to make more of these rules conscious and to do so for a number of very good reasons.

For one thing, grammar is interesting. Language is fascinating when you come to understand that its grammar is a remarkably coherent piece of human knowledge and that most human activities would be impossible without the subtle riches of linguistic communication. More important, however, the study of basic grammar can help you to improve your writing by reminding you of how it works. For example, if you know that a verb must agree with its subject, you are less likely to write "The humour and personal concern of Mr. Jones, my sociology professor, *is* what I like best about the course." Moreover, knowing grammatical terms can help you discuss your writing with instructors who are trying to make it more effective. If an instructor suggests that you *use subordinate clauses for subordinate ideas*, the suggestion will not get through to you if you do not know a clause from a hammock.

In Part 2 of this book, "An Index to Usage and the Principles of Effective Writing," you will find many suggestions for improving your writing. In order to use that index intelligently, you will need to understand the basic grammar we are about to discuss. We begin here with words and sentences, then go on to clauses and phrases.

Words

Words have been traditionally placed into classes called *parts of speech* according to their forms and the way they communicate meaning in sentences.

Before we begin to study the characteristic features of these classes, it is important to point out that some words can fall into more than one class, depending on how they are used in the sentence. For example, consider this group of sentences:

The *light* is hurting my eyes.

Let's *light* the Christmas tree.

Kathy has a *light* complexion.

She wore a *light* brown dress.

If your native language is English, you can make out the different meanings of these sentences quite easily. The fact that you *can* make out the different meanings is partly due to your ability to understand the word *light* in a different way in each sentence. In other words, in each sentence you are identifying *light* as a member of a different class, because in each sentence *light* has a different function.

You should be aware that hundreds of words can behave the way *light* does in those four sentences. Good dictionaries always define such words according to each of the various ways in which they can be used, and as we go along you will be able to see the logical process governing the classification of these words. But you need to know the characteristic features of the various classes.

Nouns

A noun is a word used to name something: a person, a place, an object, an idea. Words like *apple*, *car*, *table*, and *freedom* are nouns.

The following features of nouns will help you identify them:

1 Nouns can be made into plurals, usually by adding *-s* or *-es*.

    cars   peaches   taxes

2 Nouns can be made into possessives, usually by adding an apostrophe and *-s*.

    Danny's shoes

    Education's advantages

    a *car's* engine

3 Nouns can be preceded by words like *a*, *an*, *the*, *my*, *each*, *this*, *that*, or even another possessive noun. When you see such a word, you know a noun is coming.

    a horse

    this chicken

    Brian's computer

4 Nouns fit into the noun position in a sentence.

    The_____is beautiful.   The *house* is beautiful.
    I bought a_____.   I bought a *car*.
    I fought with my_____.   I fought with my *brother*.

5 Some nouns are formed by adding the suffixes (characteristic word endings) either to other nouns or to other parts of speech.

    store + *age* = storage

    deny + *al* = denial

    young + *ster* = youngster

TEST YOURSELF ON

Identifying Nouns

Circle the nouns in each of the following word groups.

  1. An African elephant

  2. The blue notebook.

3. I saw the light.

4. Cheese is available in New Brunswick

5. The Blue Jays are a good team.

6. Alligators are fond of dating crocodiles.

7. I have a boat on the lake.

8. A message from my nose to my brain tells me it's spring.

9. I am going to invite Conservatives to my party.

10. The fire is blazing in the fireplace.

Verbs

A verb is used to describe an action or a state of being.

> Carl *plays* basketball. (describes action)

> Carl *is* tall. (describes a state of being)

To be a sentence, a group of words must include at least one verb. Here are the features of verbs that will help you identify them and understand their functions:

1 Verbs can be single words *(sings, touched)* or they can consist of several words in a *verb phrase (has gone, will be working, might have been murdered). Has, will, might, have, be,* and *been* are called *auxiliary* or *helping verbs.* See pages 10–11 for more information about auxiliaries.

2 Verbs can change form to indicate a change of time. When verbs change form this way we say they have changed *tense.*

> Alice *is walking* to the movies.

> Alice *walked* to the movies.

The word in the sentence that can be changed to indicate a change of time—that's the verb.

3 Verbs have certain persistent forms. Nearly all have an *-ing* form (runn*ing*, jump*ing*). All third-person-singular present-tense verbs in the indicative mood end in the letter *-s* (pushe*s*, live*s*, grow*s*). Many verbs form their past tenses by adding *-d* or *-ed*.

4 Verbs in ordinary use always follow the subject in the sentence.

George *drives* a car. (George is the subject.)

Spring *came* early this year. (Spring is the subject.)

TEST YOURSELF ON

Identifying Verbs

Circle the verbs in the following sentences. Keep in mind the features of verbs you have just read about.

1. Margaret plays the piano.

2. A civil engineer earns a good salary.

3. My sister is jumping rope.

4. Carlita waited in the rain for an hour.

5. She trusted Jean to show up.

6. I called her apartment, but she had left.

7. The mail will be late today.

8. Mom has given Dad perfect instructions on how to use the camera.

9. Her teacher told her that she would graduate with the rest of her class.

10. I am curious about the history of racism in this country.

TEST YOURSELF ON

Identifying Verbs by Changing Tenses

Identify the verbs in the following sentences by changing their tenses.

Example: Tom *played* basketball for his team.
Tom *plays* basketball for his team.
Verb: played.

1. Tom played basketball for his team.

2. Rajit passes his examination easily.

3. The apples were delicious.

4. Your help makes a lot of difference to me.

5. He seemed unhappy.

6. In fact, Arthur works for his father.

7. She will be happy with his birthday present.

8. Frank understood the lesson.

9. The piano piece will end the program.

10. She has taken her father's car to school.

11. We will sit at different tables.

12. He has taken a vacation.

5 Verbs can either be *linking verbs* or *action verbs*. All verb forms of the verb *be* and such other verbs as *seem*, *appear*, *become*, and *feel* are *linking* verbs. They link together the subject of a sentence with another word describing the state of being of that subject.

Frank *felt* anxious.

You *are* beautiful.

Aunt Rosa *seemed* quiet.

Fred *is* a dancer.

Action verbs, on the other hand, describe action. They are either *transitive* or *intransitive*, depending on whether they act on something or not. When a verb is transitive, it acts on something, which is called the *direct object* of the verb.

Gravity *moves* the *planets*. *(Planets* is acted on by *gravity.)*

Women *date men*. (*Men* is acted on by *women*.)

An intransitive verb also describes action, but it does not act upon an object. It describes an action performed *by* the subject that also applies *to* the subject and nothing else.

Jacqueline *dresses* stylishly.

Patricia *sat* down.

Some verbs can be used transitively in one sentence and intransitively in another.

Enzo *works* hard. *(intransitive)*

Enzo works the tractor. *(transitive)*

6 Verbs have a property called *voice*. When the verb is in the *active* voice, the subject performs the action. When the verb is in the *passive* voice, the subject receives the action.

John *ate* a rabbit. (The rabbit went into John's stomach.)

John *was eaten* by a rabbit. (John went into the rabbit's stomach.)

7 Verbs also have a feature called *mood*, to indicate the manner or mode in which they are used. The *indicative* mood is used for ordinary statements of fact and questions, the *imperative* for issuing commands or giving directions, and the *subjunctive* for statements that are contrary to fact or that express potential or possibility.

I *gave* him five dollars. (indicative—statement of fact)

Can you *give* me a lift? (indicative—ordinary question)

Give me five dollars. (imperative—a command)

Turn left at the overpass. (imperative—a direction)

If I *were* a millionaire I would be happy. (subjunctive—contrary to fact)

TEST YOURSELF ON

Identifying Types of Verbs

Circle all the verbs you can find in the following sentences. Above each circle, write T if the verb is transitive, I if the verb is intransitive, and L if the verb is a linking verb.

1. I feel wealthy.

2. René smokes too much.

3. He is riding his motorcycle.

4. My father plays golf every Sunday.

5. The bomb exploded.

6. Bill loves hats.

7. My brother needs a job.

8. Lawyers are officers of the court.

9. Judges make rulings.

10. My fitness instructor is very slender.

11. Jane played the piano.

12. Students read all day long.

Auxiliaries

An *auxiliary* verb is also called a *helping* verb. Frequently, auxiliaries signal a reader that a verb is coming. *Is*, *did*, *have*, *was*, *can*, *may*, *would*, and *had* are all examples of auxiliaries.

The following features of auxiliaries will help you understand their form and functions:

1 Auxiliaries have different meanings and change the meanings of the verbs they couple with in various ways. For example, they indicate time and therefore change tense.

He *is* playing.   He *was* playing.

A subgroup of auxiliaries called *modals (should, would, could, can, may, might, must, ought to, have to, shall, will)* add meanings that suggest possibility, ability, obligation, and so forth.

He *can* play.   He *should* play.   He *must* play.

Notice that this group of auxiliaries is always used with the present tense stem of the verb.

2 Auxiliaries are widely used in asking questions.

Did you go?   *Must* you go?   *Can* you go?

3 The auxiliary that always appears with verbs ending in *-ing* is the verb *be*, in any of its forms:

He *is* playing.

I *was* playing.

He *has been* playing.

They *will be* playing.

4 Only two auxiliaries, *be* and *have*, are used with past verb forms such as *known, played, gone, remembered.*

I *am remembered.*   She *has gone.*   It *has been known.*

TEST YOURSELF ON

Identifying Auxiliaries

Write the proper auxiliary in each of the blank spaces in the following sentences.

1. You _____ visit your sick friend.

2. We _____ need some cream for our coffee.

3. He _____ planning to take a course in physics.

4. He says they _____ trying to climb the rocks.

5. When _____ you take the exam?

6. She _____ gone to the hairdresser's.

7. _____ you continue playing the piano?

8. _____ he see what we_____doing with the fish?

9. He _____ decided to find out if they _____ taken.

10. She _____ laughing and we _____ crying but nobody

_____ paying attention.

Adjectives

Adjectives modify nouns, making them more specific. A hamburger is good, but if we call it a *juicy* hamburger, we have said more about it. The following important features of adjectives will help you identify them and understand their functions:

1 Adjectives can be changed in form to compare two or more objects. The *comparative* form can be made by adding the ending *-er* to the basic adjective (called a *positive* form). The *superlative* can be formed by adding the ending *-est* to the positive form.

Positive	Comparative	Superlative
happy	happier	happiest
young	younger	youngest

However, some adjectives form the comparative and the superlative by adding the words *more* and *most*.

Positive	Comparative	Superlative
beautiful	more beautiful	most beautiful
honest	more honest	most honest
recent	more recent	most recent

Also, some adjectives form the comparative and the superlative irregularly.

Positive	Comparative	Superlative
good	better	best
bad	worse	worst
many	more	most

The comparative form is used to compare two objects.

He is *happier* than I am.

Her cat is *more beautiful* than mine.

My cold is *worse* today (i.e., "than it was yesterday").

The superlative form is used to compare more than two objects.

I am the *happiest* man in the world.

Here is the *most beautiful* hat I've seen.

She is the *best* player on the team.

2 Adjectives in a sentence appear after a linking verb or before a noun.

He was *happy*.   A very *happy* girl arrived.

3 Many adjectives have characteristic endings that can help you identify them. Here are a few:

-al (international)

-ant, -ent (resistant, excellent)

-able, ible (affable, irresistible)

-ar, ary (solar, ordinary)

-ive (attentive)

-ous (generous)

-y (funny)

-ish (foolish)

For more information on adjectives, see **Modifiers** and **Dangling Modifiers** in Part 2.

TEST YOURSELF ON

Identifying Adjectives

Identify all the adjectives you find in the following sentences.

1. My computer has a better memory than yours.

2. She seems courageous.

3. My father was kind to my mother.

4. She made him happier than he had ever been.

5. It is childish to be greedy.

6. The engine in this car is sound, but the body looks old.

7. She was athletic, girlish, and sensitive.

8. The greatest figure-skater I ever saw was Brian Orser.

9. That's a funny costume!

10. I get nervous when I have to take an exam.

Adverbs

Adverbs modify verbs, adjectives, other adverbs, and whole sentences.

Old people *often* sit. (modifies the verb *sit*)

She was *rarely* unhappy. (modifies the adjective *unhappy*)

I ate *too* quickly. (modifies the adverb *quickly*)

Unfortunately, we can't have a vacation this year. (modifies the whole sentence)

The following important features of adverbs will help you identify them and understand their functions:

1 A few adverbs, like adjectives, can change form to compare degrees or qualities by adding the endings *-er* and *-est*.

Positive	Comparative	Superlative
soon	sooner	soonest
quick	quicker	quickest

However, most adverbs form the comparative and superlative by adding the words *more* and *most*.

Positive	Comparative	Superlative
often	more often	most often
rapidly	more rapidly	most rapidly

A few adverbs form the comparative and superlative irregularly.

Positive	Comparative	Superlative
badly	worse	worst
well	better	best

2 Adverbs can often be moved from one position in the sentence to another without changing the meaning of the sentence. This is in contrast to adjectives, which must remain relatively fixed if the sentence is to make sense.

Adverbs	Adjectives
Often she was lucky.	*Lucky* she was often.
She *often* was lucky.	She *lucky* was often.
She was *often* lucky.	She was *lucky* often.
She was lucky *often*.	She was often *lucky*.

You can see that all the sentences under *Adverbs* make sense even though in each the word *often* is in a different position. On the other hand, only the last two sentences under *Adjectives* make sense.

However, not all adverbs are as moveable as *often*. For more on how to control the placement of adverbs, see **Misplaced Modifiers** and **Dangling Modifiers** in Part 2.

3 Adverbs frequently end in the suffix *-ly*, and many adverbs are formed by adding this suffix to an adjective.

Adjective + -ly = Adverb	
rapid	rapidly
sweet	sweetly
brave	bravely

The difficulty is that not all words ending in *-ly* are adverbs. Some nouns add *-ly* to form *adjectives*. There are not many of these, but they are important. Here are a few:

Noun + -ly = Adjective	
beast	beastly
father	fatherly
love	lovely
saint	saintly

TEST YOURSELF ON

Identifying Adverbs

Take this test by changing the conditions indicated in each of the sentences below. That is, change the manner (*rapidly* to *slowly*), the time (*now* to *then*), or the place or direction (*here* to *there*, *up* to *down*). The word you change is the adverb.

Example: Carla walked *slowly* into the lion's cage.
Carla walked *quickly* into the lion's cage.

1. Carla walked slowly into the lion's cage.

2. She drove in.

3. He went up.

4. He put the apple here.

5. He answered the question sweetly.

6. She is often absent.

7. He did his homework sloppily.

8. She lived upstairs.

9. He is never happy.

10. She walked over.

Verbals

Verbals are words which are derived from verbs but which function differently from verbs. They are distinct enough that they almost qualify as parts of speech. The three types of verbals are called participles, gerunds, and infinitives.

1 *Participles* are verb forms used with auxiliaries to form certain tenses.

He is *playing*.   He has *played*.

Playing is the present participle of the verb *to play*. *Played* is the past participle. (See **Verbs**, pages 6–10.)

However, participles are **true verbals** only when they are used as adjectives, to modify nouns. The following examples of participles will help you understand their form and function.

Skiing in the five kilometre race, Paul felt his heart *beating* wildly.

Skiing modifies the noun *Paul*. *Beating* modifies the noun *heart*. Both *skiing* and *beating* are thus true verbals.

Paul had *coated* his skis with the *required* wax.

Coated is a past participle, but not a true verbal. *Required* is a true verbal, modifying the noun *wax*.

The spectators *watching* Paul's progress cheered him on.

Watching is a participle, a true verbal. *Watching Paul's progress* is a participial phrase modifying the noun *spectators*. Notice that participles can take objects.

2 *Gerunds* look like participles, but they are used only as nouns. The following examples will help you understand their form and function:

Skiing is Paul's obsession.

Paul considers the *waxing of skis* an essential skill.

Waxing of skis is a gerund phrase serving as the object of the verb *considers*. Notice that gerunds, like participles, can take objects. If you have difficulty distinguishing between gerunds and participles, try putting a possessive pronoun before the word in doubt. "Paul considers *his* waxing of skis . . ." functions grammatically: *waxing* is a gerund. "The spectators *their* watching Paul's progress . . ." does not make sense: *watching* is a participle.

A possessive pronoun used before a gerund is called the *subject of the gerund*. Note that while a possessive pronoun is correct when used before a gerund, a personal pronoun usually is not. For example, sentences such as "*My* skiing is important to me" and "Do you object to *my* sitting here?" are correct; "*Me* skiing is important to me" and "Do you object to *me* sitting here?" are unacceptable. However, the apparent rule is not hard and fast: 'His friends were stunned at *him*, a man obsessed with competitive skiing, *sitting* out the race.''

3 *Infinitives* are the base forms of verbs and are usually preceded by the word *to: to ski, to compete, to win.* They look like verbs, and they can act in the same way that verbs do by taking subjects, objects, and complements.

> Paul asked his fans *to stand* back and *give* him air.

Fans functions as the subject of *to stand* and (to) *give.*

> Paul was eager *to catch* his breath.

His breath functions as the object of *to catch.*

> Paul wanted his fans *to be* considerate.

Considerate functions as the complement of *to be.*

However, although they resemble verbs, infinitives really function as nouns, adjectives, and adverbs. The following examples will help you understand how they work.

> *To catch his breath* was his main concern.

The infinitive phrase acts like a noun, serving as the subject of the verb *was.*

> Crossing the finish line was a moment *to treasure.*

The infinitive acts like an adjective, modifying the noun *moment.*

> The crowd pressed too close *to allow him breathing space.*

The infinitive phrase acts like an adverb, modifying the adverb *close.*

Like the other verbals, infinitives can take objects.

TEST YOURSELF ON

Identifying Verbals

Identify all the verbals you can find in the following sentences.

1. I would rather be sailing.

2. My goal is a career in the performing arts.

3. A prejudiced judgement of the singing would be unfair.

4. Judith wanted to become a bus driver, which left her old-fashioned grandmother puzzled.

5. Thinking it over, Ed decided to resist the proposed law.

6. The following is a shining example of good writing.

7. Choosing to do unto others as you would have them do unto you is a sign that you have matured.

8. Did the Conservatives' gambling their re-election on the free trade issue seem to make sense?

9. Ground between her teeth for a whole evening, the pencil was clearly the worse for wear and had to be thrown away.

10. They were required to go home at midnight or, failing that, to telephone.

Prepositions

A preposition connects a noun or a pronoun with other parts of the sentence.

> The man *in* the truck drove away. (connects *man* and *truck*)
>
> She passed him *by*. (connects *passed* and *him*)

A preposition forms a prepositional phrase when it is followed by a noun, with or without an article (*a, the*) or a possessive pronoun (*my, her*) in between.

> *in* the truck   *to* Alberta   *at* her house.

In these phrases, we would call the word *truck* or *Alberta* or *house* the *object of the preposition*—the word that the preposition connects to the rest of the sentence. (More on the prepositional phrase will be found on pages 38–42.)

Prepositions usually denote direction or position, as you can see from this list:

abroad	behind	from	through
about	below	in	throughout
above	beneath	inside	till
across	beside	into	to
after	besides	like	toward
against	between	near	under
along	beyond	of	until
alongside	by	off	up
amid	concerning	on	upon
among	despite	onto	with
around	down	over	within
at	during	since	without
before	for		

In addition to these, there are a number of prepositions in English that consist of more than one word. Here are some:

according to	by way of	in spite of
ahead of	contrary to	in view of
apart from	due to	instead of
as for	in addition to	on account of
as well as	in case of	out of
away from	in front of	up to
because of	in place of	
by means of		

All the words in the first list *may* be used as prepositions. Some words on the list—*during, among, with,* and others—are regularly prepositions, but most of the words are also used as other parts of speech. For example, you may recall that the words *in, over,* and *by* were adverbs when used in the following ways:

She drove *in*.

She drove *over*.

She drove *by*.

But the same words are prepositions when used in these ways:

She drove *in* the truck.

She drove *over* the bridge.

She drove *by* the house.

Prepositions occupy certain typical positions in sentences. Notice the positions occupied by the prepositions italicized in the following sentences:

The house *across* the road is mine.

The name *on* the door is my mother's.

She wrote an essay *on* Shakespeare.

He was carrying a bag *of* potatoes.

She went *to* her class.

He lived *in* my building.

Notice that there is nearly always an article or a possessive pronoun (*the, his, my*) between the preposition and the following noun to form what we call a prepositional phrase (see page 39 for more on this structure).

TEST YOURSELF ON

Using Prepositions

Using the following list of nouns, select twenty of the prepositions listed above and make prepositional phrases by using an article or a possessive pronoun (*the, a, my, his, her, your*) where appropriate.

Nouns

farm	tomato	day
apple	pizza	camp
newspaper	chopsticks	lake
automobile	burglary	room
ferry	television set	cage
chair	stadium	planet
horse	football field	

Example: beyond the lake

Conjunctions

Conjunctions are words that act to join together words, groups of words, or whole sentences. Different conjunctions do different jobs, and there are three different classes of them to consider.

1 Co-ordinating Conjunctions

This group consists of the seven words *and, or, but, yet, for, nor*, and *so*. All are commonly used to join together two independent clauses (see pages 33–38), while suggesting a relationship between them.

> She was poor, *but* she felt rich in spirit. (suggests an unexpected contrast)

> He was happy, *for* he had passed his exams. (suggests cause)

Note: The punctuation of such sentences is important. You will find more on the subject in Part 2 under **Comma Rules**.

But and *yet* are frequently used to join pairs of adjectives in suggesting unexpected contrast.

> She was angry *yet* calm.

> She was aggressive *but* gentle.

In addition to the co-ordinating conjunctions, there are four pairs of *correlatives: both . . . and, not only . . . but also, either . . . or*, and *neither . . . nor*.

> *Both* apples *and* peaches are delicious.

> *Not only* apples *but also* peaches are delicious.

> He was *either* young *or* inexperienced.

> He was *neither* young *nor* inexperienced.

2 Conjunctive Adverbs

Conjunctive adverbs are a group of words used to connect independent clauses; they act in a sentence like the word *therefore*.

> The school was over; *therefore*, he decided to take a long vacation.

> The children were playing in the yard; *therefore*, he took a nap.

The following words are commonly used as conjunctive adverbs:

besides	hence	indeed	subsequently
consequently	however	moreover	therefore
furthermore	in fact	nevertheless	thus

He ate the whole pie himself; *furthermore*, he was not sorry.

He ate the whole pie himself; *moreover*, he was not sorry.

He ate the whole pie himself; *nevertheless*, he was not sorry.

Note that conjunctive adverbs can change position in the sentence and still act as connectors.

The clock struck twelve; *therefore*, Meng got ready to leave.

The clock struck twelve; Meng, *therefore*, got ready to leave.

The clock struck twelve; Meng got ready to leave, *therefore*.

Note too that when words like *and* join two sentences together, they are preceded by a comma; when words like *therefore* join two sentences together, they are preceded by a semicolon or a period and followed by a comma. (For more detailed information on punctuating with conjunctive adverbs, see **Comma Rules, Fragments**, and **Semicolon** in Part 2.)

3 Subordinating Conjunctions

Subordinating conjunctions are words used to join a word or a word group to a sentence by subordinating that word or word group—by making it less important.

Writer A says: *Although John doesn't sing well*, he is a member of the church choir.

Writer B says: *Although he is a member of the church choir*, John doesn't sing well.

Writer A is emphasizing one kind of disparity and Writer B another. Each is modifying his main declaration—the part of each writer's sentence that follows the comma—in a different way. Each has therefore *subordinated* a different idea by introducing it with a subordinating conjunction.

It's important to note that the subordinated portion can begin or end the sentence.

John doesn't sing well *although he is a member of the church choir*.

Although he is a member of the church choir, John doesn't sing well.

Subordinating conjunctions generally act like the word *although*. Depending on the meaning you want to convey, you can use any of the following words as subordinating conjunctions:

after	provided	whatever
although	since	when
as	that	whenever
because	though	where
before	unless	wherever
if	until	whether
lest	what	while

TEST YOURSELF ON

Using Conjunctions

1. Write ten sentences in which a co-ordinating conjunction joins two sentences. Try to use each of the seven co-ordinating conjunctions at least once.

2. Write eight sentences in which you use each pair of correlatives at least once.

3. Write a dozen sentences in which you use each of the conjunctive adverbs on page 23 at least once.

4. Take the sentences you just wrote and change the position of the conjunctive adverb in each sentence.

5. In how many of the sentences that you have written in response to exercise 3 can you substitute a co-ordinating conjunction for a conjunctive adverb? Try the substitution and find out.

Pronouns

Pronouns are words that can replace nouns. Such words as *he, she, him, her, them, somebody, mine,* and *this* are all pronouns. An important word associated with pronouns is *antecedent.* Consider these examples:

I just saw *Alice. She* seems fine.

Richard put *his* money into real estate.

In the first example we say that the word *Alice* is the antecedent of the pronoun *she*. In the second example we say that the word *Richard* is the antecedent of the pronoun *his*.

Not all pronouns have antecedents in all cases, but you will want to keep the term in mind and be sure that pronouns agree with their antecedents in your writing. For more details on this subject, see **Pronoun References** in Part 2.

All pronouns can occupy some of the typical noun positions in sentences, although not all can occupy every noun position.

Sentence with a Noun
The *man* is over there.

Pronouns Substituted for the Noun
He is over there.

Mine is over there.

Somebody is over there.

Neither is over there.

Sentence with a Noun
I know the *man*.

Pronouns Substituted for the Noun
I know *him*.

I know *hers*.

I know *somebody*.

I know *neither*.

Here are the chief kinds of pronouns and the names they are known by:

1 Personal Pronouns

I	me	my, mine
you	you	your, yours
he	him	his
she	her	her, hers
it	it	its
we	us	our, ours
they	them	their, theirs

2 Reflexive Pronouns

myself	ourselves
yourself	yourselves
himself	themselves
herself	
itself	

3 Relative Pronouns

who	which
whose	that
whom	

Relative pronouns are used to connect a subordinate word group to another part of the sentence.

John, *who* sings well, is a member of the church choir.

The foreign country *that* I like best is Italy.

The antecedent of *who* in the first example is *John*, and the antecedent of *that* in the second example is *country*.

Sometimes a relative pronoun is omitted but understood in a sentence.

The car [that] I liked was a Toyota.

4 Interrogative Pronouns

who	which
whom	what

Interrogative pronouns are used to ask questions.

Who is your friend?

Which would you like?

What did you say?

5 Demonstrative Pronouns

this	these
that	those

Demonstrative adjectives *point* to a noun, but they may also be used by themselves as demonstrative pronouns.

> *This* hat is mine. (pointing to a noun)
>
> *This* is mine. (as a pronoun)

6 Indefinite Pronouns

Common indefinite pronouns are the following:

one	everybody	everything	neither
no one	nobody	something	none
anyone	somebody	nothing	most
everyone	other	all	more
someone	another	few	
anybody	anything	either	

7 Reciprocal Pronouns

> each other
>
> one another

TEST YOURSELF ON

Using Pronouns

A Use each of the following words in two sentences.

1. many	3. that	5. either	7. all
2. his	4. few	6. several	8. three

B Replace each of the italicized words in the sentences below with a pronoun. In some cases you will have to drop a few words from the sentence.

Example: My *grandmother* needs false teeth.
          She needs false teeth.

1. My *grandmother* needs false teeth.

2. My grandmother needs false *teeth*.

3. My *boss* complained to me.

4. *People* are funny.

5. *Members of Parliament* are politicians.

6. The *sea* can never be emptied.

C Underline all the pronouns you can find in the following sentences. Some sentences have more than one.

1. His shoes are brown.

2. Mine are black.

3. Everybody knows something.

4. You should be honest with yourself.

5. My brother wanted him to be nice to everyone.

6. Anyone can tell that you have a sunburn.

7. Students are friendly to one another.

8. Nothing bothers me when I am by myself.

9. She put herself in his position.

10. Much will be gained and nothing lost if you go swimming with us this afternoon.

11. Neither will be enough.

12. Several will be fine.

Sentences

Now that we have discussed words, we must begin to consider sentences. Sentences can be commands or directions on how to do something or go somewhere (imperative sentences):

Turn on the lights. Make a left turn.

Or they can be questions (interrogative sentences):

Who are you?

Or they can be statements (declarative sentences):

I saw Uncle Antoine this morning.

In this section, we will be concerned mainly with sentences that are statements.

Basic Sentence Facts

1 Every sentence can be divided into two parts because every sentence accomplishes two things: (1) it names something (an object, an idea, a person, a place), and (2) it says something about what it has just named.

Part 1 (What Is Named)	Part 2 (What Is Said About It)
Dogs	bark.
Birds	are beautiful.
Babies	drink milk.

The thing named we call the *subject* of the sentence; what is said about the subject we call the *predicate*.

In a sentence like *The large, tropical birds are beautiful*, we say that the *complete subject* is *the large, tropical birds* but that the *simple subject* is *birds*. The simple subject *birds* is the thing about which something is being said. The complete subject, *the large tropical birds*, *includes* the simple subject and other words that describe it more exactly. A complete subject can also look like this: *the birds in the trees*, where *birds* is the simple subject.

2 Every predicate contains at least one verb. A single verb may contain several words, also called a *verb phrase* (examples: *has been married, should be married*). A sentence can never have only an *-ing* verb.

3 To find the subject of a sentence, first find the verb. You can do this by locating the word in the sentence that denotes action or a state of being, the word that can change tense.

George *feels* good.   George *felt* good.

Clearly, *feel* is the verb because it changes tense. Now if we ask the question *who* (or in some sentences *what*) *feels*, and refer to the sentence for our answer, we must reply *George*. And *George* is the subject.

In the sentence *George and Pierre travelled to Europe together*, the verb is *travelled*. When we ask *who travelled*, we get the answer *George and Pierre*. Sentences like this one, therefore, are said to have a *compound subject*. A compound subject has more than one part.

TEST YOURSELF ON

Locating Subjects of Sentences

A In each of the following sentences, underline the subject. To find the subject, first locate the verb—the word that denotes action or a state of being and that can change tense. Then ask the question *who* or *what* (of the verb). The answer will be the subject.

1. Whisky burns my tongue.

2. She is beautiful.

3. My father is a policeman.

4. Hot dogs taste good sometimes.

5. Parents sometimes scold their children.

6. The truck driver and his helper quit early.

7. Misery loves company.

8. You and your brother look happy.

9. The pipe blows bubbles.

10. Everybody seemed sad.

B In the following sentences, underline the complete subject, and circle the simple subject.

Example: Big, friendly (bears) live in the woods.

1. The charming English teacher gave us an assignment.

2. The man in the blue suit looked sinister.

3. The beautiful old woman was fascinating.

4. Sensible young people think ideals are as important as material

   wealth.

5. My mother's old college roommate came to town.

Basic Sentence Parts

Depending upon the kind of verb in the sentence—transitive verb
or linking verb—we can conveniently identify the following basic
parts:

1 Predicate Noun and Predicate Adjective
A predicate noun or predicate adjective completes the sense of a
linking verb, suggesting an equivalence between the subject and the
predicate noun or predicate adjective.

> My mother is a *police officer*. (subject + linking verb + *predicate
> noun*)

> Allan is *friendly*. (subject + linking verb + *predicate adjective*)

My mother is what? and *Allan is* what? are the questions to ask to
locate the predicate adjective or predicate noun.

2 Direct Object and Indirect Object
Direct and indirect objects occur with action verbs. The direct object
is the part of the sentence that *receives* the action of the verb. Consider
this sentence:

> André threw the ball.

Threw is the verb (it denotes action and can change tense). Who
threw? André, the subject. André threw what? The ball—so *ball* is
the direct object of the verb.

The italicized portions of the following sentences are all direct objects:

> Mechanics repair *automobiles*. (Automobiles are repaired.)
>
> My aunt lent me her *car*. (The car was lent.)
>
> The professor taught her students *biology*. (Biology was taught.)

Now for the sake of keeping in practice, locate the verb and the subject of each of these sentences, using the who-what method we've been discussing.

The indirect object is the person or thing in the sentence *to* or *for whom* the action is performed.

> My brother gave his friend a camera.

The action performed in the sentence is the brother giving the camera. *Camera* is the direct object. It was *given*. *To whom*? To his friend. *Friend* is the indirect object.

3 Object Complement (Noun or Adjective)

The object complement completes the meaning of the direct object by identifying it more exactly. A noun can do this; so can an adjective.

> subj.   verb   dir. obj.   obj. comp., noun
> We considered the cowboy a hero.
>
> subj.   verb   dir. obj.   obj. comp., adj.
> We considered the cowboy foolish.

TEST YOURSELF ON

Identifying Basic Sentence Parts

A Underline the simple subjects of the following sentences once and the predicates twice.

1. My mother is a good cook.

2. We elected Anne our spokesperson.

3. He had an idea.

4. Everybody likes ice cream.

5. Some do not.

6. Sally taught her sons arithmetic.

7. All Ottawa politicians are the same.

8. Your friendly local shopkeeper is really a small businessperson.

9. Unknown composers often write famous songs.

10. He gave me his heart for Christmas.

11. That film made my friends angry.

12. The big, grey clouds are drifting slowly.

13. Summers are too long.

14. The boys considered the girls intelligent.

B Describe each word of the predicates you underlined in A by writing above each word VL (for linking verb), VT (for transitive verb), VI (for intransitive verb), PA (for predicate adjective), PN (for predicate noun), DO (for direct object), IO (for indirect object), OCN (for an object complement that is a noun), and OCA (for an object complement that is an adjective).

Clauses and Phrases

Clauses and phrases are groups of words. Sentences are frequently made up of phrases and clauses.

Clauses

A clause is a group of words having both a subject and a verb. A clause can be either *independent* or *dependent*. Another word for *dependent* is *subordinate*. Another word for an *independent clause* is a *sentence*.

Independent Clause/Sentence = Subject + Verb = Can Stand Alone

Dependent/Subordinate Clause = Subject + Verb = Cannot Stand Alone

Dependent clauses can act as parts of sentences, as adjectives, adverbs, and nouns.

1 Adjective Clauses

Cats are animals *that can scratch.*

The italicized portion of the sentence is an adjective clause. It is a clause because it has a subject, *that*, and a verb, *can scratch*. It is dependent because it cannot stand alone. The word *that* makes it dependent on being hooked to something else—a noun (in this case *animals*), which it modifies. It is, therefore, an adjective clause.

An adjective clause can modify a noun regardless of where the noun appears in the sentence.

Chairs *that are covered in velvet* look elegant. (modifies *chairs*)

Three points about adjective clauses are worth noting here:

A We usually make this distinction in using *who* and *which*: when the noun being modified refers to a person, we use *who*; when it does not, we use *which*. But we often use *that* instead of either one.

She is the athletic star *that* (or *who*) the nation has hoped would appear.

The decision *which* (or *that*) the Supreme Court made in 1988 ruled unconstitutional any law discriminating against a woman's choosing to have an abortion.

B Frequently, in both speech and writing, we use adjective clauses but omit the subordinating conjunction.

The loan ~~that~~ I negotiated will be paid off in two years.

C Sometimes a *which* clause can modify a whole sentence—not just a single noun in it.

It was a great party, *which everyone agreed was a pleasant change for a Saturday night at Robert's.*

2 Adverb Clauses

Babies drink milk *when they are hungry*.

The italicized group of words is an adverb clause. It modifies the word *drink* by answering the question, *When* do babies drink milk? They don't drink it all the time, only *when they are hungry*. The adverb clause differs from the adjective clause in two ways: (1) its connecting word (*when*, in this cause) is not part of the clause but stands at the beginning of it; (2) it can be moved around in the sentence and still do its job.

Babies drink milk *when they are hungry*.

When they are hungry, babies drink milk.

Adverb clauses begin with one of the subordinating conjunctions listed on page 24 (words like *whenever, although, if, until, unless*, and so forth).

3 Noun Clauses

What I am eating tastes good.

The italicized group of words is a noun clause. Occupying the place of a noun, it is the subject of the sentence. You can test to see if this is true by asking the question: *what* tastes good? The only satisfactory answer is *what I am eating*. Therefore, the clause is the subject. But the noun clause can also occur in most of the other positions typically occupied by nouns (that is, as predicate noun, as direct object, or in the position of a noun in a prepositional phrase).

That is *what I am eating*. (predicate noun)

I love *what I am eating*. (direct object)

I am satisfied with *what I am eating*. (object of a proposition)

Noun clauses are very commonly signalled by words like *whoever, whatever*, and *what*.

I can supply *what you need*.

Whoever runs will be short of breath.

Whatever needs fixing can go to the repair shop.

TEST YOURSELF ON

Clauses

A Using the word *who, whom, which,* or *that,* construct a clause that modifies each word or group of words below:

Example: money
money *that I spent yesterday*

1. money

2. people

3. little boys

4. apples

5. laws

6. women

B Using a word such as *although, unless, because,* or any of those listed on page 24, construct a clause to go with each of the following simple sentences.

Example: The scholarship fund gave me what I asked for.
Although my grades weren't as good this year as they were in 1987, the scholarship fund gave me what I asked for.

1. The scholarship fund gave me what I asked for.

2. It has hair on it.

3. Onions give me indigestion.

4. I can see my brother.

5. Exams make me nervous.

6. The office was empty.

C Underline the clause in each of the following sentences and above each write ADV if the clause is acting as an adverb, N if it is acting as a noun, or ADJ if it is acting as an adjective.

1. What I want for supper is fish.

2. Until you come home, I have to babysit with our little brother.

3. The car that pleases me most uses the least gas.

4. Whatever you do is all right.

5. The man whom I pointed out is my uncle.

6. I don't know what will happen next.

7. Although I came early, the show was sold out.

8. I am disappointed because my grades were not higher last term.

9. The basketball court that is in the gym is occupied day and night.

10. The thing that hurts most is indifference.

D Below are printed ten sentences. Part of each sentence is in *italics*. Place an I over the part that is independent, a D over the part that is dependent. After that, decide whether the clauses marked with a D are adjective, adverb, or noun clauses; label each as ADJ, ADV, or N.

1. *The man* who was here yesterday *was Judy's father*.

2. *Although I never went past the tenth grade*, I can write well.

3. Whenever you cross the yellow line in the centre of the road, *you're in danger*.

4. *Whoever asks* should be directed to the Administration Building.

5. I can guess *what you're thinking*.

6. The doctor *whom I saw* said I'd recover in a week.

7. *The tractor*, which I bought last year, *is in terrible condition*.

8. You'd better look *before you leap*.

9. I'll wait for you *until nine o'clock*.

10. Because he was late getting up, *he missed the bus*.

Phrases

A phrase is a group of words having neither a subject nor a verb. Phrases can be used as adjectives, adverbs, and nouns.

1 Phrases Used as Adjectives

The woman *in the blue suit* spoke quietly.

The birds *flying toward the barn* are beautiful.

My father was a man *known for his kindness*.

I need shoes *to wear to the wedding*.

The italicized part of each example is a phrase being used as an adjective. By function, each is an adjective phrase in the sentence. However, it is convenient to learn to recognize adjective phrases by what they look like—that is, by the first word (or headword) of the group.

The italicized phrase in the first sentence is a *prepositional phrase* because its headword *in* is a preposition and it looks like the prepositional phrases we spoke of on pages 19–21. The second phrase is a *participial phrase* because it begins with a participle, *flying*. The third is also a participial phrase because it begins with the participle *known*. The fourth is an *infinitive phrase* because it begins with the infinitive form of a verb, *to wear*. Each of the names we gave the phrases in this paragraph is a name given by form, by what the phrases look like. But each phrase is the same in function: each acts as an adjective.

2 Phrases Used as Adverbs

She spoke *in the afternoon*.

The italicized group of words has the form of a prepositional phrase (preposition + the + noun), but it answers the question *when* and functions as an adverb modifying the verb *spoke*.

To avoid fatigue, he rested.

Here we see another kind of phrase that can be used as an adverb—an infinitive phrase (*to avoid fatigue*), modifying *rested*.

3 Phrases Used as Nouns

Riding a motorcycle can be dangerous.

The italicized group is a phrase used as a noun—the subject of the sentence. (Test this by asking *what* can be dangerous. The only satisfactory answer is *riding a motorcycle* because the sentence does not say that *riding can be dangerous* or that *a motorcycle can be dangerous*.)

In form, this is called a *gerund phrase*. (See Verbals.) It is named after the *gerund*, the *-ing* form of the verb that acts as a noun (for example, as the word *swimming* does in the sentence *Swimming is fun*). In function, it is a noun phrase.

A gerund phrase can go in other noun positions in the sentence. Here it is the direct object of the verb *like*.

I like *riding a motorcycle*.

An infinitive phrase can also be used as a noun.

To ride a motorcycle can be dangerous.

I like *to ride a motorcycle*.

Occasionally, a prepositional phrase is used as a noun in the position of the subject of the sentence:

Over the fence is out.

After supper is all right.

TEST YOURSELF ON

Phrases

A Underline each phrase you find in the sentence below, and above each write ADJ if the phrase is being used as an adjective, ADV if it is being used as an adverb, or N if it is being used as a noun. Some sentences have more than one phrase.

1. She travelled in the afternoons.

2. The cameras carried in stock were all cheap.

3. After a few minutes, he saw the sun set over the trees.

4. Known for his pure tenor voice, he often gave concerts in the park.

5. To love deeply is my goal in life.

6. I saw him riding a bicycle.

7. Come up to my house for an hour.

8. He wants to study chemistry.

9. I saw the shoplifter running down the street.

10. She stood next to my brother.

B For each of the sentences or parts of sentences given below, construct the type of phrase that is called for to serve the given function.

Example: The man (participial phrase: adjective) looked sinister.
The man *walking alone* looked sinister. (The phrase acts as an adjective modifying *man*.)

1. The man (participial phrase: adjective) looked sinister.

2. Karen travelled (prepositional phrase: adverb).

3. (Participial phrase: noun) should be a pleasure.

4. She looked like a student (participial phrase: adjective).

5. He talked (prepositional phrase: adverb)

6. (Infinitive phrase: adverb), he broke up with his girl.

7. She typed (prepositional phrase: adverb).

8. He loved (participial phrase: noun).

9. She begged me (infinitive phrase: noun).

10. She was a woman (participial phrase: adjective).

C First, go through the passage printed below and underline all the phrases you can find. Then answer the questions that follow the passage.

In the morning, James is at his best. He snorts out of bed with a whoop and a shout and beams a smile at everyone in the house. Flying through the air with the greatest of ease, he usually stops first at his trapeze. There he gets the kinks out of his kinkless muscles and beats a tattoo on the ceiling with his straining toes as he soars higher and higher. After this, to make sure that nobody in the household is still sleeping, he puts a rock and roll tape into his portable stereo player, turns the volume up loud and aims it up the stairs. Now he'd like to tell a few jokes. Determined to find a willing listener, he jumps on a few adult shoulders and shouts directly in their ears ''Wanna hear a joke?'' Each of James's manoeuvres lights up the house with the sights and sounds of vitality and confirms us in our perception that a new day has arrived and all's right with the world.

1. Can you point to a participial phrase that functions as an adjective?

2. Point out two examples of a prepositional phrase.

3. How many infinitive phrases are there in the passage? How does each one function in the sentence?

4. Is there a phrase in the passage acting as a noun?

5. Point out two examples of phrases acting as adverbs and specify whether each is prepositional, participial, or infinitive.

TEST YOURSELF ON

Recognizing Parts of Speech

From the following passage, find at least two examples of the parts of speech named below and write them in the space provided.

Sometimes I think that I'm the world's sloppiest person. I can't seem to keep my little office in any kind of reasonable order. Papers accumulate on my desk, overflow onto the floor in great piles, get put on shelves but fall out of them down onto the floor again, and, finally, force me out of my office and into the nearest empty one. My inclination is to spread out, I guess. A woman who knows me pretty well says I'm determined to fill up empty space; however, she doesn't quite understand that filling up empty space is painful to me. When the papers start to pile up, I agonize over them. And when I have filled up several offices, I go into a real tailspin. For that's when I must go back to my own place and start cleaning up, filing some things, throwing other things out, and generally restoring order. It's no use, because no sooner do I succeed in that restoration than the whole cycle starts again.

Nouns _____

Adjectives _____

Adverbs _____

Verbs _____

Auxiliaries _____

Verbals _____

Pronouns _____

Prepositions _____

Conjunctions _____

If you have worked your way carefully through this part of the book, you should now be ready to tackle any of the entries in Part 2. These entries all focus on specific writing problems or principles of effective writing. Many of them cannot be understood without reference to some of the ideas discussed in Part 1. Thus you should continue to use this part as a reference. The improvement it can make in your writing is worth the effort.

Part 2

An Index to Usage and the Principles of Effective Writing

Note: Cross-references in **boldface** type are to other entries in Part 2. Cross-references in regular type are to sections in Part 1.

Abbreviations

Over the years there has developed a set of conventions that tell us when we may and when we may not use abbreviations in essay writing. Here they are divided into the appropriate and the inappropriate.

Appropriate

Forms of Address and Titles

It is permissible to use such abbreviations as *Mr., Mrs., Ms., Messrs.* (plural of *Mr.*), *Mmes.* (plural of *Mrs.*), *St., Jr., Sr., M.D.* (Doctor of Medicine), *D.D.S.* (Doctor of Dental Surgery), *B.A.* (or *A.B.*, Bachelor of Arts), *M.A.* (Master of Arts), *Ph.D.* (Doctor of Philosophy), and *H.E.* (*His* or *Her Excellency*, a title appropriately used only by the Governor General, ambassadors and bishops).

Conventional Foreign Words and Phrases

The following abbreviations of certain useful foreign words and phrases may be used:

c *or* ca (about)	i.e. (that is)
cf. (compare)	v. (see)
e.g. (for example)	viz. (namely)

Technical Terms

The following technical terms may be abbreviated:

BTU (British Thermal Unit)	cm (centimetre)
cc (cubic centimetre)*	g (gram)

*cm^3 is preferable in technical writing.

km (kilometre)   mph (miles per hour)
km/h (kilometres per hour)   rpm (revolutions per minute)
CPU (central processing unit)

Organizations, Institutions, Government Agencies, Trade Unions
It is common practice to abbreviate the names of institutions. Occasionally, an abbreviation forms an *acronym*, that is, a pronounceable
word, such as WHO for World Health Organization. In an essay,
first write out the whole name of the organization; subsequent references to it may be abbreviated.

> The Committee on Dental Education (CODE) issued a stern warning
> about the use of kangaroo flakes in toothpaste. CODE officials noted
> that very few kangaroos have had good checkups this year. CODE
> stated that fluorides are the most effective additives for toothpaste.

Here is a brief list of some common abbreviations for well-
known groups:

NHL (National Hockey League)
CBC (Canadian Broadcasting Corporation)
NDP (New Democratic Party)
NFB (National Film Board)
RCMP (Royal Canadian Mounted Police)
SPCA (Society for the Prevention of Cruelty to Animals)
UN (United Nations)
UNESCO (United Nations Educational, Scientific, and Cultural
    Organization)

Expressions of Time
These may be abbreviated:

1434 BC (before Christ)
AD 953 (anno domini; in the year of Our Lord)
8 a.m.
7:29 p.m.
NST (Newfoundland Standard Time)
AST (Atlantic Standard Time)
EST (Eastern Standard Time)
CST (Central Standard Time)

MST (Mountain Standard Time)
PST (Pacific Standard Time)
YST (Yukon Standard Time)
DST (Daylight Saving Time)

A

Inappropriate

It is inappropriate to abbreviate in the following ways in a written text (many of these abbreviations are acceptable in addresses and certain short references):

Titles

Wrong   *Prof.* Tremblay and *Sen.* Tremblay are brothers.
Right   *Professor* Tremblay and *Senator* Tremblay are brothers.

Given Names

Wrong   Geo., Wm., Thos., Ed., Jas., Theo.
Right   George, William, Thomas, Edward, James, Theodore

Places

Wrong   I plan to spend my vacation in *Sask.*
Right   I plan to spend my vacation in *Saskatchewan.*

Wrong   Of all the underdeveloped areas, *S.A.* has the highest economic growth rate.
Right   Of all the underdeveloped areas, *South America* has the highest economic growth rate.

Wrong   To get to Sarah's, take County *Rd.* to Manawaka
Right   To get to Sarah's, take County *Road* to Manawaka.

Wrong   Paulo lives at Elm *St.* and Carson *Ave.*
Right   Paulo lives at Elm *Street* and Carson *Avenue.*

Days of the Week, Names of the Months, and Holidays

Wrong   The King died on *Tues.*
Right   The King died on *Tuesday.*

Wrong   The academic calendar runs from *Sept.* to *Apr.*
Right   The academic calendar runs from *September* to *April.*

A

Wrong   For *Xmas*, I'd like a new bathrobe.
Right   For *Christmas*, I'd like a new bathrobe.

Academic Courses

Wrong   Richard is failing *phil* and *psych* this term.
Right   Richard is failing *philosophy* and *psychology* this term.

Miscellaneous Items

Do not use an ampersand (&) unless it is part of an official company name, for example, *Earl H. Rovit & Son., Inc.* In ordinary circumstances, use *and* in place of &.

Do not abbreviate ordinary words through laziness or because you are uncertain about their spellings. Do not, for example, substitute *thru* for *through*, *tho* for *though*, *yrs* for *yours*, or *mtns* for *mountains*.

TEST YOURSELF ON

Abbreviations

By using abbreviations where appropriate, correct the errors in the following sentences. Place the letter C next to the sentences that you think are correct.

1. _____ Mister Tuten took the stand and stated that at 8 ay em, when the accident took place, he was travelling at 55 kilometres per hour.

2. _____ The physician on duty administered 100 cubic centimetres of insulin.

3. _____ He said he was able to get through the winter by taking a short vacation in Florida at Christmastime.

4. _____ By using the Panama Canal, ships can avoid going around the tip of S.A.

5. _____ The Canadian International Development Agency is committed to giving aid to third world countries. When asked, a spokesperson for the Canadian International Development Agency said that last year's budget had been in excess of $2,000,000 and that this year's budget figures would be available by St. Patty's day.

6. _____ Many species of fish inhabit this lake, e.g., pike, perch, and catfish; some specimens have measured as much as forty-five centimetres and weighed as much as six and a half kilograms.

7. _____ On Mon., Wed., and Fri. I go from psych to phil and then on to gym.

8. _____ Driving west toward Alberta you can pass through Man. and Sask.

9. _____ Before I started my diet on Thurs., I weighed 100 kgs.

10. _____ The mtns look toward Alta. on one side and B.C. on the other.

11. _____ Gail & Grace have both broken up with their boyfriends.

12. _____ His parents hope that Vincent de Marco, Junior, will grow up to be like Vincent de Marco, Senior.

A

Active Voice

See **Voice**.

Adjectivals

An adjectival is any word, phrase, or clause that can act as an adjective in a sentence. See **Modifiers**.

Adverbials

An adverbial is any word, phrase, or clause that can act as an adverb in a sentence. See **Modifiers**.

Ambiguity

When something can be read in two or more ways, then we say it is ambiguous, that is, it has ambiguity. *Mail leaves tomorrow* could mean that *the mail will leave tomorrow* or that the writer of the message wants *his leaves* mailed tomorrow. See **Modifiers, Pronoun References, Shifts**.

Antecedents

An antecedent is what a pronoun may sometimes refer to and must always agree with. See **Pronoun References, Shifts**; Pronouns.

Apostrophe

The apostrophe is a mark used by convention (agreement) to signal contractions, possessives, and certain special plurals.

Contractions

The rule for contracting two words into one is to use the apostrophe in place of the missing letter or letters.

are not = aren't
Roger is = Roger's (see also Possessives, below)
cannot = can't
it is = it's (but *its*, without the apostrophe, is possessive)
let us = let's
we have = we've
would not = wouldn't
you will = you'll

Possessives

In English, there are two ways to express possession, ownership, and similar relationships when using nouns.

> The *office of the manager* is located at the top of the stairs.

> The *manager's office* is located at the top of the stairs.

Both ways are correct. In general, we would use the first method (using the word *of*) for nouns that stand for something inanimate and the second (using an apostrophe and -s) for nouns representing something animate.

> **Animate**   Rose's room; Nick's office; Brenda's eyes; Colin's book
> **Inanimate**   the light of the moon; the colour of the paint; the score of the game

Nevertheless, it is valuable to know that both forms mean the same thing: possession. If you are having trouble with the apostrophe -s (*'s*) form, you can determine whether or not the *'s* is needed by

A

using the fact we've just noted. For example, suppose that one of your essays contained the following phrases, and that you were unsure whether an apostrophe were needed in any of them:

1. Charles horse
2. Clarences cross
3. Janes boss
4. Marks loss
5. the Smiths went

Using the fact previously noted—that the *of* form and the *'s* form both mean the same thing—we can try to see whether any of the five phrases can be turned into the alternative *of* form.

1. Charles horse $=$ the horse of Charles
2. Clarences cross $=$ the cross of Clarence
3. Janes boss $=$ the boss of Jane
4. Marks loss $=$ the loss of Mark
5. the Smiths went $\neq$ the went of Smith

We can see clearly that the first four examples *can* be changed into the alternative form and therefore need an apostrophe in the original form—as follows:

1. Charles' horse (or Charles's horse)
2. Clarence's cross
3. Jane's boss
4. Mark's loss

Example 5 needs no apostrophe because it contains no possessive.

TEST YOURSELF ON

Changing from One Form of Possession to the Other

Using the rule you have learned, change the following into the alternative possessive form:

1. the outcome of the game

2. the tirade of Jenny

3. the argument of the mayor

4. the future of the girl

5. the impatience of my father

6. the wit of Mario

7. the engine of Phil

8. the winged chariot of time

9. the ale of Gail

10. the acting of Raoul

Forming the Possessive of Singular Nouns and Indefinite Pronouns

In order to form the possessive of singular nouns and indefinite pronouns* that do not end in -s simply add *'s*.

my father's cigarette	a doctor's appointment
my mother's comb	anybody's game
TV Guide's features	teacher's pet
everybody's future	nobody's fault

Forming the Possessive of Plural Nouns

To form the possessive of plural nouns, add *'s* to nouns with an irregular plural (e.g., *children, men, women*), and add *only* an apostrophe to plurals ending in -s.

Irregular Plurals	*Regular Plurals*
men's clothing	the *boys'* hats (the hats belong to more than
women's liberation	one boy)
children's growth	his *parents'* devotion (the devotion of two
	people: mother and father)
	students' grades (the grades of more than
	one student)

Note: Never use an apostrophe for any of the possessive personal pronouns. That is, *his, hers, its, yours, ours, theirs, mine* already indicate possession and need no additional marks to indicate that fact.

A

Forming the Possessive of Nouns Ending in -s, -x, and -z

The rule here is the same as the previous one for plurals ending in -s.

Marx' philosophy	the Joneses' garage
Lefty Gomez' career	Ulysses' voyage
the boss' daughter	Venus' orbit

However, you have a spelling option based on how you pronounce these possessives. For example, if you actually say *boss-es* in pronouncing *boss'* then you may spell it to conform with the pronunciation. Thus the following alternative spellings would also be correct:

Marx's philosophy

Lefty Gomez's career

the boss's daughter

Forming the Possessive of Two or More Nouns

Place the *'s* after the last item in a series of nouns if you want to indicate joint ownership; place the *'s* after each item if you want to show individual possession but talk about both items in the same sentence.

I stayed at *Ted and Ed's* house. (They own the house together.)

I have sympathy for *Ted's and Ed's* troubles. (Each man's troubles are his own; the speaker declares sympathy for that which belongs to each man—and does so in the same sentence.)

Forming the Possessive of Compound Nouns

In a compound noun, the last word takes *'s*:

my mother-in-law's generosity

the Attorney General's order

my brother-in-law's book

Special Plurals

The apostrophe is used to form the plurals of certain signs, numbers, letters, and words.

Count up all the + *'s* and − *'s*.

On her quizzes, she had all *8's* and *9's*.

he had trouble pronouncing his *s's* and his *th's*.

Don't use too many *which's* in your writing.

Also, the apostrophe is sometimes used for plural dates: "The 1800's were a time of change." However, it is preferable to write *1800s* for this kind of date.

TEST YOURSELF ON
The Correct Use of the Apostrophe

Each of the sentences below has an apostrophe problem for you to correct. Except for a few that are placed correctly, the apostrophe is either misplaced, superfluous, or missing and badly needed.

1. The womens' liberation movement grew stronger year by year because of it's militant posture.

2. During the 60s, many young people would'nt obey societys rules; their's was the age of rebellion.

3. Charles horse had a charley horse before Tuesday's race's.

4. The Provincial Attorney Generals office is flooded with work; street crime's seem to be taking place at a record rate.

5. If you get 90s and 100s on your exams, your grade point average this term will be higher than Max's.

6. If she wont give you her book's, thats all right; Grandmas grammars are hers to give.

7. Its in your pant's pocket.

8. My mother-in-laws kindness to others has made her famous in Summerside.

A

9. Scott's and Neil's book is likely to be published this year.

10. Mrs. Shiraz's uncles cousin was the first member of his family to arrive in Canada.

11. My father-in-laws' storytelling is always fascinating.

12. I'm tired of Corey Harts; play someone elses records.

13. Anybody's troubles are my trouble's.

14. Bacon and egg's is my favourite breakfast.

15. Peoples interests are determined by the complicated fact's of their lives.

Appositives

An appositive is a noun, or some structure that can take the place of a noun, that is set right next to another noun to further explain or define it. It is set in *apposition*—in the next position in the sentence—to the noun on which it will expand. An appositive can be a single word or a group of words. In the following examples, the first noun is in italics and the appositive is in boldface.

The *teacher*, **Davis**, spoke slowly. (word)

Wayne Gretzky's *skill*, **shooting a puck into a net**, earns him a large salary. (phrase)

The *teacher*, **a physics professor**, spoke slowly. (noun phrase)

An appositive can occur in a sentence in various positions where nouns occur.

That was *Danielle*, **my friend**.

He liked my *car*, **a '57 Chevy**.

A useful fact to understand about the appositive is that this structure is really an abbreviated clause.

The *teacher*, **Davis**, spoke slowly. (The appositive *Davis* is really a part of the clause *whose name is Davis*.)

Wayne Gretzky's skill, **shooting a puck into a net**, earns him a large salary. (The appositive, *shooting a puck into a net* is really a part of the clause *which is shooting a puck into a net*.)

A

There is another important fact about appositives that you should understand. Some are not essential to complete the meaning of the sentence; these are therefore called *non-restrictive*. They are set off by commas. The appositives are italicized in the examples:

The doctor, *Allan Peters*, treated me for the flu. (The essential meaning is "The doctor treated me for the flu.")

For Christmas, I got a camera, *a Pentax Reflex*. (The essential meaning is "For Christmas, I got a camera.")

However, some appositives *are* essential to the meaning of the sentence; these are called *restrictive*. They are *not* set off by commas because they *belong* to the noun they are set beside.

The mechanic *John* gave my car a lube job. (The essential meaning here is not that *the* mechanic gave my car a lube job, but that the mechanic named John did the job—there were several mechanics and *John* identifies the correct one.)

I was helped through college by my Aunt *Marie*. (If the speaker had had only one aunt, then the word *Marie* would have been non-essential; as it is, *Marie* identfies one of the aunts and is an essential word.)

(See also **Comma Rules**, 5, for more on restrictives and non-restrictives.)

TEST YOURSELF ON

Appositives

The following sentences all contain appositives, but they are all improperly punctuated. First, underline the appositive; then decide whether or not to set it off by a comma or commas. *Remember*: if the appositive is essential to the sentence (restrictive), do not use the comma or commas; if the appositive is non-essential (non-restrictive), do use the comma or commas.

A

1. We slept that night in the tent an old piece of canvas with a dozen holes in it.

2. The colonel Thomas Jones commanded the regiment as if he were a drill sergeant.

3. The police arrested two people a pickpocket and a burglar.

4. My aunt who lives in Nova Scotia Rebecca Rose writes historical romances.

5. We had to read *War and Peace* a book by someone named Tolstoy.

6. The constable we liked best Singh treated us like human beings.

7. We were in the hands of the mediator the one who would decide.

8. Arthur Hopkins was a law professor a position he had attained at a very young age.

9. The fighter we were eager to see O'Sullivan was up against a tough opponent.

10. The author of the book Alice Munro will be autographing copies at Eaton's today.

Auxiliaries

Auxiliaries, or helping verbs, are the following: forms of the verb *be (am, is, are, was, were); has, have, had; do, did; can, could; be able to; may, might; would; should; must; ought to; shall* and *will*. For detailed information on how auxiliaries are used, see Part 1, Auxiliaries.

Capitalization

The use of capital and lower case (small) letters follows a number of clear rules. We can number these for convenience as follows:

1 Beginning a Sentence
Capitalize the first words of sentences.

> *L*asagna and cannelloni are Italian delicacies.
>
> *T*ravel agents are now offering charter flights to Mars.

2 The Pronoun *I* and the Interjection *O*
Capitalize these no matter where they occur in the sentence.

> Doug says *I* am a space cadet.
>
> From far and wide, *O* Canada, we stand on guard for thee.

3 Days of the Week, Months, Holidays
Capitalize all of these no matter where they occur in the sentence.

Tuesday	April	Remembrance Day
Friday	August	Easter
Sunday	January	Christmas

4 Titles of Books, Plays, Films, Television Shows, Short Stories, Poems
Capitalize all of these no matter where they occur in the sentence. Articles and conjunctions are not capitalized unless they begin the title.

> *Who Has Seen the Wind* (book)
>
> *The Ecstasy of Rita Joe* (play)
>
> *Roxanne* (film)
>
> *The Journal* (television show)
>
> "Boys and Girls" (short story)
>
> "Lycidas" (poem)

Important note: These titles should also be either italicized or enclosed in quotation marks, as they are above. See **Italics** and **Quotation Marks** for further information.

C

5 Proper Names, Proper Adjectives, and Titles

Capitalize the names of persons or geographical entities. Capitalize an official title only when it is used with the title-holder's name.

Kathy Roe	Fredericton, New Brunswick
Middle East	Mars
Italian	Maritimer

Senator Pitfield is unavailable. The *senator* is late today.
The government appointed a *senator* today.

6 Historical Events, Historical Terms, Historical Artifacts

Use a capital letter for items such as the following:

War of 1812	the Enlightenment
the British North America Act	the Augustan Age
the Magna Carta	the Battle of Vimy Ridge

7 Terms Associated with Colleges and Universities

Use a capital letter for courses that are specifically designated by number. Use a lower case letter for those that are not so designated (except languages, which are always capitalized). Use a capital letter for academic titles when they are used with the title-holder's name.

Biology 137

Math 11

French

anthropology (as in, ''I am taking anthropology this term.'')

Dean Linda Marcus

Professor Pat Merrivale

Dr. Dennis Turner

When a specific person's title is used without the surname, capitalization of the title is optional.

Dean Marcus left the meeting. The dean (or Dean) had another important appointment and could delay no longer.

8 Miscellaneous Items

Use a capital letter for the names of public or private buildings.

the Parliament Buildings	the CN Tower

the Lion's Gate Bridge	the Château Frontenac
Fortress Louisbourg	the West Edmonton Mall

C

Use a capital letter for the names of both private and public organizations.

Agriculture Canada	the Red Cross
the United Nations	the Modern Language Association
the Edmonton Oilers	Statistics Canada

Use a capital letter for virtually all references to things religious; deities, churches, adjectives based on these.

God	the United Church
the Lord	Jewish
Anglican	the Bible
Christ	Rama
Moses	the Koran

Use a capital letter for products referred to by brand name.

Xerox	Rice Krispies	Bombardier
Scotch tape	Kleenex	Sony

TEST YOURSELF ON
Capitalization

Read carefully each of the following sentences. Where there is an error in capitalization, indicate the error by writing CAP in the space provided. Then correct the error. If the sentence is correct, write C in the space.

1. _____ On friday we are taking the venus Special to Mars.

2. _____ Bernard LeBlanc MP made his maiden speech in parliament today; the member spoke on rock 'n' roll.

3. _____ To be mayor of New York is a little crazy.

4. _____ He didn't say i was a federal government employee —he said I was a snivel servant.

C

5. _____ An arabian knight is oil right.

6. _____ Prime Minister Mulroney favours a policy of lasting peace in the Middle East.

7. _____ The level of pollution in lake Erie is superseded only by the level of pollution in the Love canal, according to measurements made last january by Environment Canada.

8. _____ The work of a university president would be no challenge to my History Professor.

9. _____ Next semester, I plan to take chemistry, Biology 101, mathematics, History 98, and Physics.

10. _____ The community colleges in this province are enjoying increases in student enrolment.

Case

Case refers to the function of a noun or pronoun in a sentence. In the sentence *He lent me his father's car*, the nominative case form *he* shows it is being used as the subject; the objective case form *me* indicates that the pronoun is an object; the possessive case form *father's* shows that the noun is possessive.

Case endings of nouns were once important in English but have now all but disappeared. Nouns have just two case forms: (1) the common form, for example, *doctor*, and (2) the possessive form, *doctor's*. It is the case of pronouns—where there are three cases: nominative, objective, and possessive—that requires the writer's attention.

Nom.	I	we	you	he	she	it	they	who
Poss.	my	our	your	his	her	its	their	whose
	mine	ours	yours		hers		theirs	
Obj.	me	us	you*	him	her	it*	them	whom

Following are the rules for the proper use of each case.

Nominative

1 Use the nominative case for the word in the subject position in the sentence. We need hardly say more about this rule, since few of us are likely to write sentences like "*Us* have a date tomorrow" or "*Me* want an apple."

2 Use the nominative case *who* in a clause where it is clearly the subject of the verb; do not be tempted into using *whom* by the words that intervene between *who* and its verb.

clause

There is a professor *who I know works hard to make contact with students*. (*Who* is here the subject of *works*; you should not make the error of thinking that *whom* should replace it because of the words *I know*.)

clause

He saw some men in uniform *who he thought were Mounties*. (*Who* is the subject of *were*; do not think that *whom* should replace *who* because of the words *he thought*.)

3 In formal writing, use the nominative case after forms of the verb *be (is, are, was, were*, and so forth). Many good writers and speakers use the objective case, but formal writing requires the nominative.

Formal It is *I*. It might be they.
Informal It's *me*. It might be *them*.

4 Use the nominative case, in formal writing, after the conjunctions *as* and *than*. In these constructions, the pronoun is the subject of an omitted verb. In informal writing and in speech the objective case is frequently used.

*As you can see, *it* and *you* do not change in the objective cases, only in the possessive.

C

Formal   He is hungrier *than I* [am]. (*Am* in this sentence is omitted but understood by the reader, and *I* is the subject of *am*; therefore, *I* must be in the nominative case.)

Informal   He is hungrier *than me*. (Here the conjunction *than* is made into a preposition, with *me* as its object.)

Formal   We are as intelligent as *they* [are]. (*Are* is omitted but understood by the reader, *they* is the subject of *are* and is therefore in the nominative case.)

Informal   We are as intelligent as *them*. (*As* is made into a preposition, with *them* as its object.)

5 Use the nominative case when the pronoun appears as part of a compound subject.

Jack and *he* played cards last night. (The compound subject of this sentence is the words *Jack* and *he*; the whole sentence really combines two sentences: "*Jack* played cards last night" and "*He* played cards last night.")

6 Use the nominative case of a pronoun in an appositive where the pronoun explains or further identifies a noun that is either the subject or the predicate noun.

appositive

It was the *coach, he alone*, who held the team together. (*Coach* is the predicate noun; therefore, *he*, the appositive pronoun, is in the nominative case.)

appositive

Those *two*—the policeman and *he*—prevented a robbery. (*Two* is the subject; therefore, *he*, the pronoun in the appositive, is in the nominative case.)

Note: Not all pronouns in appositives are in the nominative case. See **Objective** for examples of appositive pronouns in the objective case.

Possessive

1 Use pronouns in the possessive case to indicate possession, source, authorship, and similar relationships.

I liked *her* speech very much.

I know *whose* house that is.

The committee made *its* recommendations quickly.

2 In formal writing, use the possessive case of a noun or a pronoun before a *gerund*. A gerund is the *-ing* form of a verb that is used as a noun; for example, *swimming* is a gerund when used in the sentence ''Swimming is fun.'' (See Verbals.) In informal writing, you will sometimes see the objective case used instead of the possessive.

> ***Formal***   There was a good reason for *his* working hard.
> ***Informal***   There was a good reason for *him* working hard.
>
> ***Formal***   She was glad about *Michel's* organizing the concert.
> ***Informal***   She was glad about *Michel* organizing the concert.

Notice the subtle difference in meaning in the last pair of examples. In the first, the emphasis is on the organizing of the concert. In the second, the emphasis is on Michel.

See description of gerunds in Part 1.

Objective

1 Use the objective case where the pronoun is the object of a verb.

> The weird noise troubled *him*. (*Him* is the object of *troubled*.)
>
> *Whom* did you invite? (*Whom* is the object of the verb.)

It is important to understand that where the object is a compound construction containing, say, a proper name and a pronoun, the pronoun must be in the objective case.

> The club elected Sheila and *me* co-chairpersons. (*Sheila* and *me* are the objects of the verb *elected*; therefore, *me* is in the objective case; do not say ''Sheila and *I*'' in a construction like this. You would not say, ''The club elected *I* chairperson.'')

2 Use the objective case when the pronoun is the object of a verbal. A verbal is either a verb ending in *-ed* or *-ing*, or is an infinitive, that is, a verb with the word *to* preceding it (*to work, to play*, and so forth). (See Verbals.)

C

Knowing *him* was a pleasure. (*Him* is the object of *knowing*.)

Whenever I see babies, I want to kiss *them*. (*Them* is the object of *to kiss*.)

Note: An exception to this rule occurs when the infinitive is *to be* and its subject is unexpressed; then formal usage requires that the nominative case be used after the infinitive.

Formal   I wouldn't want *to be he*.
Informal   I wouldn't want *to be him*.

3 Use the objective case for a pronoun that is the object of a preposition.

Three of *us* went to the movies last night. (*Us* is the object of the preposition *of*.)

She is the professor for *whom* I worked hardest. (*Whom* is the object of the preposition *for*.)

It is important to note that on occasion two pronouns will be objects of the same preposition. Both must then be in the objective case.

Bob and I both wanted the job; the boss would have to choose between *him* and *me*. (Both *him* and *me* are objects of the preposition *between*).

4 In formal writing, use the objective case *whom* in a clause where it is clearly the object of the verb. In informal writing, *who* is widely used instead of *whom*.

Formal   She is the visitor *whom* we expected. (*Whom* is the object of *expected*.)
Informal   She is the visitor *who* we expected.

Formal   *Whom* are you criticizing? (*Whom* is the object of *are criticizing*.)
Informal   *Who* are you criticizing?

The word *whom* is now used less and less, even among well-educated writers and speakers. Still, in certain cases, *whom* is the much-to-be-preferred formal choice.

Whom do you want to see?

Whom are you waiting for?

Note: Whom is *always* used when the pronoun directly follows a preposition.

> *For whom* are you waiting?

> *To whom* do I pay my dues?

5 Use the objective case of a pronoun following the conjunctions *as* and *than* if that pronoun is the object of a verb that has been omitted from the sentence.

> He likes her more *than* [he likes] *me*. (*Me* is the object of *likes*.)

> I treated her as fairly as [I treated] *him*. (*Him* is the object of *treated*.)

6 Use the objective case of a pronoun that appears in an appositive when that pronoun explains or further identifies a noun that is an object.

>   appositive
> The coach fired two players, *Colin and me*. (*Me* is in the objective case because it further identifies the noun *players*, the object of *fired*.)

Note: Do not use the reflexive pronoun *myself* in place of the objective pronoun *me*.

> **Wrong** My aunt willed her estate to my brother and *myself*.
> **Right** My aunt willed her estate to my brother and *me*.

TEST YOURSELF ON
Using the Correct Case of Pronouns

Select the proper case of the pronoun from the choices in parentheses in each of the following sentences. Make your choices in accordance with correct formal usage.

1. She talked to Tracey and (I, me) for a long time.

2. I can't imagine (his, him) accepting the job.

3. He didn't look it, but Paul was as tired as (I, me).

C

4. The mayor, (she, her) alone, was responsible for the success of that clean-up campaign.

5. The blue jeans fitted Bob as well as (I, me).

6. Somehow, Richard thought he was better than (I, me).

7. When Linh ran to answer the phone, she knew it was (he, him).

8. They never found out the names of the vandals (who, whom) they believed were destroying the highway signs.

9. Chris and (he, him) got drunk together last night.

10. The two of them—Gabrielle and (he, him)—drove to Dawson City in three days.

11. I can do the job without (his, him) instructing me every minute.

12. The girls considered Jim and (I, me) the most attractive single men they knew.

13. (Who, Whom) are you waiting for?

14. They gave medals to two swimmers, Janet and (me, I).

15. After the party, the host was as tired as (I, me).

Coherence

The word *coherence* means "a sticking together." When we use it to refer to writing, we mean (1) that the parts of a sentence stick together to form a correct and logical utterance; (2) that the sentences in a paragraph are in logical and smoothly connected order; and (3) that each paragraph in a piece of writing is logically and smoothly connected to the ones that precede and follow it.

Achieving Coherence in Sentences

Many different kinds of errors contribute to the lack of coherence in sentences. Some of these are discussed in separate entries. (**Dangling Modifiers; Diction** (especially the section on idioms, pages 110–113); **Misplaced Modifiers; Parallel Construction; Pronoun References; Shifts**). In order to achieve coherence in a sentence, it is also necessary to avoid the following kinds of errors.

1 Avoid Split Constructions

A Do not needlessly separate the subject of the sentence and the verb.

> **Poor**   *Lisa*, after gathering together her clothes, books, and papers, *packed*.
> **Better**   After gathering together her clothes, books, and papers, Lisa packed.

B Do not needlessly separate the verb and its complement.

> **Poor**   The truck driver delivered, after driving all night in a terrible rainstorm, the new boiler we had ordered.
> **Better**   After driving all night in a terrible rainstorm, the truck driver delivered the new boiler we had ordered.

C Do not needlessly split an infinitive. To do so may destroy the coherence of the sentence. A split infinitive, however, does not always lead to incoherence; sometimes it cannot be avoided and produces perfect clarity.

> **Awkward**   He asked me *to as quickly as possible drop over* to his house.
> **Correct**   He asked me *to drop over* to his house as quickly as possible.
>
> **Awkward**   I promised *to immediately try out* for the football team.
> **Correct**   I promised *to try out* for the football team immediately.
>
> **Appropriate**   IBM expects *to more than double* its business this year.
> **Appropriate**   *To just miss* the train is a bad start for anybody's day.

C

2 Avoid Illogical Subjects and Complements

A Do not carelessly use a modifying phrase or clause as the subject of a sentence.

Wrong *Because he drove too slowly* made him miss the first inning of the game. (The adverb clause cannot be the subject of *made*.)
Right Because he drove too slowly, he missed the first inning of the game.
Right Driving too slowly made him miss the first inning of the game.

Wrong *By using power tools* will save a lot of hard work. (The italicized phrase cannot be used as the subject of *will save*.)
Right Using power tools will save a lot of hard work.
Right The use of power tools will save a lot of hard work.

B Do not use *when* or *where* as part of the complement of the verb *is*.

Wrong The thing I like to do most at parties *is when* I'm dancing.
Right The thing I like to do most at parties *is dance.*

Wrong A vacation *is where* you relax.
Right A vacation is *a period of relaxation.*

3 Avoid Using Mixed or Incomplete Comparisons

A Do not use comparisons that mix two comparative constructions.

Mixed My biology course is as interesting, *if not more interesting* than, my chemistry course. (The italicized modifying phrase is misplaced, making the main clause read: ''My biology course is as interesting than my chemistry course.'')
Unmixed My biology course is as interesting as my chemistry course, if not more interesting.
Correct (but stilted) My biology course is as interesting as, if not more interesting than, my chemistry course.

Mixed Willie Mays was one of the greatest, if not the greatest, players in all of baseball history.
Correct Willie Mays was one of the greatest players in all of baseball history. He may even have been *the* greatest.

B Do not use inexact or incomplete comparisons.

> *Inexact*   Toronto is farther from Ottawa than Kingston. (Confusion: which place is farther from which?)
> *Exact*   Toronto is farther from Ottawa than Kingston *is*. (Both terms of the comparison are filled in here.)
> *Exact*   Toronto is farther from Ottawa than *it is* from Kingston. (Again, the comparison is now exact.)

> *Inexact*   I like to watch television because it has more varied entertainment. (More varied than what?)
> *Exact*   I like to watch television because it has more varied entertainment *than other media.*

> *Incomplete*   Her prospects for a job after graduation looked lower than a labourer. (Is a labourer *low*?)
> *Complete*   Her prospects for a job after graduation looked lower than a *labourer's.*
> *Complete*   Her prospects for a job after graduation looked lower than *those of a labourer.*

4 Avoid Omitting Necessary Words

A Do not omit words that are necessary to maintain parallel structure in the sentence. (See **Parallel Construction** for a complete explanation of the term.)

> *Wrong*   He told her that she was intelligent but she lacked confidence. (The omission of *that* between *but* and *she* makes it uncertain whether she was told she lacked confidence or whether she thought so herself.)
> *Right*   He told her *that* she was intelligent but *that* she lacked confidence.

B Do not omit necessary parts of verbs. When the two parts of a compound construction are in different tenses or there is a change of number between them, be sure to include all the parts of *both* verbs.

> *Wrong*   The balancing of Federal and Provincial power *has* and always *will be* a contentious issue in Canadian politics. (*Be* goes properly with *will* to form the future tense; but *has* needs *been* to form the present perfect.)

C

Right   The balancing of Federal and Provincial power *has been* and always *will be* a contentious issue in Canadian politics.

Wrong   Jack *was fishing* and the other men *sleeping*. (*Jack* is singular and properly takes the singular auxiliary *was; men* is plural and needs the plural *were*.)

Right   Jack *was fishing* and the other men *were sleeping*.

Note: It is permissible to omit parts of compound verbs when both parts of the construction are in the same tense.

She *had read* the assigned books and [*had*] *done* the required term paper. (The tenses are the same, so the bracketed *had* may be omitted.)

C Do not omit words through sheer carelessness; careful proofreading can usually pick up these errors. Notice how a careless omission can make a sentence incoherent and result in misreading.

Omission   The psychiatrist showed emotional behaviour unrestrained by any rational controls leads to trouble. (Prior to reaching the verb *leads*, a reader may believe that the psychiatrist him- or herself showed unrestrained emotional behaviour.)

Complete   The psychiatrist showed *that* emotional behaviour unrestrained by any rational controls leads to trouble.

TEST YOURSELF ON

Revising Incoherent Sentences

Each of the following sentences is plagued by one of the problems we have been discussing in this section. Analyze each problem, and then write out what you consider to be a good revision of the sentence; be prepared to explain why you think your version is superior.

1. In the basket is where I put the apples.

2. Because cheating the consumer is so widespread that we need a permanent Ministry of Consumer and Corporate Affairs.

3. Jack, after the heat, the crowds, and the excitement, fainted.

4. The doctor wanted, because he suspected a kidney problem and needed to be sure, a urine sample.

5. The invitation said that I was to only reply if I couldn't make it.

6. A good disco is where they play music for dancing.

7. Professor Gould is one of the best, if not the best, teachers in the department.

8. A Toyota is built better and uses the least gas.

9. The actor's makeup looked like a clown.

10. *Québécois* are just as friendly as the Maritimes or the West.

11. Loneliness is when you are starved for intimacy.

12. The bookcase I built myself cost far less than a carpenter.

13. The music instructor told her that she had talent but she needed to improve her technique.

14. In Vancouver are a trio of mountains reaching toward the clouds and which provide great sightseeing for millions of visitors.

15. He was working and still does at the packing plant.

Achieving Coherence in Paragraphs

Most kinds of writing require that sentences be written one after another to form coherent paragraphs. A coherent paragraph is one in which (1) there is a logical order to the sentence—a definite principle governs the location of each sentence in the paragraph—and (2) there are clear connections—smooth bridges—between these sentences.

1 To ensure that your paragraphs have coherence, choose the appropriate logical plan with which to govern the order of your sentences. Usually, the subject of your paragraph will suggest the right plan to follow. If you are telling a story, a common plan is the chronological one: you order your sentences according to time. If your paragraph is describing something, say a house, then a common plan of organization would have you describe the house from the inside out or vice versa: we call this a spatial plan. Here are examples showing the difference a plan can make in the coherence of your paragraphs.

C

Incoherent (sentences without order)

Last night, my father discovered that our car had been stolen. The
detectives didn't hold out much hope for its return, but they said
they would be in touch if there were any news. They took down all
the information about the car and were very polite. My father asked
my mother if she thought I had taken it without permission, but she
assured him I hadn't. He just couldn't believe it wasn't parked in
the usual place, and ran down the hill to see if maybe the brakes
had given out and it had rolled down. When he was finally convinced that the car had been stolen, he phoned the police. After they
left, my father was depressed.

Coherent (Chronological order imposed)

Last night, my father discovered that our car had been stolen. He
asked my mother if she thought I had taken it without permission,
but she assured him I hadn't. He just couldn't believe it wasn't
parked in the usual place and ran down the hill to see if maybe the
brakes had given out and it had rolled down. When he was finally
convinced that the car had been stolen, he phoned the police. The
detectives took down all the information about the car and were very
polite. They didn't hold out much hope for its return, but they said
they would be in touch if there were any news. After they left, my
father was depressed.

Incoherent (sentences without order)

A spiral ramp hugging the wall goes whirling up as far as the eye
can see, leaving a huge cone of space in the center. The entrance
hall is also very dramatic. When you first approach the museum,
you notice that it's very different from the buildings around it—
ordinary high-rise apartment houses. It is low, first of all, almost
squat in appearance. The squat impression made by the outside is
lost on the inside. The building is made of massive geometric forms:
cones, tubes, rectangles, and squares, all solidly connected to form
a unitary, dramatic mass of concrete, with here and there a strange
vertical slit in the façade. Everything inside is airy and light, turning
and curving. From the top of the ramp, what you see is so slender
and spacious you can hardly believe it's the same building you saw
from the outside.

Coherent (spatial order imposed)
When you first approach the museum, you notice that it's very different from the buildings around it—ordinary high-rise apartment houses. The museum is low, first of all, almost squat in appearance. It is made of massive geometric forms: cones, tubes, rectangles, and squares, all solidly connected to form a unitary, dramatic mass of concrete, with here and there a strange vertical slit in the façade. The entrance hall is also very dramatic. A spiral ramp hugging the wall goes whirling up as far as the eye can see, leaving a huge cone of space in the center. Everything inside is airy and light, turning and curving. From the top of the ramp, what you see is so slender and spacious you can hardly believe it's the same building you saw from the outside.

C

TEST YOURSELF ON
Making Coherent Paragraphs

A Write a coherent paragraph that incorporates all the following information about Robertson Davies. Begin your paragraph with sentence 1.

1. Robertson Davies, the distinguished Canadian writer, was born in Thamesville, Ontario in 1913.

2. His broad experience as a dramatist, journalist, critic, and teacher has provided him with a wealth of literary material.

3. From 1942 until 1962, he was editor of the *Peterborough Examiner*.

4. As a novelist, he may be best remembered for the "Deptford Trilogy" of novels, including the much admired *Fifth Business*, which he published during the 1970s.

5. He received the prestigious Stephen Leacock medal for humour in 1955.

6. Fourteen plays have been published by this prolific author.

7. In the "Deptford Trilogy," Davies' fascination with psychology, myth, magic, and theatre combine.

C

8. Davies published his first book, called *Shakespeare's Boy Actors*, in 1939, but it wasn't until he had transformed his Peterborough experiences into the "Marchbanks" novels during the 1950s that he began to acquire major distinction.

B Both of the following paragraphs are incoherent because the sentences are poorly arranged. Impose an orderly plan on each and make coherent paragraphs of them.

1. Most Canadians have become increasingly interested in leisure activities these days. There is so much intensity in these activities that we can fairly say Canadians now have two jobs: one is real work, the other real play. Jobholders work fewer hours and thus have more leisure. Besides, Canadians have always been sociable, in a reserved sort of way, and sociability goes hand in hand with leisure. The reasons have to do with changes that have taken place in Canadian life in the last twenty-five years. Interest in health has grown, and this has led many to take an active role in sports. Moreover, the idea has gained prominence that self-fulfilment means gaining skills in pleasurable leisure activities like photography, sailing, woodwork, painting, and many others.

2. The outside of the building is typical of old farmhouses in this part of the country. So is the blackened tin funnel that was once used to lead cooking fumes to the outside. Inside, the house has been modernized—a new stove, a refrigerator, wall heaters— but the old wood stove is still there. A chimney squirts into the air from the top of each addition. Even a faded photograph on the living room wall, showing the original house without the additions, testifies that what used to be is not entirely gone. The furniture also reflects the original identity of the house. It is a white frame square, with two little additions—afterthoughts— sloping off either side of the square.

2 To ensure that there are clear connections between your sentences, you must keep in mind the following four considerations.

A Present your ideas from a consistent point of view. This means that you must speak, in each sentence, from the same position or vantage point. You must not needlessly shift tense, number, or person within a paragraph.

Shift in Tense
In the story, Tom *went* to the Northwest Territories to make a life as a hunter and trapper. Then he *goes* to the Yukon to search for gold. His restlessness *was* emphasized repeatedly. Thus by the end of the story, he *is* a sad man.

Shift in Number
Young *people* who look for security in their jobs rather than satisfaction are likely to be disappointed. A young *person* needs to choose a career that will stimulate his or her imagination while it is young and responsive. *They* can always gain security later on, at the appropriate age. *He or she* must be wary of experiencing the worst possible regret: looking back on life and knowing *he or she* hasn't lived.

Shift in Person
Now more than ever, *parents* need to pay close attention to children's gaining basic skills like reading, writing, and mathematics. *You* need to do more than help them with their homework. *You* cannot expect children to honour those skills if you don't. Therefore, a *parent* must set an example for *children*.

B For the purpose of presenting parallel or co-ordinate ideas, use parallel construction in sentences that follow each other.

My mother has passed along to me certain rules for getting along with others. Don't argue with parents; they'll think you don't love them. Don't argue with children; they'll think themselves victimized. Don't argue with husbands and wives; they'll think you're a tiresome mate. Don't argue with strangers; they won't want to be friends. My mother's rules can be summed up in two words: don't argue.

Most of us feel the troubles we encounter are not of our own making. We think that the system has failed us. We think that our loved ones have failed us. We think that circumstances have failed us. It rarely occurs to us that the failure has been our own and that it might be temporary and perhaps even reparable.

(See **Parallel Construction** for more information.)

C

C Repeat key words and phrases to keep the flow of your thought before the reader. If you fail to do this, gaps in your thought are created. Pronouns referring precisely to their antecedents can also serve this bridging function.

> A *magic show* works by carefully directing our *attention*: But the *show directs* our *attention* where the *magician wants* it to be. *He wants* us to look away from the *place* where his transformations go on. For that *place* has no *magic*; it's a *work place*. The *magical* quality of the *show* depends on our not seeing the *work*. When we do not look at that *work*, we see the *magic*, and our *attention*— focused on the right *place*—is well rewarded.

D Use transitional devices where they are necessary to further this bridging function between sentences. A transitional device is a word or a phrase that can serve as a point of reference (*finally, at last*) or that can actually indicate the relationship between one sentence and the next (*consequently, as a result*).

> Soon, he was able to walk. *Afterward*, he was even able to swim a little and he managed a few minutes in the pool every day. *Consequently*, when spring came, his physical condition had improved considerably. He was stronger, could walk without tiring, and was able to swim as long as he wanted to. *However*, he was still depressed by the ordeal of the accident and the recuperation period during which he was unable to work. *On the whole, though*, he had much to be thankful for.

Here is a list of some of these transitional devices, classified according to meaning:

Time after a while, afterward, at last, at the same time, in the meantime, immediately, later, soon

Place here, there, nearby, close by

Addition again, also, besides, further, furthermore, in addition, likewise, moreover, next

Result as a result, accordingly, consequently, hence, therefore, thus

Comparison likewise, similarly, in such a manner

Contrast after all, and yet, however, in contrast, in spite of, nevertheless, on the contrary, on the other hand, otherwise

Concession   it may be true, I admit, naturally, of course
Summary   in brief, in short, on the whole, to conclude, to sum up, finally, to summarize
Illustration and Example   for example, for instance, to be specific, in particular, indeed, in fact, that is, to illustrate

See also **Transitions**.

TEST YOURSELF ON

Revising Incoherent Paragraphs

The following paragraphs contain confusing shifts in person, tense, or number, or lack smooth transitions. Eliminate the shifts wherever they appear and add transitions where necessary to make them all coherent.

1. My parents always argue with me about my wanting a moped. They said the machines were dangerous, but I believed they were not. Mopeds go only thirty kilometres an hour. It ran cheaply and was not very expensive to insure. They have been sold cheaply too.

2. Cooking is both easy and fun if one observes certain basic rules. First, you should have the right utensils. As the saying goes, ''a cook is only as good as his pots.'' A cook should buy only fresh ingredients. You ought to learn how much heat to apply to particular foods. Save good recipes.

3. A professor I know who is older than I am says that rock and roll is terrible music. I said it's just a form of what he used to think was popular music when he was young. He says rock and roll lyrics can't be heard because the music is too loud. He said the lyrics are foolish. I pointed out that though he may be right about the lyrics, they have not been more foolish than *his* kind of pop music. The degree of loudness is a matter of taste.

Achieving Coherence Between Paragraphs

As you might have expected, the rules for achieving coherence between paragraphs are identical to those that apply to achieving coherence *within* paragraphs. For example:

C

1   Structurally, there are two basic types of avalanche, a distinction noted in the Alps two centuries ago. A slab avalanche is just that— a large, cohesive mass of snow that slides, following either the failure of one of the snowpack's weak underlying layers or the failure of the bond between two layers. It is identified by an obvious fracture line left where the slab pulls away from the rest of the snowpack. Although the fracture line can be only a few inches deep and several yards long, it is often much larger, sometimes frighteningly so. In 1979, a massive avalanche in British Columbia that killed seven heli-skiers left a fracture line up to 13 feet deep (4 m) in places and a mile long (1.6 km).

2   The second type, a loose-snow avalanche, is composed of new, unconsolidated snow that slides when it reaches such a depth and weight that it can no longer cling to the slope. It starts from a single point and is characteristically a small teardrop-shaped slough of indeterminate depth.

3   Either variety can be classified further by its moisture content. A wet avalanche, created by falls of heavy, water-saturated snow or by springtime thaws, flows like a wall of mud or quick-setting cement, moving slowly but inexorably down gullies or creek beds, [burying] all that lies in its path. A dry avalanche, on the other hand, accelerates rapidly and, given enough mass and the room to run, will top 200 miles per hour (322 km/h). It is particularly dangerous because the snow in a dry avalanche begins to tumble at velocities of 25 miles per hour (40 km/h). Peter Schaerer once rode for a short distance in a dry tumbling slab before being spat out its side: "It was a strange feeling, seeing sky and snow, sky and snow, up and down, around and around. I didn't feel I could do much to help myself."

Bart Robinson, "Cold Fury, White Death," *Equinox* 31 Jan.–Feb. 1987: 54–55.

Notice in the example that the words *types, type, avalanche* constitute a bridge from paragraph 1 to paragraph 2 and that paragraph 3's development of the idea is signalled by the bridging phrase, "Either variety can be classified further. . . ."

Colloquial

See **Diction**.

Colon

The colon is a mark of internal punctuation that can be used according to the following rules:

1 Use the colon to introduce a series of items explained in the main clause of the sentence.

> In order to enjoy camping, you need the right supplies: a tent, a sleeping bag, good walking shoes, foul weather gear, waterproof matches, and the right kind of food.

> He had a bad group of symptoms: headache, nausea, fever, and an itchy rash.

2 Use the colon to direct the reader's attention to a final fact or explanation.

> You lack the one thing that rich people have: money.

> One quality is essential for the good teacher: patience.

3 Use the colon to introduce a direct quotation of some length and formality.

> The problem was clearly outlined by the city's director of planning, who put it this way: "Population increases require more living accommodation within cities, resulting in a process called densification. This means the elimination of single-family houses and their replacement by multiple-family dwellings."

Longer direct quotations can of course be introduced by a comma, too, but a comma *should* be used when the material is more informal and shorter.

> John smiled and answered softly, "You can do as you please."

4 Use a colon for the purposes of mechanical separation.

C

Matthew 8:10 (separating chapter and verse in Biblical citation)

Dear Mr. Adderly: (after the salutation in a formal letter, to separate it from the body)

2:32 a.m. (separating numbers in a time designation)

Note: Do not use a colon interchangeably with a semicolon. Do not use a colon after a verb or a preposition in a sentence to introduce a series.

Wrong My priorities *are*: home, country, and God.
Right My priorities are as follows: home, country, and God.
Right My priorities are home, country, and God.

Wrong This summer I am planning *to*: study French, get a part-time job, and swim a half-mile every day.
Right This summer I am planning to do the following: study French, get a part-time job, and swim a half-mile every day.
Right This summer I am planning to study French, get a part-time job, and swim a half-mile every day.

TEST YOURSELF ON
The Use of the Colon

In each of the sentences below, insert colons where they are needed ot change their position after inserting another word.

1. It is now 245 p.m.

2. Whatever he wanted from Suzanne, he got love, affection, kindness, money, or food.

3. The things that need repairing around the house are: the eavestroughs, the front steps, the upstairs storm windows, and the leaks in the attic.

4. What do I spend my money on? I spend my money on: food,

clothing, shelter, movies, medicine, skateboards, lobsters—a lot of things!

C

5. You need only one thing for a perfect golf swing, control.

Comma Fault

Another term for **Comma Splice**. See also **Run-on Sentences**.

Comma Rules

The comma is used to separate sentence elements. It is the most frequently used of all the punctuation marks. Its appearance signals the reader that something is interrupting the flow of the main statement (main clause), or that something is being added or subtracted, usually something that is not so closely related to that main flow of thought. The specific rules given below are aimed at ensuring that a writer's flow of thought is presented with clarity; they should be applied with that aim in mind. When there is a conflict between applying these rules and your own sense of the fitness of a comma placement, consult your instructor.

1 Use a comma to separate independent clauses joined by the co-ordinating conjunctions *and, but, or, nor, for, so, yet.*

> Greene has washed and cleaned his old car, *and* he hopes that it will attract a buyer.
>
> The plan was to leave on Sunday morning, *but* we found that we couldn't get ready on time.
>
> We can stay home and have leg of lamb for dinner, *or* we can eat out and have pizza.
>
> Jones could not give the modern names of Upper and Lower Canada, *nor* could he identify any of the Fathers of Confederation.

C

Note: A comma may be omitted between short independent clauses.

I laughed and he cried.

I asked but he didn't answer.

2 Use a comma to separate items in a series. These items may consist of words, phrases, or clauses.

Series of Words   I'd like a big bowl of fruit with *apples, pears, peaches,* and *plums.*
Series of Phrases   He liked *going to the movies, eating at fancy restaurants,* and *visiting museums.*
Series of Clauses   She liked him *when he was thoughtful, when he was kind,* and *when he was relaxed.*

Note that in each of these examples, there is a comma as well as the word *and* between the last two items in the series. In the case of items in a series, you have the option of following the practice in the above examples or of omitting the comma just before the *and* preceding the final item. Both procedures are correct; probably the retention of the comma is more formal than its omission. But whatever you choose to do, *be consistent.* Do not use one system with one series and another with a second series.

The words separated by commas in the first of the above examples are nouns. A series of adjectives can present a slightly different problem in punctuation. For example, consider the following sentences:

They were *energetic, pretty, intelligent,* and *sensitive* girls.

They had an *interesting European summer* vacation.

In the first example, we can substitute the word *and* for each of the commas—energetic *and* pretty *and* intelligent. We could also alter the order of these adjectives; it would make little difference to the sense of the sentence if we wrote "sensitive, pretty, energetic, and intelligent." Therefore, the adjectives in this example are *co-ordinate adjectives* and are properly separated by commas.

By contrast, the adjectives in the second example are not co-ordinate. We could not logically join them by the word *and* (interesting *and* European *and* summer is illogical). And we could not alter the order of these adjectives: we could not say "summer European interesting vacation." In fact, the word *interesting* really

C

modifies *European summer vacation*; the word *European* then
modifies *summer vacation* and the word *summer* modifies
vacation—there are layers of modification, so to speak. Where
we have such a series of adjectives that are not co-ordinate, we
do not use commas to separate them.

> ***Co-ordinate***   It was a *happy, productive*, and *prosperous* season in
> her life.
>
> ***Not Co-ordinate***   He was wearing a *light green* belt.
>
> ***Co-ordinate***   His remark was *foolish, rude*, and *embarrassing*.
>
> ***Not Co-ordinate***   Last night we went to a *lively little faculty* party.

3 Use a comma to separate introductory elements from the rest of
the sentence. These elements can be words, phrases, adverb clauses,
or transitional expressions.

> ***Introductory Word***   *Usually*, he took a nap after lunch.
>
> ***Introductory Phrase***   *Coming through the alley*, the car swerved to
> avoid a garbage can.
>
> ***Introductory Clause***   *Although she had already eaten dinner*, she
> sat down to have a sandwich.
>
> ***Transitional Expressions***   *In other words*, I'm in love. *On the
> other hand*, meat loaf is fattening.

Note: Certain introductory elements do not need to be followed
by a comma, if they are short and if omitting the comma does not
cause a lack of clarity in the sentence.

> *Probably* he won't win.
>
> *Naturally* he found what he was looking for.

But note too how confusion can enter a sentence when a
comma that *should* come after an introductory element is omitted:

> After he ate the horse took a romp in the fields.
>
> Because she needed to hit the catcher choked up on the bat handle.

As we have shown, introductory adverb clauses should be
set off from the rest of the sentence by a comma. The need for a
comma when the adverb clause comes at the end of a sentence
depends on the relationship of the adverb clause to the main clause
of the sentence. When the information contained in the adverb

C

clause is essential to the meaning of the sentence, no comma is needed.

I will keep knocking *until* they open the door.

The speaker here tells us that *until they open the door*, the speaker will keep on knocking; therefore, that information is essential—it gives the motive for the information in the main clause—and no comma is needed.

I came to this school *because the engineering courses are so good.*

This states the essential reason that the speaker came, and so the clauses need not be separated by a comma.

However, when the adverb clause merely gives non-essential explanatory material, a comma should be used between it and the main clause.

Our seats were in the last row of the balcony, *although we had asked for a pair in the orchestra.*

Here the italicized clause has no *essential* relationship to the main clause: it gives no *reason* that the seats were in the balcony (far from it, in fact; it suggests a contrast) nor any motive for the seats' being where they were. Therefore, it needs a comma, as if to emphasize the separateness of its information from that in the main clause.

4 Use a comma to set off a parenthetical element at the beginning of a sentence; use one comma before and one after a parenthetical or appositive element that occurs in the middle of a sentence. A parenthetical element is one which is not essential to complete the meaning of the sentence but which supplements a part or parts of the sentence.

Parenthetical Element at Beginning of Sentence
To be frank, I'm completely broke.
Certainly, he has a right to do what he wishes.

Parenthetical Element in Midsentence
The car, *you see*, is in the garage.

Appositive   Mr. Morris, *the patient in room 950*, has been wheeled down to occupational therapy.

Appositive   My uncle, *Angus MacGregor*, was a stingy millionaire.

C

It should be clear from the above examples that appositives and parenthetical elements do not affect the meaning being delivered by the sentence; they can be omitted without loss of meaning.

Notice that if only one comma is used in each of the last two examples, some confusion in meaning results.

> Mr. Morris, the patient in room 950 has been wheeled down to occupational therapy. (This may mean that the speaker is addressing a Mr. Morris and advising him that the patient in room 950 has been wheeled down.)

> My uncle, Angus MacGregor was a stingy millionaire. (Again, it is not clear that *my uncle* and *Angus MacGregor* are the same person.)

5 Use commas to set off non-restrictive elements in a sentence. Another way of talking about a parenthetical or appositive element is to say that it is *non-restrictive*: it does not *restrict* or essentially modify what it refers to; therefore, it *must* be set off by commas. On the other hand, if the element in question is *restrictive* or is essential to what it modifies, it must *not* be set off by commas.

> **Restrictive Element**   The audience *that gave him the most applause* pleased him the most. (No commas are necessary.)

> **Non-restrictive Element**   The audience, *which paid a fortune for its seats*, applauded for five minutes.

The first sentence is not about the *audience*—it is about *the audience that gave him the most applause*. Therefore, the clause must not be separated by commas from the subject word *audience*; the clause is part of the complete subject (italicized in this paragraph), and if it were separated the sentence would lose its essential meaning. On the other hand, the second sentence *is* about the *audience*; it is only incidental, not essential, information that this audience paid a fortune for its seats. Therefore, the clause in that sentence must be separated from *audience* by commas.

Try to figure out which of the following sentences contain restrictive elements and which ones contain non-restrictive elements that should be set off by commas. Answers follow immediately below.

1. People *who live in glass houses* shouldn't throw stones.
2. Students *who take this film course* are guaranteed an exciting experience.

C

3. My doctor *who is on vacation this month* leads a busy professional life.
4. The foreman at the factory *who was a conscientious worker* was taking evening courses in business administration.
5. The man *leaning over the edge of the balcony* is being reckless.

Answers: 1, 2, and 5 all contain *restrictives*. In these, no commas should be used. But commas *are* needed in 3 and 4 because they contain *non-restrictive* elements.

3. My doctor, who is on vacation this month, leads a busy professional life.
4. The foreman at the factory, who was a conscientious worker, was taking evening courses in business administration.

The reason that we need commas in these examples is that, in each, the material between the commas is not essential to the writer's message. In 3, it is only incidental that the doctor is on vacation, not essential. Similarly, in 4, the material between the commas is also incidental; it has nothing to do with the main message of the sentence—that the foreman was taking evening courses in business administration.

On the other hand, the reason we do not use commas in 1, 2, and 5 is that, in each, the italicized material is essential to what is being said about the subject.

1. People *who live in glass houses* shouldn't throw stones.

This writer doesn't mean that "people shouldn't throw stones" and that incidentally those people live in glass houses—although "People shouldn't throw stones" is a grammatical sentence and may even be a pretty good rule to live by. The writer means that *only people who live in glass houses* shouldn't throw stones; therefore, we must have *people* and all the words that follow it as one single unit, unbroken by commas.

2. Students *who take this film course* are guaranteed an exciting experience.

The writer of this sentence doesn't mean that "students are guaranteed an exciting experience," and incidentally, that those students are taking this film course. "Students are guaranteed an exciting experience" is a grammatical sentence and may even be true, but the writer of 2 really means that *only students who take this film course* receive the guarantee. Therefore, we must take these words as a single unit, unbroken by commas.

Try analyzing 5 as we have just analyzed 1 and 2.

6 Use a comma to separate a contrasting element from the rest of the sentence; a comma emphasizes the contrast.

> He came to the dance with me, *and not with you.*
>
> She says she loves exercise, *but doesn't do it.*

7 Use a comma to achieve clarity, even in places where you ordinarily might omit it.

> In brief, dresses will be longer this year.
>
> People who like to see wild birds, walk through the woods.
>
> Whatever he did, did no good.
>
> The soldier dropped, a bullet in his leg.

8 Use a comma in dates, addresses, and letter forms.

> ***Dates***   August 4, 1989 (or 4 August 1989); Friday, November 30, 1992
>
> ***Address***   Moose Jaw, Saskatchewan
>
> ***Letter Forms***   Dear Mary, (after the salutation in an informal letter, to separate it from the body)
>
> > Yours sincerely,

TEST YOURSELF ON
The Use of the Comma

A Write your own sentences to test your ability to use commas correctly.

1. Construct five compound sentences, each with two independent clauses; use the co-ordinating conjunctions *and, but, or, nor,* and *so* once each—and place commas in the correct positions.

2. Construct five sentences, each beginning with an adverb clause and followed by a simple main clause. Place the commas in the correct positions.

C

B Some of the following sentences use the comma correctly; next to these, place the letter C. In the others, either there is a comma missing or too many commas are used. Supply those that are needed; cross out those that are superfluous.

1. _____ The boys in the back of the room are noisy.

2. _____ Teenagers, who are very poor drivers should have their licences revoked.

3. _____ During the summer days are long.

4. _____ Above all the storm clouds are dark and threatening.

5. _____ I saw you talking to a pretty slim girl.

6. _____ I'd like to be rich married secure and famous.

7. _____ The ship, which docked yesterday is the *Queen Elizabeth II*.

8. _____ People, who live beyond their incomes, shouldn't complain about money.

9. _____ I will keep taking the test, until I pass it.

10. _____ I need to buy a grey, summer suit and a pair of white cotton pants.

11. _____ Wherever you're going to get there requires planning and purpose.

12. _____ On Friday, November 30, 1983, I met my wife, and my life, has not been the same, since.

13. _____ In fact I stole the books.

14. _____ George, who is very nearly my age, is much further along in his career than I am in mine.

15. _____ The revolution in education which so many educators talk about has yet to take place.

16. _____ A university really consists of a group of students who want to learn, a group of teachers who want to teach, and a good collection of books.

17. _____ I paused but he went on.

18. _____ Either he goes or I go.

19. _____ He eats drinks and talks too much.

20. _____ Usually living alone is a matter of personal choice.

Comma Splice

When two independent clauses are joined only by a comma, and *not* by a comma and a co-ordinating conjunction, we call the error a comma splice or comma fault.

For a detailed discussion of this problem, see **Run-on Sentences**.

Contractions

When two words are joined together with one or more letters omitted and an apostrophe in its place, we have a contraction.

do not = don't   is not = isn't   we will = we'll

See **Apostrophe** for more detailed information.

D | *Dangling Modifiers*

A dangling modifier is a phrase or a clause that either modifies no word in the sentence or refers to the wrong word.

> ***Dangling Participial Phrase***   *Walking home from school*, the fire engine came screeching around the corner.

The thing to notice about this example is that it *says* one thing but *intends* to say another. Because *walking home from school* modifies *fire engine*, it *says* that the fire engine, as it was walking home from school, came screeching around the corner. Clearly this is ridiculous.

It *intends* to say that as *someone* was walking home from school, the fire engine came screeching around the corner, or that walking home from school, *someone saw* the fire engine come screeching around the corner.

Therefore, to correct the dangling phrase, we must get *someone* into the action. We can accomplish this by giving the phrase something to modify in the main clause (*the fire engine came screeching around the corner*):

> Walking home from school, *I saw* the fire engine come screeching around the corner. (Now the phrase modifies the word *I* in the main clause.)

Alternatively, we can turn the phrase into a dependent clause and get the *someone* into the action that way:

> *As I was walking home from school*, the fire engine came screeching around the corner. (Now someone—*I*—has been brought into the action by appearing in the italicized clause.)

How you decide to correct this dangling modifier depends on where you want to place the emphasis. Since emphasis naturally falls on the subject of the main clause, you would use the first revision if you wanted to emphasize the speaker, I, and the second if you wanted to emphasize the fire engine.

You can avoid dangling modifiers if you proofread carefully. Learn to recognize and correct the various kinds of dangling modifiers likely to appear in your work.

1 Recognize and Correct Dangling Participial Phrases.

These are similar to the example just discussed.

D

> **Dangling** *Smoking a cigar*, the horse stood on its hind legs. (The phrase seems to modify *horse*—the wrong word.)
>
> **Revised** *As I was smoking a cigar*, the horse stood on its hind legs. (Phrase turned into a clause—a person getting into the action.)
>
> **Revised** Smoking a cigar, *I saw* the horse stand on its hind legs. (Now the phrase clearly modifies the new subject of the main clause: *I*.)

> **Dangling** Our summer passed happily, *swimming and playing baseball*. (Note that the dangler can come at the end, not just at the beginning of the sentence; the summer did not swim and play baseball—*we* did; therefore, the phrase modifies the wrong word.)
>
> **Revised** We passed our summer happily, swimming and playing baseball. (Note that the addition of the word *we* as the new subject does the correcting job nicely.)
>
> **Revised** *Because we were swimming and playing baseball*, our summer passed happily. (The phrase has been converted into a clause.)

> **Dangling** *Lying on my back on the raft*, the stars burned brightly in the sky. (It is not the *stars* that are lying on the speaker's back: the phrase is modifying *stars*, the wrong word.)
>
> **Revised** *As I was lying on my back on the raft*, the stars burned brightly in the sky. (The phrase is turned into a clause.)
>
> **Revised** Lying on my back on the raft, *I could see* the stars burning brightly in the sky. (Adding the words *I could see* to the main clause gives the phrase the correct word to modify: *I*.)

2 Recognize and Correct Dangling Gerund Phrases.

A gerund is an *-ing* word that functions as a noun. A gerund implies the presence of a *someone*.

> **Dangling** *After filling my cavity*, my tooth stopped aching. (The *tooth* did not do the *filling*.)
>
> **Revised** *After the dentist filled my cavity*, my tooth stopped aching. (The phrase is now a clause.)
>
> **Revised** *After filling my cavity*, the dentist stopped my tooth from aching. (Now the phrase refers clearly to the new subject of the main clause: *dentist*.)

D

> ***Dangling***   *In planning a college education*, careful preparations are
> needed. (*Careful preparations* cannot do the *planning*; a *someone* is
> needed.)
>
> ***Revised***   *In planning a college education, a student* needs to make
> careful preparations. (The *someone*, in the form of *a student* has
> been added to the main clause; now the phrase correctly modifies
> *student*.)

3 Recognize and Correct Dangling Infinitive Phrases.

An infinitive phrase has for its headwords the *to* form of a verb: *to
play, to work, to love,* and so forth.

> ***Dangling***   *To become a movie star*, talent and luck are needed. (*To
> become a movie star* does not logically refer to *talent and luck*, the
> subject of the main clause; people become movie stars.)
>
> ***Revised***   *To become a movie star*, one [or *a person*] needs talent
> and luck. (Now the phrase refers logically to *one*—or *a person*.)
>
> ***Revised***   *If you want to become a movie star*, you need talent and
> luck. (The phrase has been converted into a clause.)

> ***Dangling***   *To make a delicious stew*, fresh ingredients must be
> used. (The *ingredients* do not cook the stew; people do.)
>
> ***Revised***   *To make a delicious stew*, you must use fresh ingredients.
> (We have supplied the subject in the main clause, *you*, to which the
> phrase can logically refer.)
>
> ***Revised***   *If you want to make a delicious stew*, you must use fresh
> ingredients. (The phrase has been converted into a clause.)

4 Recognize and Correct Dangling Elliptical Clauses

An *elliptical* expression has words missing. An *elliptical clause* is
missing either a subject or a verb; these are understood instead of
being stated. You can correct dangling elliptical clauses either by
making the subject of the elliptical clause agree with the subject of
the main clause or by supplying the missing subject and verb.

> ***Dangling***   *When driving*, my seat belt is always fastened. (The *seat
> belt* is not *driving*; the italicized clause is missing the words *I am*,
> so the implied subject, *I*, does not agree with the *seat belt* of the
> main clause.)
>
> ***Revised***   *When driving*, I always fasten my seat belt. (Now the
> implied subject, *I*, is the same as the new subject of the main
> clause.)

D

Revised *When I am driving*, my seat belt is always fastened. (With the missing words supplied, the clause is expanded and refers, properly, to *is fastened*.)

Dangling *When at the age of six*, my Uncle André gave me my first haircut. (*Uncle André* was not *at the age of six* when the haircut was given—the speaker was: *I was* are the missing words.)
Revised *When at the age of six*, I was given my first haircut by my Uncle André. (The implied subject of the clause now matches the new subject—*I*—of the main clause.)
Revised When I was at the age of six, my Uncle André gave me my first haircut. (The missing words supplied expand the clause and make it modify, properly, the verb *gave*.)

Note: Some verbal phrases do not intend to modify any single portion of the main clause. Rather, they make statements about the whole sentence. These are called *absolute constructions*; using them puts the writer in no danger of creating a dangling modifier.

Considering the time, we're not doing badly.

Parking regulations having been suspended, we decided to leave the car on Queen Street.

The air being nippy, we brought along our parkas.

Winning being impossible, we figured we'd just have fun playing.

TEST YOURSELF ON

Recognizing and Correcting Dangling Modifiers

Some of the following sentences are correct; place a C next to them. For those that have dangling modifiers, underline the dangling modifier; then correct it according to the methods just discussed.

1. _____ Before ~~leaving~~ *I left* for Winnipeg, hotel reservations must be made.

2. _____ Being Canadian his knowledge of Mauritius was limited.

3. _____ Arriving in Charlottetown his suitcase was in Vancouver.

D

4. _____ To understand one's spouse, good communications should exist.

5. _____ After putting my son to sleep, I settled down with a good book.

6. _____ After changing my shoes, my girlfriend took me out to dinner.

7. _____ To understand true happiness, you need to know true love.

8. _____ Although planning to get married, my girlfriend's parents didn't know it.

9. _____ His eyes caught the glint of a strange seashell walking barefoot on the beach.

10. _____ Listening to the concert, the Talking Heads seemed like the funkiest group in the world.

11. _____ My examinations were passed, sweating and praying.

12. _____ To travel in grand style, money is essential.

13. _____ Driving through Ontario, I decided to stop in Wawa.

14. _____ If sleepy, your car can be very dangerous.

15. _____ Before going up for a parachute jump, the airplane was thoroughly inspected.

Dash

The dash is a mark of internal punctuation that has the separation effect of the comma or parentheses but that confers emphasis on what follows it. (See **Parentheses** for a brief discussion of the differences in the use of the three marks.)

If you use a typewriter, the dash is made by striking the hyphen key twice: --. If you write by hand, make the dash twice as long as the hyphen. In either case, do not leave a space before or after the dash—run it directly up against the letters of the preceding and following words. The dash may appropriately be used in the following circumstances.

1 Use the dash to set off a final appositive that is short and would benefit from emphasis.

> What was in the package was what he feared and desired—poison.
>
> After he read the thesis, one word came to mind—nonsense.

2 Use the dash to set off non-restrictive appositives that would benefit from emphasis or that need dashes for clarity.

> My doctor—my friend for thirty years—always told me the truth.
>
> Three girls—Jackie, Leslie, and Denise—came to my birthday party.

Note that we could replace the dashes in the last example with commas, but see what confusion might result if we did:

> Three girls, Jackie, Leslie, and Denise, came to my birthday party.

In this sentence, we cannot be sure that the names given are those of the three girls; it is possible, in this case, that six people came and that Jackie and Leslie are men. The dashes, however, clear up any possible confusion.

3 Use a dash to set off a series of items, occurring either at the beginning or the end of a sentence, where the items are separated by commas.

D

> ***Beginning of Sentence***　Love, friendship, caring for children, personal fulfilment, protecting nature's bounties, concern for others—these are the values that enlightened human beings strive for.
> ***End of Sentence***　We look for the same qualities in an athlete that we find in a soldier—agility, stamina, strength, courage, and competitiveness.

4 Use a dash to set off parenthetical elements that abruptly interrupt the sense of the sentence.

> In the blackness of the mine shaft, we started climbing slowly—what else could we do?—until at last we saw a pinpoint of light.

> The cultural makeup of the community—a blend of Asian, Caribbean, East Indian, and European—makes the annual Winter Carnival an exciting event.

TEST YOURSELF ON
The Use of the Dash

Use the dash to improve the clarity, emphasis, and meaning of the following sentences.

1. You owe me one thing, loyalty.

2. There is a possibility that we who have paid our rent will be evicted from our apartment.

3. The pilgrims went devoutly to Rome Catholicism's holy city.

4. That's what I would call it a crying shame!

5. The crises in his life, divorce, separation from his children, the loss of his job, the attack of pneumonia, these were all too much for him.

6. I notified the dean of my decision, resignation.

7. Job training programs, increased educational opportunities in

the professions, improved day-care facilities, all these are necessary to begin the attack on poverty.

8. The defeat of communicable diseases and the increase in the food supply these have been partly responsible for the rise in world population.

9. One of the world's great religions Islam was begun by an Arab merchant, Mohammed.

10. He drove in a cold fury not for one minute taking his eye off the prisoner beside him.

Diction

Diction means "the use of words." The use of words always involves choice, and in this entry we will discuss the considerations that govern a writer's choice of words. Before we do so, however, we must consider two preliminary matters: (1) the sources where writers can find words and (2) the standards commonly applied to the use of language.

Sources

1 Dictionaries

The dictionary is an invaluable source of words. It is not just an alphabetical list of definitions: for each word, a good dictionary will also give such information as the part of speech the entry belongs to (i.e., noun, verb, preposition, etc.), its level of usage (archaic/obsolete, informal/colloquial, non-standard, dialect, slang, etc.), plural spelling, pronunciation, synonyms and antonyms, and more. You

D

should become familiar with the dictionary and take advantage of what it has to offer. The following are recommended in the event that your instructor does not suggest a particular dictionary:

The *Concise Oxford Dictionary* (1982)
A Dictionary of Canadianisms on Historical Principles (1967)
The *Dictionary of Newfoundland English* (1982)
Funk and Wagnall's *Standard College Dictionary*, Canadian Edition (1976)
The *Gage Canadian Dictionary* (1983)
Holt, Rinehart and Winston's *Compact Dictionary of Canadian English* (1976)
The *Random House Dictionary of the English Language* (1981)
Webster's II New Riverside University Dictionary (1984)
Webster's Ninth New Collegiate Dictionary (1984)

A specimen entry from the *Gage Canadian Dictionary*, a book in the Dictionary of Canadian English series (W.S. Avis, R.J. Gregg, M.H. Skargill. Eds. P.D. Drysdale, V.E. Neufeldt. [Toronto: Gage, 1983] 8.) is reproduced below.

ac·claim (ə klām′) *v. n.* —*v.* **1** show satisfaction and approval by words or sounds; shout welcome to; applaud: *The crowd acclaimed the fireman for rescuing two people from the burning house.* **2** announce with signs of approval: hail: *The newspapers acclaimed the fireman a hero.* **3** *Cdn.* elect to an office without opposition: *The voters acclaimed her mayor.*
—*n.* a shout or show of approval; applause; welcome.
[< L *acclamare* < *ad-* + to + *clamare* cry out]

ac·cla·ma·tion (ak′lə mā′shən) *n.* **1** a shout of welcome or show of approval by a crowd: applause. **2** an oral vote: *The club elected him president by acclamation.* **3** *Cdn.* the act or an instance of electing without opposition: *There were acclamations in five ridings.* **by acclamation,** *Cdn.* without opposition in an election: *Since no candidate opposed him, Mr. Kress was elected by acclamation.*
[< L. *acclamatio* a shouting. See ACCLAIM.]
☛ *Hom.* **acclimation**.

Here we find two main boldface entries of related words, each followed by standard lexical (i.e., dictionary-style) descriptions. Directly following the main entry for **acclaim** are parentheses enclosing ə *klām′*, which indicates pronunciation. Referring to the pronunciation key elsewhere in the dictionary, we find that ə is pronounced like the *u* in the word *circus* and that the *ā* is like the *a* in *face*. Next, in italics appear the letters *v, n.* —*v.*, indicating that the word

D

serves as both verb and noun and that its meaning as a verb is being considered first. Its meaning as a noun is signalled later by the appearance of —*n*.

The definitions that immediately follow are separated by bold-face numerals and proceed from the most common senses (1 and 2) to a later accretion (3), in this case a specifically Canadian use, shown by the *Cdn.* preceding the definition. In fact, **acclaim** and **acclamation** are words that will serve to test how accurately a dictionary reflects Canadian usage. Although these words are in common use throughout the English-speaking world, elections that are said to be won ''by acclamation'' are described in other countries—such as Great Britain and the U.S.A.—as being won ''without contest'' or ''with no contest.''

At the end of each entry, within square brackets, is the etymology, or derivation, of the word. We see that **acclaim** derives from the Latin word *acclamare*, to cry out, and that **acclamation** derives from *acclamatio*, a shouting.

2 Dictionaries of Synonyms and Antonyms

Dictionaries of synonyms and antonyms are especially valuable in helping you to expand and enliven your vocabulary and to choose the exact and accurate word—a crucial aspect of good diction. Two kinds of synonym dictionaries are available. One simply lists under the word you are looking up a whole group of words having similar meanings. A second type discriminates between synonyms by way of a discussion of shades of meaning. The following are recommended:

Norman Lewis, *The New Roget's Thesaurus of the English Language in Dictionary Form* (hardcover, lists synonyms)
Webster's New World Dictionary of Synonyms (hardcover, makes discriminations)
Roget's II: The New Thesaurus (hardcover, lists synonyms)
The Merriam-Webster Thesaurus (softcover, lists synonyms)
The Merriam-Webster Dictionary of Synonyms (softcover, makes discriminations)

3 Other People's Writing

An important source for fresh and lively words is your reading. When you read, do so with a sharp eye for what is well said. It is not only

D

permissible, it is desirable, to use—in your own way—words and expressions that other writers have used well. This does not mean that you should, in response to a writing assignment, *lift* (plagiarize) a whole essay or even a couple of sentences from someone else's writing and try to pass them off as your own; rather it means that you should feel free to incorporate into your own work the best words and expressions that other writers have used and that seem to you especially eloquent.

Standards

Good English is a relative term. Linguists define it as the level useful to the particular situation in which it is spoken and written. Thus good English varies from one social or regional group to another and from one particular kind of writing and speaking to another. What is *good* for speakers and writers in southern Australia differs from what is good for users of the language in western Ireland—or Canada. Many kinds of variations have been described for speakers of our language, but the most important for our purposes are the distinctions made between *standard* and *non-standard* English, and, within standard English, the distinction between *formal* and *informal*.

Standard English is the spoken and written language used by well-educated people when they wish to communicate as effectively as they can. People who use standard English enjoy a certain measure of social prestige; their language is used routinely in business, law, science, the humanities, and whenever an occupation or a profession requires written communication. Journalism, literature, and the great bulk of printed matter also use standard English. On the other hand, *non-standard* English is the term given to the speaking and writing characteristics of the relatively uneducated. Writers and speakers of non-standard English have usually had little opportunity to use written communication, and, more often than not, they have had little formal education.

Standard

Most people today feel politically powerless. A relatively small group participates in nominating candidates for office, and not many more go to the polls to elect these candidates. More important, few citizens have access to government at any level. Thus politicians are not in touch with the real needs of their constituencies. The people know it, and this is the source of the feeling of powerlessness. Unfortunately, that feeling leads to apathy.

D

Non-standard

We was asking ourselfs the other day what we would be doing if we was rich. Gordie didn't have no idea, he says it couldn't never happen anyway, so whats the difference. Bruce said he buy himself a car—a Cadillac—a house, a boat, and so many pair of shoes he couldn't never wear them out, cause he couldn't never wear em at all. Me, I say if I was rich, I just keeps on *buying*. I don't care *what*.

The advice given in this book is directed toward helping you to achieve competence in standard English. Since most students using this book will be seeking to enter the world where standard English is considered the appropriate level of spoken and written communication, we adhere to this standard. What we mean by good diction, then, will refer to standard English.

Within standard English, good diction depends on three basic considerations: the use of language that takes into account both your subject matter and your audience—in other words, the levels of usage called *formal* and *informal* and the appropriate uses of the *colloquial* and *slang*; the use of the *exact* word that will convey your *exact* meaning; and the use of words that are fresh, clear, and concrete.

Levels of Usage: Subject Matter and Audience

1 Formal

The formal level is appropriate whenever you want to establish an impersonal relation to your subject and your audience. It is the most useful level for conveying a serious attitude to an audience expecting precise information, because formal writing strives to be clear and exact. Most of your writing for courses at the post-secondary level —university or community college—and, later, most of what you write as part of your job, will be written at a formal level. Serious books and articles in science, social science, technology, law, and the humanities employ formal style. So do proposals and reports written for governments and businesses. Typically, such formality is found mainly in writing, but it is also used in speeches, lectures, and discussions, such as those commonly held at formal meetings. Formal writing is characterized by seriousness of tone, relatively complex sentence structure, and frequently, a specialized vocabulary. This does not mean, however, that formal writing is pedantic, unnecessarily complex, or dependent on jargon. While an audience may be uninformed, it will not appreciate being considered unintelligent and will reject pomposity and obscurity. Your chief intention is to convey exact information. Good writing always aims at conveying the writer's meaning as simply and directly as possible, no matter what the occasion.

> Ginseng is the perennial herb *Panax* native to North America and Asia. Asiatic ginseng (*Panax schinseng*) has been known in Asia for centuries and particularly prized by the Chinese as an important item in their herbal formulary. They have used ginseng as a virtual panacea, prescribing it for conditions ranging from flatulence to pneumonia. The demand for ginseng in North America is a recent development. For the purpose of export, China and Korea have developed the North American *Panax quinquefolius*. Here ginseng root is also virtually a panacea, but most users employ it to enhance natural vitality.

2 Informal

In recent years, it has become increasingly difficult to separate formal from informal usage. Still, there are distinct differences. The informal level is the level of everyday language employed by well-educated people. It is the language used in private letter-writing, ordinary conversation, and even books and articles that aim to catch the attention of an audience that feels at home with a familiar tone.

> Policemen make friends with other policemen. It isn't that they're not friendly; they're just busy. In fact, they spend so much time on the job, they don't have much time for socializing. So they just naturally tend to be friendly with the people they see most: other policemen. Most policemen enjoy each other's company, but most wish they had a wider range of acquaintances.

Note that this sample of informal writing is conversational in tone; that it has a speaker's vocabulary, uses contractions, and has a less complicated sentence structure than the formal sample. All but the

D

most sternly academic, scientific, or legal writing has some informal cadences in it.

An important thing to bear in mind—regardless of whether your writing is formal or informal—is to maintain consistency of tone, except when you are so well in control of your material that you are able to mix tones on purpose.

Unintentionally Mixed Tones

The beauty of the uninhabited desert regions *doesn't do a thing for me*.

Revised to Maintain Formality

The beauty of the uninhabited desert regions *does not impress me*.

Intentionally Mixed Tones

The Prime Minister's tour of European capitals must be described as a *bust*—considering that he failed to negotiate any of the trade agreements he and the *backroom boys* had hoped for.

Some discussions (and some dictionaries) regard the *colloquial* level as synonymous with informal or non-standard or both. But the word *colloquial* really means *spoken* and can be used to describe a wide range of language that appears in standard, non-standard, formal, or informal writing.

Here is a small list of words and expressions that are considered colloquial, along with their more informal counterparts:

Colloquial	More Formal
boss	superior, supervisor
bug	germ
brainy	intelligent
flunk	fail
hunch	premonition
job	position
kid	child
snooze	nap
splurge	spend lavishly
stump	puzzle
alibi	excuse
funny	strange
phone	telephone
guy	man
slob	unkempt person

3 Slang

D

Slang is highly informal language, mostly spoken, rarely used in written standard English—but not always absolutely forbidden. Slang consists of both newly coined words and expressions and new and extended meanings attached to older words. It develops from attempts to find fresh and colourful language—funny, pungent, surprising. It also develops as a kind of shorthand, and that is frequently at the root of its downfall. As shorthand, slang comes to be so overused that it falls into disuse. For example, *heavy*, a "heavy" expression of the late sixties and early seventies, is no longer in frequent use by those who habitually use slang. *Groovy* has also been banished by many slang users, and *let's tip*, meaning *let's leave* (on the analogy of "let's tiptoe out"), is so short a piece of shorthand that it never really caught on.

Nevertheless, slang has its place in both formal and informal writing and it is unwise to suppose that slang is "bad" English. In fact, many words and expressions that began as slang have passed into general (formal) usage, and our language is richer for having them. The use of slang, like the use of other words, should be determined by audience and subject matter. Some purists would object to a slang expression like the following:

> The new Steve Martin movie is *an absolute must-see*

although, conceivably, it might prove a highly effective concluding sentence for a first paragraph reviewing that movie, especially if the review were addressed to a suitable audience (the subject matter is certainly suitable for slang expression).

> Steve Martin is a jaunty firechief; Daryl Hannah is a stunning grad student in astronomy; *Roxanne* is a hilarious and touching film that depicts the progress of a romance between a small-town good guy with the strangest nose and a bright young woman who can see beyond the surface. And on top of it all, the film was shot in Nelson, B.C., and really put that town on the international map. Even high-brow critic Pauline Kael fell in love with the setting. Conclusion: *the new Steve Martin movie is an absolute must-see.*

Examine carefully the following three examples. Are these effective uses of slang? Can you think of a way to improve the one or ones you think are ineffective? Can you think of contexts in which one or more of them might be effective?

I didn't want to get hung up in a 9–5 grind but I needed the money that this gig had to offer, so I rapped about it with my old lady and got a good handle on the whole shebang. Then I said okay.

To me his apartment was pure raunch. It looked like he had really pigged out there over the weekend.

Man, don't get all bent out of shape!

TEST YOURSELF ON
Identifying Slang and Colloquial or Informal Language

Using your own sensitivity to language, put a C or an I next to those words or expressions below that strike you as colloquial or informal, and an S next to the ones that seem to be slang. After you have marked all of them, look each of them up in a good dictionary and check the dictionary labels against your answers. How many did you get?

1. bitch (verb)
2. freak (fan, enthusiast)
3. uptight
4. jazz (verb)
5. bust (verb)
6. cool it
7. beef (verb)
8. cop (noun)
9. scat
10. funky
11. slob
12. feisty

TEST YOURSELF ON
Selecting the Proper Level of Usage for a Specific Piece of Writing

Think about each of the specific pieces of writing given below and for each one choose the proper level of usage. Prepare to defend your choice with a logical argument.

1. A report to the Board of Directors of IBM Corporation on the sales prospects of a new product: a tiny, portable minicomputer.

2. A review of the movie *The Decline of the American Empire* written for an underground newspaper.

D

3. An introduction to the form of popular music known as heavy metal, written for *Maclean's* magazine.

4. The same—written for the editorial section of a small-town newspaper.

5. An article for the campus newspaper on a recent budget crisis at your community college.

6. An account of your basketball (or hockey) team's ninth consecutive loss—written for your school newspaper.

7. An essay written for a course in sociology giving an account of how your family (including aunts, uncles, and cousins) celebrates weddings.

8. A speech at a fraternity or club dance announcing the dissolution of the club or fraternity.

9. A basic explanation of enzymes for a scientific journal.

10. A review of children's literature published in the past year—for a journal of psychology.

Using Exact Words to Convey Exact Meaning

Writers who care about their work—which is another way of saying writers who care about their readers—will expend the time and energy necessary to write with precision; that is, they will go over what they have written to make sure that the words they have used convey their exact meaning.

1 Precise Expression

Writers who want to increase the precision of their word choices must be prepared to acquire the habit of rereading and then revising their written work. They must develop the habit of *seeing* and changing constructions like the following:

> *Inexact*   My father is *totally* interested in sports.

It's hard to say exactly *what* this sentence intends to express; it may mean something like "My father is *completely* interested in sports" but more likely a word like *exclusively* or *solely* or *only* was intended, instead of either *totally* or *completely*. The writer may have meant to say that "My father has an *absorbing* interest in sports," but the failure to be exact asks the reader to consider many possibilities.

D

> **Inexact**   Lisa was asked to testify as an *uninterested* observer of the burglary.

Here the writer simply confuses two words: *uninterested*, which means "without interest," and *disinterested*, which means "free of bias; impartial." Obviously, then, the exact expression would be "Lisa was asked to testify as a *disinterested* observer of the burglary."

> **Inexact**   We swam until we were tired, played volleyball on the sand, ate too much seafood, and got bad sunburns. We had a *nice* time.

Here the offending word is *nice*; it's simply too vague and doesn't in the least describe what has gone before. Better would be "we had an *exhausting but exhilarating day*."

TEST YOURSELF ON
Using Exact Expressions

In each of the following examples, the italicized word or phrase is not as exact as it should be. Supply a better expression in each case.

1. Corruption in the Federal Cabinet was *first known* in *The Globe and Mail*.

2. He *fulfilled* the court orders.

3. By the time the summer was over, he *knew* his desires.

4. Summer jobs for students were *not easy*.

5. Unemployment was an important *fact* in our economy.

6. Many of those who were flower children have *lost their appeal* for homesteading.

7. Her *immaturity* may improve as she gets older.

D

8. The rural atmosphere *subjects* a person to the beauties of nature.

9. She decided to *expect* the job.

10. After the meal, he felt *nice*.

---

2 Idioms

An idiom is an expression whose meaning cannot be determined by the ordinary meanings of the words used in it. Native speakers of English have no trouble recognizing the idiom in the sentence "A gunman *held up* the supermarket." They would not think that the gunman *lifted high*, but rather that he had *robbed*, the supermarket. Thus we could not literally translate *held up* into, say, Swedish, and expect a Swede to understand it to mean *robbed*. Logic also offers no help in understanding idioms. Because it is *customary* in English to say, "He was acquitted *of* the charges" rather than "he was acquitted *from* the charges," we say that the use of certain prepositions after certain words is idiomatic—that is, not logical but just peculiar to our language.

Although most native speakers of English automatically use idiomatic expressions, some writers have difficulty with verbs or adjectives that must be followed by particular prepositions in order to deliver their intended meaning. Here is a brief list of some troublesome combinations.

absolved by, from   I was *absolved by* the court. I was *absolved from* blame.

accompany by, on   I was *accompanied by* Tom. I was *accompanied on* my trip by Tom.

acquitted of   He was *acquitted of* all charges.

adapted to, from, by   The gasoline engine can be *adapted to* air-conditioners. The movie script was *adapted from* a novel; it was *adapted by* Mordecai Richler.

agree to, on, with   We agree *to* the terms. We agree *on* a course of action. He *agreed with* me.

angry with, at, about   Terry was *angry with* me, *angry at* her mother, and *angry about* her situation.

argue with, for, against, about   I *argued with* Marc *about* air pollution; he *argued for* and I *argued against* government controls.

D

capable of He was *capable of* being deceitful.

compare to, with *Compared to* me, he's a saint. She *compared* a Volkswagen *with* a Toyota.

communicate with, about I asked her to *communicate with* me soon. The two countries *communicated about agriculture*.

confide in, to Can I *confide in* you? Then I want to *confide to* you that I broke the law once.

conform to, with You must *conform to* (or *with*) this standard.

conformity with You must act in *conformity with* prevailing customs.

connect by, with The hose is *connected by* a coupling. I am *connected with* the English Department.

correspond to, with I *correspond with* my colleagues regularly. A French province *corresponds* roughly *to* a Canadian province.

describe as, to It was *described as* a blessing. I *described to* him my latest project.

despair of He *despaired of* ever understanding algebra.

differ about, from, with We *differ about* the best wine to drink with fish. My ideas *differ from* hers. I beg to *differ with* you.

different from* My plans are very *different from* yours.

enter into, on, upon We *entered into* an agreement. Canada *entered on* (or *upon*) a new era in foreign relations.

free from, of We were *free of* him at last. I need to be *freed from* my obligations.

identical with Your hat is *identical with* mine.

independent of She is *independent of* her family.

interest in He *interested* himself *in* politics.

live at, in, on He *lives at* 525 Pine Avenue. He *lives in* an elegant mansion. She *lives on* her independent income.

listen to, at He *listened to* nobody. She *listened at* the door.

necessity for, of The *necessity for* vitamins has been proven. There is no *necessity of* your catching cold.

object to I don't *object to* your statement.

overcome by, with Sarah was *overcome by* sadness. Arthur was *overcome with* admiration.

parallel between, with There is a *parallel between* his attitudes

---

*Different than is the colloquial usage when a clause is the object of the prepositional phrase. *Formal*: The farm looks different *from what* I had expected. *Colloquial*: The farm looks *different than* I had expected.

D

and his behaviour. The course of her career ran *parallel with* mine.

persuade of, to   I was *persuaded of* the rightness of his argument. I was *persuaded to* accompany him on the trip.

preferable to   Hawaii is *preferable to* Baffin Island for a vacation.

superior to   Her stereo set is *superior to* mine.

vary from, in, with   Ideas *vary from* one another just as shoe sizes *vary in* width. My mood *varies with* changes of weather.

worthy of   He is *worthy of* my sympathy.

Idiomatic expression also requires that some verbs be followed by a gerund and some by an infinitive.

Infinitive	*Gerund*
able to go	capable of going
like to go	enjoy going
eager to go	cannot help going
hesitate to go	privilege of going
need to go	purpose of going
ask to go	consider going
consent to go	deny going
want to go	put off going

TEST YOURSELF ON
Using Correct Idiomatic Expressions

In each of the blank spaces, write the correct idiomatic expression needed for the sentence. The expression required may be a preposition, an infinitive, or a gerund.

1. With fish dinners, drinking white wine is preferable _____ drinking red.

2. I hesitate _____ him what I think of him. (Use a form of *tell*.)

3. She lives comfortably _____ her pension.

4. They argued _____ who would do a better job as major.

D

5. He was described _____ me as a liberal, which was quite different _____ what I had been led to believe.

6. She was capable _____ making her feelings known.

7. Because she was angry _____ me, I was overcome _____ guilt.

8. I was not eager _____ (use a form of *leave*) school, but there was a necessity _____ doing so.

9. We entered _____ a contract; therefore we were legally connected _____ each other.

10. George confided _____ his friends that he was breaking up with Kathy.

Fresh, Specific, and Concrete Language

A writer's language should be fresh, specific, and concrete; it should avoid clichés and try to make a vivid impression on the reader. Plain language can do this if it strives for a proper balance between the abstract and the concrete, the general and the specific.

1 Clichés

The word *cliché* (pronounced *clee-shay*) comes from the French word for stereotype plate or printing block. Hence any word or expression whose freshness or clarity has been lost through constant usage is called a cliché, a stereotype. Such words or phrases are also called tired, stale, trite, or worn out. Writers who habitually use clichés not only use tired words but also present the reader with tired ideas.

Nevertheless, we all use clichés in ordinary conversation. In those circumstances, they are frequently forgiven—perhaps because we make up for the tired expression with a lively presence. In any case, whether your writing is formal or informal, you should develop an ear for clichés and avoid using such expressions as the following:

the beginning of the end	the last straw
better late than never	mother nature
bigger and better	neat as a pin
cool as a cucumber	on balance
a crying shame	pretty as a picture
deep, dark secret	right on
do justice to	rotten to the core
free as a bird	sadder but wiser
hard as nails	tell it like it is
hot under the collar	variety is the spice of life
last but not least	viable options

Writers who persistently use clichés are not in control of their material. Writers who are in control of their material can *use* clichés to make fresh points.

The fact that Aaron was so often late for appointments made it obvious that he would never be known as *a regular guy*.

My response to what you've just proposed is *wrong on*.

The bigger the better simply does not apply to things like budget deficits and the headaches they invariably bring on.

TEST YOURSELF ON

Identifying Clichés

Circle any words or expressions you find in the following passages that you think are clichés; then supply better—fresher—words or expressions to replace them.

1. Although I was financially embarrassed, I decided to eat out

   anyway. I didn't care that I was getting to be fatter than a pig; I

   wanted to do justice to a great meal—and the bigger the better.

   I settled on McDonald's and started eating like there was no

   tomorrow. I had six Big Macs, four large orders of fries, and

   three large shakes. Last but not least, I topped the whole thing off with four apple turnovers. That, however, was the last straw. My stomach really started to growl, and later on that evening I realized that I had eaten myself sick. The next morning I was, believe it or not, sadder but wiser.

2. In this day and age, getting set for life in the fast lane demands that university and college students get on the ball and learn more than just the stuff taught in classes. Students should get out and mingle. This is the only way to develop a well-rounded personality and the ability to get along with others. There are all kinds of things students can do to become more interesting personalities. They can join a club, attend dances, or just start being friendly —straight from the shoulder—with their fellow students in class. Hitting the books isn't the only way to go through school. If you want to get what you pay for, you have to pass the acid test. Beyond a shadow of a doubt, if you want to get more out of life, you have to put more into it.

2 Concrete and Abstract Language

Writers should use concrete language wherever possible. A concrete word is one that appeals directly to the senses—it points to something that exists. Thus *engine* is a concrete word: we can see, hear, and feel an engine when we lift the hood of a car. But what the engine supplies, *power* (or *energy*), is abstract: power cannot be directly perceived. Many concrete things deliver power: an engine, a turbine, a locomotive, a football fullback, and so forth. We would not say, giving the reason for not buying a specific car, ''The Ford had no power'' if we meant that it had no engine—but we might say ''The Ford had no power'' if we meant that its engine wasn't efficient. So both abstract and concrete language have their uses. But the advice still holds: writers should use the concrete word whenever they can, because the mind's ability to picture a concrete word makes the writing more vivid. This policy also applies to sentences. Sentences with abstract ideas can be made clearer by supporting them with concrete illustrations.

> **Sentence Containing Needlessly Abstract Words**
> The *grounds* were *sloppy* and the *planks* on the porch were *bad.*
> **Revised to Supply Concrete Words**
> The *front yard* was *littered with broken furniture and rusted tools* and the *steps* of the porch were *rotted and splintered.*

Frequently, the pattern of abstract-concrete shows up in good writing as the form of a paragraph; that is, the first sentence is an abstraction that the following sentences seek to make concrete.

> **Abstract First Sentence of a Paragraph**
> When dealing with institutions, people are made to feel small.
> **Concrete Follow-up Sentence**
> They are made to fill out needlessly complicated forms, to spend long hours waiting in line, and frequently to visit an office several times in order to get what they came for.

3 Specific and General Language

The terms *specific* and *general*, applied to words or expressions, mean much the same as is meant by the labels *concrete* and *abstract*—with this difference: *specific* and *general* attest to the relative degrees of concreteness of a particular set of words.

    meat—poultry—chicken
    animals—primates—gorillas
    military—soldier—Corporal Kim
    foliage—trees—oak
    clothing—trousers—blue jeans

Note that as you read from left to right, the words become more specific; the reader is better able to *picture* the concrete object. Though we would not say that the words in the left-hand column are abstract, they are *more general* terms than those in the other two columns. Good writing requires that the writer use the more specific term whenever possible. Although it is true that good writers use general terms as well as specific ones, more often than not there is a loss of freshness and clarity in writing when writers abandon control of their work and use constructions like the following:

D

> *General* Shade was provided by a big *tree* on the *grass*.
> *Specific* Shade was provided by a *spreading maple* on the *lawn*.

> *General* College students are forced to waste a lot of time.
> *Specific* A college student must often waste time waiting in registration lines, filling out forms, and making more than one trip to a professor's office to obtain a grade. (Notice how this idea is expanded when it is made more specific.)

TEST YOURSELF ON

Using Specific, Concrete Language

A For each of the italicized words in the sentences below, find at least two other words that convey a more specific meaning.

1. She *slept* for half an hour.

2. He *ate* his food as if it were his last meal.

3. He decided not to *tell* that he'd had an accident.

4. She *called* for help.

5. Al didn't want to *show* his feelings.

6. He *ran* all the way home.

7. She *worked on* her essay for an hour; then she gave up.

8. Out of the corner of his eye, he *noticed* someone approaching.

9. He *walked* lazily down to the corner store.

10. They *wrote* their compositions in class.

B Follow each of the general statements in the sentences below with two sentences, giving concrete details to illustrate them.

Example: When I woke up this morning, I felt as if I'd been drugged.

D

Follow-up with concrete details: My head ached dully, and my vision was blurred. When I tried to move, it felt as if I were walking through water.

1. When I woke up this morning, I felt as if I'd been drugged.

2. My garden is growing beautifully.

3. I don't think my parents understand that I'm an adult.

4. The physically disabled have special problems

5. Registering for classes at this college takes its toll on a student.

Double Negative

The use of an additional negative to reinforce an early negative statement is called a double negative and is not acceptable in standard English. Usually, the writer of a double (or even a triple) negative is intent on being emphatic in his or her no-saying, and several hundred years ago this usage was acceptable, but not now.

Double Negative   Nobody loves me no more.
Revised   Nobody loves me *any more*.

Double Negative   He can't hardly walk any more.
Revised   He *can* hardly walk any more. (*Hardly* is the negative.)

Double Negative   Scarcely none of my friends likes reggae music.
Revised   Scarcely *any* of my friends like reggae music. (*Scarcely* is the negative.)

Triple Negative   He never had no faith in nobody.
Revised   He never had faith in *anybody*.

One form of the double negative *is* acceptable, however, and its use is a form of stylistic choice. For example, we could say, "He was frequently late for my classes," or to achieve a slightly different emphasis, "He was *not in*frequently late for my classes." Another example: "She said she was willing to go out on dates with Tom," or "She said she was *not un*willing to go out on dates with Tom." The slightly different emphasis in the two sentences using the acceptable double negative is one of qualification. The two negatives cancel each other, which adds an ironic lack of commitment.

TEST YOURSELF ON
Eliminating Unacceptable Double or Triple Negatives

Each of the sentences given below contains an unacceptable double or triple negative. Correct them in the spaces provided.

E-H

1. I don't want nothing to do with you.

_____

2. There was never nobody like him.

_____

3. She never had no reason to give nobody a present.

_____

4. He didn't hardly have any friends.

_____

5. There wasn't scarcely a soul in the library when I was there on Saturday night.

_____

Ellipsis

The omission of a portion of quoted text is called ellipsis. Spaced dots (an ellipsis) are used to indicate where text has been omitted.

The Full Text Being Quoted
Mr. Ross Alexander's play moves across the stage like a dream of yesterday, stinging us with its wit and wisdom, arguing our case

before an ethical court, lifting our spirits as we contemplate our
battered selves.
Edward Quinn

A Portion Quoted from This Text with Some Words Omitted
Quinn says "Alexander's play moves . . . like a dream . . . arguing
our case . . . lifting our spirits . . ."

E

The spaced dots in this quoted portion are called an ellipsis. When
the ellipsis comes at the end of a sentence, use a period followed
by three spaced dots to indicate omitted material.

An ellipsis is also used to indicate a pause or an unfinished
statement, especially in dialogue.

"Be careful, John. If you're not . . ."

"I don't know . . . I just don't know."

End Punctuation

The punctuation marks that end sentences—periods, exclamation
marks, and question marks—suggest how a reader is to understand
the whole sentence. Internal punctuation (colons, commas, dashes,
parentheses, and semicolons) indicates relations of the parts of the
sentence. See **Colon, Comma, Rules, Dash, Exclamation Mark,
Parentheses, Period, Question Mark, Semi-colon**.

Examination Skills

See **Study and Examination Skills**.

Exclamation Mark

The exclamation mark (!), which always signifies strong emphasis,
is very rarely used in formal writing, which usually adopts an even

tone. Exclamations most frequently occur in simulated speech, where they are used as follows:

1 Use the exclamation mark to signify the end of an exclamatory sentence, phrase, or clause. An exclamatory expression is an abrupt, forceful outcry—very emphatic.

> How he must be suffering! (sentence)
>
> What a tragedy! (elliptical clause, i.e., one with words missing: full clause is "What a tragedy this is!")
>
> No kidding! (phrase)

A single exclamation mark does the job. Don't use more than one for extra emphasis.

2 Use the exclamation mark to emphasize a form of direct address or an interjection when there is strong feeling being conveyed.

> Nicole! I need help!
>
> Hurray! We won!

3 Use an exclamation mark to add emphasis to an imperative sentence (a command) where strong feeling is being conveyed.

> Shut your mouth!
>
> Stay away from me!
>
> Give me an answer now!

4 Do not use an exclamation mark for (a) statements that are not exclamatory, (b) ordinary forms of address, (c) unemphatic interjections, or (d) mild commands.

> ***Wrong***   That's too bad!
>
> ***Wrong***   Nicole! I'd like to speak to you.
>
> ***Wrong***   Well! we've arrived.
>
> ***Wrong***   Turn left at the corner!

Note: When the exclamation mark is overused, it gives your writing an air of forced excitement—almost hysteria—and robs you of the opportunity to provide real emphasis where it is needed. Use the exclamation mark sparingly.

E

TEST YOURSELF ON

Using the Exclamation Mark Appropriately

Some of the sentences below use the exclamation mark appropriately; next to these, place the letter C. In the rest, strike out the exclamation marks that are unnecessary.

F

1. _____ War is hell!

2. _____ How the mighty have fallen!

3. _____ College courses ask too much of a student!

4. _____ Get your hands off me!

5. _____ How he must have suffered!

6. _____ This coffee is terrible!

7. _____ I need aspirin!

8. _____ What a crazy man!

9. _____ Turn the car around!

10. _____ What big teeth you have, Grandma!

Fragments

The word *fragment* means a piece or a part; therefore, a sentence fragment is a piece of a sentence. Beginning writers frequently write pieces of sentences because they distrust the *length* of what they are writing, and they think that if they insert a period after they have written a certain number of words their writing will "look" better. This is an error. Length is not the main factor in determining when to end one sentence and begin another.

> [A] Whenever I try to hold a long and serious conversation with my parents about my career. [B] They get me angry by raising irrelevant issues and arguments.

The writer of this material decided to place a period after the word *career* because the string of words looked long. In fact, however, the portion that is marked A is an incorrect *sentence fragment*. The reason it is a fragment is that it is a *dependent clause*; that is, it has a subject (*I*) and a finite verb (*try*)—which all sentences need—but it also has a subordinating conjunction, *whenever*. The whole structure hangs from this conjunction—which signals us that the structure must be connected to an independent clause—and therefore A cannot stand alone.

F

We can make A independent and therefore able to stand alone by eliminating *whenever*; this detaches the clause from what it depends on and makes it a whole sentence—an independent clause.

The second method of correcting the fragment error is to take the fragment, A, and hook it to an independent clause. This we can do by substituting a comma for the period after *career* and making the capital letter in *they* into a lower case letter, for the B portion of the example *is* an independent clause. (If you have forgotten the meaning of dependent and independent clauses, go back to Part 1, pages 33–38, and study the subject.)

Original Example
Whenever I try to hold a long and serious conversation with my parents about my career. They get me angry by raising irrelevant issues and arguments.

Example Corrected by the First Method
I try to hold a long and serious conversation with my parents about my career. They get me angry by raising irrelevant issues and arguments.

Example Corrected by the Second Method
Whenever I try to hold a long and serious conversation with my parents about my career, they get me angry by raising irrelevant issues and arguments.

Which of the corrections do you think is better? In this case, the second method is better because retaining the word *whenever* establishes a clear relation between the two parts.

Fragment
While I was listening to some rock on the stereo the other night. Someone came along and stole my car.

Corrected by First Method

I was listening to some rock on the stereo the other night. Someone came along and stole my car. (Grammatically correct, but gives no sense of how the two parts are related.)

Corrected by Second Method

While I was listening to some rock on the stereo the other night, someone came along and stole my car. (Also grammatically correct, but a better correction because the two parts are better related.)

F

TEST YOURSELF ON

Correcting Sentence Fragments

The following are all incorrect. Rewrite each as a complete sentence.

1. They wouldn't let Jodi on the basketball court. Because she wasn't wearing sneakers.

2. I'm worried about my final exams. Which come in about three weeks.

3. Professor Urban took me out for an expensive dinner. Although he had mentioned to me that he was short of money.

4. Unless I'm given the salary I want. I won't take the job.

5. Whenever he hears the Beatles sing ''Yesterday.'' He's reminded of the sixties.

Another kind of sentence fragment is made when beginning writers mistake verbals for verbs and think that the structure containing a verbal can stand alone. (See Phrases.)

                                    verbal
Incorrect   Sandra has an overwhelming desire. *To leave town.*

                                      verbal
Incorrect   Arthur believes he has one purpose in life. *To teach.*

                                      verbal
Incorrect   Uncle Armand is happy doing only one thing. *Running.*

Even if you haven't written much, you would not be likely to make the errors in these examples, because in each case the verbal is limited to just a few words. The problem remains the same, however, when these verbals are extended into long verbal phrases.

> ***Incorrect***   Sandra has an overwhelming desire. *To leave town in order to start a new career.*

> ***Incorrect***   Arthur believes he has one purpose in life. *To teach youngsters the fundamentals of mathematics.*

> ***Incorrect***   Uncle Armand is happy doing only one thing. *Running ten miles a day to prepare himself to compete in marathon races.*

F

The italicized phrase in each of these examples is dependent and cannot stand alone. Each must be connected, with or without a comma, to the sentence that precedes it. Besides having no subjects, these phrases have no finite verbs—only verbals—and a sentence must have a subject and a finite verb.

A third type of fragment appears when you punctuate prepositional phrases as if they were complete sentences (see Phrases). Only complete sentences should be punctuated as such.

> prepositional phrase
> ***Incorrect***   Financial aid at this college is given. *To students.*

> prepositional phrase
> ***Incorrect***   Financial aid at this college is given. *To students who show need.*

> prepositional phrase
> ***Incorrect***   Financial aid at this college is given. *To students who show need and whose records are outstanding.*

Once again, it is unlikely that beginning writers will make the error shown in the first example, because the prepositional phrase there consists of only two words. But in the other two examples, the possibility is greater because the number of words is greater. In all three examples, of course, the period after the word *given* is incorrect and creates the fragment that follows it.

A fourth type of fragment is created when you fail to recognize that a portion of what you are writing is really a final appositive and not a sentence.

> ***Incorrect***   This summer, I'm spending my vacation with George.
> appositive
> *A friend.*

> ***Incorrect***   This summer, I'm spending my vacation with George.
>   appositive
> *A friend, a sportsman, a very funny guy.*

The first example contains an error that a beginning writer probably won't make, because the appositive consists of only two words. But the error in the second example is more likely to be made because the appositive has more words. In fact, appositives can be quite long and complicated, but no matter how long they are, they cannot stand as sentences. To correct the fragments above, change the period to either a comma or a colon.

F

TEST YOURSELF ON

Recognizing and Correcting Sentence Fragments

A Turn the following sentence fragments into sentences by crossing out a word in the fragment.

1. Until I reached home.

2. Although he seemed like a nice enough man.

3. Whenever I have gone to the theatre.

4. Unless my uncle gives me some financial support.

5. Because you have dry skin.

6. If I saw her at a party.

7. After the doctor changed my bandage.

8. Since he wasn't a practising Christian.

9. While the cows were being milked.

10. As my mother walked through the door.

B Correct the following fragments by adding an independent clause to the beginning or the end of each:

Example

> *Fragment*: Which cost me twelve dollars.
> *Fragment connected: His birthday present was a book*, which cost me twelve dollars.

1. Which cost me twelve dollars.

2. Although I rarely eat at a restaurant.

3. If I never buy another automobile again.

4. Running along the side of the road.

5. To understand auto mechanics.

6. In the woods behind my house.

7. A friend, a teacher, an adviser.

8. To students who are able to undertake advanced studies.

9. Unless I hear from you tonight.

10. To people who are interested in art.

11. Travelling all over the world.

12. Enough time, enough equipment, enough spirit.

C Read carefully each of the following examples. Underline a sentence fragment wherever you see one, and correct it. Some of the examples are complete sentences, containing no fragments; next to these, write C.

1. _____ Horses racing together through the surf.

2. _____ When college students graduate, they usually celebrate with a party or a dance.

3. _____ Her father had one goal. To leave her a considerable inheritance.

4. _____ She cooked a large and elaborate dinner. To impress her husband's parents.

5. _____ Last summer we visited Niagara Falls and then crossed over into the United States. Which is what I have always wanted to do.

6. _____ Although I am not at all sure what I will do after graduation. I am very sure that I want to spend four years studying ecology.

7. _____ They drove 4,800 kilometres across the country to see their son's graduation. An event that they had yearned to see for four long years.

F

8. _____ The black experience in South Africa has been a frightful one. Which accounts for the revolutionary tone of most black South African writing.

9. _____ Although television programming seems innocuous, its effects are not.

10. _____ I'm not leaving here. Until I get my money back.

TEST YOURSELF ON
Correcting Fragments by Proofreading

The following passage contains eight sentence fragments. By careful proofreading, find and correct each one.

My father was a farmer. Although he'd gone to college, where he studied technology. Life on the farm was hard, but my father was ingenious, probably because of his training as a technician, and he took delight in solving mechanical problems. Problems that would come up with the tractors or the milking machines or even the plumbing in our house. He never had time for long vacations. Which doesn't mean he ever in any way felt "burnt out." The way so many of us feel today when we work for long periods without appropriate rest. My father's secrets were two: he was a champion at resting whenever rest periods came—at night, for example. When he'd settle down with the weekly paper by the fire after a good supper. The other secret was the real sense of joy he took in his work. No aspect of the work on the land or with the livestock ever seemed to bore him. Although some of the tasks required constant repetition. In fact, whenever he needed to leave the farm to be present at ceremonial occasions. He'd be nervous and irritable for all the time he was away. It would be fine if all of us could live a work life like my father's. Loving the labour we performed.

H

Free-writing

See **Prewriting**.

Homonym

A homonym is a word identical in sound with another word but different in origin, meaning and, sometimes, spelling. Examples are *sun* and *son, bear* and *bare*, and so on. See **Spelling**.

Hyphen

The hyphen is used between words or between prefixes and words to indicate that the hyphenated structure should be taken as a unit (*twenty-two, low-level*); to separate prefixes from words when the combination is spelled like a word with another meaning (e.g., *re-creation*, "a creation again," and *recreation*, "leisure"); and to divide a word at the end of a line of text to show that it continues on to the next line. This last use is a matter of convention; we will begin with it.

1 Use a hyphen when you must divide a word at the end of a line of text and continue it on the next line. When you must do this, place the hyphen between syllables. A syllable is a unit of spoken language consisting usually of a vowel alone or a vowel with one or more consonants. Good dictionaries give the proper syllables of a word in each entry. Here is the proper syllabication of a few multi-syllable words. Notice that each syllable is pronounceable.

a-bove	con-ver-sa-tion	pic-ture
ac-tor	dis-trib-ute	rev-er-end
bap-tism	hy-dro-gen	ref-u-ta-ble
bi-cy-cle	op-po-nent	res-to-ra-tion
bur-y	pa-tience	sep-a-ra-tion

Here are examples of proper word divisions at the end of a line.

It turned out on Friday that our *conversa-*
tion had been unnecessary. We were really agreed on everything.

After graduating from college, Donald became an *ac-*
tor, something I had not thought possible when I knew him.

If you are unsure of the proper syllabication of a word, consult a good dictionary. But never leave a single letter on one line even if it *is* the proper syllabication. And never divide a word of one syllable, such as *France* or *trout*.

Wrong   There was a line of low, threatening clouds *a-*
bove the mountains.
Right   There was a line of low, threatening clouds
above the mountains.

Wrong We decided it would be in our best interest to *bur-y* the hatchet and be friends again.
Right We decided it would be in our best interest to *bury* the hatchet and be friends again.

Wrong In the fall, when we finally left for *Fr-ance*, we were very excited.
Right In the fall, when we finally left for *France*, we were very excited.

H

2 Use a hyphen to join words or words and prefixes together. The hyphen used in this way is, in most cases, a transitional mark. For example, usually (but not always), when words are first linked to each other, they are written separately—as in *basket ball*. Later, this word became *basket-ball*, and it is now, of course, always written *basketball*. Thus, just how to use the hyphen for any compound word at any particular moment is difficult to determine because usage is continually changing and even good, recently published dictionaries are likely to be behind the times. Still, the dictionary is the soundest authority and should be consulted when the writer is doubtful about a particular hyphenation.

The following rules were accurate when this book was written:

A Words beginning with *all, self*, and *ex* (meaning *former*) are always hyphenated.

He is a *self-made* man.

In Washington, the President's staff is *all-powerful*.

The *ex-Prime Minister* usually has little to say.

B When the root word is a proper noun or proper adjective, use a hyphen to separate prefixes.

anti-Semitic   un-American   pro-Thatcher

C Prefixes ending in a vowel are frequently hyphenated, especially if the root word begins with the same vowel.

anti-intellectual   semi-invalid   pre-election
re-educate   de-escalate   re-evaluate
co-ordinate   anti-abortion

D Certain prefixes are hyphenated to avoid confusing a word with another whose spelling is identical.

A work of art is a *re-creation* of experience. (to avoid confusion with *recreation*, "leisure")

Since the math teacher couldn't follow his logic, the student had to *re-prove* the theorem. (to avoid confusion with *reprove*, "rebuke")

Now that I have emptied our closets, we have to *re-store* all our things. (to avoid confusion with *restore*, "return to a former condition")

H

3 A good many compound nouns are hyphenated; a good many others are not; and some are written as single words. (A compound noun is one that consists of more than one word.)

Hyphenated	Unhyphenated	Single Words
air-brake	dream life	blackbird
bee-sting	diving board	database
bull's-eye	first cousin	headache
cave-in	high school	landslide
free-for-all	ice cream	madman
merry-go-round	oil spill	newsstand

Remember: If you are unsure about a particular case, consult a good dictionary.

4 Compound adjectives—groups of words that when taken together act like a single-word adjective—are usually joined together by hyphens.

able-bodied seaman	*low-level* official
devil-may-care attitude	*middle-of-the-road* politician
double-parked car	*out-of-work* actor
fence-busting outfielder	*two-tiered* stadium

Note: When these adjectives are in the predicate adjective position, following a linking verb, the hyphen is omitted.

The actor is *out of work*.

Her car was *double parked*.

5 Hyphens are used between parts of compound numbers—twenty-one to ninety-nine—and in specifying fractions. Hyphens are also frequently used to connect numbers in specifying dates.

This is my *twenty-second* birthday.

My professor is only *thirty-one* years old.

He is taxed *two-fifths* of his income.

The meetings will take place September *4-11*.

My vacation runs *July 31-August 14*.

Note: Do not use a hyphen in non-compound numbers.

one hundred twelve

H

TEST YOURSELF ON

The Appropriate Use of the Hyphen

Some of the sentences below contain uses of the hyphen that are correct; next to these, write C. Some sentences, however, contain word groups that need a hyphen. Insert a hyphen wherever you think one is missing.

1. _____ Sarah is a well trained teacher, but she would rather be a well paid researcher.

2. _____ Resort the laundry so that we can get all the white things together.

3. _____ Everything Jeffrey does is self-serving.

4. _____ Call in a carpenter; those bookshelves are not a doityourself job.

5. _____ Ed's colourblindness is due to a genetic defect.

6. _____ In the 1950s, many leftleaning U.S. citizens were labelled unAmerican.

7. _____ Coal mine caveins are preventable.

8. _____ The actor used to be an able bodied seaman.

9. _____ Exdiplomats frequently write their memoirs.

10. _____ The all-powerful Revenue Canada takes two-fifths of my income in taxes.

11. _____ My friend was a semiinvalid and a proTurner psuedoliberal.

12. _____ She scored a bull'seye in target shooting, but he was uninterested.

I-M

Idiom

See **Diction**.

Internal Punctuation

See **End Punctuation**.

Italics

Italics is the name given to the typeface in which these words are printed. On the other hand, the typeface in which these words are printed is called roman. In hand-written manuscripts or typescripts, underlining is the equivalent of italics. Italics are conventionally used in the following special cases.

1 Use italics for the names of books, plays, films, television shows, newspapers, magazines, ships, aircraft, long musical compositions.

Shakespeare's *Hamlet*

Melville's *Moby Dick*

Saturday Night (magazine)

The Calgary *Herald* (Note that the name of the city is not in italics here; although it is for some newspapers, e.g., *The Vancouver Sun.*)

S.S. Rotterdam, Queen Elizabeth II

The City of Birmingham (name of aircraft)

Beethoven's *Ninth Symphony*

The Grey Fox (film)

Venture (television show)

2 Use italics for foreign words and phrases that have not become part of the English language.

He lived in North Bay but kept a small *pied-à-terre* in Toronto. (*pied-à-terre* = temporary or secondary lodging place)

Writing poems was his whole *raison d'être*. (*raison d'être* = reason for being)

Leo is known as a *bon vivant*. (*bon vivant* = a person who enjoys good food and other pleasant things)

Note: Some foreign words and phrases *have* become part of the English language and should not be italicized. Here is a small list of them:

| cliché | gamin | guru | genre | lacuna |
| café | bona fide | ensemble | elite | Gesundheit |

3 Use italics for words and phrases considered as themselves.

The word *elegant* is derived from Old French.

The term *end of the line* is a cliché.

4 Use italics for scientific terms in Latin.

The constellation Great Bear (*Ursa major*) is in the northern hemisphere.

For genetic research, the species of mosquito known as *anopheles* is most useful.

5 Use italics for giving special emphasis to ordinary words. You should achieve emphasis by placing the important word or words in an emphatic position in the sentence, not by carelessly using italics. Italics should be reserved for words that cannot be emphasized enough by ordinary work on structure.

Weak   I'm talking about *love*, as an emotion.
Revised   Love is what I'm talking about. (Here the position of *love* as the subject gives it enough emphasis without italics.)

Weak   He said he would *never* marry.
Revised   Questioned as to when he would marry, he replied with one word: never. (The final position of the word in the rewritten sentence is very emphatic: note, too, that the sentence has been designed to emphasize *never*.)

Proper Use of Italics   What's important is not what she *was*, but what she has *become*. (Italics point up the contrast between *was* and *become*.)
Guido is henpecked not because he has a wife but because *his wife has him*. (Italics call attention to the reversal.)

TEST YOURSELF ON

The Use of Italics

Some of the following sentences show the correct use of italics. Next to each of these, write C. Some sentences, however, need to have italics added or removed; in these, make the appropriate corrections.

1. _____ The current craze for *nostalgia* knows no limits.

2. _____ The expression freaked out is slang.

3. _____ The Vancouver Sun has only one competitor.

4. _____ Great books like Moby Dick and Anna Karenina occupy the mind long after we've read them.

5. _____ My Aunt Alicia is on the cover of *City Woman* this month.

6. _____ The program includes Beethoven's Sixth Symphony and his Fidelio Overture.

7. _____ I felt much better after I spoke to my *guru*.

8. _____ The porcupine anteater belongs to the family *echidna*.

9. _____ Event magazine published Diana's first story.

10. _____ We're sailing on the *S.S. Rotterdam*.

11. _____ She worked as a *fille de chambre* [lady's maid].

12. _____ It was his last performance as Hamlet.

L

Logic

Clear and forceful writing always involves clear thinking and the presentation of honest evidence. Therefore, in this brief treatment of a complex subject, we shall deal with aspects of logic useful to writers who wish to impart to their work the rigour and strength of solid thought. The topics to be covered are these: (1) fairness in argument, (2) the careful use of evidence, (3) methods of clear reasoning, and (4) errors in thinking.

Fairness in Argument

To be sure that your arguments or generalizations (or thesis statements) are fair and not prejudiced, you should avoid the errors discussed here.

1 Avoid basing your argument on belief rather than knowledge.

Prejudice is prejudgement, before the facts are known. We may *wish* to believe something is true and argue a case using that something as a generalization. But we would only be displaying prejudice.

Deirdre doesn't know how to drive a car. I always see her sitting in the back seat of her parents' automobile. (How does the speaker know that Deirdre isn't just following family custom by sitting in the back?)

She must have a sugar daddy somewhere. Every time I see her, she's wearing a new outfit. (The speaker is merely *assuming*. Deirdre may have money that is *not* the gift of an "admirer" but that she has earned or been given as a gift by a relative.)

These leaps in logic are frequent in ordinary conversation or in careless discourse elsewhere. They are prejudicial and lead to serious distortions. Consider the way that racial prejudice follows the same model of slack thought: for example, all Italians are loud, Chinese poor drivers, Jews rich and stingy, and so forth.

2 Avoid arguing by discrediting an opponent or his idea.

This is known as *argumentum ad hominem*, or "arguing to the man." It is a form of non-evidence that fails to notice a person might be wrong about one thing and right about another.

Don't believe Quinn when he says our college isn't doing right by its students. He never went to school himself. (Quinn may have been wrong in avoiding a formal education—although we can't tell from what the speaker says—and right in his analysis of the way the college functions.)

Tuten is wrong about the town's need for more roads. He's a contractor and naturally he wants the money. (Tuten doesn't *know* he'll get the contract; besides, he could be right about the need for roads.)

The examples given show that the speaker in both cases is arguing to the man rather than to the issues involved.

3 Avoid making capital by associating your idea or argument with a great name.

This is called the *argumentum ad verecundiam*, where it is hoped that the association of one's position or thought with a great name will transfer the authority or prestige of that name to one's own thought. It also works in reverse. By associating an opponent's ideas with some person or movement of low prestige, one discredits one's opponent.

If Lester Pearson were alive today he'd be promoting aid for the Third World.

Like all revolutionaries, he believes in sharing the wealth.

TEST YOURSELF ON
Judging the Fairness of Generalizations

Read carefully each set of statements printed below. Then prepare for each a discussion of its fairness or unfairness according to the discussion you've just read.

1. The Bible says "honour thy father and thy mother," so I never disobey mine.

2. College students don't work as hard as they did in my day. Nowadays all they do is listen to music.

3. Business is nothing but thievery. How else could they make so much money?

4. Black people make terrific athletes.

5. I would never hire an ex-convict to work for me. Once a thief, always a thief. That's what I say.

The Careful Use of Evidence

Instead of using prejudice and unfair tactics, the logical writer employs evidence that appeals not to passion but to reason.

Good evidence is the proper use of facts, opinion, or statistics. Evidence honestly and carefully used supports a generalization (a thesis statement) in such a way as to persuade a reader that the case being presented is solid to the point of being unassailable.

Failure to be careful leads to errors in handling evidence, and these usually fall into the following categories:

1 Biased Evidence
This is a form of evidence so unreliable that it is sure to do the argument more harm than good. If you were to argue, on the basis

of a poll taken among construction workers in Edmonton, that the Canadian people are in favour of the federal government spending large sums of money to subsidize the construction of an oil pipeline to the Arctic Ocean, your evidence would be biased. These people would not necessarily favour building *only* pipelines, although surely they are saying they want more work. Nor could they be considered representative of Canadians as a whole. Similarly, if you were to argue that northerners' objections to such a pipeline are irrelevant, citing the need of urban southerners for energy compared to the northerners' need for caribou herds, you would also be arguing from biased evidence. Conservation of the caribou is the responsibility of all Canadians.

Biased evidence is frequently the mainstay of advertising and other forms of commercial presentation. There the evidence is made biased by taking things out of context. Some companies which advertise their soft drinks as sugar-free (good) do not, in the same advertisement, acknowledge that those drinks contain disreputable sugar substitutes (bad).

The testimony of character witnesses at trials can also be seen as a form of biased evidence, for such witnesses are always prepared to say only good things about a defendant.

Advertising blurbs and character witnesses are, among others, notoriously deliberate employers of biased evidence. But writers need to be careful that they do not inadvertently use such material. The way to avoid this trap is to use only the most rigorously impartial and respectable sources.

2 Insufficient Evidence

It is December in southern Manitoba. For three days, the temperature hovers around 12 degrees. A native exclaims, ''We're having a mild winter.'' This is a clear case of insufficient evidence. What about the other days between December and March?

Another case: if after your first week of college you have failed to make a friend, are you justified in thinking, ''This school is a drag; everybody's unfriendly''? Not really. You have insufficient evidence because it has only been a week and you haven't been exposed to *all* the possible friends you might make.

Thus insufficient evidence most frequently involves having too few cases on which to build a generalization. Writers must be sure to make their evidence plentiful enough to be convincing.

3 Poorly Evaluated Statistics

Faulty evidence in the form of poorly evaluated statistics is easy to present if the writer is not wary. For example, Statistics Canada issues a statistic on unemployment for a particular month: 8.7 percent. Before citing this figure in support of an argument that the Canadian economy is performing about as well as expected, you had better consider this question: as well as expected with regard to whom? For buried in that single 8.7 percent statistic there may be others—for example, that teenagers suffer an unemployment rate of 26.7 percent and native teenagers an even higher rate. The economy does not perform for all the people all the time.

Another example, closer to home, will make this issue even clearer. Suppose you've been working during all of 1989 at your usual part-time job for the salary of $100 a week. Then in 1990, your boss recognizes your true value (at last) and starts paying you at the new rate of $200 a week. Can we assume that you now have twice as much money? Would that be a fair way to make inferences from the statistics? Not at all. It should be fairly obvious that you've jumped into a new tax bracket, that more taxes are being withheld from your pay cheque, and that larger Unemployment Insurance payments are being deducted as well.

The point is that all of us need help with statistics. For this reason, although statistics are very useful in an argument, we need to be wary about how we use them.

TEST YOURSELF ON

Recognizing Biased, Insufficient, and Statistically Unreliable Evidence

Each of the following groups of statements is a case of evidence poorly conceived. Give a name to the error in each case.

1. Twelve percent of Canadians earn 50 thousand or more dollars a year. Let's look for the rich ones on this campus: there are 3,000 of us, so there must be 360 who earn that much.

2. Everybody I know is buying a motorcycle. They must be terrific.

3. If you live in Whitehorse, you must have warm blood.

4. I read that the lumberjacks in British Columbia want to cut down more trees. That must mean nobody in the province is interested in ecology.

5. My sister's not doing well in math. Women can't handle math and sciences.

6. The price of cars has doubled in the past ten years. Windsor must really be raking in the money.

7. A beer ad showing two lean and lithe tennis players taking a break from their game to drink a can of beer.

8. I can't hire that ex-convict; he might steal something.

9. Now that I've bought a car, I need a bigger allowance.

10. Inflation last year was 8 percent; this year it's 16 percent; next year, it'll be 24 percent.

Methods of Clear Reasoning

Logic refers to clear reasoning, and reasoning involves two basic processes called *induction* and *deduction*.

Induction is the name we give to a process involving rational movement from particular facts to general statements. Scientists and the scientific method rely on induction. For example, when a number of cases of influenza are diagnosed in the same part of the country (particular facts), we can say (make the generalization) that there is a flu epidemic there. Similarly, when a physicist determines, after a number of experiments, that metal *A* is a better conductor of electricity than metal *B*, the determination (the generalization) is made possible by the many experiments (particular facts). Induction can also be thought of as an ordinary mental process—the way we are influenced by experience. If a number of attempts to make friends with Nick come to naught and we think to ourselves that Nick is unfriendly, we are only making use of the inductive process. Similarly, one important way in which the thesis statement comes into being is induction: we examine the facts and make a generalization from them.

However, a warning must be given here about induction. First, we can never be as sure about a conclusion based on a certain number of facts as we can about a conclusion based on all of them. When a scientist says that water freezes at 0 degrees Celsius, he means that having observed it to do so on a number of occasions, he predicts that it will normally do so. Similarly, if you should conclude, having met seven bright graduates of York University, that *all* York graduates are bright, your certainty will still be limited by the principle involved: it is never an absolute certainty when one leaps from *some* to all. Still, we can be surer that physical nature is uniform than we can that human nature is.

Thus in inducing a generalization, the writer must bear this warning in mind: he must at least be sure that he has a sufficient number of cases (facts) on which to base his conclusion (generalization), that these are typical cases (e.g., that the York graduates were not all people who graduated with first class honours but just ordinary graduates), and that exceptions can be explained (e.g., one of the York graduates seems not so bright when you ask her a tough question; is it true that she is not bright or is it that when you asked, she had been without sleep for a few days and wasn't performing well on that one occasion?)

Deduction, on the other hand, is a kind of thinking that proceeds from a generalization to a particular fact. From the generalization that people who are underweight tend to die earlier than those who are not, you can deduce that it is best to watch one's diet carefully. Or if you know that a particular restaurant serves wonderful food (generalization), you can deduce (particular fact) that it would be a good place to take a friend to dinner.

You may now understand that there is a relationship between induction and deduction, and so there is. For example, sound conclusions reached through scientific induction may be just the useful generalizations from which to make particular deductions—about health for instance. The Canadian Medical Association can produce records showing causes of death in millions of cases; it has concluded (induced) that death by heart attack is hastened by the intake of cholesterol-rich foods. From that generalization, you can deduce that it is bad for your health to eat too many eggs or too much cheese or red meat.

In order for the inductive process to yield a true generalization, the facts must be true; similarly, in order for the particular fact deduced to be true, the premises from which it was made must be true.

In the case of deduction, there is a process for testing the validity of conclusions; in its most familiar form, the deductive form is exemplified by the *syllogism*. A *syllogism* is nothing but a little argument in the form of two premises and a conclusion drawn from them.

Major premise   All citizens pay income taxes.
Minor premise   All Canadians are citizens.
Conclusion   All Canadians pay income taxes.

To understand why the conclusion in this syllogism is valid, we can think of those mentioned as belonging to classes and begin to represent these classes visually.

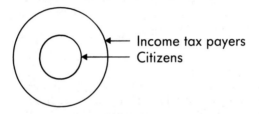

This is a visual representation of the major premise. Within the outer circle are all those who belong to the class of income tax payers. The inner circle encloses the class of citizens. Now let us represent the minor premise in the diagram.

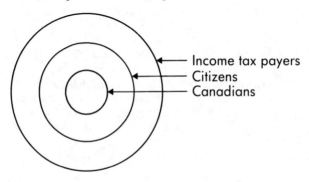

Now the innermost circle encloses the class of Canadians. That circle is enclosed not only within the circle of citizens but also in the circle of those who pay income tax. Hence it is clear visually that all Canadians pay income tax (are a class included within the class of income tax payers). But notice that if we had started with a major premise stating that "some citizens pay income tax," our conclusion could not be so straightforward.

Now we would need to conclude that *some Canadians pay income taxes*.

Some Canadians pay income taxes.

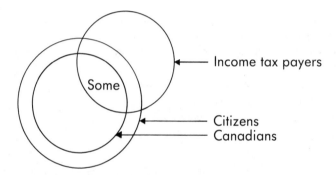

You will rarely if ever encounter a syllogism either in written work or in conversation. More likely in conversation there is the appearance of part of a syllogism: Either one of the premises or the conclusion is missing.

The Grey Fox is playing at the movies. I hate Westerns. (Conclusion missing: I won't go to the movies.)

It's Tuesday, so I'd better go to work. (Missing premise: Tuesday is payday.)

But a syllogism is not useful unless our premises are true, because a syllogism can validate an untruth. For example, here's a syllogism that provides a perfectly valid conclusion:

All cats are grey.
All grey things are stupid.
All cats are stupid.

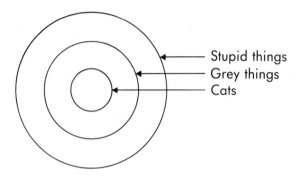

Stupid things
Grey things
Cats

It certainly follows from the premises that all cats are stupid, but it's not true because the premises are not. This is an obvious example, and you are not likely to make this kind of error. But take another syllogism:

L

> Conservative doctors oppose government bans on extra-billing.
> Dr. Singham opposes government bans on extra-billing.
> Dr. Singham is a conservative doctor.

Here is a visual representation:

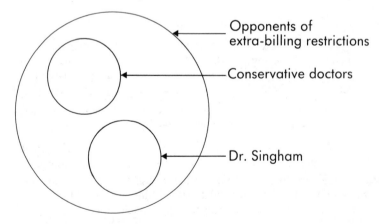

Opponents of
extra-billing restrictions

Conservative doctors

Dr. Singham

Notice that Dr. Singham is not included in the class of conservative doctors. He doesn't have to be. If the major premise had been that *only* conservative doctors oppose government bans on extra-billing, the conservative doctors' circle would lie virtually on top of the one enclosing those who oppose extra-billing restrictions and Dr. Singham would have to be included. But common sense will confirm, as the diagram indicates, that many others oppose extra-billing restrictions for many reasons: they don't like the alternatives so far proposed; they don't like government interference in all avenues of our lives; and so on. But Dr. Singham need not be conservative either; that is, his objections to the bans may not lie in the area of venality presumably ascribed to the conservative doctors. Perhaps he's a young physician just starting out and honestly feels he's entitled to a large financial reward for the many years he spent preparing for an exacting profession. Perhaps he believes that extra-billing restrictions will result in mass emigration of Canadian doctors to the U.S. In any case, it is clear that although the premises here are true— conservative doctors *do* oppose extra-billing restrictions as does Dr. Singham—the conclusion is clearly false.

L

Thus in addition to using the diagram method of checking syllogistic deduction, the writer needs to check carefully the truth of his premises. The writer must check his evidence, the facts from which he draws his conclusions. The writer needs to check the support that underlies his evidence, and this involves induction.

TEST YOURSELF ON
Applying Induction or Deduction

A *Induction*: Below are five sets of factual statements, each followed by a conclusion induced from them. Consider the value of the conclusion in the light of the foregoing discussions. Is the conclusion a reasonable one? Why? Why not?

1. Richard was an assistant to a deputy minister. He is used to taking responsibility, engaging in long-range planning, dealing effectively with large numbers of subordinates, executing policy. Therefore, he would make a good business executive.

2. This year the Canadian dollar reached the highest value it has held against the U.S. dollar in years. The Federal Conservatives are in power for the first time in years. The Conservative government must be good for the Canadian economy.

3. Carla's family is always calling on her for help, and I'll be involved in it. Look what happened to Joe after he married Anna! I'm not going to marry Carla.

4. I heard that Professor Brodsky always springs surprises when she gives exams. I'm not going to study for them.

5. The average temperature in Athens in the summer is 26 degrees. So I think I'd better take light cotton clothing on my trip.

B *Deduction*: Below are five syllogisms. Make a visual representation of each and check the conclusions. Are they valid? After you have checked on the valid conclusions, ask yourself whether these valid conclusions are also true.

1. All cats are independent.
   No independent animal likes humans.
   Cats don't like humans. (*conclusion*)

2. Most Quebeckers are friendly.
   Most friendly people are hospitable.
   Most Quebeckers are hospitable. (*conclusion*)

3. All Irishmen like to drink whisky.
   Ed Quinn likes to drink whisky.
   Ed Quinn is an Irishman. (*conclusion*)

4. Violence is wrong.
   War is violence.
   War is wrong. (*conclusion*)

5. Some actors are out of work.
   Out-of-work people are usually a little desperate.
   Some actors are a little desperate. (*conclusion*)

Errors in Thinking

Even the most reasonable people make errors when they think, so we must take the time to deal with some common forms of thinking errors called *fallacies*.

1 Post Hoc Ergo Propter Hoc

This fallacy is known by its Latin name, meaning "after this, therefore because of this." Do not think that because event *B* follows or comes after event *A*, event *A* was the cause of event *B*. The conclusion that Dimitra started to be unhappy after she married Kostas is not necessarily a criticism of her marriage to Kostas. Her unhappiness may have nothing to do with Kostas *or* the marriage. It might be that her career has taken a critical turn and she is under great pressure at her job. Or it is possible that her health is deteriorating, something entirely unrelated to the marriage.

The need to avoid this fallacy becomes even clearer when we consider public questions.

> This town started to deteriorate rapidly after Mayor Campbell was elected.

This conclusion is especially pernicious because the so-called evidence (the deterioration) is visible and on that account may seem convincing. But a moment's thought will show that the conclusion is false. Deterioration, especially in an urban setting, is not an instantaneous process; it takes time. Ignoring the general nature of the accusation, we can extrapolate from what we know that deterioration takes place in a number of separate areas—housing, transportation, an increase in crime, and so on. It is a complex of events that cannot be attributed to the mayoral term of one man; its seeds were no doubt planted long before Campbell's nomination. If anything, Campbell arrived in the middle of all this. He did not cause it.

2 Non Sequitur

This Latin term means "it does not follow." This fallacy occurs when the writer either leaves out steps in the thought process or draws conclusions that do not follow from the premises.

> She's the best teacher I've ever seen, and she should be made head of the department.

The conclusion doesn't follow. Is it a fact that very good teachers make very good department heads? How so? And even if this were true, how many teachers has the speaker or writer seen?

> Ronald Reagan was a Republican president; that's why he stalled on controlling acid rain in Canada.

The conclusion does not follow, because steps have been omitted in the writer's reasoning process. That is, he or she has not let the reader in on these steps:

1. Ronald Reagan was a Republican president.
2. Like other Republicans in recent decades, Reagan focused attention on helping American industrial interests maintain or increase their profits.
3. Important among these interests were certain industries producing the fumes that contributed to acid rain.
4. The investment required to install devices to eliminate the acids from these fumes would have reduced profits.
5. That's why he stalled on controlling acid rain in Canada.

To avoid non sequitur, you should be sure that, in your papers, all steps in the thinking process are included.

L

3 Hasty Generalization

This fallacy is a form of using insufficient evidence. For example, if you know a seventeen-year-old who refused to get a job when his father asked him to and an eighteen-year-old who wouldn't observe his mother's 2 a.m. curfew, you do not have enough evidence to conclude that young people today are a bad lot because they don't obey their parents. Such a conclusion makes a statement about millions of individuals on the basis of a couple of cases—a bad business. If your main proposition is based on such evidence, you would do well to reconsider the whole thing.

4 False Analogy

Analogies are useful in clarifying certain points under discussion, but they are seldom enough to win an argument because *alike* does not mean *identical*. Still, they are useful. For instance, we may compare the negotiation of a trade agreement between two nations to an athletic game such as football or soccer. We may speak of the need for a *level playing field*, suggesting that one side shouldn't have a marked advantage, or of *knowing where the goalposts are*, suggesting that the final objectives should not be arbitrarily changed. Indeed, two teams do meet to discuss the matter; each team is seeking to promote its nation's interests to the maximum; each team has a strategy for achieving its objectives; and so forth. However, the likenesses have the power to explain an international trade negotiation in only a limited way. The analogy doesn't hold up entirely. When an athletic competition is over, that's the end of it, but there is much more to relations between sovereign nations than a single trade agreement. If a negotiation is to be successful, neither one side nor the other can expect to *win* in the same way an athletic team would hope to. The final goal is to reach an agreement that is of mutual benefit. The difference from an athletic contest is crucial.

Analogies are useful, then, to illustrate certain points under discussion, but they are not enough to resolve an argument. When using an analogy, be careful not to create a false parallel.

5 Begging the Question

In this fallacy, the writer or speaker assumes in his or her thesis the validity of something that really needs to be proven. To say, *He's an idiot because he says stupid things* is neither explanation nor proof. The word *idiot* in this context means *someone who says stupid things*. Thus the original utterance means, *He's someone who says stupid things because he says stupid things*. We would have to hear these so-called stupid things before we accepted the declaration of idiocy. On the level of formal argument, a statement like, *The crucially important hospital should be built* is a similar type of statement. That is because *crucially important* here simply means *should be built*. Thus the statement means *The hospital which should be built should be built*. We need to know why it should be built. Otherwise, the statement begs the question.

TEST YOURSELF ON

Recognizing Logical Fallacies

Examine each set of statements below and point out the logical errors in the thinking behind each.

1. Ever since those Greeks moved into the neighbourhood, the crime rate has gone up. They must be responsible.

2. Nowadays, it's a crime to waste food.

3. It's a vital necessity that everyone get out and vote on Election Day.

4. He'd make a great Defence Minister. He's spent all his life in the army.

5. My two little cousins don't like candy. I guess children don't like sweets.

6. It's Tuesday. I'd better not skip work today.

7. All I can say is, he wasn't an alcoholic *before* he married Rachel!

8. Professors are like pieces of toast; they should be buttered up.

9. My aunt and uncle love to visit the Soviet Union. They must be Communists.

10. The film I saw last night was wonderful. It should easily win an Oscar.

M

Misplaced Modifiers

A misplaced modifier is a word, phrase, or clause that does not point clearly and directly to what it is supposed to modify. It resembles a dangling modifier (see page 92), except that the word or words modified are present in the sentence. When using modifiers, be sure to place the word, phrase, or clause close to the word or words it actually modifies, since the meaning changes with the placement of the modifier.

> He *almost* had a heart attack every time he looked at his bank statement. (He almost had the attack—but not quite—every time he looked.)
>
> He had a heart attack *almost* every time he looked at his bank statement. (He actually had the attack—sometimes, but not every time he looked.)

1 Be careful to place the adverbs *almost, even, hardly, just, merely, only, nearly,* and *scarcely* close to the words they modify. Misplacing words like *almost* and *only* occurs quite often in informal writing, but you should learn to be careful about their placement because misplacing them can often confuse the reader badly.

Misplaced Word   I *only* told the jury what I had seen. (The choices here are three: *I only*—and nobody else—told the jury; *I told only* the jury—and nobody else; or I told the jury *only what I had seen.*)
Revised   I told the jury *only* what I had seen.
Revised   I told *only* the jury what I had seen.
Revised   *Only* I told the jury what I had seen.

Misplaced   I *nearly* went halfway to Florida.
Revised   I went *nearly* halfway to Florida.

Misplaced   I *almost* ate half the pie.
Revised   I ate *almost* half the pie.

2 Be careful to place modifying phrases close to the word or words they modify.

Misplaced Phrase   My history professor made it clear why wars take place *on Tuesday*. (The *wars* take place on Tuesday?)
Revised   *On Tuesday*, my history professor made it clear why wars take place.

Misplaced Phrase   Airlines serve martinis to passengers *in little bottles*. (The *passengers* are in little bottles?)
Revised   Airlines serve passengers martinis in little bottles.

Misplaced Phrase   Environmental groups protested the oil leaks *all over the country*. (Were there *oil leaks* all over the country?)
Revised   Environmental groups *all over the country* protested the oil leaks.

3 Be careful to place modifying clauses close to the word or words which they modify.

Misplaced Clause   Sid bought a book for his library *that cost $19.04*. (Did his *library* or his *book* cost that much?)
Revised   Sid bought a book *that cost $19.04* for his library. For his library, Sid bought a book *that cost $19.04*.

A special case of the misplaced modifier is called a *squinting modifier* because it looks in two directions at the same time; that is, it "squints."

Squinting Modifier   To be beautifully dressed *often* pleases my wife. (Is she *often pleased* or *often beautifully dressed*?)

Revised   It *often* pleases my wife to be beautifully dressed. It pleases my wife to be beautifully dressed *often*.

Squinting Modifier   Lucia said *when she was on her way* home she would stop and buy the vegetables. (Did she say it while travelling home? Or did she say that sometime on her way home she would stop?)

Revised   When she was on her way home, Lucia said that she would stop and buy the vegetables. (*Said* while on her way home.) Lucia said that on her way home she would stop and buy the vegetables. (She will *stop* on her way home.)

M

TEST YOURSELF ON
Revising Misplaced and Squinting Modifiers

Some of the following sentences contain well-placed modifiers; next to these, write C. Others, however, have misplaced or squinting modifiers; correct these, even if it means recasting the sentence.

1. _____ With the calculator, I can show you how to make a

   million dollars in twenty seconds.

2. _____ The sick patient wanted to live happily.

3. _____ The sunset that we loved completely stunned us.

4. _____ We made plans to leave over the weekend.

5. _____ Professors who teach rarely get rich.

6. _____ Subconsciously, Cam wanted to become famous.

7. _____ Caesar was stabbed in the heyday of his glory.

8. _____ He just left for a minute.

9. _____ For Christopher's sake, I decided to go to

   Newfoundland.

10. _____ The Crown penalizes those who commit murder for good reason.

11. _____ Ed Broadbent just arrived here last week.

12. _____ The father heard the news that his son had been born with joy.

13. _____ *True Confessions* appeals to readers with scandalous stories.

14. _____ Those who jog slowly develop heart trouble.

15. _____ The ugly face scared him that looked through the window.

M

Modifiers

In Part 1, we noted that adjectives and adverbs act to modify or further describe members of other word classes: nouns and verbs. Adjectives and adverbs are called modifiers. But the question of modification is a bit more complicated than you may have imagined from reading about it in Part 1. Here we shall discuss the complications by discussing other words that can act as adjectives and adverbs. These other words are called *adjectivals* and *adverbials*.

Other Words Used as Adjectives: Adjectivals

Some words are nearly always used as adjectives: *old, young, happy, proud*, and so forth. But other words, ordinarily belonging to other parts of speech, can also act as adjectives. So, of course, can phrases. All are entitled to be called adjectivals.

1 Nouns Used as Adjectives

We looked into the *bear* cage. (modifies *cage*)

She was wearing her *party* dress. (modifies *dress*)

We went to the *baseball* game. (modifies *game*)

2 Verbs Used as Adjectives

A whole class of verbs are commonly used as adjectives. These are the participles: the *-ing* forms (present participles), the *-d* or *-ed* forms (past participles), and the irregular past participles (*gone, broken, kept*, and so forth).

The *fleeing* suspect was caught by the police. (modifies *suspect*, the subject)

The *broken* arrow was useless. (modifies *arrow*, the subject)

He seemed *defeated*. (acts as predicate adjective)

The job was *finished*. (acts as predicate adjective)

3 Adverbs used as Adjectives

The apartment *below* is mine. (modifies *apartment*)

The road *ahead* is closed. (modifies *road*)

4 Phrases and Clauses Used as Adjectives

Phrase   The men *in the truck* were tired. (modifies *men*)
Phrase   The planes *flying overhead* are bound for Europe. (modifies *planes*)

Clause   The people *who rented my house* will stay until August. (modifies *people*)
Clause   I bought a Toyota, *which runs like a top*. (modifies *Toyota*)

Other Words Used as Adverbs: Adverbials

Some words are nearly always used as adverbs: *often, soon, rarely*, and so forth. But other words, ordinarily belonging to other parts of speech, can also act as adverbs, as can phrases and clauses. All these are entitled to be called adverbials.

M

1 Nouns Used as Adverbs

I went *home*. (modifies *went*)

She arrived *yesterday*. (modifies *arrived*)

2 Verbs Used as Adverbs

Because he was in a hurry, he decided to eat *standing*. (modifies *to eat*)

Sonia played *to win*. (modifies *played*)

3 Phrases and Clauses Used as Adverbs

Phrase   We are staying *at a hotel*. (modifies *are staying*)

Phrase   We are impatient *to leave for the theatre*. (modifies *impatient*)

Clause   *Although we were tired*, we couldn't fall asleep. (modifies the whole of the main clause)

Clause   *When they saw the shark*, they were frightened. (modifies *were frightened*)

M

TEST YOURSELF ON

Recognizing Modifiers: Adjectivals and Adverbials

Identify each of the italicized words or word groups as either an adjectival or an adverbial.

1. We were going on a *holiday* trip.

2. We would arrive *in the afternoon*.

3. He went *home*.

4. *When she spoke softly*, we had to strain to listen.

5. He gave the apples to the man *in the raincoat*.

6. She was promoted to *plant* manager.

7. The book, *which cost $18*, was overpriced.

8. The man *who sent her the flowers* was in love with her.

9. He was a *broken* man.

10. They were a *defeated* team.

11. The *purring* cat likes its milk.

12. The man *in the gray flannel suit* looks like my brother.

Number

See **Shifts**.

Numerals

Whether your writing is formal or informal, the basic guideline in handling numerals is to be consistent in your usage: either use numerals or spell the numbers out in words—do not mix the two. There are several basic rules for handling numerals in formal writing.

N-P

1 Spell out numbers that require no more than two words. In other cases, use numerals.

There were *seventy-five* cases of swine flu reported.

The population of Montreal is less than *four million*.
but
My income tax refund amounted to *$88.37*.

Note: In business and technical writing, numbers from 10 up are often written as numerals.

2 In writing dates, addresses, percentages followed by %, page numbers, or the time of day followed by *a.m.* or *p.m.*, use numerals.

Date   October 19, 1926 *or* 19 October 1926

Address   55 East 9th Street, Apartment 7K

Percentages   Sales at IBM declined 27.3% during the last quarter of 1987.
but
This bank pays five percent interest.

Page Numbers   See Chapter 3, page 112.

Time of Day   11:30 p.m. *but* three o'clock

3 Use numerals for quantities in scientific and technical writing.

The barometric pressure is *101.2* kpa.

The specimen was *1.37* centimetres in length.

4 It is appropriate to use in the same sentence a combination of words and numerals where such a combination will make your writing clear.

You may take only *one* 30 centimetre salmon each day.

The cashier counted out *70* one-dollar bills.

5 Do not begin a sentence with a numeral that is not spelled out.

Wrong   *250,000,000* is the approximate population of the U.S.S.R.
Right   The population of the U.S.S.R. is approximately 250,000,000.

Wrong   *6* kilometres from here there is a gas station.
Right   *Six* kilometres from here there is a gas station.

Note: If your text includes a great many numbers or a mixture of whole numbers and decimals, it is preferable to use numerals for all the numbers.

N

TEST YOURSELF ON

Using Numerals Correctly

Each of the following sentences contains errors in handling numerals. Correct them.

1. 2,000 years ago, an important event took place in Palestine.

2. Including finance charges, this new car would cost you ten thousand six hundred and thirty-eight dollars.

3. They live at nine-0-eight Queen Street East, apartment three E.

4. Marc drinks about 36 cases of wine every year.

5. The father is 40, the mother is 37, and their children are 12 and ten.

6. 3 years ago I owned a Volkswagen.

7. The average annual rainfall in the Mato Grosso district of Brazil is one hundred twelve point seven three centimetres.

8. On February second, nineteen twenty-two, she managed to publish a book of some seven hundred pages.

9. On page five, there is a good description of a corrupt man.

10. Her author's royalties amounted to twelve percent of the price of the book.

Organization and Planning

Organization and planning are essential to good writing. An essay that is disorganized is incoherent, but achieving proper organization takes planning. This entry is devoted to both.

Organization

An essay is commonly organized into three parts: an introduction, a main body, and a conclusion. The main body is the most important of these parts, for in it the writer treats the main ideas of the essay. The organization of the body of the essay is treated under **Unity, Paragraph Development**, and **Coherence**.

Here we are interested in introductions and conclusions, but before we take up these important items, let us consider a whole essay—including introduction, main body, and conclusion:

My Disaster at First-year Registration
[1] If you have ever wondered why you see so many prematurely grey-haired first-year students on this campus, this little story will answer your question.

[2] Bright and early on the first day of registration, I showed up at the Registrar's Office at 8 a.m. to pay my fees. The line at Window 1 snaked halfway around two corners to the lobby of the Administration Building. But I was patient. After a half-hour, I was at the promised land—the grilled window. I paid. They stamped my receipt. I was pushed out of the way.

[3] Suddenly, it dawned on me that I didn't know what to do next. I looked around, utterly confused. A passer-by took pity on me. "Window 2 for your timetable," he snapped.

[4] So there I was, back in line. Another half-hour passed before I arrived back at the grill. I showed my receipt. They gave me—a *torn* calendar and a blank timetable sheet. I was shoved out of the way again. But the calendar might have been ripped into shreds for all I cared; the crazy abbreviations and symbols were nearly unreadable. How would I ever figure out how to register?

[5] This problem seemed small when I arrived at the main registration area in the gymnasium, because there it became a matter of survival. The physical contact here made the shoving at the Registrar's Office seem like gentle caresses. Again, a friendly person intervened; I found an adviser who explained that I needed to go to each departmental desk and register for courses one by one according to the days and hours I preferred.

[6] By this time, afternoon was crawling toward late afternoon. As I pondered my choice, I decided I had better get cracking before I died of starvation. So I ran to the English Department desk to register for Composition 101. But I was twenty yards away from the desk—without having registered—before I realized I didn't understand what they'd meant when they told me I'd been "closed out."

[7] I will spare you the catalogue of further pains I endured that long day. You will learn whatever else you need to know about the registration experience by looking for me on campus. I'm the stooped, greying male first-year student you see arriving for an 8 a.m. math class, the same one you see leaving after his 5 p.m. biology lecture.

The *introduction*, paragraph 1, opens the essay by proposing a challenge to the readers, and it does so in a humorous vein. It also tunes the readers in to the nature of what they are about to read: a short, personal story. Further, it gives the tone of the piece and its main idea in brief.

The *main body* consists of paragraphs 2 to 6 and includes everything that actually happened; this portion of the paper is the centrally important part of what the writer has to say.

The *conclusion*, paragraph 7, ends the piece by returning to an idea presented in the introduction. It also gives a climactic end to the story by telling the reader the kind of schedule the poor student managed for himself—a long, ten-hour day.

The main body here is a little story—a piece of narration. Under **Paragraph Development**, other types of development are explained. See that entry to study more about how to handle a main body according to your specific purpose in writing a particular paper. For now, we will continue with more on introductions and conclusions and go on to planning an outline.

Introductions

Introductions are important because they are the first of your words that a reader sees. Effective introductions perform a number of different tasks. Perhaps the most important is to catch the reader's interest and attention; right behind this come the tasks of identifying the subject and setting some sort of limit on it. A good introduction also sets the tone for the rest of the piece—it advises the reader how you, the writer, intend to treat the subject.

Here are a number of introductions, each identified by the method the writer employs:

Using the Writer's Personal Experience
There was, I think, only a brief period in my life when I actually turned heads. It was the summer of my seventeenth year when, newly graduated from a private girls' school, I was in that transition stage between being an old child and a young woman, a state of half and half that men of all ages apparently find disarmingly erotic. Anne Taylor Fleming, ''In Defense of Flirting''*

---

* Throughout this handbook, where sample paragraphs such as this have been carried over from the American edition, the form of their documentation differs from that of samples new to the Canadian edition. The new samples are documented according to the style recommended by the Modern Language Association (1984); the old are not.

Making an Unusual Statement

A strange place it was, that place where the world began. A place of incredible happenings, splendours and revelations, despairs like multitudinous pits of isolated hells. A place of shadow-spookiness, inhabited by the unknowable dead. A place of jubilation and of mourning, horrible and beautiful.

It was, in fact, a small prairie town.

Margaret Laurence, "Where the World Began," *Heart of a Stranger* (Toronto: McClelland, 1976) 213

Offering a Strong Opinion

The current terrorist epidemic has mystified a great many people, and various explanations have been offered—most of them quite wrong.

Walter Laqueur, "Terrorist Myths"

Stating and Illustrating the Main Idea

The dedicated baseball fan is a man who likes to kid himself. He'll get to a World Series game early, see a ballplayer yawning and take it as a sign of nervousness. He'll see a nervelessly relaxed body leaning against a batting cage and consider it merely feigned indifference. He'll watch an outfielder casually scratching his nose and count it as a tic. He's wrong. In fact, what looks like boredom on behalf of the people involved in the World Series is most often just that.

Jim Bouton, "A Few World Series Sinkers"

Opening with a Challenge to the Reader

If you want your mate to stop guessing about your feelings and motives, you have to be prepared to reveal yourself.

Nena and George O'Neill, "Communicating with Yourself"

Conclusions

A good conclusion to an essay leaves the reader feeling that they have enjoyed a satisfying, rounded-off reading experience. It does this in one of the following ways:

1 By concluding with a reiteration, often in some varied form, of your thesis statement or main idea. A paper called "Abolish Mandatory Retirement" might end like this:

 If mandatory retirement is abolished, as has been argued, then many fields will continue to benefit from expertise that would otherwise have been relegated to a park bench.

2 By concluding with a summary of your main points, thus reinforcing in the readers' minds the effective things you have said. A possible ending for ''Nuclear Energy Versus Solar Power'' might go as follows:

> Nuclear energy presents us with the prospect of dangerous operation, deadly waste products, and sinister accidents, but the sun—as we have known all along—is an endless source of pleasure, enduring and powerful.

3 By making a climatic point. This type of conclusion is effective when you present a series of points in ascending dramatic order and finish with a particularly high note.

Planning

Planning an essay—even a five-hundred-word essay—begins with note-taking, jotting down ideas as you ask questions about your subject. Say it's ''first-year student registration.'' What time did I get there? *Awful. Arrived at eight in the morning.* Then what happened? *Got in line at Registrar's Office to pay fees.* Next? *Didn't know what to do—had to get in line again to ask*! Ask enough questions, and you may wind up with a list that looks something like this:

1. Awful. Arrived at 8 in the morning.
2. Got in line at Registrar's Office Window 1 to pay fees.
3. Had to line up again—find out what to do next!
4. Closed out of English.
5. Had to ask what ''closed out'' means.
6. Found out I needed to go to Window 2 for timetable and calendar.
7. Calendar torn.
8. Couldn't read it, anyway.
9. Entered registration area and was shoved and pushed for five minutes before I found an adviser.
10. Lost my timetable sheet.
11. Finally got classes that begin at 8 and end at 6, four days a week.

Outlines

The most useful tool for planning an essay is an outline, and although the notes do not exactly constitute an outline, you couldn't start to make an outline without them, and very little effort will enable you to make an outline from the notes. They have, embedded within them, just what you need for *controlling* and *directing* the way your essay will proceed.

For one thing, a quick glance at the notes tells you that there is a main point here—registration is a shocking, traumatic experience for an uninformed and inexperienced first-year student. Furthermore, the fact that two areas are mentioned—the Registrar's Office and the registration area—provides a way of dividing the essay and beginning to organize an outline:

I. The Registrar's Office
    A. Got in line to pay fees
    B. Got in line again for timetable and calendar
        1. Calendar torn
        2. Couldn't read it
II. The registration area
    A. Got pushed and shoved before finding adviser
    B. Got closed out of English
        1. Found out what "closed out" means
        2. Missed lunch
    C. Got labourer's 8–6 schedule

This outline would help you to control your writing. It is an aid in keeping your plan in mind, indicates the order in which you will discuss things, and manages to suggest the relative importance of the two places on the day of registration, by assigning a greater proportion of space to one (registration area) than to the other.

In order to become competent at making useful outlines, you should know something about the formal principles of outlining and the different types of outlines that can be used.

Types of Outlines

The three types of outlines most commonly employed are the topic outline, the sentence outline, and the paragraph outline. In a *topic outline*, each entry is a word or a small group of words. In a *sentence outline*, which has the same basic structural pattern as the topic outline, the words are replaced by complete sentences. In a *para-

graph outline, there are no divisions, headings, and subheadings, as in the others, but only a list of paragraph topic sentences. Some writers feel that the paragraph outline is most suitable for short papers, and the others for longer papers. A writer using a sentence outline is likely to keep in closer touch with the points because of the fuller information contained in sentences.

Whatever you do, decide beforehand which kind of outline you plan to use, and then follow its requirements systematically: use *only* sentences in the sentence outline; be sure you have topic sentences for the paragraph outline. And check your outline to be sure that it is consistent with the principles that apply to all outlines.

Here are samples of each kind of outline, for a paper on ''The Energy Crisis on Oil and Two Alternate Sources of Power'':

Topic Outline
I. The Arab oil embargo of 1973
  A. Shortage of oil
  B. Dwindling of resources
II. Alternative of nuclear power
  A. Expensive
  B. Dangerous
  C. Likely to run out
III. Solar power
  A. Inexpensive
  B. Not dangerous
  C. Limitless supply
  D. Needs technology

Sentence Outline
I. The Arab oil embargo of 1973 pointed up the need for Canada to find alternate sources of fuel.
  A. The embargo produced a shortage of oil.
  B. It reminded us that all our fossil fuel resources are limited.
II. Nuclear power as an alternative, though widely favoured, is not likely to be the answer.
  A. It's very expensive—both for new plants and fuel processing.
  B. It's very dangerous.
  C. It's also likely to prove a limited resource.

III. Solar power is probably a more attractive alternative.

    A. It's relatively inexpensive except for start-up costs.

    B. It's easy to handle and not dangerous.

    C. The supply is limitless.

    D. The technology is, however, expensive and not yet in place.

Paragraph Outline

1. The Arab oil embargo of 1973 pointed up the need for Canada to find alternate sources of fuel, by creating a shortage of oil and reminding us that oil was in any case in very limited supply—a dwindling resource.

2. Nuclear energy is widely favoured as an alternative source of power, but it has many serious drawbacks.

3. Solar power is probably a more attractive alternative because it is cheap, limitless in supply, and relatively inexpensive.

4. It may be that solar energy will not be adopted because of industry's reluctance to provide the expensive technology.

Testing the Outline

Use the following criteria to be sure that your outline is logical and consistent:

1 Use a conventional form of notation. The following example is a useful one; it is rarely necessary to subdivide more than is shown:

    I. . . . .

       A. . . . .

          1. . . . .

             a. . . . .

             b. . . . .

          2. . . . .

       B. . . . .

    II. . . . .

2 Be sure that your outline covers your subject adequately. The major headings in your outline should include enough material to satisfy the expectations provoked by your subject. For example, consider these two outlines:

The Microcomputer

Inadequate Material	*Adequate Material*

I. Hardware
II. Software

   I. Hardware
      A. Central Processing
         Units
      B. Keyboards
      C. Video Monitors
  II. Software
      A. Operating Systems
      B. Applications
 III. Users
      A. Business
      B. Personal

Obviously, the outline on the left shows the writer's failure to consider the entire subject; of course this is a simple exercise, but checking your outline against this criterion of completeness can save you a great deal of trouble.

3 Be sure that your outline is in logical order. All the heads and subheads in your outline indicate parts. No category of head or subhead, therefore, can have only one part—if the essay or part is brief enough to be considered one part, it doesn't need to be outlined. Every outline must have at least two main headings, and wherever you divide one of these (I, II), you must divide it into at least two parts. If a I has an A, it must have a B. If an A has a 1, it must have a 2, and so forth.

    Moreover, the order of your parts (the progression from I to II to III) must follow some consistent principle: chronology is one, cause and effect another. Do not mix your principles.

Consistent Time Order
   I. Selecting the date
  II. Inviting the guests
 III. Preparing the menu
 IV. Cooking the food
  V. Setting the table

Mixed Order
Crime
   I. Its increase since the seventies (time order)
  II. Its causes (cause-and-effect order)
 III. Robbery versus rape (order by classification)

If your outline fails to meet this criterion, you are probably uncertain of your whole approach and need to re-examine your central idea or thesis statement.

4 Be sure to cast groups of headings and subheadings in parallel grammatical form. This will ensure that the parts of the outline are clearly related to one another. Notice in the sentence outline on page 166 that I A and I B are parallel (in B, the pronoun *it* stands for *the embargo*), but that they are not parallel with II A, II B, and II C—which are parallel with one another. (*Note*: it is only due to the nature of the subject that III A, III B, and III C are parallel with the same group under II; in most cases, they need not be and will not be parallel.)

TEST YOURSELF ON
The Principles of Outlining

P

A Using one of the manageable titles given at the end of **Subjects for Essays** (page 262, exercise A), construct three outlines for it: a topic, a sentence, and a paragraph outline.

B Choose one of the topics in exercise B on page 262, give it a manageable title, and construct a sentence outline for it.

Paragraph Development

Adequate development is one of the three criteria for an effectively written paragraph. (For the other two, see **Unity** and **Coherence**. Also discussed under **Unity** is the important idea of the *topic sentence*: if you are not familiar with the topic sentence, read **Unity** before reading further here.)

A paragraph that is adequately developed is one that gives reasons, details, illustrations, or examples to fully support its topic sentence. The failure to give full development to every topic sentence leads to a series of short, choppy statements—not paragraphs—and leaves readers with the impression of a hasty and ill-thought-out composition.

> The United Nations, which was established to maintain peace, does not do so. Since 1945, there have been many wars—Korea, the Middle East, and Vietnam, to name just a few.
>
> Besides, the United Nations is an instrument for propaganda. The Soviets use it constantly for this purpose.

Obviously, this writer opposes the United Nations, but the first "paragraph" gives inadequate development to the topic sentence because not enough examples of the U.N.'s failure are given. Similarly, the second "paragraph" fails to be specific enough; it doesn't give examples of *how* the Soviets use the U.N. for propaganda.

> With nuclear energy, there is still the possibility of accidents. The big one at Chernobyl caused many deaths.
>
> Moreover, there is also the problem of waste materials. Some of those waste materials have toxic effects for as long as 150,000 years!

P

The one example given in the first fragment is unpersuasive. Has there been only one? If not, how many? Also, how many people were killed? What damage was caused to the environment? The emphatic exclamation point in the second fragment does not hide the fact that the fragment is undeveloped. What is being done now with waste materials? Why is it inadequate? The fragment is badly in need of development.

TEST YOURSELF ON

Developing Fragmentary Paragraphs

Each of the following sets of sentences is badly in need of further development. Develop each.

1. The more money you make, the more money you spend. When your income is low, you yearn for more—but learn to be restrained.

As soon as your salary rises, however, you begin to give in to your desires.

2. Television tends to make us passive. The reason for this is that we have nothing to *do* as television viewers. It's all done for us.

3. Woodworking is not as difficult as it appears. The first thing you need is a reliable set of tools.

Development is not a haphazard process, but one that depends on your topic sentence: that is, it depends on the nature of the subject you are dealing with in your paragraph. Therefore, it is important to be clear about what you're writing and to try to determine the best way to express and develop your thought. Most well-constructed paragraphs follow one or another of the following basic developmental plans: chronological, spatial, or logical (also called expository).

Chronological Order

Use chronological order wherever time and sequence are important. In the example that follows, the author achieves clarity by constant reference to time, date, and season in an orderly manner.

The *Terra Nova* sailed from London 15th June 1910 and from New Zealand 26th November. She was fearfully overloaded; on deck, as well as the motor-sledges in their huge crates, there were 30 tons of coal in sacks, 2 1/2 tons of petrol in drums, 33 dogs, and 19 ponies. She rode out a bad storm by a miracle. "Bowers and Campbell were standing upon the bridge and the ship rolled sluggishly over until the lee combings of the main hatch were under the sea . . . as a rule, if a ship goes that far over she goes down." It took her thirty-eight days to get to McMurdo Sound, by which time the men were in poor shape. They had slept in their clothes, lucky if they got five hours a night, and had had no proper meals. As soon as they dropped anchor they began to unload the ship. This entailed dragging its cargo over ice floes which were in constant danger of being tipped up by killer whales, a very tricky business, specially when it came to moving ponies, motor-sledges and a pianola. Then they built the Hut which was henceforward to be their home. Scott, tireless himself, always drove his men hard and these things were accomplished in a fortnight. The *Terra Nova* sailed away; she was to return the following summer, when it was hoped that the Polar party would be back in time to be taken off before the freezing up of the sea forced her to leave again. If not, they would be obliged to spend a second winter on McMurdo Sound. Winter, of course, in those latitudes, happens during our summer months and is perpetual night, as the summer is perpetual day. The stunning beauty of the scenery affected the men deeply. When the sun shone the snow was never white, but brilliant shades of pink, blue and lilac; in winter the aurora australis flamed across the sky and the summit of Mount Erebus glowed.

Nancy Mitford, "A Bad Time," from *The Water Beetle**

Spatial Order

Use spatial order when it is necessary to describe physical reality and the spatial relationships between persons, things, or parts of things. A spatial ordering can proceed from inside to outside, top to bottom, up to down, and so forth. This description of a turtle crossing a road is a classic one.

P

The sun lay on the grass and warmed it, and in the shade under the grass the insects moved, ants and ant lions to set traps for them, grasshoppers to jump into the air and flick their yellow wings for a second, sow bugs like little armadillos, plodding restlessly on many tender feet. And over the grass at the roadside a land turtle crawled, turning aside for nothing, dragging his high-domed shell over the grass. His hard legs and yellow-nailed feet threshed slowly through the grass, not really walking but boosting and dragging his shell along. The barley beards slid off his shell, and the clover burrs fell on him and rolled to the ground. His horny beak was partly open, and his fierce, humorous eyes, under brows like fingernails, stared straight ahead. He came over the grass leaving a beaten trail behind him, and the hill, which was the highway embankment, reared up ahead of him. For a moment he stopped, his head held high. He blinked and looked up and down. At last he started to climb the embankment. Front clawed feet reached forward but did not touch.

* Reprinted by permission of A.D. Peters & Co. Ltd.

The hind feet kicked his shell along, and it scraped on the grass, and on the gravel. As the embankment grew steeper and steeper, the more frantic were the efforts of the land turtle. Pushing hind legs strained and slipped, boosting the shell along, and the horny head protruded as far as the neck could stretch. Little by little the shell slid up the embankment until at last a parapet cut straight across its line of march, the shoulder of the road, a concrete wall four inches high. As though they worked independently the hind legs pushed the shell against the wall. The head upraised and peered over the wall to the broad smooth plane of cement. Now the hands, braced on top of the wall, strained and lifted, and the shell came slowly up and rested its front end on the wall. For a moment the turtle rested. A red ant ran into the shell, into the soft skin inside the shell, and suddenly head and legs snapped in, and the armored tail clamped in sideways. The red ant was crushed between body and legs. And one head of wild oats was clamped into the shell by a front leg. For a long moment the turtle lay still, and then the neck crept out and the old humorous frowning eyes looked about and the legs and tail came out. The back legs went to work, straining like elephant legs, and the shell tipped to an angle so that the front legs could not reach the level cement plain. But higher and higher the hind legs boosted it, until at last the center of balance was reached, the front tipped down, the front legs scratched at the pavement, and it was up. But the head of wild oats was held by its stem around the front legs.
John Steinbeck, *The Grapes of Wrath**

Logical or Expository Order

Use logical or expository order to present illustrative details, examples, or reasons in supporting a topic sentence. There are a number of methods of expository order. They are the methods by which paragraphs and whole essays are organized for their specific purposes. One of these methods will be suitable for your particular paragraph or your particular purposes. The chief methods are (1) illustrative details and examples, (2) comparison and contrast, (3) definition, (4) classification, (5) process analysis, and (6) causal analysis.

1 Illustrative Details and Examples

A common and sturdy way of explaining and making vivid a generalization is to offer concrete details or examples to support the topic sentence. Most of the other methods also include use of this technique at one point or another.

> This conversation seemed welcome. His father-in-law appeared to follow it. He nodded, and on his narrow, elongated, bluish, post-human face there were traces of old expressions. An expression of shrewd and dignified concern, suspicion of advertising and of foreign cars and car dealers. There was even a suggestion of doubt—as in the old days—that David could be trusted to handle such things well. And relief that he had done so. In his father-in-law's eyes David would always be somebody learning how to be a man, somebody who might never learn, might never achieve the steadfastness and control, the decent narrowness of range. David, who preferred gin to whiskey, read novels, didn't understand the stock market, talked to women, had started out as a teacher. David, who had always driven small cars, foreign cars. But that was all right now. Small cars were not a sign of any of the things they used to be a sign of. Even here on the bluffs above Lake Huron at the very end of life, certain shifts had registered, certain changes had been understood, by a man who couldn't grasp or see.
>
> Alice Munro, ''Lichen,'' *The Progress of Love* (Toronto: McClelland, 1986) 51–52.

P

To illustrate a general concept, the writer can name a specific member of the general class: a **herring** is a **fish**. **A Toyota** is a *car*. He can also specify how something operates: **Hitler was a mad dictator**; *during World War II, he ordered the deaths of 6 million Jews*. The specification of parts is another technique for giving details, illustrations, and examples. Narrating one's story in detail illustrates very well one's conclusion about the kind of a day one had, and there are a number of other approaches as well.

2 Comparison and Contrast

Where your need is to set two items alongside each other for the purpose of noticing their similarities or differences, comparison and contrast are the developmental methods of choice. By using either of these methods, you can also isolate one of the items as being the

better of the two—thus advancing an argument, or you can isolate
for study the lesser known of the two items (say the U.S. Congress)
by comparing it with the better known (say the Canadian Parliament).

> Riel spoke indeed for the grievances of the Métis, but what he tried
> to establish was not a traditional order—based on the precedents of
> the buffalo hunt—of the kind that Dumont and Father André were
> to create in 1873 when they established their local government
> among the hunters of St. Laurent; it was rather an establishment for
> Assiniboia (and he tended to attempt a repetition of the same pattern
> for Saskatchewan half a generation later) devised on the lines of the
> responsible governments which the Canadian provinces inherited
> from pre-Confederation days. There is no reason to suppose that,
> when the province of Manitoba was created, Riel was ever disap-
> pointed with the constitutional results of his efforts. The fact that
> the rights of the Métis had been insufficiently protected certainly did
> not immediately occur to him, and when it did he doubtless assumed
> that the right legislation would immediately rectify matters. He was
> a very modern man in his illusion that within a cage of political
> action one might preserve the vanishing splendours of a free and
> natural life.
>
> Dumont, in contrast, was so much the free and natural man
> that even in 1869 the Red River seemed over-civilized to him. He
> preferred the farther prairies where the buffalo hunt had still half
> a generation to go. The people whose leader he became in the ear-
> lier 1860s were not refugees from the Canadian penetration into the
> Red River colony, though later on many of these came to the Sas-
> katchewan. They were the free hunters who had avoided the settled
> life of the environs of Fort Garry and who had moved constantly
> farther into the West as the buffalo herds were hunted out of the
> eastern prairies, and who would continue to do so until they fol-
> lowed into history the great beasts they pursued.
> George Woodcock, *Gabriel Dumont* (Edmonton: Hurtig, 1975) 12.

On the road close companionship may be little more than three
trucks moving in convoy across the time zones. Indeed, one of the
most astonishing phenomena of the long run is the identification that
can develop when two strangers pace each other for a certain distance, feeling comfortable at the same speeds, sharing the same
sense of risk and prudence, abstract from behind or in the rear-view

mirror but oddly intimate. If man to man, it's like a good game of
squash. If man to woman, it's like dancing together. Either way,
aloneness often makes the experience feel like love, and invariably
it explodes into a disappointing nothingness at the next exit.

The road, strangers, aloneness: they are the best and the worst
of long distance driving. On the one hand, they offer freedom,
adventure, and time to think. On the other, they offer ennui, aliena-
tion, and forlorn country-and-western tunes about the miles to go till
Mama. And what is true for driving is ten times truer for hitchhik-
ing. The experience of random encounters intensifies the highs of
the road, while the frequent periods of frustrated thumbing intensify
its lows. Usually, however, what is revealed by chance more than
makes up for the dangers of being mugged, raped, or stuck in
Wawa, Ontario.

Byron Graham, ''On the Road,'' *Saturday Night* January 1987: 20.

To develop a paragraph or an essay in this method, you would
proceed by selecting points of comparison that could be applied to
each member of the pair you are working with. For example, if you
were comparing a North American car and a foreign car, you might
select as points the initial costs of the cars, subsequent costs of
maintenance, convenience of service, economy with respect to energy,
and ease of handling. The comparison essay reveals something about
one member of the pair (by comparing a known item to an unknown
one) or decides which is best by measuring their respective merits.

3 Definition

Essays frequently require paragraphs defining important terms or
objects. Definition can be an important aid to the reader in understanding complex matters, especially where highly connotative words
or terms are being employed.

The *satire* is a verbal caricature which distorts characteristic features
of an individual or society by exaggeration and simplification. The
features picked out for enlargement by the satirist are, of course,
those of which he disapproves: ''If Nature's inspiration fails,'' wrote
Juvenal, ''indignation will beget the poem.'' The comic effect of the
satire is derived from the simultaneous presence, in the reader's
mind, of the social reality with which he is familiar, and of its
reflection in the distorting mirror of the satirist. It focuses attention
on abuses and deformities in society of which, blunted by habit, we

were no longer aware; it makes us suddenly discover the absurdity
of the familiar and the familiarity of the absurd.
Arthur Koestler, *The Act of Creation*

Where is the north, exactly? It's not only a place but a direction,
and as such its location is relative: to the Mexicans, the United
States is north, to Americans Toronto is, even though it's on
roughly the same latitude as Boston.

Wherever it is for us, there's a lot of it. You stand in Windsor
and imagine a line going north, all the way to the pole. The same
line going south would end up in South America. That's the sort
of map we grew up with, at the front of the classroom in Mercator
projection, which made it look even bigger than it was, all that pink
stretching on forever, with a few cities sprinkled along the bottom
edge. It's not only geographical space, it's space related to body
image. When we face south, as we often do, our conscious mind
may be directed down there, towards crowds, bright lights, some
Hollywood version of fame and fortune, but the north is at the
back of our minds, always. There's something, not someone,
looking over our shoulders; there's a chill at the nape of the neck.

The north focuses our anxieties. Turning to face north, face
the north, we enter our own unconscious. Always, in retrospect,
the journey north has the quality of dream.
Margaret Atwood, "True North," *Saturday Night* January 1987: 143.

To define a word like *religion*, which most people need to define
for themselves since there is no general agreement on its full implications, the writer would plan to give examples of *religion*; he would
also include a lexical definition of the term, separating it from other
terms that were near it in meaning by giving its distinctive properties
and perhaps would also say what *religion* is *not*. The wiser writer
of definitions uses the full range of explanatory resources.

4 Classification

The grouping of persons, things, or ideas according to some principle
or order frequently sheds new light on those things. Thus the paragraph that classifies also explains.

Symbolic immortality is an expression of man's need for an inner
sense of continuity with what has gone on before and what will go
on after his own limited biological existence. The *sense* of immor-

tality is thus more than mere denial of death, and grows out of compelling, life-enhancing imagery of one's involvement in the historical process. This sense of immortality may be expressed *biologically*, by living on through one's sons and daughters and their sons and daughters, extending out into social dimensions (of tribe, organization, people, nation, or even species); *theologically*, in the idea of a life after death or of other forms of spiritual conquest of death; *creatively*, through "works" and influences persisting beyond biological death; *naturally*, through identification with nature, with its infinite extension into time and space; or *transcendentally*, through a feeling-state so intense that time and death disappear.
Roberty Jay Lifton, "The Struggle for Cultural Rebirth," *Harper's*, April 1973

But who, then, is the desirable man—the patron who will cajole the best out of the writer's brain and bring to birth the most varied and vigorous progeny of which he is capable? Different ages have answered the question differently. The Elizabethans, to speak roughly, chose the aristocracy to write for and the playhouse public. The eighteenth-century patron was a combination of coffee-house wit and Grub Street bookseller. In the nineteenth-century the great writers wrote for the half-crown magazines and the leisured classes. And looking back and applauding the splendid results of these different alliances, it all seems enviably simple, and plain as a pikestaff compared with our own predicament—for whom should we write? For the present supply of patrons is of unexampled and bewildering variety. There is the daily Press, the weekly Press, the monthly Press; the English public and the American public; the bestseller public and the worst-seller public; the high-brow public and the red-blood public; all now organized self-conscious entities capable through their various mouthpieces of making their needs known and their approval or displeasure felt. Thus the writer who has been moved by the sight of the first crocus in Kensington Gardens has, before he sets pen to paper, to choose from a crowd of competitors the particular patron who suits him best. It is futile to say, "Dismiss them all; think only of your crocus," because writing is a method of communication; and the crocus is an imperfect crocus until it has been shared. The first man or the last may write for himself alone, but he is an exception and an unenviable one at that, and the gulls are welcome to his works if the gulls can read them.
Virginia Woolf, "The Patron and the Crocus," from *The Common Reader*

P

The writer selects a principle of order according to his interest, bearing in mind the need to arrive at logical categories that are informative for a reader. Using the principle of gender to divide your English class into men and women is not very useful, but interest in writing or previous grades in English composition or reading habits would all yield significant categories and significant information. A writer's purpose in classification essays is usually to inform, but it can also be to entertain: classifying the kinds of bores you know can be fun.

5 Process Analysis

Process analysis is a method of separating some complex whole into its component parts—usually a mechanical process. A paragraph that explains in detail how something functions or how a machine is put together is filled with explanatory power. Process analysis is also useful in giving direction as to how to do something, and paragraphs using this method of development frequently employ chronological or spatial order.

> These solitary wasps are beautiful and formidable creatures. Most species are either a deep shiny blue all over, or deep blue with rusty wings. The largest have a wing span of about four inches. They live on nectar. When excited, they give off a pungent odor—a warning that they are ready to attack. The sting is much worse than that of a bee or common wasp, and the pain and swelling last longer. In the adult stage the wasp lives only a few months. The female produces but a few eggs, one at a time at intervals of two or three days. For each egg the mother must provide one adult tarantula, alive but paralyzed. The mother wasp attaches the egg to the paralyzed spider's abdomen. Upon hatching from the egg, the larva is many hundreds of times smaller than its living but helpless victim. It eats no other food and drinks no water. By the time it has finished its single Gargantuan meal and become ready for wasphood, nothing remains of the tarantula but its indigestible chitinous skeleton.
> Alexander Petrunkevich, "The Spider and the Wasp," *Scientific American*, August 1952

> The three absolute acts of the tragedy are first the entry of the bull when the picadors receive the shock of his attacks and attempt to protect their horses with their lances. Then the horses go out and the

second act is the planting of the banderillos. This is one of the most
interesting and difficult parts but among the easiest for a new bull
fight fan to appreciate in technique. The banderillos are three-foot,
gaily colored darts with a small fish hook prong in the end. The
man who is going to plant them walks out into the arena alone with
the bull. He lifts the banderillos at arm's length and points them
toward the bull. Then he calls ''Toro! Toro!'' The bull charges and
the banderillero rises to his toes, bends in a curve forward and just
as the bull is about to hit him drops the darts into the bull's hump
just back of his horns.

By-Line: Ernest Hemingway, ed. William White

Those who write to tell others how to do something are usually
very careful about several things. First, they are careful to demarcate
the stages in the process. Second, they take into account how much
the reader knows or doesn't know, so that they are quick to define
terms that may not be familiar to the reader. Finally, though their
essays are heavily factual, they make sure that a thesis statement
controls what they write.

6 Causal Analysis

P

This method also separates something into its component parts, but
here the something is some specific event or other human situation,
and the aim of the writer is to suggest the causes that produced some
particular result.

The transistor was the outcome of purely scientific curiosity. At first
glance it looks extremely simplistic in design—a germanium crystal
soldered to a metal disk, contacted on its other face by two tungsten
wires slightly more than a thousandth of an inch apart—but it
resulted from an elaborate experiment. Shockley stumbled upon the
principle while investigating the behaviour of semiconductors. These
substances (of which germanium is one) behave unlike familiar elec-
trical conductors such as copper or silver or familiar insulators such
as rubber. Shockley found a way to alter the conductivity of germanium so that it let current flow rapidly in response to a signal. To
understand its conception, it helps to review the functions of the
electronic tube and the way in which electric current is conducted
by a solid.

Mar Jean Olson, Ph.D., ''The Transistor Turns 40,'' *Canadian Electronics
Engineering* February 1988: 29.

Undoubtedly the single most important difference between a voluntary organization and a business is that the former has no market mechanism. In a business, survival depends on whether the customer buys and pays for the goods or service provided. There is a direct link between the organization's outputs and its inputs. For most non-profit organizations, this direct link is absent. The clients of the voluntary organization generally do not supply the funds needed to keep it going. Instead, funds are provided by government agencies, private foundations, businesses, and the general public donating directly or indirectly through agencies such as the United Way. These groups often have interests and priorities very different from those of clients.

V.V. Murray, "Why Can't Voluntary Organizations Be More Businesslike?" *Canadian Business Review* 14.1 (1987): 20.

The attitude of Americans towards their north, and indeed towards the rest of the world, may be seen in developmental rather than symbolic terms. This is a vision of the north which does not depend on symbols and dreams, but instead on practical exploitation and development, either, as originally, for commercial purposes, or, as in the last fifty years, increasingly for military purposes. Because the American north is small compared to the Canadian, because Canadians have shied away from active participation in their own north, and because the Canadian north has been seen as vital to the defence of the continent, Americans have tended over the past hundred years to fill a vacuum there. Though the main thrust of nineteenth-century Manifest Destiny was to the south and west, it did lead some Americans northward as well. This process, which became evident almost from the moment the United States acquired territory in the north, is particularly evident today in the search for new petroleum resources in the Arctic region. Thus the history of the Canadian north is in part a history of the relations of two differing national concepts of the north, in which the active, developmental concept, as represented by the Americans, interacts with the more passive or symbolic concept of sovereignty represented by Canada. Moreover, for over a century now it has often been intrusions by Americans which have stimulated Canadians to take action in their north. The phlegmatic Canadian beaver was only with difficulty persuaded to challenge the eagle.

William R. Morrison, "Eagle over the Arctic: Americans in the Canadian North 1867–1985," *The Canadian Review of American Studies* 18.1 (1987): 62–63.

To enter into a discussion of why some complex human event took place, the writer must generate his materials by asking a great many questions of his subject, thus arriving at an essay that declares the multiplicity of cause and effect in the world. The writer must also be wary of simplistic thinking in other ways: for example, because event A happened *before* event B it is not necessarily the cause of it. Writing the cause-and-effect essay also requires that you use a solid chain of reasoning. (See **Logic**, pages 137–152.)

TEST YOURSELF ON

Understanding Methods of Paragraph Development

A Which method of development would be most suitable for making a paragraph out of each of the following topic sentences? Give reasons. Then select one topic sentence and develop it into a paragraph.

1. Marijuana is not more harmful than alcohol, though my parents seem to think so.

2. The Parliament Buildings look like a Gothic cathedral.

3. Unexpected things happen to new students on this campus.

4. Television commercials don't care what they do as long as they sell, sell, sell.

5. Intelligence is the capacity to face what you do not know how to handle.

6. There are three kinds of English teacher on this campus.

7. Lung cancer is a result of certain environmental pressures on the respiratory system.

8. My troubles with mathematics began in 1985.

9. The secret to treating raw wood to look like fine furniture finishing is patience.

10. Foreign cars and North American cars differ in crucial ways.

B Write three separate paragraphs using the following topic sentence:

My attitudes toward teachers have changed since I came to college.

In the first paragraph, explain *why* this change has taken place. In the second paragraph, explain *how* these attitudes have changed. Finally, in the third paragraph, compare and contrast two sets of attitudes toward teachers, the ones you had in high school and the ones you have now.

Parallel Construction

Wherever grammatical structures—words, phrases, or clauses—are repeated, we have a parallel construction.

> **Words** Jasmine *whispered* in David's ear, *touched* his arm, *winked* at him, then *walked* away. (parallel verbs)
> *Impetuously, bravely, daringly,* Sundip drove to the hoop and stuffed the ball through. (parallel adverbs)
>
> **Phrases** *To think clearly, to act ethically, to love completely*— these were Deirdre's goals. (parallel infinitive phrases).
>
> **Clauses** *When you have learned who you are, when you have experienced the world, when you have come to respect others*—then you are entitled to be called an adult. (parallel adverbial clauses)

The advantage of parallel construction is that it binds ideas together and allows the reader to grasp each point because he or she has been prepared for the second and third points by the *form of the first*. You may not want to use parallel construction to the extent that it is used in the above examples, but ineffective writing results when you *begin* to use parallel construction and then abandon it. You must be sure either to use it or avoid it—and not use it partly, as in the following examples:

>   1   2   3
> **Partly Parallel** Melissa was *bright, beautiful,* and *a person who had great consideration for others.* (1. single-word adjective; 2. single-word adjective; 3. noun + adjective clause)
> **Revised** Melissa was *bright, beautiful,* and *considerate.*

P

Partly Parallel   The Prime Minister favoured *a revised income tax*¹ *schedule,*² *simplifying the criminal code,* and *less money for*³ *judges of the Supreme Court.* (1. adjective + compound noun phrase; 2. gerund phrase; 3. adjective + noun + prepositional phrase)

Revised   The Prime Minister favoured *a revised income tax schedule, a simplified criminal code,* and *a lowered salary for the Supreme Court judges.*

The problem with the partly parallel examples above is that they set up an expectation in the mind of the reader and then don't fulfil that expectation. The result is confusion.

In order to avoid incomplete parallels, you should make sure that whatever grammatical construction follows the word *and* (or any of the other co-ordinating conjunctions) in your sentence construction also precedes it. If you have a construction like *. . . and a policeman,* you would need a noun to parallel *a policeman* before the word *and (a doctor and a policeman).* Similarly, if one of your sentences contained *. . . and which always haunted him,* you would need the same kind of construction *before* the word *and (which always followed him and which always haunted him).*

P

TEST YOURSELF ON

Filling in the Other Side of and, but, *or* Constructions

What could go on the other side of the words *and, or,* and *but* in each of the following examples?

1. . . . and snake oil.

2. . . . and whose mother came from Italy.

3. . . . and that hasn't been seen since.

4. . . . but who thinks of himself as a gentleman.

5. . . . and lovely.

6. . . . or to live longer.

7. . . . but never wanted to live there.

8. . . . but hates whisky.

9. . . . and tries everything.

10. . . . or went alone.

TEST YOURSELF ON
Making Constructions Parallel

Now that you have had some practice in making the sides of co-ordinating conjunctions parallel, try your skill at whole sentences. First locate the co-ordinating conjunction in each of the following examples. Then, if the constructions on either side of the conjunctions are not parallel, revise the sentences to make them parallel. If the sentence is correct, write C beside it. Make sure you underline all parallel constructions, whether or not the sentence is correct.

1. _____ The purpose of this meeting is to review past procedures, recognize what we have to do in the future, and so that we can get to know each other better.

2. _____ This term I learned philosophy, biology, and how to write a term paper.

3. _____ My mother is neat, patient, and a person who is filled with pride.

4. _____ Bob liked falling in love and to write poetry.

5. _____ She was happy but nervous.

6. _____ Whenever I visit my relatives, I'm nervous, exhausted, and I feel like I am disoriented.

P

7. _____ Travelling in Italy makes you aware of art and the food is wonderful for your taste buds when you eat there.

8. _____ Having a sprained ankle and then to try to walk is excruciatingly painful.

9. _____ Joking with my friends, swimming in the lake, and horseback riding in the woods—those are the things I like to do on my vacation.

10. _____ At the party, I spoke to a sociologist, a detective, a stockbroker, and this man who repaired television sets.

P | *Parentheses*

Parentheses is the plural of the word *parenthesis*. *Parentheses* signifies *both* curved marks: ( ). Parentheses are used to set off material that is not absolutely essential to complete the meaning of the sentence pattern but that supplements or further explains a part or parts of that sentence. We call such material *parenthetical elements*; these elements can be appositives or other non-restrictive phrases or clauses.

But since parentheses, commas, and dashes can all be used to set off parenthetical material, you need to learn the difference between these marks when they are used for this purpose.

Dashes are used either to set off material that is emphatic or to set off material you decide to emphasize. In other words, using dashes gives emphasis; your material should match the emphasis given.

My friend Louis—*who drove his pickup into the lake last night*—is a complete madman.

What happened last night—*if you believe him*—was an accident.

Commas are used to signal that the parenthetical material is more nearly a part of the sentence than materials set off by dashes or parentheses—that the material interrupts the flow of thought only slightly.

The signs of the storm, *lightning and thunder*, frightened him.

You can, *if you wish*, rent a cheaper model.

Parentheses signal that the enclosed material is not emphatic and that its nature is supplemental.

The Corsica is a model of the Chevrolet (*built by General Motors*).

Most students pay heavy tuition charges (*though there are a few exceptions*).

As you can see, the choice of which punctuation to use can be a matter of taste. Nevertheless, the following general rules are good guidelines:

1 Use parentheses to set off material that is not essential to complete the meaning of the sentence and that is unemphatic and supplemental. Such material may include words, phrases, whole sentences, or even several sentences.

1. At that time, the chairperson (Bohaychuk) had very little power.
2. At that time, the chairperson (Bohaychuk, a gruff old man from Regina) had very little power.
3. At that time, the chairperson had very little power. (Bohaychuk, a gruff old man from Regina, understood this well.)
4. At that time, the chairperson had very little power. (Bohaychuk, a gruff old man from Regina, understood this well. It was, perhaps, Bohaychuk's understanding of the situation that later prompted Thomas Gunn, also from Saskatchewan to try to raise the status of the position.)

P

Note that, in the third example, a full sentence is enclosed within the parentheses. In such cases, *the period comes before the closing parenthesis*. Note that there *is* a space before the opening parenthesis, but there *is no* space between the opening parenthesis and the first word or between the period and closing parenthesis.

Another point about punctuation with parentheses: *where the parenthetical material is a part of the sentence, the period goes outside the closing parenthesis*.

At that time, the chairperson was Bohaychuk (a gruff old man from Regina).

Note: Do not use parentheses for essential material.

Wrong   The men were dog tired; the lieutenant (*therefore*) called a halt to the march.

Wrong   I'm going to keep on taking that examination (*until I pass it*).

2 Use parentheses to set off cross-references and figures denoting lifespan.

It will become clear later (*in Chapter 7*) that James Joyce (*1882–1941*) was not exactly kind to his brother.

TEST YOURSELF ON
Using Parentheses Correctly

Some of the sentences below have parenthetical material correctly set off by dashes and commas; next to these sentences, write C. However, some of the sentences should have parentheses *instead* of the commas or dashes; change these. In addition, where you see essential material enclosed within parentheses, eliminate those parentheses and, if necessary, substitute other punctuation.

P

1. _____ I think, if you don't mind, I'll take my nap now.

2. _____ Sheldon—a good friend of mine—left for Calgary yesterday.

3. _____ The power of the media—with its enormous audience—is hard to overestimate.

4. _____ We whizzed along the highway, all of us on our bicycles, enjoying the breezes and the sunshine.

5. _____ The author—authors?—of Genesis spoke the stories with reverence.

6. _____ I won't go to the party (unless you come with me).

7. _____ She had (probably) a logical mind.

8. _____ The magician—a most amazing sleight-of-hand artist—had us all on the edges of our seats.

9. _____ Then it rolled through the grating, my last coin, and I was destitute.

10. _____ He was born in 1235, or somewhat earlier, and died about forty-five years later.

Passive Voice

See **Voice**.

Period

The period, which is sometimes (especially in British usage) called the *full stop*, is a mark of end punctuation. It signals the end of a *declarative* or mildly *imperative* sentence and is used in most abbreviations. (Spaced periods (. . .) also have special uses; see **Ellipsis**.)

1 Use a period to end declarative and imperative sentences. A declarative sentence makes an assertion; an imperative sentence issues a command.

> I am going to the movies tonight. (declarative)
>
> Go to the movies tonight. (imperative—this one a very mild command)

Note: For strongly imperative sentences, consider using the exclamation mark. Example: *Get out of my sight!*

2 Use a period after an abbreviation.

Mr. Buckley	Ms.
Dr. Figueroa	U.S.
Ph.D.	a.m.

Note: The period following Mr, Ms, or Mrs is optional; you can omit it, as has been done in this sentence.

Person

See **Verbs** and **Shifts**.

Possessives

See Nouns, Pronouns; **Apostrophe**, **Case**, and **Pronoun References**.

Prewriting (including Free-writing)

Prewriting is what we call the initial stage of the writing process. This stage begins when you find out you will be required to write an essay, and it ends when you're ready to write a first draft. Some writers disagree on exactly when prewriting ends, but this is a good approximation.

The Prewriting Process

What you do first during prewriting depends on what your instructor has asked you to do.

Few instructors will simply ask you to "write something." If one does, however, your first task in the prewriting stage will be to choose something to write about. More often than not, instructors will be more specific in their writing assignments and will ask you to write in a general subject area or ask you to write using a specific form of organization (see **Paragraph Development**, pages 169–183). In other words, in prewriting you must either choose a subject or explore one that you have more or less in hand.

In either case, prewriting is the stage at which you get started. If you are choosing your own subject, you need to explore possibilities, either from the fund of experience you already have or from the experience you can arrange for yourself for the specific purposes of this writing assignment.

You can search your past experience and look over the incidents, the people, and the places that have figured in your life. Think specifically about individuals—lists of friends, relatives, acquaintances, fellow workers. These lists will produce specific memories that might be fruitful. You can also take the chronological approach. Do a year-by-year survey of what you did and whom you met, the jobs you held, the trips you made, the milestones in your life, the high notes and the low.

Reviewing this lode of experience will lead you to possibilities for your subject.

A second source of possible paper subjects is the experience you can arrange. That is, you can undertake to observe something— to examine the physical world, for example, landscapes, buildings, works of art, man-made things. Or you can study communities, peoples, situations, events, or issues. You can, in fact, observe items of the latter group more systematically by doing formal research (see Part 3 for a discussion of research methods).

The prewriting we have discussed so far involves your using a pen and paper to make lists or notes. Another way to use pen and paper for invention, that is, for the purpose of generating ideas for papers—and more—is called free-writing, and it involves something other than lists and notes. Peter Elbow, who has written extensively on the subject, suggests that free-writing is one of the most efficient techniques available in the prewriting stage.

Free-writing

In free-writing, you put your pen to paper for a specified period of time—say ten minutes—and you don't stop until the ten minutes are up. Move the pen along at a brisk pace without actually hurrying. The main rule is *don't stop*. If you go absolutely blank, it's perfectly all right to write ''I'm absolutely blank'' and to keep on writing that or similar things until you begin to produce something else. It is very important to continue to write without stopping, without thinking, and especially without going back to correct mistakes—or what you think of as mistakes in spelling, grammar, or syntax. It is also important that you do not try to ''stick to the subject.'' If you wander onto another topic, so be it. Eventually, you can get back to the original subject easily enough.

You could be inhibited, as many are, by the need to explore a subject area and to keep a watchful eye on grammar and spelling— *all at the same time*. Through the hand-mind connection, free-writing helps you to loosen your capacity to think. By relieving you of the necessity of being grammatically and syntactically correct *as you write*, free-writing enhances your capacity to explore the corners of your mind. Thus free-writing is a primary aid to invention.

Free-writing to Explore a Subject

To explore a specific subject, begin with the word or words that characterize your subject and take off from there. Work for ten minutes by the clock. After you've finished, set the pages aside for a few hours. Then examine what you've written for ideas and for directions you might take with your subject. (See also Choosing a Topic and Limiting a Topic in **Subjects for Essays**, pages 259–262.)

Free-writing is not meant to be read by your instructor or by anyone else for the purpose of evaluating it or criticizing it. You may, if you wish, ask your instructor or a friend to read it, without comment, just so you'll know that someone out there has read it. The free-writing that you do is for *your* benefit. It is a resource that you can examine for possible topics for your paper, directions you might want to take with your paper, useful ideas to support what you want to say, or, in fact, indications of *what* you want to say.

Free-writing to Keep the Instrument Sharp

Free-writing is also worth using as a form of pre-writing that generates fresh, usable words, phrases, and sentences. Every piece of free-writing can be *mined* for the fresh language this exercise often produces. In other words, free-writing is a useful habit for keeping sharp your writing instrument—the instrument that is alive and well in the unexplored corners of your mind. Since you are a student whose courses often demand writing in one form or another, you might find regular free-writing sessions helpful, say three or four times a week, just to keep your instrument alive. In a writing course, you should consider free-writing a useful technique whenever (a) you are given a subject for a writing assignment, (b) you are blocked at a stage in the writing process, or (c) you need a way to stimulate the free flow of ideas you never quite realized you had.

TEST YOURSELF ON
Free-writing

Do **one** of the following free-writing exercises, using either pen and paper, a typewriter, or a word processor.

A Simply take out your notebook, turn to a fresh page and, without further ado, start writing. Continue for ten minutes, by your watch, without stopping and without taking the trouble to correct misspelling or errors in punctuation or grammar. Don't lift your pen from the page or your fingers from the keyboard. Just write.

B Start writing—as directed in ''A'' above—but begin with these words: ''Free-writing is like playing basketball without a hoop.''

C Start writing—again as directed in ''A'' above—only this time begin with these words: ''Apples are good for your complexion.''

P

Pronoun References

A pronoun sometimes does its work by referring back to another word or group of words. What the pronoun refers back to is called its *antecedent*.

The following guidelines will be useful to you in making sure that your pronoun references are clear and consistent:

1 Pronouns must *agree* in person and number with their antecedents.

A In referring to persons, places, and things, use pronouns that agree in person and number.

> I saw *John* yesterday; *he* seemed depressed.
>
> The *dog* wagged *its* tail.
>
> When I saw the *Smiths* yesterday, *they* were on *their* way to the movies.

B Use a singular pronoun in referring to antecedents like the following: *any, anybody, anyone, each, every, everybody, everyone, either, neither, man, woman, person, nobody, none, someone, somebody*. In informal speech we frequently find plural pronouns referring to some of these, but formal usage requires the singular.

> ***Formal (writing)***   *Everybody* has *his* dreams.
> ***Informal (speaking)***   *Everybody* has *their* dreams.
>
> ***Formal (writing)***   Mathematics requires *each* of us to use *his or her* intellect.
> ***Informal (speaking)***   Mathematics requires *each* of us to use *our* intellect.

P

C In the case of a collective noun used as an antecedent, use a singular pronoun if you are thinking of the group as a unit; use a plural pronoun if you are thinking of the members separately.

> The *team* raised *its* batting average by ten points.
>
> The *team* came through when *their* friends began urging *them* on.

D When two or more antecedents are joined by *and, or*, or *nor*, the following rules apply: (1) when two or more singular antecedents are joined by *and*, use a plural pronoun; (2) when two or more singular antecedents are joined by *or* or *nor*, use a singular pronoun; (3) when one of the antecedents joined by *or* or *nor* is singular and one plural, use a pronoun that agrees with the nearer of the two.

> 1. *Paulo* and *Lisa* did *their* work together.
> 2. Neither *Lisa* nor *Grace* has *her* hat on.
> 3. Neither the *conductor* nor the *musicians have* held *their* rehearsal.

TEST YOURSELF ON

Pronoun Agreement

Make all the pronouns in the following sentences agree with their antecedents according to the principles of formal usage.

1. Anybody who knows their music would know Bob Marley.

2. The committee did their work in private.

3. Neither the new professor nor the first-year students knew his way around the campus.

4. Anybody who likes their morning coffee cold is peculiar.

5. When the team scored a touchdown, the band raised its instruments to play.

6. Everybody has a right to their own opinion in politics.

7. If a drugstore or a supermarket opened in our neighbourhood, they would do well.

8. Neither of them could do their homework in the middle of all that noise.

9. Every cook thinks their recipes are best.

10. None of the students in biology could identify the specimens under their microscope.

P

---

2 Do not use pronouns ambiguously. *Ambiguous* means "able to be understood in more than one way." Therefore, an ambiguous pronoun reference occurs whenever the pronoun you use can refer to more than one antecedent.

> ***Ambiguous***   My father told my brother that *he* had to go to Halifax. (Who had to go? the father or the brother?)

Clear   My father said to my brother, ''I have to go to Halifax.''
My father said to my brother, ''You have to go to Halifax.''

Ambiguous   When Donna looked at Lisa, *she* blushed. (Who
blushed? Donna or Lisa?)
Clear   When she looked at Lisa, Donna blushed.
Clear   Donna blushed when she looked at Lisa.
Clear   Lisa blushed when Donna looked at her.
Clear   When Donna looked at Lisa, Lisa blushed.

3 Do not use pronouns with remote references. A pronoun that is
too far away from what it refers to is said to have a remote reference
(or antecedent).

Remote   As for the Concorde, we did everything we could to stop
the plane from landing at Mirabelle Airport, including sending people out to picket the field and writing letters to our MPs. *It* is
obscene. (The *it*, referring to the airplane, is too far away, too
remote, from its antecedent, *Concorde*.)
Revised   As for the Concorde, *it* is obscene, and we did everything
we could to stop the plane from landing at Mirabelle Airport,
including sending people out to picket the field and writing letters to
our MPs.

Remote   Billy gave up smoking and, as a result, temporarily gained
a lot of weight. *It* was very bad for his health.
Revised   Billy gave up smoking because *it* was very bad for his
health and, as a result, temporarily gained a lot of weight.

4 Do not use pronouns with faulty broad reference. A pronoun with
broad reference is one that refers to a whole idea rather than to a
single noun. When the pronoun refers to more than one idea, it
has a faulty broad reference. The vague use of *this, that*, and
which most frequently results in faulty broad references.

Faulty Broad Reference   He planted a line of tall shrubbery to stop
people from looking into his garden. *That* is not easy. (What is not
easy? the planting or stopping the people?)

Sometimes, adding a noun can make the loose reference clear.

Revised   He planted a line of tall shrubbery to stop people from
looking into his garden. *That job* is not easy. (Now the *job* refers
clearly to the *planting*.)

Faulty Broad Reference   He spent his time getting help with his income tax forms, *which* his wife considered unfair. (What does she consider unfair? that he spends his time that way? that he gets help? Or does she consider the forms unfair?)

In faulty references involving a *which* clause, it is sometimes necessary to recast the sentence, getting rid of *which*.

Revised   His wife considered it unfair that he spent his time getting help with his income tax forms.

Now we can see that what his wife considers unfair is the way in which he spends his time.

Despite the fact that writers are prone to errors of broad pronoun reference, the use of the broad pronoun reference is not prohibited. Frequently, such references are perfectly appropriate —where they are perfectly clear.

I'll take the cash to the bank. *That's* the safest thing.

We need to save money. *This* is the only way to stay solvent.

5 Do not use pronouns with implied antecdents; that is, do not let the pronoun refer to a noun or a whole idea that is absent from the sentence. The vague use of *it, you, they,* and *them* most frequently causes this error.

P

Implied Antecedent   *It* says in my notebook that China has the biggest population in the world.
Revised   My notebook says that China has the biggest population in the world.

Implied Antecedent   I could have supplied the answer if I had thought about *it*.
Revised   I could have supplied the answer if I had thought about the question.

Implied Antecedent   At some colleges, it is not easy for *you* to live off campus.
Revised   At some colleges, students find that it is not easy to live off campus.

Implied Antecedent   *They* have mostly an agricultural economy in Southeast Asia.
Revised   The economy in Southeast Asia is mostly agricultural.

Implied Antecedent   I go to Maple Leaf Gardens because I like to watch *them* play.

Revised   I go to Maple Leaf Gardens because I like to watch the Leafs play.

TEST YOURSELF ON

Pronoun References

Some of the sentences below have perfectly clear pronoun references; next to these, write C. Others, however, have faulty pronoun references; correct these, even if you have to recast the sentence.

1. _____ The Boston Bruins were soundly beaten by the Montreal Canadiens on their home ice last night.

2. _____ She carried a briefcase, which looked as if it had cost her a hundred dollars.

3. _____ During the Riel rebellion, they struggled over the question of native land rights.

4. _____ The idea that Peter broached to Marc was one that he had thought of some years earlier.

5. _____ For the first time in months, we went up to the farm last weekend; we cleaned out the barn, pruned the apple trees, and swam in the creek. It was wonderful.

6. _____ Driving through Jasper National Park, you are likely to see a bear.

7. _____ Georgia's mother died when she was twenty-three.

8. _____ Michael and Barbara came to the wedding in a

horse-drawn carriage, which somewhat amused the other guests.

9. _____ Tony and Johanna are broke, but Arthur is rolling in it.

10. _____ Mira started out to study medicine because society needed them.

11. _____ A great many service professionals do not offer their clients a touch of humanity but only a rule for efficient living. It is a great necessity.

12. _____ Lee stole things because she had no other way of earning a living, and she went to jail for it. It was a shame.

13. _____ I dropped a pebble in the gas tank and heard no splash. That proved we were out of gas.

P

14. _____ I never buy clothes at Lipton's because they are expensive.

15. _____ Michel balanced himself 400 metres above the ground, which is a hard thing to do.

Proofreading

Proofreading is the stage in the writing process during which the writer goes over his or her pages with painstaking care for the purpose of making final, detailed improvements. The physical act of proof-reading involves using a pen or pencil as a pointer while reading every word on a page and every page of a piece of written work. (Those who work with word processors may proofread on a printout or by using a pointer directed at the screen display.) Experienced writers usually proofread with certain goals in mind: to make sure that their sentences flow smoothly from one to the next; to make last minute improvements in the choice of a word or a phrase; and to catch any inadvertent errors in spelling, grammar, or punctuation. Less experienced writers should make a checklist for themselves. For each item on this checklist, they should proofread their papers once.

The important things to remember about proofreading are that (1) it should always be done with a pen or a pencil pointing directly at each word and that (2) it is essential not to skip this stage. Proof-reading assures that all the preceding hard work you've done will amount to something. You will be delivering your work in a state that allows for effective communication.

Below is a checklist which you may use as is, or on which you may want to base one of your own.

P

Proofreading Checklist

1. Is the paper legible? If written by hand, does a reader have to strain to decode it? Make it legible—even if you must re-copy.
2. Have you, in the heat of composition, omitted necessary words? Supply them.
3. Do your sentences flow smoothly from one to the next? If not, supply transitions. (See **Transitions**.)
4. Is your spelling correct?
5. Are the grammar and punctuation correct?
6. Are there habitual errors here, ones you tend to make regularly? Catch them.
7. It's not too late to sharpen a phrase with a better word or words.
8. It's not too late to make a more precise point, or illustrate an idea in a clearer way.

TEST YOURSELF ON

Proofreading Technique

Make up a proofreading checklist of four or five items that apply especially to the writing you do at this stage of your life. Then proceed to proofread the following paragraphs, going over them once for each item on your personal checklist.

A. Armies of Canadians are undertaking to make healthy improvements in the way they live, they are hitting the road, jogging to protect their hearts and blood vessels. Their breaking down the doors of health food stores, looking for tofu and beans and other unprocesed foosd with low sodium and low sugar and low fat contents. They also avoiding smoking like the plage, all over the country there are butttout programs. These activities are having good affects on the nation's death rates and especially on ther rates of death from heart disease and lung cancer and cancer of the stomach.

B. The best way to stop smoking is to undergo whats called aversion thwerapy, it really works. Its based on the simple idea that we will have an aversion toward anything we associates with pain or displeasure. The psychological theory is called behaviorism. When we are rewarded we are reinforced to continue doing what brought us the reward. When we are punished, we experience the opposiet. It sounds like fascism but smoking is really the pits

P

and we must all give it up. The program involves a series of controlled experiences in which the smoker is made to experience their smoking habit with distasteful things. Eventually, he or she gets so turned off by these things they give it up.

Question Mark

The question mark is used to end a sentence that asks a direct question.

> Where is Malcolm going?
>
> He asked where Malcolm was going. (indirect question)
>
> *Did he* ask where Malcolm is going? (a direct question, indicated by the italicized phrase)

Question marks can also convert declarative sentences into questions.

> Aviva went to the football game? (Imagine this sentence spoken with the emphasis on *football*.)
>
> Dimitra loves David? (emphasis on *David*)
>
> Sean and Frances are getting married? (emphasis on *married*)

An imperative sentence may also be converted into a question.

Q-S

> Pass the sugar?
>
> Give you the newspaper?

A question mark is used between parentheses to indicate the writer's uncertainty about some detail.

> Her mother was born in 1893(?) and died in 1972.
>
> Shakespeare was born in 1564 on April 23(?).

It is also permissible, for emphasis, to place a question mark after each question in a series.

> Did you tell her you loved her? get interested in her work? try to work out your differences?

Note that this example constitutes a single sentence and that there is no capital letter following the question marks.

For treatment of the question mark in quotations, see **Quotation Marks**.

TEST YOURSELF ON
The Use of the Question Mark

A Convert each of the following into questions by placing a question mark in the proper place; in some, you may have to change the pronouns.

1. Marcia ran the school.

2. Give me your pen.

3. Take off your coat.

4. Jorge likes apples.

5. Susannah likes parties.

B Some of the following sentences are properly punctuated and some are not. Next to the correct sentences, write C. Supply question marks in the others where needed.

1. _____ He asked me if I would go to the ball game with him.

2. _____ He asked me, ''Would you come with me to the ball game.''

3. _____ Did she take you seriously read your paper give you a tutoring session grade you fairly?

4. _____ She mentioned to me—did I understand her correctly—that she was going to Scotland next summer.

Q

Quotation Marks

Quotation marks always appear twice ('' ''): once at the beginning of the quoted material, once at the end. *Note:* Don't forget that second use; proofread your paper to make sure you haven't, because confusion always results when you do.

Uses of Quotation Marks

Quotation marks are used in the following cases:

1 Use quotation marks wherever you quote directly someone's *written or spoken* words.

> Placing the poet on the literary stage, Clara Thomas wrote: ''But Bliss Carman, with his mane of white hair and his wide-brimmed hat, *looked*, in mild and romantic eccentricity, the way people expected a poet to look.'' The reading public wanted poets to look the part during that period of Canadian literary history.

> ''Well,'' Ron said, ''I wouldn't be surprised if Lila took off for Yellowknife and surprised us all.''

The first example offers a quotation of someone's (in this case Thomas') *written* words. In the second example, a writer quotes what Ron has *said* about Lila. Take careful note of the position of the quotation marks and the position of the other punctuation marks *in relation to the quotation marks*.

Q

2 Although you use a pair of regular (double) quotation marks ('' '') to enclose direct quotations, use a pair of single quotation marks (' ') to enclose a quote within a quote.

> ''Frankly,'' Eric said, ''Carmella answered my inquiry with 'no comment, I'm busy.' ''

> Louise said, ''The answer Donald gave was 'I don't know.' ''

3 Quoting dialogue—conversation between two or more people— requires certain special conventions: (1) use a separate paragraph when reporting each person's speech; (2) include in the same paragraph such phrases as *he said, she replied,* or *he answered*;

(3) punctuate according to the practice in this sample passage, and note especially that the first word of a quotation is always capitalized if the quoted material itself is a full sentence.

The policeman came running up to me, and I could tell he was furious.

"Do you own this robot?" he asked.

I was startled. "I never saw him before in my life!"

"Then how come," said the policeman, "he just winked at you?"

Sure enough, the robot's green-lit eye was blinking at me. "I think he's just friendly," I replied.

"He just leaked oil on my shoes," said the policeman, menacingly.

"Am I my robot's keeper?" I pleaded.

4 Use quotation marks for titles of short stories, essays, short poems, songs, articles from periodicals, book chapters, or other parts of books.

"Two Fishermen" (short story by Callaghan)

"Soldiers Home" (short story by Hemingway)

"Politics and the English Language" (essay by Orwell)

"Cariboo Horses" (poem by Al Purdy)

"Yesterday" (song by the Beatles)

"The Pollstergeists" (magazine article)

In Chapter 4, "The Myth of the Poet," the author examines a modern dilemma.

Modern socialism is attacked in Part 2, "The Return."

5 Use quotation marks to give special emphasis to a word or a phrase or where you speak of a word *as* a word.

Johnny had a "system" for beating the dealers in Las Vegas.

He had a "hands-off" attitude.

"Bad dude" is slang for "splendid chap." (*Note*: Italics may also be used in cases like this one.)

6 Do *not* use quotation marks for indirect quotations. An indirect quotation is one that reports what a speaker said but not necessarily in the speaker's exact words.

> David asked Dimitra why she wanted to earn a Ph.D. (indirect)
> David asked Dimitra, ''Why do you want to earn a Ph.D.?'' (direct)
>
> Paul said that he liked my book. (indirect)
> Paul said, ''I like your book.'' (direct)

Quotation Marks with Other Punctuation

Be sure to position quotation marks correctly when they are used with other punctuation marks.

1 Place commas and periods *inside* quotation marks.

> ''I wanted to quit early,'' he said, ''but I couldn't think of an excuse.'' (The only mark *outside* is the one used to separate *he said* from what follows those words.)
>
> Police work is an example of a ''high-risk occupation,'' and policemen are paid accordingly.
>
> She had ''the common touch.''

2 Place colons and semicolons *outside* quotation marks.

> She had ''the common touch''; consequently, people in all walks of life responded warmly to her.
>
> Tom said that to have a good time he needed the right ''equipment'': congenial company, enough leisure, and peace of mind.

Q

3 Place question marks and exclamation marks inside quotation marks if they are actually part of the quote; place them outside if they are not.

> She leaned out the window and shouted, ''Fire!''
>
> Did you say, ''I don't know''?

Note that although the exclamation mark in the first example applies to ''Fire'' and the question mark in the second applies to the whole sentence, neither sentence takes any additional punctuation marks at the end.

Misuse of Quotation Marks

Quotation marks should not be used for the following purposes:

1 Do not make a practice of overusing quotation marks for emphasis.

> *Inappropriate*   The cowboys in the movie were strong ''men.''
> *Inappropriate*   I thought Tony was a ''wise guy.''
> *Inappropriate*   People like Jean are a ''dime a dozen.''

The first example needs no quotation marks around *men* (or *strong*) to convey its message; the quotation marks in the third example just point up a tired expression which should not have been used in the first place, and the quotation marks in the second are better left out too—though the expression *wise guy* is also trite by now.

2 Do not use quotation marks as an excuse to include an unacceptable slang expression in a piece of formal writing. If the slang expression is appropriate, use it without quotation marks; if it is not, do not use it at all.

> *Inappropriate*   At that point, President Reagan simply ''flipped out'' and sent in the Marines.
> *Inappropriate*   Most of the patients at the clinic are children who have ''gone ape.''
>
> *Appropriate*   He was displaying a common twentieth-century hang-up: paranoia.
> *Appropriate*   The carnival atmosphere can only be described as raunchy.

Q

3 Do not use quotation marks to excuse using a word that does not say precisely what you mean.

> *Imprecise*   My sister used to ''get'' me about the braces on my teeth.
> *Precise*   My sister used to tease me about the braces on my teeth.
>
> *Imprecise*   The cards in the library are kept in a wooden ''box.''
> *Precise*   The cards in the library are kept in a card catalogue.

TEST YOURSELF ON
The Use of Quotation Marks

A Some of the following sentences contain direct and some indirect quotations. Change the direct quotations to indirect ones, and change the indirect quotations to direct ones.

1. The student said that he considered me one of the best professors in the English Department.

2. ''Ling's ceramics are elegant,'' said Mark.

3. Matt said, ''In my opinion, Sabina's a talented actress.''

4. Jim said the policeman asked him why he was speeding.

5. Maria told Jean she wanted to see her over Easter.

6. Lou reminded Frank that they were brothers.

B Some of the following sentences have quotation marks correctly placed. Next to them, write C. The others need quotation marks in one place or another. Supply them.

1. _____ We read a short story called ''Spit Delaney's Island,'' and our professor said that Jack Hodgins, the author, had been a high school teacher.

2. _____ In the poem Sailing to Byzantium, what is the significance of the line The salmon-falls, the mackerel-crowded seas?

3. _____ When we say that a recording has a lot of wet, we mean that it contains many echo effects.

4. _____ In a moment of frenzy, Vito wrote: "Elephants can be housed in a car garage just as well as in a regular cage."

5. _____ That song Snowbird was a winner.

6. _____ Part 2 of his book is called "An Analysis of Urban Problems."

C Place quotation marks correctly in each of the following sentences.

1. You made a fool of me, Margaret said, and I won't forgive you for it. The name of my article is not Childhood Reams but Childhood Dreams.

2. She had written, I don't care for the climate in the tropics, but when I saw her in Edmonton she said, I'm looking forward to visiting Cuba for the second time.

3. Can you lend me a hundred dollars? she asked timidly. Slapping his hand down hard on the table, he replied, I think not, madam. I never saw you before in my life.

4. Imagine, he said, that you are in a strange environment and you are surrounded by alien creatures. What thoughts go through your mind as you try to integrate yourself into this scene? he went on.

5. She said to me, He smirked, you're a loser, and I was startled, to say the least.

6. Who said so? I asked.

Q

Revising and Editing

At a certain stage in the writing process, you have produced, let us say, two typewritten pages in response to an assignment, but you are by no means ready to hand these in to your instructor. Ideally, these pages have lain in your desk drawer for a couple of days, a procedure that is useful in detaching you from the work and enabling you to examine it critically. We would call these hypothetical pages a *first draft* and say that you were now ready for *revising* and *editing*.

Revising describes the process of making such substantial changes as rewriting or recasting sentences, deleting sentences from a paragraph or adding them to it, moving paragraphs to new positions in the essay, or inserting freshly written ones into your text. *Editing* is a term we usually reserve for smaller changes, such as substituting one word for another, changing mechanical things like capital letters, and adjusting spelling and punctuation.

Revision and editing are most difficult to undertake when your papers are handwritten. Revising and editing handwritten papers always involve a good deal of recopying. The way to make revision and editing less laborious is to make several xerox copies of your first draft and use the cut and paste technique. That is, use scissors to cut pieces of your xerox copies and then Scotch tape to assemble the good pieces into a new draft.

The same technique can be used when you type your essays, although retyping revised and edited drafts is not as laborious as recopying by hand.

R

The word processor is, of course, a most efficient machine to assist with revising and editing. In using a word processor, we generate a text that we "save" (or record) on a diskette. The text is displayed on a screen where the writer is able to perform many varied tasks of revision and editing with just a few strokes on the keys.

Regardless of what mechanical means you use, however, revising and editing is best done with some plan in mind. Individual writers will have their own favoured methods of proceeding, but most writers, whether or not they are aware of it, go about reworking their drafts in some methodical fashion or other.

A useful plan might be to go over your draft, revising and/or editing, once, or more than once, on behalf of the items given under each number listed here:

1 *Considering large matters*: does the general shape of your essay conform to your original plan? If it doesn't, should it? Or is it better the way it is now? Do you go on too long in any given section? Does a particular section need filling in with more detail? Do your paragraphs follow each other smoothly? Are there good transitions between them? When a transition between paragraphs looks rough, consider whether one or the other paragraph belongs where it is: should it be moved? Does your introduction do its job? How about your conclusion?

2 *At the paragraph level*: look at each of your paragraphs, one by one. Does each one have unity? Or are there sentences that don't belong?

Delete what doesn't belong. Cut it out if it's handwritten or typewritten; "select" it and delete it if it's displayed on a word processing screen.

3 *At the paragraph level*: does each sentence run smoothly into the next? Check the transitions between sentences. Make sure you carry your reader carefully over sturdy verbal bridges.

4 *Looking at sentences*: do your sentences say what you want them to say? Are they worded as crisply and as leanly as possible?

5 *At the level of words*: are you sure your tone is what you want it to be? That is, is your diction satisfactory for the specific purposes of your essay? Change words and phrases wherever you need to in order to sustain the appropriate tone.

6 *Grammar and punctuation*: if you make characteristic errors in grammar, check to be sure that those are not here. Have you put periods in the right places? Commas? Closed quotations? Apostrophes?

R

TEST YOURSELF ON
Revising and Editing

A Consider the following paragraphs in the light of numbers 2–6 above. That is, do what you can to revise and edit the paragraphs so that they make their points more sharply and correctly and thus make better reading.

I think that the transplantation of the baboons heart inside the baby was justified because the Doctors were trying to save the infant's life. Wouldn't you like someone to try to save your life? I would. I'm not sure they had much of a choice. Where were they going to get a tiny little heart from a human so fast as they needed the thing? It might have been cruel to the baboon, we have to think more about what we're saying when we say "cruel to the baboon."

This thing was also justified because the parents said it was all right and they're really the ones who have the right to say what is right for the baby. Another reason why I think the thing was right is that the transplantation was done for Medical Science. If we're ever going to treat heart disease better we have to have more information and a thing like this obviously gives quite a bit more information than you'd get without it.

R

Run-on Sentences

A run-on or fused sentence is an error in punctuation in which one or more periods are omitted between sentences (or independent clauses).

My Aunt Meg is a great cook she always provides the food at big family dinners.

The writer of this sentence has failed to recognize that there are two independent clauses in the construction: *my Aunt Meg is a great cook* and *she always provides the food at big family dinners*.

The run-on sentence is a serious error because it confuses and disorients a reader. Equally serious is the error known as the comma splice or comma fault. This error occurs when the writer separates the two clauses with *only* a comma:

> My Aunt Meg is a great cook, she always provides the food at big family dinners.

In both the run-on sentence and the comma splice there is not enough punctuation to link the sentences. There are four ways to punctuate two independent clauses correctly.

1 Use a period:

> My Aunt Meg is a great cook. She always provides the food at big family dinners.

2 Use a comma followed by a co-ordinating conjunction *and, but, or, for, so, nor, yet*):

> My Aunt Meg is a great cook, *and* she always provides the food at big family dinners.

3 Use a semicolon, which would provide enough stopping power to properly separate the clauses but would also indicate that the two clauses are closely related and belong together in the same sentence:

> My Aunt Meg is a great cook; she always provides the food at big family dinners.

4 Use a semicolon followed by a conjunctive adverb (*anyway, besides, consequently, finally, furthermore, however, instead, meanwhile, moreover, nevertheless, otherwise, subsequently, therefore, thus,* and so forth). The conjunctive adverb acts to relate the two clauses more precisely:

> My Aunt Meg is a great cook; *therefore*, she always provides the food at big family dinners. (Note how this additional word brings the clauses into closer relation.)

Note: There is usually a comma following the conjunctive adverb, but the strong linkage between the clauses is provided by the semicolon.

TEST YOURSELF ON

Linking Independent Clauses with a Co-ordinating Conjunction

Link the pairs of sentences below with a comma followed by one of the co-ordinating conjunctions: *and, but, or, nor, for, yet, so.*

1. Charles was head of the Ethics Committee. He carried out his duties with high purpose.

2. He couldn't increase the speed of the car. There was a motorcycle policeman waiting at the exit.

3. Carla couldn't type. The paper was due the next morning.

4. Foreign policy was a pressing issue. The Prime Minister knew he had to deal with it.

5. She could take the train to Montreal. She could stay later and take the air shuttle.

6. He had no money for the bus. He decided to walk.

7. In many ways she annoyed him. He thought he wanted to date her.

8. He thought she was kind. She had done him many favours.

9. The snowmobile was dangerous. She planned to go up the mountain in it.

10. Hockey players work a very long season. They are well paid for it.

11. Roller-skates are ugly. They are fun to use.

12. They are getting married. They are very much in love.

R

TEST YOURSELF ON

Linking Independent Clauses with a Semicolon and a Conjunctive Adverb

Try linking the pairs of sentences below with a semicolon. After you have done so, look at the list of conjunctive adverbs given above and see if the addition of one of those might create a better relation between parts. *Remember*: a comma follows a conjunctive adverb, but the strong link is made by the semicolon.

1. Cam had confidence in his ability to write. He sat down and wrote a book.

2. Painters have the urge to arrange form, line, colour, and mass. They paint pictures working with these principles.

3. National parks are a part of our heritage. We have a tradition of protecting wildlife and its habitat.

4. He had just changed the spark plugs and the points. The car was in good running condition.

5. Benjamin's tax refund came on July 25. On August 1, he began his European vacation.

R

6. His father wrote that he could no longer pay Thanh's tuition. Thanh had to get a part-time job.

7. Concetta's first novel was well received. Her second work received even greater recognition.

8. Shut the windows during a heavy rainstorm. Your apartment will be flooded.

9. The muscles in her legs were crying out with pain. She pressed on, walking and limping up the trail.

10. He knew he should stay at home and write his paper. He dressed up and went to the dance.

Let us return for a moment to the run-on sentence with which we began this discussion:

> My Aunt Meg is a great cook she always provides the food at big family dinners.

A fifth way to correct this run-on sentence is to change one of the independent clauses to a dependent clause—and separate the clauses with a comma.

> *Because my Aunt Meg is a great cook*, she always provides the food at big family dinners.

The addition of the word *because* changes the independent clause to a dependent clause and makes a comma the correct punctuation to separate it from the main (independent) clause.

TEST YOURSELF ON

Recognizing and Correcting Run-on Sentences and Comma Splices

R

Some of the sentences below are run-on sentences or comma splices and some are correct. Next to the correct sentences, write C. Correct the other sentences by one or another of the methods discussed in this entry.

1. _____ I love to swim, there is no better exercise.

2. _____ I had to be in Vancouver on the 18th, therefore I decided to leave Montreal on the 12th.

3. _____ Crime does not result from the inborn tendency of individual criminals; rather, it is a complex social

problem, having to do with social environment and economic status.

4. _____ Many Nova Scotians fish, it's important to their economy.

5. _____ Because she had always been careful about money in her youth, she could look forward to a secure old age.

6. _____ The term *arson* should apply to a fire that someone has set even if the fire isn't set deliberately the results are the same.

7. _____ Potential students are no longer flocking to colleges the job market no longer requires so many college graduates.

8. _____ Pacific coast Chinook salmon stocks are depleted what we need now are reserves of goodwill if we are to prevent their extinction.

9. _____ Marriages are not made in heaven, divorces are not made in courts.

R

10. _____ He looks like my brother, he talks like my enemy.

TEST YOURSELF ON

Proofreading to Catch Run-on Sentences and Comma Splices

Read carefully the following paragraphs, and wherever you see a run-on sentence or comma splice, correct it.

Hospitals can really be depressing, it's depressing seeing all those sick people in beds. Of course, some of them get well and go home to their families, but it's depressing knowing that some of them will die in those beds. It doesn't matter hospitals are still depressing places.

The white walls are gloomy, the beds are small and narrow. Some nurses are snobbish and make your stay impossible with their aloofness some of them are so nice you hate to leave. But doctors are so busy that they have no time for you personally, they treat you like an experiment most of the time. As for the food, it too is depressing it's supposed to make you healthy but it really makes you sick just to look at it, even the way its prepared, the way it looks, causes that depressed feeling.

Some people enter the hospital with a minor illness by the time they have been there a few days, they have a major problem, remember the movie *Hospital* they had it right.

Of course, it's not all bad, the candy and fruit your family and friends bring can lighten your day, and you may finally be able to read the novel you were given for your birthday.

S

Semicolon

The semicolon (;) is a mark of internal punctuation that is equivalent to a period in its power to bring an independent clause to an end.

1 When the semicolon is used to separate independent clauses, it can be used with or without the conjunctive adverb (words such as *nevertheless, moreover, thus, subsequently, consequently, therefore*, and others; see **Conjunctions** for a longer list of these words).

> The car wouldn't run on regular gas; *therefore*, we filled the tank with unleaded.

> Sid never liked home cooking; he preferred to eat out every night.

2 The semicolon can also be used to set off items in a series if they are very long or contain other kinds of internal punctuation.

> What she objected to in his character was that he was angry, wilful, and stubborn; that he had no capacity to develop or sustain a professional or vocational interest that would lead to him taking or holding a job; and that he was incapable of having easy relationships with either his peers, his family, or his neighbours.

> We were divided into three groups: (1) those who could sing, dance, act, or play a musical instrument; (2) those who had carpentry or other technical skills; and (3) those who had some kind of business experience or advertising and public relations skills.

Note: Where you use quotation marks, the semicolon goes outside the closing quotation marks:

> He thinks of himself as ''progressive''; he voted for Crosbie.

> Tom said, ''Stagecraft is vital to any study of Shakespeare''; he meant it, too.

For more on the semicolon, see also **Fragments** and **Run-on Sentences**.

TEST YOURSELF ON
The Correct Use of the Semicolon

Each of the sentences below is poorly punctuated because it needs a semicolon for one reason or other. Some of the sentences consisting of two independent clauses could also use a conjunctive adverb after the semicolon. For each sentence, add one or more semicolons where needed.

1. My father thinks I'm lazy he'll only give me my allowance if I do chores around the house.

2. The news we heard on the radio was bad, we went out and got drunk.

3. We could have insisted they cancel the reservation and give us back our deposit so that we could go to another hotel, we could have stayed there without making a fuss and spent three miserable nights sleeping on lumpy mattresses and listening to the sound of the freight trains, or we could have gone quietly away, taken our sleeping bags out to the trailer park, and camped underneath the beech trees by the lake.

4. The elevator shakes and rumbles as it goes up, the inspector says it's safe.

5. Christmas is only three weeks away, this year I don't care.

6. Professors care only about their own lectures, their students' producing a great deal of work for them, their status, and their vacations, students care only about snap courses, getting high grades however they can, and enjoying midwinter and summer breaks, administrators care only about budgets, reputations, and no emergencies.

7. He was given a long prison sentence, he had never been arrested before.

S

8. Six men were killed in an accident, the mine owners instituted stringent safety regulations.

9. I have a six-figure income and a house that's all paid for, I have investments in real estate and oil wells.

10. I exercise too hard and long, I get muscle aches.

Sentence Length and Variety

Avoiding Monotony

Variation in the length and kinds of sentences you write helps to avoid giving your readers the impression of monotony. There are a number of ways to achieve this variation in sentence structure and length, but let us first consider what to avoid.

1 Avoid writing a series of short, simple sentences. Children write this way, but that is because their minds are not yet developed to the point where they can understand the relations between ideas.

> *Weak*   We went to the movies. It was a Western. We bought popcorn. It made noise. The other people were mad. They told us to stop.
>
> *Revised*   Because there was a Western playing, we went to the movies. We bought some popcorn, but we made so much noise eating it that the other patrons got angry and asked us to stop.

The series of weak sentences constitutes a simple example—something a child might write—but there are occasions when more mature writers fall into the same pattern.

> *Weak*   The house was dark. We walked up the steps. We went through the door. There was a noise. We paused and listened. We decided it was only the wind.

S

Revised   The house was dark as we walked up the stairs and through the door. There was a noise, and we passed to listen more carefully, but it was only the wind.

(For further information on combining short sentences into more complex structures, see **Subordination**.)

2 Avoid writing long, excessively compounded sentences—sentences that join together, willy-nilly, a number of independent clauses using *and* or other co-ordinating conjunctions.

Weak   We drove up to the park, but we saw that the gate had been locked for the night, and so we changed our plans and turned around and headed for Kamloops.

Revised   As we drove up to the park, we saw that the gate had been locked for the night. Changing our plans, we turned around and headed for Kamloops. (First independent clause is made into a subordinate clause by the use of *as*; third clause is made into a phrase; second and fourth clauses become main clauses of two separate sentences.)

Weak   He was the faculty adviser of the campus newspaper, and he was a professor in the English Department, but he was never too busy with his duties to consult with students.

Revised   The faculty advisor of the campus newspaper, who was also a professor in the English Department, was never too busy with his duties to consult with students. (First clause becomes a phrase which is the subject of the new sentence; second clause becomes a subordinate clause; third clause becomes the predicate of the sentence).

S

The excessively simple pattern and the excessively compounded pattern have one thing in common: they are both monotonous. They present independent clauses in the regular order of subject-verb, and they present only one type of sentence—the declarative. To achieve variety, you must occasionally interrupt these patterns—by beginning or ending sentences with subordinate structures or by interrupting a sentence with an appositive.

TEST YOURSELF ON

Revising Sentences of Monotonous Length

A Revise the following groups of short sentences.

1. Television commercials are annoying. They insult the intelligence. They waste one's time. They should be banned from the airwaves.

2. President Reagan was from California. He was an actor there. He was formerly Governor of California. He brought many business leaders to Washington.

3. She wanted to be a doctor. She studied chemistry. She studied biology. She worked for good grades. She put in long hours. Her final year arrived. She applied to medical school. She was accepted.

4. The doctor came. He took my temperature. He checked my heart. He took my blood pressure. He prescribed some medicine. Then he said I'd probably recover in a few days.

5. I needed a job. I looked at the want ads. I went to employment agencies. I even visited a number of factories and offices. I got very tired. But I finally landed a job.

B Revise the following sentences. Eliminate excessive joining together of independent clauses by creating subordinate clauses and phrases.

1. The train entered the station, and I got ready to board but then I found I'd left my bag in the checkroom and I ran back inside the waiting room to get it.

2. The *Star Wars* trilogy was a very successful series and broke many box office records and this goes to show that science fiction adventure films appeal greatly to the movie-going public.

3. There are thousands of Canadian university students, and most of them believe that they need this education to get better jobs, but the job market is not encouraging the hopes of these students, and some of them might do better in vocational training.

4. Members of the volunteer fire department are really dedicated and they give much of their time in public service, but they are not appreciated enough and often feel bitter because of this.

5. For a while, soccer was the fastest growing sport in North America and as many as 70,000 fans turned out for one game, but even Pele's giving the sport a boost did not save the NASL from decline and eventual collapse.

Achieving Sentence Variety

So far we have looked at what to avoid: a series of short, simple sentences, and a sentence composed of many independent clauses strung together with co-ordinating conjunctions. Both types of sentence tend to produce monotony when used exclusively because both begin with the subject of the sentence. This is not a bad thing to do—more than half of your sentences will probably begin that way—but such a practice produces monotony when followed exclusively. Therefore, variety is achieved by changing the order of words in your sentences. Variety is also achieved by occasionally departing from the declarative sentence and using the question or the command. You should undertake these changes with great care, however, since altering the order of words in a sentence always involves a slight alteration of meaning. Choosing the proper alteration is a matter of carefully considering your subject matter and the meaning you want to convey. Here are the principal means of achieving sentence variety.

1 Vary the beginnings of your sentences. Suppose you have one sentence that looks like this:

> The miners worked purposefully in the tunnel, and they were unaware of the storm outside.

Or, suppose you have two sentences that look like this:

> The miners worked purposefully in the tunnel. They were unaware of the storm outside.

In either case, you can produce variations looking like these:

> *Working purposefully in a tunnel*, the miners were unaware of the storm outside. (beginning with a verbal phrase)

> *In the tunnel*, the miners worked purposefully, unaware of the storm outside. (beginning with a prepositional phrase)

> *Because the miners were working purposefully in the tunnel*, they were unaware of the storm outside. (beginning with an adverbial clause)

> *There* were miners working purposefully in the tunnel, unaware of the storm outside. (beginning with an expletive)

> *And* the miners worked purposefully in the tunnel, unaware of the

S

storm outside. (Beginning with a co-ordinating conjunction is perfectly acceptable, but usually the meaning of the sentence depends on something that has gone before.)

2 Reverse the usual order of subject-verb or subject-verb-object. But to do this is to create a distinctly emphatic order, and you should do so only where your aim is to achieve such emphasis.

Subject-Verb	*Verb-Subject*
The mouse ran up the wall.	Up the wall ran the mouse.
Michael's letter rested in the mailbox.	In the mailbox rested Michael's letter.

Subject-Verb-Object	*Object-Subject-Verb*
Joanna loves pizza.	Pizza Joanna loves.
I never saw him.	Him I never saw.

3 Occasionally use a question or a command instead of a declarative sentence, but only when it is appropriate to do so.

Imperative (command)   *Imagine a fine tapestry*, interwoven with various attractively coloured threads, and you will have a picture of the diversity and beauty in the fabric of Canadian life.

Question   *What is the purpose of an education*? One purpose is to train the mind to perceive fine distinctions.

TEST YOURSELF ON

Achieving Sentence Variety

Revise the following sentences by revising their beginnings.

1. The car had broken down the night before, and they had to take the bus to school.

2. The Liberal party held a fund-raiser at the Château Laurier and it attracted a surprising number of young people.

3. His grades were poor, and his scholarship money was almost gone, and he knew he had to do something.

4. The rescue team worked all night at the site of the cave-in, and they were unable to stop for dinner.

S

5. Readers with lively imaginations read *The Hobbit* and project themselves into its adventurous moments.

6. Governments are less inclined to give in to hijackers' demands these days, but hijackings continue anyway.

7. She knew she would have to save money regularly for next year's tuition, and she opened a savings account and began to make regular deposits.

8. Nobody knew where the cat had gone, but everybody began searching furiously.

9. Big-time professional sports can accommodate very few athletes, but many Canadian youngsters still dream of a career in the big leagues.

10. Inflation has made money worth less, and it is more expensive to live in Canada than it used to be.

11. The man in black stood against the wall.

12. The mouse ran into my computer.

Shifts

When you begin a sentence by saying "He *begged* and *pleaded* for the loan and. . . ," the reader immediately tunes in to *begged* and *pleaded* as verbs in the past tense. The reader's expectation is that if any other verb appears in the sentence, it too will be in the past tense. So if the sentence is completed with ". . . *asks* the bank manager to have some sympathy" (present tense verb), the reader will be shocked, disappointed, and confused because you have *shifted* gears.

It is not easy, but it is absolutely essential, to maintain the kind of consistency that is missing in the above example. In fact, both beginning and experienced writers shift gears in a number of different ways. A writer should understand that achieving consistency requires consistent proofreading—until they are sure they are incapable of producing the various kinds of shifts.

Reread carefully the sentence you have just read (beginning with "A writer"). Notice that the sentence begins with a *singular* subject, *writer*, but that after the dash, the second and fifth words, *they*, are plural pronouns. Here we see another kind of shift, a shift in *number* from singular to plural. We can also see shifts in *tense* (as in the first example given in this entry), *person, mood, voice,* and *point of view*. Below is a discussion of each kind of shift.

Tense

Perhaps no other shift is so annoying to a reader as this one, because a verb carries not only meaning but a sense of time, and the writer who uses verb tenses inconsistently interferes with the reader's sense of a consistent time pattern.

> **Inconsistent**   In the novel *The Stone Angel*, the narrator and main character, Hagar Shipley, finally *confronts* herself. She *discovered* she *was* dying of cancer and, stunned, *wandered* the streets. Waking up in a deserted cannery, she *had been joined* by Murray Lees, a social outcast, who *helped* her by sharing her life's troubles. Eventually, she *found* her way to a hospital bed, and after much self-examination, *accepts* herself for the person she is.
>
> **Consistent**   In the novel *The Stone Angel*, the narrator and main character, Hagar Shipley, finally *confronts* herself. She *discovers* she *is* dying of cancer and, stunned, *wanders* the streets. Waking up in a deserted fish cannery, she *is* joined by Murray Lees, a social outcast, who *helps* her by sharing her life's troubles. Eventually, she *finds* her way to a hospital bed, and after much self-examination, *accepts* herself for the person she is.
>
> **Inconsistent**   When I *go* to the seashore for my vacation, I *went* to the beach right away because I *loved* to swim. I *see* the lifeguard and I *asked* him if it *was* all right to swim. *Jaws makes* me frightened to go in the water.
>
> **Consistent**   When I *went* to the seashore for my vacation, I *went* to the beach right away because I *love* to swim. I *saw* the lifeguard and I *asked* him if it *was* all right to swim. *Jaws made* me frightened to go in the water.

S

Person

The English verb system recognizes three *persons*: the first person (*I* recognize, *we* recognize), the second person (*you* recognize [both singular and plural]), and the third person (*he, she,* or *it* recognizes; *they* recognize). Most shifts in person occur because writers use the second person (*you*) carelessly.

> **Inconsistent**   *People* shouldn't expect to be dependent all their lives. *You* have to take care of *yourself* in adult life.
> **Consistent**   *People* shouldn't expect to be dependent all their lives. *They* have to take care of *themselves* in adult life.

> **Inconsistent**   When *you* have a cold, *one* should get plenty of rest and drink fluids.
> **Consistent**   When *you* have a cold, *you* should get plenty of rest and drink fluids.

Number

Errors in consistency can happen when writers begin with a singular noun and shift to a plural pronoun—or vice versa.

> **Inconsistent**   The Canadian *medical student* abroad *has* special problems because *they* have to do *their* work in a foreign language.
> **Consistent**   Canadian *medical students* abroad *have* special problems because *they* have to do *their* work in a foreign language.

> **Inconsistent**   Business is so good at Canadian Tire that *no one* loses *their* job there.
> **Consistent**   Business is so good at Canadian Tire that *no one* loses *his* job there.

> **Inconsistent**   *Lawyers* seem to have an easy life, because every time *he* goes into court *he* makes a fat fee.
> **Consistent**   *Lawyers* seem to have an easy life, because every time *they* go into court they make fat fees.

S

Voice

Once you have begun to use the active voice in a sentence, do not shift to the passive voice, and vice versa. (See also **Voice**.)

Inconsistent   We *leave* for the beach at eight o'clock, *swim* from nine-thirty to eleven, and lunch *is eaten* at twelve.
Consistent   We *leave* for the beach at eight o'clock, *swim* from nine-thirty to eleven, and *eat* lunch at twelve.

Inconsistent   *Dig* a hole for the seeds, *drop* them in and cover them with loose soil, and then the ground is lightly *watered*.
Consistent   *Dig* a hole for the seeds, *drop* them in and cover them with loose soil, and then *water* the ground lightly.

Mood

Do not shift from the indicative to the subjunctive mood, or vice versa. Maintain consistency by sticking with one or the other, bearing in mind that in formal writing the subjunctive is preferred where it is called for. The indicative mood is used for statements of fact or other kinds of assertions or questions; the subjunctive mood is used for statements contrary to fact or those expressing possibility or potential.

Inconsistent   If I *were* a rock star and I *was* making a lot of money, I'd give a lot of free concerts.
Consistent   If I *were* a rock star and I *were* making a lot of money, I'd give a lot of free concerts.

Inconsistent   The Red Cross representative prefers that the donations *be* given by cheque and that the amounts *are* entered on their special form.
Consistent   The Red Cross representative prefers that the donations *be* given by cheque and that the amounts *be* entered on their special form.

S

Point of View

A point of view is a position from which an observation is made; it is also the place from which an idea springs. You should be consistent in making your observations from the same place (point of view) and should be sure the reader knows whose ideas belong to whom— that is, that the place the ideas come from is consistently named.

Inconsistent Observation

Lying face down on the pavement, I could see the collected debris of the day—cigarette butts, candy wrappers, odd bits of paper—*and then came the sound of the ambulance and I could see it approach.* (Obviously, the writer could not see the ambulance if he were lying face down on the pavement.)

Consistent Observation

Lying face down on the pavement, I could see the collected debris of the day—cigarette butts, candy wrappers, odd bits of paper—*and then came the sound of the ambulance and I knew it was getting closer.*

Inconsistent Assignment of Ideas

Most people understand that animals need space in which to live. Malin Himes, the anthropologist, says that the acquisition of such space is connected to the amount of power the animal has. How we fight for space—and thus gain the necessary power to get it—is determined by our cultural training. The current conflict between the Soviet Union and the United States over outer space exemplifies this idea. (The reader does not know to whom the ideas in the third and fourth sentences belong.)

Consistent Assignment of Ideas

Most people understand that animals need space in which to live. Malin Himes, the anthropologist, says that the acquisition of such space is connected to the amount of power the animal has. *Himes asserts that* how we fight for space—and thus gain the necessary power to get it—is determined by our cultural training. *Himes offers as an example of this notion* the current conflict between the Soviet Union and the United States over outer space.

S

TEST YOURSELF ON

Correcting Shifts

Correct all the unnecessary shifts you find in the sentences below. Some sentences are correct as they stand; next to these, write C.

1. _____ People need to be praised when we work hard and accomplish our goals.

2. _____ Ian argued with his counsellor about the curfew and asks him to make an exception.

3. _____ She goes up to the cashier's window and asked for three tickets.

4. _____ Anybody who cares about his or her health can have themselves examined by a doctor twice a year.

5. _____ My wife said she was thirsty and would I please get her a glass of water.

6. _____ According to Knight, Shakespeare is the greatest writer in English. Shakespeare takes in all points of view.

7. _____ We arrive in London on Tuesday, leave for Paris on Thursday, and then the rest of the week is spent in Rome.

8. _____ Johnny Carson is known to all because he sparkles on television every night.

9. _____ Every basketball player has their own way of driving to the hoop.

10. _____ He went to the movies, sees *King Kong*, is terribly frightened, and was afraid to go home.

11. _____ Finally, we added the icing, and then it was baked for fifty minutes.

S

12. _____ Jean-Paul said that he liked Laura and would she care to have dinner with him.

13. _____ From the top of the CN Tower the people looked like toy figures, strutting mechanically along, smoking their cigars.

14. _____ I was told that cigarette smoking would ruin my lungs and that you should give it up if you wanted to avoid heart trouble, too.

15. _____ Wagner recommended that admissions standards be raised and students warned about their poor preparation for college.

Specific/General

See **Diction**.

S

Spelling

Most readers think of misspelling as a sure sign of inadequate writing. The impression is nearly impossible to dispel, despite the fact that many fine writers have had trouble spelling. Whether one is a naturally good speller or not, accurate spelling is essential. Fortunately, there is hope for poor spellers. The way you spell is a habit and one that you can change.

The Spelling Problem

The spelling problem can be divided into two parts: (1) you and (2) the conventions of spelling.

You

The burden of improving your spelling rests squarely on you; a teacher cannot help much in your discarding the old habit and taking on the new. Only an increased consciousness that improvement is possible combined with a disciplined approach can help. To begin, take note of the following suggestions on how to proceed, and design your program based on them.

1 Be aware when you are in doubt about the spelling of a word. If you are *not* aware of your doubts, you cannot dispel them by consulting a good dictionary and will continue to make the same mistake.

2 When you have found the correct spelling of a word, don't try simply to memorize it. Eye-hand co-ordination needs to be practised. Try to visualize the word before you write it out. Then write it out correctly several times. After you've been able to write the word correctly three times, construct five sentences, using the word in each. This practice will reinforce your new spelling habit.

3 Make note of the words you misspell; make a list of them and keep the list handy. Notice if there are types of words that you persistently misspell, and work through the rule that applies to the group. (See Spelling Rules.)

4 Don't reserve certain words for writing and others for speaking. Try to use your whole vocabulary in both speaking and writing. This is useful because the correct pronunciation of words often helps you to visualize the correct spelling.

5 Proofread everything you write at least once for spelling errors alone.

6 Develop your own special methods to help you in the learning process. Some students use flash cards; others tack lists of troublesome words on the walls of their rooms. Be creative. There are many ways to approach the problem.

S

The Conventions of Spelling

We no doubt misspell a few words because we habitually mispronounce them.

math*e*matics	NOT math*m*atics
heigh*t*	NOT heigh*th* (by analogy with *eighth*)
disa*s*trous	NOT disas*ter*ous

The dictionary often helps by giving the correct pronunciation of such words. However, English pronunciation and spelling are notoriously eccentric. Therefore, you must use pronunciation cautiously. For instance, English offers dozens of words with analogous spellings, e.g., *through* and *bough* are not pronounced the same way. Such spellings must simply be learned.

Canadian Spelling

Canadians face a special spelling problem: our usage is influenced by the practice of both the Americans and British, and Canadian usage is not uniform. Should you write *colour* or *color*, for example, *centre* or *center*, *cheque* or *check*, *kerb* or *curb*? You would probably not hesitate to choose *curb* from the last example, demonstrating how American spellings are increasingly common among Canadian writers. On the other hand, the British *centre*, not the American *center*, predominates in Canada. If you are in doubt, the best Canadian source to consult is the *Gage Canadian Dictionary*, the authority recommended by the Department of the Secretary of State of Canada. Where Gage offers alternatives, that listed first predominates.

The **our/or** endings sometimes present an exception. An order-in-council dated June 12, 1890, records that "in all official documents, in the Canada Gazette, and in the Dominion Statutes, the English practice of *our* endings shall be followed." Writers of government documents continue to abide by this policy. On the other hand, daily newspapers from coast to coast had changed from *our* to *or* as early as 1887. Robert J. Ireland has shown that, in common usage, preference for one or the other depends on where you live. In Ontario, approximately 97% use the spelling *colour*; in New Brunswick, about 52%; in Alberta, about 27% (*Canadian Spelling: An Empirical and Historical Survey of Selected Words* [Diss., York University, 1979] 173). For further information on this subject, see *In Search of the Standard in Canadian English* (W.C. Lougheed, ed., Occasional Papers, No. 1 [Kingston: Queen's University, 1985]).

Your choice of spelling style will depend on what you are writing and whom you are writing it for. What is important to remember is that, whichever style of spelling you choose to use in a piece of writing, the style should be used **consistently** throughout the piece.

Spelling Rules

The first place to begin your disciplined study is with the following rules.

Rule 1: *ie* **and** *ei*
Memorize this famous jingle:

> *i* before *e*
> except after *c*
> or when sounded like *a*
> as in *neighbour* or *weigh*.

i *before* e	ei *after* c	ei *as in* neighbour *and* weigh
achieve	deceit	freight
cashier	receive	reign
believe	ceiling	sleigh
exceptions	*exceptions*	*exceptions*
either	financier	sleight
neither	species	height
seizure		eider
sheik		
leisure		
weird		

S

TEST YOURSELF ON

ie and ei

Complete the spelling of the following words by using either *ie* or *ei* in the blank spaces.

1. fr_____nd   3. bel_____f

2. conc_____ve   4. ach_____vement

5. exper_____nce

6. rec_____ving

7. th_____r

8. f_____ld

9. effic_____ncy

10. conven_____nce

11. aud_____nce

12. dec_____t

13. misch_____f

14. p_____ce

15. y_____ld

16. sl_____gh

17. w_____ght

18. forf_____t

19. v_____n

20. h_____nous

Rule 2: Final Silent -e

1 Final silent -e is usually dropped before adding a suffix that begins with a vowel.

argue—arguing   dare—daring
baste—basting   give—giving
charge—charging

2 Final silent -e is usually retained when adding a suffix that begins with a consonant.

arrange—arrangements   hate—hateful   like—likeness
love—lovely   sore—soreness   sure—surely

Note the following exceptions:

S

A Final silent -e is retained after soft c (as in *dance; colour* has the hard c) and soft g (as in *rage; glove* has the hard g) when adding suffixes beginning with a or o. Because c and g are generally hard before a, o, and u, we keep the silent -e in order to keep the consonant soft.

charge—charging—chargeable
stage—staging—stageable
slice—slicing—sliceable

B In some words, the final silent -e must be retained before the suffix -ing in order to prevent mispronunciation or ambiguity of meaning.

singe—singeing (to scorch; retains *e* to prevent confusion with *sing—singing*.)

dye—dyeing (to tint; retains *e* to prevent confusion with *die—dying*.)

C Final silent *-e* is retained when the letters *ye*, *oe*, or *ee* precede the suffix *-ing*.

free—freeing	shoe—shoeing
hoe—hoeing	tree—treeing
see—seeing	eye—eyeing

TEST YOURSELF ON

Final Silent -e

Complete the spelling of the following words by using an *e* to fill in the blank space in each. If no *e* is needed, leave the space blank.

1. mov_____ing

2. prov_____ing

3. mov_____ment

4. peac_____able

5. chang_____able

6. liv_____ly

7. manag_____ment

8. sens_____ible

9. realiz_____ation

10. ton_____al

11. receiv_____ing

12. bor_____ing

13. bor_____dom

14. car_____ing

15. car_____ful

16. dy_____ing (to tint)

17. rang_____ing

18. rag_____ing

19. troubl_____some

20. bar_____ness.

S

Rule 3: Final -*y*

Followed by a suffix other than one beginning with the letter *i*, final -*y* is usually changed to an *i*.

marry—marriage   beauty—beautiful   busy—business

When the suffix begins with an *i*, retain final *-y*.

cry—crying   enjoy—enjoying

Some exceptions
day—daily   lay—laid
pay—paid   say—said

TEST YOURSELF ON
Final -y

Complete the spelling of the following words by using either *y* or *i* or *ie* to fill in the blank spaces.

1. occup_____ing
2. lonel_____ness
3. anno_____ing
4. pl_____s
5. turke_____s
6. fr_____s
7. plo_____s
8. repl_____ing
9. cr_____s
10. pra_____s

11. theor_____s
12. stor_____s
13. bur_____ing
14. histor_____s
15. histor_____'s (belonging to history)
16. accompan_____ing
17. opportunit_____s
18. happ_____ness
19. modif_____ing
20. def_____ance

S

Rule 4: Final Consonants and Doubling
When adding a suffix that begins with a vowel, double a final single consonant under either of the following conditions:

a. when it ends a monosyllabic word, as in *bat* or *run*.
b. when it appears after a single vowel at the end of a word that is stressed on the last syllable, as in *preFER*.

beg—begging	alLOT—alLOTTing
beGIN—beGINNing	forGET—forGETTing
comPEL—comPELLed	ship—shipping

Without these conditions, the consonant is *seldom* doubled.

BENefit—BENefited	GALlop—GALloping

Notes on Word Endings

The following notes about noun and verb endings and other suffixes will supplement the above rules.

Note 1: Noun Plurals and Third Person Singular, Present Tense Verbs

A When a noun ends in a sound that allows a pronounceable final -*s, add* -*s* to form its plural. For verbs having this capacity, add -*s* to form the third person singular, present tense.

Nouns	*Verbs*
stone—stones	trust—trusts
pill—pills	know—knows
drawer—drawers	hope—hopes

Some Exceptions	
tomato—tomatoes	veto—vetoes
buffalo—buffaloes	echo—echoes

B When a noun ends in a sound that does not allow a pronounceable final -*s*, add -*es* to form its plural. For verbs without this capacity, add -*es* to form the third person singular, present tense.

Nouns	*Verbs*
lunch—lunches	pass--passes
tax—taxes	wish—wishes

C To form the plural of a noun ending in *y* preceded by a consonant, change the *y* to *i* and add *-es*. For a verb with the same ending, do the same to the third person singular, present tense.

Nouns	***Verbs***
company—companies	carry—carries
party—parties	fly—flies

D When a noun ending in *y* is preceded by *a*, *e*, *o*, or *u*, form the plural by adding *-s*. For a verb with the same ending, do the same to form the third person singular, present tense.

Nouns	***Verbs***
day—days	buy—buys
boy—boys	pay—pays
toy—toys	enjoy—enjoys
key—keys	

E Certain nouns borrowed from other languages frequently form their plurals by retaining the plural form of the original language.

alumna—alumnae	datum—data
alumnus—alumni	phenomenon—phenomena
basis—bases	

However, good writers have tended to anglicize some of these, and dictionaries frequently list two plural forms. See what your dictionary says is the acceptable plural form of each of these:

beau   focus   index   radius   stadium

S

Note 2: Suffixes to Preserve Hard *c*

To preserve the hard sound of *c*, words ending in that letter add a *k* before a suffix ending in *e*, *i*, or *y*.

panic—panicked—panicking
mimic—mimicked—mimicking
traffic—trafficked—trafficking

Note 3: Four Special Words and the *eed* Sound

A *Supersede* is the only word in English that ends in *-sede*.

B *Exceed*, *proceed*, and *succeed* are the only words in English ending in *-ceed*.

C Thus all other words in English ending in the *-eed* sound are spelled *-cede*.

accede	precede
concede	recede
intercede	secede

TEST YOURSELF ON

Spelling Rules 1–4

Complete the spelling of the words with blanks in the exercise below by filling in the blank spaces according to one or another of the rules or notes explained in this section. Some blanks do not need filling in.

1. She is occasional_____y absent.

2. The Sh_____k of Araby

3. A sens_____ible commit_____ment

4. Pro_____to jail; do not pass go; do not collect two hundred dollars.

5. He perc_____ved a sunset.

6. Cake top_____ing

7. I like the ic_____ing.

8. The c_____ling is cracking.

9. The grain is ship_____ed to China.

10. The water is boil_____ing.

11. A terrible argu_____ment

12. She stud_____ed hard.

13. He went swim_____ing.

S

14. He was stop_____ing me from drop_____ing my

    p_____ce of cake.

15. The lovel_____ness of the flowers

16. It is occur_____ing often.

17. A bus_____ness appoint_____ment

18. Standing around ey_____ing girls

19. Legislative assembl_____s are provincial.

20. My brother is dy_____ing

Word Lists

One or both of the following lists of words may be useful to you in working on your spelling problem.

1 Words that Sound Alike but Mean Different Things (Homonyms)

The following pairs of words sound alike or look somewhat alike, but are spelled differently. Of course, their meanings are different, too. To master this list, you should write out sentences, using each word correctly in a number of different ways.

S

After each word is an abbreviation indicating the part of speech to which it belongs (*n.* for *noun*; *v.* for *verb*; *adj.* for *adjective*; *adv.* for *adverb*; *prep.* for *preposition*; *conj.* for *conjunction*; *pro.* for *pronoun*; *poss.* for *possessive*; *contr.* for *contraction*). This is followed by a definition.

accept *v.* to receive
except *prep.* not included
except *v.* to leave out

advice *n.* counsel; information offered
advise *v.* to give advice or counsel

affect   *v.* to have an effect on; to influence
effect   *n.* the result of some action
effect   *v.* to accomplish or execute

all ready   *pro.* + *adj.* all are prepared
already   *adv.* at or before this time

all together   *pro.* + *adj.* all in the same place
altogether   *adv.* entirely

allusion   *n.* a reference
illusion   *n.* a false impression

altar   *n.* a special place for religious ceremony
alter   *v.* to change

always   *adv.* constantly; at all times
all ways   *adj.* + *n.* in every manner

ascend   *v.* to rise or go up
ascent   *n.* a movement upward
assent   *n.* an agreement
assent   *v.* to agree

assistance   *n.* help given
assistants   *n. pl.* helpers

beside   *prep.* by the side of
besides   *prep. and adv.* in addition to

boarder   *n.* a person paying for subsistence in someone's house
border   *n.* a boundary

born   *v. (always passive)* given birth to
borne   *v.* carried; given birth to

breath   *n.* air inhaled or exhaled
breathe   *v.* to inhale and exhale

S

canvas   *n.* a heavy, coarse cloth
canvass   *v.* to search for, examine, or solicit

capital   *n.* a city that is a seat of government; an upper case letter;
   money
capital   *adj.* principal; first-rate; upper case
capitol   *n.* a building used by a U.S. state legislature

choose   *v.* to select
chose   *v. (past tense of choose)* selected

cite   *v.* to quote; to charge with an offence
site   *n.* a place or location
sight   *n.* the faculty of seeing

coarse   *adj.* rough; not refined
course   *n.* school subject; a way or a path

complement   *n.* something that completes
compliment   *n.* praise
compliment   *v.* pay compliment to, praise

conscience   *n.* part of the mind that rules on moral questions
conscious   *adj.* awake or alert

council   *n.* a deliberative body
counsel   *n.* advice given; a lawyer
counsel   *v.* to give advice

dependant   *n.* a person who depends on someone else
dependent   *adj.* relying on another for support

descent   *n.* a downward movement
dissent   *n.* disagreement
dissent   *v.* to disagree

desert   *n.* a dry, barren area of land
desert   *v.* to abandon
dessert   *n.* final course of a meal

device   *n.* something contrived
devise   *v.* to prepare, originate, or make a contrivance

do   *v.* to perform
due   *adj.* owing; with *to* specifies the cause of something
dual   *adj.* twofold
duel   *n.* a formal fight between two people

eminent   *adj.* famous
imminent   *adj.* about to happen

envelop   *v.* to enclose
envelope   *n.* a paper container used for mailing

extant   *adj.* still existing
extent   *n.* the degree of something

farther   *adv. and adj.* usually refers to distance
further   *adv. and adj.* usually refers to time, quantity or degree

S

foreword *n.* short preface to a book
forward *adv., adj., v., and n.* toward the front, to help along, one at the front

formally *adv.* in a formal manner
formerly *adv.* at an earlier time

forth *adv.* forward; onward; out
fourth *adj. or adv.* the one following the third

human *adj.* pertaining to people
humane *adj.* compassionate or kindly

idle *adj.* not occupied or employed
idle *v.* to spend time in idleness
idol *n.* a likeness of something, usually a god, for worship

ingenious *adj.* resourceful, clever
ingenuous *adj.* showing innocent or childlike simplicity

its *poss. pro.* belonging to it
it's *contr.* it is

know *v.* to understand, recognize, have experience of
no *adv.* expressing the negative
now *adv.* at the present time

lead *n.* (pronounced *led*) the metal
lead *v.* (pronounced *leed*) to show the way; to conduct
led *v.* (past tense of *lead*) showed the way; conducted

loose *adj.* not tight
lose *v.* to misplace; to be defeated

maybe *adv.* perhaps
may be *v.* possibly may exist or happen

moral *adj.* relating to right or wrong
morale *n.* the mental or emotional condition of a person or group

passed *v.* past tense and past participle of *pass*
past *n.* an earlier time
past *prep.* at the farther side of

peace *n.* not war
piece *n.* a part of

personal *adj.* relating privately
personnel *n. pl.* a group of persons employed

S

principal   *n.* chief; head of a school; capital owned
principal   *adj.* most important
principle   *n.* rule or doctrine

prophecy   *n.* a prediction
prophesy   *v.* to predict

quiet   *adj.* not noisy
quit   *v.* to depart from; resign
quite   *adv.* rather; almost completely

respectfully   *adj.* showing deference
respectively   *adv.* each in the order given

right   *adj.* correct or suitable
rite   *n.* a ceremony or ritual

stationary   *adj.* fixed or immobile
stationery   *n.* paper for writing or typing

than   *conj.* a comparative term
then   *n. or adv.* indicates time

their   *poss. pro.* belonging to them
there   *adv.* a place; also used as expletive at beginning of sentences
they're   *contr.* they are

to   *prep.* indicates direction
too   *adv.* excessively; overmuch
two   *n.* the number

weather   *n.* climate
whether   *conj.* expresses alternatives

were   *v.* past tense plural of *to be*; also subjunctive form
we're   *contr.* we are
where   *adv. or pro.* indicates place or position

who's   *contr.* who is or who has?
whose   *poss. pro.* belonging to whom?

your   *poss. pro.* belonging to you
you're   *contr.* you are

2 Words that Are Troublesome to Spell

The following list consists of words that are habitually troublesome to spell. The part or parts of each that are the sources of the trouble are printed in boldface or noted in parentheses, or both. The best way to use this list is to write sentences using each of the words; write as many as five sentences for each word, and in that way embed in your hand, eye, and brain the correct spelling of each word. Proceed gradually. If you do a mere five words a day, you will master the whole list by the end of the semester.

a lot of (three words)
absence
academy
acceptable
acceptance
accessible
accidental
accidentally
acclaim
accommodate
accompaniment
accompanying
accomplish
accumulate
accuracy
accurate (one *r*)
accustom
achievement
acquaintance
acquire
actuality
actually
admittance
adolescence
adolescent
advertising (no *e* after *s*)
advice/advise
affect/effect
alleviate
allotted
allotment (one *t*)
all right (two words)
all together (two words)

already (one *l*)
altar/alter
altogether (one word; one *l*)
amateur
analysis
analzye
annually
apologetically
apology
apparent
applies
appreciate
appreciation
appropriate
arctic
argument (no *e* after *u*)
arguing (no *e*)
arise
arising
arouse
arrangement
article
athlete (no *e* after *h*)
attack (no *t* after *k*)
attempts
attendant
attended
audience
authority
autumn

bargain
basically

S

beauteous
beauty
becoming (no *e*)
before
beginner
belief
believe
beneficial
benefited (one *t*)
boundary
breath (no final *e*)
breathe
brilliance
burial
business
busing, bussing
busy

calendar
capitalism
career
careful (one *l*)
carried
carrying
category
cemetery
changeable
chief
children
Christian
choice
choose (double *o*)
chose
cigarette
clothes
coming (no *e* after *m*)
commercial
committee
communist

comparative
compatible
concede
conceivable
condemn
connotation
conscience
conscientious
conscious
consequently
continuously
controlled
controversy
convenience
correlate
criticism
criticize
cruelly
cruelty
curiosity
curious
curriculum

dealt
deceive
definitely
dependent
description
desirability (no *e* after *r*)
despair
detriment
devastating
device/devise
different
dilemma
disastrous (no *e* after *t*)
disciple
discipline
discrimination

S

disillusioned
dissatisfied
dominant

effect/affect
efficiency
eighth
eliminate
embarrass
emphasize
endeavour
environment
equipment (no *e* after *p*)
escapade
escape (no **x**)
especially
exaggerate
except
exercise
explanation
extremely

fallacy
familiar
families
fantasies
fantasy
fascinate
fictitious
foreigners
forty (no *u* after *o*)
fourth
friendliness
fulfil
further

gaiety
government
governor

group
guaranteed

harass
height (no *h* after *t*)
heroes
heroine/heroin
hindrance (no *e* after *d*)
hospitalization
huge
humour
humorist
humorous
hypocrisy
hypocrite

ignorant
imagine
immediately
immense
importance
incidentally
independence
indispensable
individually
industrious
initiative
intellect
intelligence
interrupt
irrelevant
irresistible
irritable
its/it's

jealousy
judgement

know/no/now

S

laboratory
labourer
laboriously
laid
leisurely
library
licence (n)
license (v)
lieutenant
lightning (no *e*)
likelihood
literature
liveliest
livelihood
liveliness
loneliness
lonely
loose/lose
losing (no *e*)
loss
luxury

magazine
maintenance
manoeuvre
marriage
material
maybe/may be
meant
medieval
melancholy
millennium
miniature
minuscule (not *i*)
mischief
mischievous (no *i* after *v*)
moral/morale
morally
mysterious

narrative
necessary
ninety
noticeable
noticing (no *e*)
numerous

occasion
occurred
off/of
omit
opportunity
opponent
opposite
optimism

paid
pamphlets
parallel
parliament
paralyzed
passed/past
perceive
persistently
personal/personnel
phase/faze
phenomenon
piece
plausible
pleasant
politician
possession
precede
preferred
prejudice (no *d* before or after *j*)
presence
prestige
prevalent
procedure

S

pro**ceed**
profession (one *f*)
professor (one *f*)
pro**noun**ce
pronu**n**ciation (no *o* after *n*)
prophec**y**/prophes**y**
psychoanalysis
psychology
psychosomatic

qui**et**/qu**it**e

rec**ei**ve
re**cog**nize
re**comm**end
refe**rr**ing
rel**ie**ve
remem**br**ance
remini**sc**e
res**our**ces
rhythm
ridicule
roo**mm**ate

s**c**ene
s**ch**edule
s**ei**ze
sentence
separate
serg**ea**nt
shep**h**erd
signifi**cance**
sopho**m**ore
sta**bi**lization
stren**gth**
stud**y**ing
substantial
sub**t**le
subtl**y** (no *e*)

suc**ceed**
succe**ss**ion
suffi**cient**
su**mm**ary
su**pp**ress
su**r**prise
sus**c**eptible
suspense
symb**ol**
synon**y**m

te**ch**nique
tend**ency**
than/then
th**eir**/th**ere**/th**ey're**
themsel**ves**
therefore
th**orough**/th**rough**
though**t**
to/**too**/**two**
transfe**rr**ed
tremend**ous**
tried
trie**s**
tyran**ny**

undoub**t**edly
u**nn**ecessary
unus**ually**
us**e**ful
us**e**less
us**ing**

va**cuu**m
val**uab**le
var**ies**
various
veng**ea**nce

S

warrant   write
weather/whether   writing
weird
where/were   yield
whose/who's   your/you're
woman/women

TEST YOURSELF ON

Catching Spelling Errors by Proofreading

Proofread carefully each of the following paragraphs. There are five spelling errors in the first and seven in the second. See if you can find and correct them all.

1. In order to achieve one's academic goals, one must lead a disciplined life as a student. The arrangment of one's time is of first importance. The student should set aside regular hours for studing: so many hours per week for reading, so many for writing papers, so many for gainful employment, and so on. It helps if the same hours are set aside for each activitie, for the mind is best trained by regularity. Nor should liesure time be neglected; a balanced life is best for any kind of achievement. Discipline also requires that the student appear promptly for confferences with instructors and that he or she, in fact, be mature enough to ask that instructors meet with him or her. Reaching one's academic goals thus requires discipline *and* maturity.

2. Most of us, when we see on the calender that Christmas is approaching, are paniced if we haven't completed our shoping. To avoid that sinking feelling in the pit of your stomach, take a few tips from me. (1) Inteligent gift givers will feel that old urge at the first sign of a nip in the air; begining with the first fall frost, start buying. (2) Paralell with an early start should go a slow start: buy one gift at a time, leaving that long list at home and crossing off names as you go. If you will heed these two simple rules, you will save money—prices are usually lower *before* the season starts—and the anxiety of the Christmas rush. Instead, you'll have given yourself the gift of peace.

S

Study and Examination Skills

To acquire and retain study skills, you should be aware that studying requires the virtues of organization, clarity, concreteness, logic, and concentration.

Preparation

The physical items and mental attitudes necessary to get ready to study are the following:

1 The proper materials: all the texts and notes you need, together with paper, highlighting magic markers, and the like.

2 An appropriate place for studying: a quiet room, a section of the library—any place where you can concentrate.

3 Concentration. If you have trouble concentrating for a reasonable period of time, you need to rid your mind of distractions that prevent concentration and to learn how to increase your concentration. Try this method of increasing concentration: sit down on a Monday at two o'clock (or some other convenient hour) and concentrate by reading for as long as you can before you feel you must give up. Note how long you lasted—perhaps five minutes. On Tuesday, extend the time to seven minutes; on Wednesday, to nine minutes. Continue the pattern until you are able to go on for half an hour (or some other length of time that seems productive). You need not be afraid of taking little breaks, though; they help your overall concentration by releasing tension.

4 Proper goals. During a study session, you should aim to master a manageable concept—the concept of I.Q., for example, rather than half of your psychology text—and should not dwell on long-term goals, such as getting an A in the course.

5 A schedule. Divide your week, all 168 hours, into periods when you sleep, eat, rest, work—and have fun (drudgery is not the answer). A schedule helps by enabling you to absorb your experience in manageable segments and allowing you the time you need for each of your activities.

S

6 An understanding that the mind can only process limited bits of information at any one time.

7 An understanding that you must associate what you learn in one course with whatever else you learn, either in another course or outside your classes. This broader perspective will help you to retain what you learn.

8 The determination to engage in periodic review or reinforcement of what you've been learning. Protect your investment in study time. Don't let your hard-won knowledge slip away.

9 A determination to avoid cramming. Cramming is an inefficient way to get the job done. At best—when it works—it affords you a short-term grasp of information, which lasts just long enough for one exam.

Reading

Everything we learn, we learn by analogy. *Something* is there to assist us: a model, a fragment of similar information, an idea. When you read a text, it is important to do so in an organized way so that you can begin with a model, however fragmentary. You should not begin by plunging into a text with a close reading.

First, *skim* the chapter or section. Examine the boldface or italicized subheads. Get into your mind the general area of study; prepare yourself with a model or analogy onto which you can hook those numerous concrete details. The goal in skimming is to gain a *general* idea of the author's organization and major ideas. You might, in skimming, go through a process like the following:

S

1 What does the chapter title mean? Can you relate the subject to anything else you know?

2 Read the first few paragraphs and then the last few: frequently, these summarize the major ideas. What are they, roughly? Say them aloud to yourself, in your own words.

3 Skim the chapter from heading to heading, subhead to subhead. Can you feel what the author's getting at? how he or she is proceeding?

4 Look a little more carefully at any maps, diagrams, charts, graphs, tables, pictures, or schematics. Do these add anything to your first grasp?

5 Pause and think over what you've learned so far. See if you can tell yourself in your own words what the major idea or ideas are.

As soon after your skimming as possible, read carefully through the chapter or section with a view toward grasping the ideas or groups of related ideas and understanding the concrete details out of which these ideas arose. Follow a procedure something like the following:

1 As you read, try to distinguish the main ideas from the supporting evidence or ideas. To help you, stop after a paragraph or a group of related paragraphs to be sure you've understood them and have been alerted to any special terms the author uses or highlights in a special typeface or colour. Remember that every discipline proceeds by *naming* its concepts. If you want to master psychoanalysis, for example, you must master terms like *unconscious*, *transference*, and *Oedipus complex*. The special language of a subject *is*, in a sense, the subject.

2 Examine the structure of the chapter as if it were a graphic guide to the author's ideas. Notice what happens as the author goes through explanatory steps, pauses for diagrams, or shifts his or her focus through extended analogies. Every once in a while, skip to the summary at the end or the introductory paragraphs at the beginning: how are you doing in understanding the ideas related there? If you are lost, go back and read a bit more carefully the section or sections you don't quite grasp.

S

3 After reading a section or sections, start annotating in the margins and highlighting with magic marker. Take the section or sections under your review and see if you can repeat the main and supporting ideas in your own words. Relate what you've learned to anything else you know. Integrate.

When you have done this, after a short period of time has intervened, do a quick review for reinforcement's sake. Check your underlinings and annotations, the special terms, the graphic material. Whatever seems foreign or unfamiliar needs rereading. Make a rough reading outline, a set of notes in outline form. Practice from head to hand is another form of reinforcement.

Taking Notes and Using Them

Going into a lecture or class discussion *cold*—without having done the assigned reading for that class—is an inefficient mistake. It robs you of that model already mentioned and thus hampers you in grasping the material to be had from the class hour.

The aim in taking class notes is (1) to reinforce what you have learned in your own reading and (2) to integrate your instructor's view of the material with your own. You *can* listen (and/or make a classroom contribution yourself) and take notes at the same time—*if* you're prepared. If not, you'll waste time writing down every word spoken, when in fact what you want is to take down main and subordinate ideas in such a way that they appear so in your notes. Thus you should block out the main ideas in larger script, the subordinate ones in smaller. Underline special terms. Above all, do not try to write down everything. First, it can't be done; second, it's unnecessary. If you do miss something, leave a space in your notebook that you can fill in later. Later, you can consult a fellow student to fill in the gaps or even ask the instructor. If you've read the material of the lecture or class, you should have even less trouble filling in. Within hours of taking notes, *go* over them for a quick skimming review, taking time to highlight important points with a special marker.

The acquisition of a "great" set of notes is useless unless they are profitably employed. Notes should be periodically reviewed; short study sessions should be set aside solely for this purpose. There are few better ways to reinforce what you know *and*, not incidentally, slowly and carefully to prepare yourself for examinations. If you don't want your notes to seem as foreign to you as a brand-new subject would be, keep up a process of periodic review and revision.

S

TEST YOURSELF ON

Improving Study Skills

Get together with two other students in one of your classes. Let the three of you read a chapter of the text, each in your own study session. Then get together again. Taking turns, each of you can present your version of the chapter's main and supporting ideas along with a definition of key terms. See which of you came nearest the mark in mastering the chapter's materials. Do the others have a way of reading that can help you? After discussing the chapter's contents, discuss study methods.

Taking Examinations

Taking an essay examination involves some of the same skills we have been seeking to acquire in pursuit of effective writing. That is, your instructor will expect you to use standard English, organize your ideas properly, and support them with effective examples or details. Although it is obvious that you cannot be as careful when you are under the pressure of time in an in-class examination as you can be when you've taken an assignment home, you can nevertheless follow the same procedures as when writing any other essay—with a few modifications.

Before the Examination
You will need to do three things before the examination:

1 Organize your notes and other materials. Reread everything. Recite out loud to yourself main ideas and supporting details. Pick out a couple of supporting details that strike you as particularly effective.

2 Review the material in a coherent way. Look at your materials in the way the instructor presented them. Then look at them in different contexts: cause and effect, advantage and disadvantage, analysis, synthesis, and so forth.

3 Test yourself. Make up test questions in several different subject areas. Actually write out the answers and check them against your notes and your text. Ask yourself to analyze, define terms, compare, and contrast. For mathematics and physical science courses, do a series of tough calculations. Students of history, economics, and the social sciences will obviously have to know causes and effects. The kind of course will suggest the kind of testing.

During the Examination
Regardless of how much time is allotted for the examination, you should proceed in an orderly manner, as if you were at home preparing an assignment: plan, write, rewrite, proofread.

1 First, read the examination question or questions carefully. If you are asked to write more than one essay, be sure to leave the most time for the question worth the most in examination points. Be sure you understand what the question asks you to do: summarize? analyze? synthesize? compare?
Note: Be prepared to answer the question precisely. It is of little use to blurt out everything you know. Instructors who ask you to write essays on examinations want you to produce something precise.

2 Next, begin to plan. Jot down on scratch paper or the back of the exam answer booklet the general outline of the subject area covered by the essay question. Bend the material to fit the essay question. Try to pluck out one of those contexts you worked with as you prepared for the exam. Jot down several good supporting ideas or other kinds of detail. Work up a thesis statement—it will help you to write cleanly and directly on the question and it will please the instructor who reads it. He or she will be impressed by your control.

3 Leave enough time to look over your essay. Read carefully to insert missing words, to make your writing more legible, to correct misspellings or grammatical mistakes, to insert a more precise or more appropriate example where you can.

TEST YOURSELF ON

S   *Taking Examinations*

A Evaluate an examination you have previously taken. Note in the margins where you went wrong. Notice your strengths and weaknesses as an examination writer. Now go back to your notes and give new answers to questions that were poorly dealt with until you feel certain that your new examination would receive a better grade than the old one.

B If your university or college has a learning skills centre, consult with the tutors or counsellors. Enrol in study skills courses.

Subjects for Essays: Choosing and Limiting a Topic

Choosing a Topic

Selecting a subject or topic is likely to become a problem for you only when a teacher asks you to invent one of your own; if you are assigned a subject or a choice of topics, the problem does not arise. In either case, your best course of action is to choose a subject that interests you, one that stimulates your imagination and that you either know something about or want to learn more about.

The place to begin is your personal experience: the things that have happened to you, the things you have done, the beliefs you hold, the skills and special interests you have nurtured.

Student writers who think they have nothing to say are mistaken. *Everyone has something to say.* In fact, we could define being human as the state of having something to say. One trouble is that we are not always aware of what we have to say until we look for it. That is one good reason why you should begin with your own experience; it will lead you to the great respository of information to write about, information you can add to what you already possess. Questions are the pathway into this storehouse.

What do I like and dislike? Who among the people I have known would be of interest to others? Whom do I admire? What interesting places have I seen? What books and articles have I read that provoked my curiosity? What films and television shows have impressed me, either pro or con? What issues concern me in my community, town, or country? Are there social conditions that need to be improved? Are there wrongs I think should be made right?

Questions like these will generate subject matter for essays. You may find yourself thinking about topics as diverse as racial discrimination in your community, legislation concerning pornography, or the predominance of melodrama on prime-time television. You'll notice that such questions may be linked to what you are studying in courses in literature, communication, physical education, the social sciences, law, history, and others. An academic research paper can be inspired by a subject of personal concern, and if you research the concrete details that give life to the subject, the essay will be thought-provoking—perhaps even inspired.

Sometimes these questions, this examination of the range of your personal experience, will lead you directly to a usable specific subject. But often the result will be a wide generalization. For example, the answer to one of the questions above ("What do I like?") might be "television comedy." Television comedy is simply too broad a subject on which to base a 500- to 900-word essay. In any case, you would have to give specific examples of television comedy in your essay in order for it to be an effective piece of writing. Your task, then, when your experience suggests a widely general topic, is to narrow it down to a manageable specific one. Instead of "television comedy," you would have to come up with an essay topic like "The Humour of 'SCTV.' "

TEST YOURSELF ON
Generating Subject Matter

A Examine your taste in television fare. Are there specific types of shows you like and watch consistently? Make a list of them. Now see if they are related. Make a list of five essay titles—possible writing assignments—suggested by the list. Examples might be such titles as "The Basic Plot of the Situation Comedy," "Is There a Bias in CBC News Analyses?" and "The Appeal in Watching Game Shows."

S

B Make a list of places or buildings you've seen and been impressed by recently—or even during the past few years. Ask yourself what features of these natural or man-made environments appeal to you most or interest you most. Now make a list of five essay titles, possible writing assignments, suggested by those places. Examples might be such titles as "A Barn with a Gambrel Roof" or "A Campsite in Banff National Park."

Limiting a Topic

Subjects should "fit" the size of the paper or essay for which they are intended. If you were assigned to write a large book, you might very well choose "The Life of Wilfrid Laurier" as your subject. Since you are unlikely to be given such an assignment, better forego that subject. In fact, for the size of the assignment you are likely to be given—say a paper 300 to 500 words—better forego all subjects on that massive scale. You can't possibly do a creditable job in 500 words of writing on topics such as "The Causes of the War of 1812" or "The Drug Culture in North America." Short papers on subjects such as these can only wind up being filled with windy judgements and vague generalities.

To limit yourself, it is necessary continually to pare down a topic until it is manageable. It is not enough to go from "The Drug Culture in North America" to "Marijuana Use in St. John's"—you must go further, for "Marijuana Use in St. John's" is quite as unmanageable in 500 words as is "The Drug Culture in North America." Another problem with large topics like these is that they probably go beyond your own experience and would require considerable research before you could plausibly do a good job on them.

The process of limiting a topic involves successive narrowings from a general topic to a usable subject for a short paper.

Suppose you have chosen the general topic of "Sports Cars." Since you probably have no knowledge of the history of sports cars—and therefore wouldn't be able to talk about Bugattis and Reos—your first narrowing would take you to "Contemporary European Sports Cars." This may strike you as exactly right until you realize that it would be folly to try to talk about the dizzying number of makes and models available from European manufacturers nowadays.

Then you get a brainstorm: you decide to talk about your own sports car. This is a shrewd decision, but you realize further that "My Sports Car" is a subject that would certainly require more than the assigned 500 words, because of the complexity of the piece of machinery you own. Try talking about a 1968 Triumph—about its basic specifications, size, equipment, road-handling characteristics, and so forth, all in 500 words. Not possible. At this point, you see that *one* of the aspects of your own car would really do nicely, and you finally (and correctly) decide on "Acceleration and Deceleration in My Triumph."

This subject is not only the right size, it is also well within the bounds of your experience—so far within, that you are a great authority on the subject, probably the *only* authority.

You may find that your method of narrowing down a general

topic requires less deliberation than the process above. Perhaps you will be able to proceed more quickly. Whatever the case, limiting a topic requires a disciplined effort to proceed toward the specific and manageable from the wide generalization.

TEST YOURSELF ON
Limiting a Topic

A Below are listed five general topics and the manageable subjects derived from each. Provide the intermediate steps between them. Use the previous analysis as a model in arriving at each stage.

1. *Clothing fashions:* The Role of Designer Jeans on Campus

2. *Education:* My Troubles at the Beginning of Biology [or some other subject] 101

3. *Television:* What David Suzuki Likes Most

4. *Student self-government:* The Duties of the Student President at My School

B Write specific, manageable titles for five of the topics listed below.

1. Basketball   6. Political parties

2. Vacations   7. The United Nations

3. Water pollution   8. Pierre Berton

4. Free Trade   9. Racial prejudice in Canada

5. Television commercials   10. Farm-price subsidies

Subject-Verb Agreement

In English, the problem of subject-verb agreement arises mainly in the present tense. To understand what it means, consider the verb *to play* and the forms of *play* in the present tense:

Subject	Verb	Subject	Verb
I	play	we	play
you	play	you	play
he, she, it	plays	they	play

The subjects in the left-hand column are all *singular*; the subjects in the right-hand column are all *plural*. All the verb forms are the same—except the third one in the left-hand column. It is a feature of the English language that whenever the subject is *he*, *she*, or *it*, in the present tense, indicative mood, the verb form that goes with it must end in -*s*.

He *considers* me his friend.

She *tells* me when to pick her up.

It *seems* like a nice day.

Most of us have no trouble when the subject is *he*, *she*, or *it*. The trouble starts when the subject gets more complicated.

My Aunt Vicky *plays* volleyball on Friday nights.

My Uncle Joe and my cousin Louis *think* she's a good player.

In these cases, once you have decided whether the subject is singular or plural, you can make the right choice. In the first sentence, you can think of Aunt Vicky as *she*; in the second, there is what we call a compound (and therefore plural) subject. Therefore, the first sentence requires a verb with an -*s* at the end, and the second does not. In the first sentence, there is a singular subject and a singular verb in the third person. In the second sentence, there is a plural (compound) subject and a plural verb form.

For some, the subject-verb agreement problem arises from a common confusion: that is, they know that *plural* nouns end in -*s*, so they make the analogy that words ending in -*s*, even verbs that end in -*s*, are all plural. But of course this is not the case. The number of the verb ending in -*s* is always singular. When the subject agrees with the verb in *number* (singular subject/singular verb; plural subject/plural verb), there is no subject-verb agreement problem.

S

TEST YOURSELF ON

Subject-Verb Agreement

A Change each of the sentences below by following the procedure of the example.

Example: Joanna's best *feature is* her eyes.
　　　　　Her *eyes are* Joanna's best feature.

1. His main interest is cars.

2. Rock and roll records are my only hobby.

3. Our greatest need is dollars.

4. Many days of non-stop studying were the cause of his breakdown.

5. Too many drinks on an empty stomach were the cause of his drunkenness.

B Change each of the sentences below by following the procedure of the example.

Example: They let me know when they want to take a break.
    She lets me know when she wants to take a break.

1. They amuse themselves when they have no toys to play with.

    He _____

2. This turns me off.

    These _____

3. It seems to like being fed by the children.

    They _____

4. That forces the argument in another direction.

    Those _____

5. They happen a lot more often than you think.

    It _____

6. She frightens me when she talks like that.

    They _____

7. She seems to profit from the time she spends in the biology lab.

    They _____

S

The Subject: Singular or Plural

You can begin to clear up the problem of subject-verb agreement by gaining an understanding of what number (singular or plural) to assign to certain subjects.

Compound Subjects

A compound subject consists of more than one noun or pronoun connected by *and* and therefore requires a plural verb.

> *Rocco*, *Vito*, and *Danny* are brothers.

> My *sister* Lucia and *I* are starting a rock band.

The use of *neither . . . nor*, *either . . . or*, or simply *or* with a compound subject produces a singular subject when both individual subjects are singular.

> Neither my father nor my mother *is* a New Democrat.

> Either biology or astronomy *is* required.

> Either Brian or John *has been* elected.

When one of the subjects is plural, use the verb that agrees with the closest one.

> Neither my uncle nor my *aunts play* pool.

> Either eggs or *cereal is* all right for breakfast.

When a compound subject consists of two items that are considered one unit, the subject can be thought of as singular.

> *Bacon and eggs is* my favorite dish.

> *I.P. Stone and Associates was* a successful company.

S

TEST YOURSELF ON

Subject-Verb Agreement with Compound Subjects and either/or, neither/nor *Subjects*

In some of the sentences below, the subject and verb agree. Next to these, write C. For the others, underline the complete subject and the verb and decide whether these are singular or plural. Correct the lack of agreement between subject and verb by changing one or the other.

1. _____ Either your father or your mother are responsible for the financial aid repayment.

2. _____ Rosie and Dom open their new bookstore next month.

3. _____ The professional and the rich man decides their own fates in the labour market.

4. _____ Coffee and croissants is fine for breakfast.

5. _____ Was the sofa and chair on sale?

6. _____ Either lung cancer or heart disease is the chief killer in Canada.

7. _____ Low-cost housing and welfare is the items needing reform in Canadian cities.

8. _____ Neither Margaret nor Maureen think their kid brother is a failure.

9. _____ Air, water, the earth, and people are all being polluted.

10. _____ Neither Gary nor the Joneses plays bridge.

Collective Nouns as Subjects
Such collective nouns as *army*, *audience*, *class*, *faculty*, *committee*, *team*, and *public* indicate a number of people, but they usually take singular verbs because they are thought of as units.

> The *team is* in first place. (the team as one whole; not the separate players)

> The *audience leaps* to *its* feet.

Collective nouns like *cattle*, *clergy*, *folks* (in the colloquial sense), *peasantry*, *gentry*, and *vermin* usually take plural verbs.

The clergy *are* not used to being treated with disrespect. (Clearly, it is a number of *individuals* who are unaccustomed to such treatment.)

Other collective nouns such as *plurality*, *minority*, *mass*, and *majority* may take either singular or plural verbs, depending on how you use them.

A minority of students *are* Greek majors. (The minority consists of separate Greek majors—a plural number.)

A minority of students *is* a force to be reckoned with. (The minority is a political unit—a singular number.)

TEST YOURSELF ON

Subject-Verb Agreement with Collective Nouns as Subjects

In each of the following sentences, determine whether the collective noun subject refers to a single unit or a plural number of individuals. Then cross out the incorrect verb in parentheses.

1. In this course, the class (decide, decides) whether to have a final exam.

2. The jury (render, renders) a verdict of *not guilty*.

3. The majority of my stamp collection (is, are) valuable.

4. The majority of my stamps (is, are) valuable.

5. Parliament (vote, votes) into law hundreds of bills each year.

6. A majority of New Democrats (vote, votes) for liberalization.

7. The Appointments Committee (settle, settles) the fate of the faculty.

8. The staff (organize, organizes) the summer program.

9. The mass of men (leads, lead) lives of quiet desperation.

10. The audience (applaud, applauds) the performance vigorously.

S

Subjects Modified by Phrases and Clauses

Sometimes the full subject of a verb is a whole string of words, consisting of the simple subject and its modifiers; these modifiers are frequently phrases, clauses, or both. But regardless of how many or what kinds of words intervene between the simple subject and the verb, the basic rule still holds: the verb must agree with the simple subject.

Subject Modified by a Phrase

Living in shared accommodation seems to encourage students' maturity.

The full subject is the italicized portion of the example. But the headword, *living*, is the simple subject; it is singular and agrees with the singular verb *seems*.

Subject Modified by a Clause

Students who butter up their professors hope to earn better grades than those who don't.

The full subject is the italicized portion of the example, but the headword, *students*, is the simple subject; it is plural and agrees with the plural verb *hope*.

We could take either of these examples and make the full subject longer and longer by adding more and more phrases and clauses, but the fact is that these long strings of words accompanying the simple subject are *modifiers*. The verb never agrees with a word or words in the modifier—only with the simple subject.

S

The *music is* beautiful. (*Music* is singular; therefore the verb, *is*, is also singular.)

The *music* of the *strings is* beautiful. (*Strings* is plural but *strings* is part of the modifying phrase *of the strings*; the verb remains singular because singular *music* is still the subject.)

TEST YOURSELF ON

Choosing the Correct Verb for Subjects Modified by Phrases and Clauses

Underline the simple subject of each of the following sentences. Then cross out the phrase or clause that modifies it and read the sentence to determine which of the verbs in parentheses agrees with that subject. Cross out the incorrect verb.

Example: <u>Actors</u> (hate, hates) to be reminded of the fact.

1. The passenger with a lumberjack's jacket and earmuffs in the aisle seat (look, looks) like my brother.

2. The patrons who are waiting in line behind the ropes (want, wants) desperately to be seated.

3. The purpose of the rules (is, are) to assure order.

4. The catch-22 in the examinations given by the Biology Department (lie, lies) in the large number of choices you are given.

5. The guard who stands at the doors of the museum (punch, punches) the tickets.

6. The difference between you and your cousins (appear, appears) to be that you are more comfortable away from home.

7. The smell of those fresh pastries (make, makes) my mouth water.

8. The progress of Ahmed's achievements at college (please, pleases) his parents.

9. Classes that meet late in the day (is, are) poorly attended.

10. Tracey's affection for politics (distract, distracts) her from her real work.

Special Cases

1 Pronouns as subjects. All of the following are singular and take singular verbs:

anybody	each	everyone	nobody
anything	either	everything	none
anyone	everybody	neither	no one
somebody	someone	something	one

Everyone with an interest in ecology *opposes* offshore oil drilling.

Each writes well.

Neither writes brilliantly.

2 Words ending in *-ics* as subjects. Words like *mathematics, economics, politics,* and *dialectics* are singular when you are speaking of the subject as a whole—as *one* thing.

Mathematics offers us a way of looking at the world.

Economics has no solution to the problem of inflation.

Where these terms refer to a number or collection of ideas rather than an academic course, they take a plural verb.

Marx's *economics do* not apply in all societies.

Since 1982, my *politics have* changed considerably.

3 *One of those which/that/who.* Where you use this or a similar structure, in which a relative clause follows a phrase containing more than one noun or pronoun, take care to be clear in your mind which verb is functioning with which subject noun or pronoun.

One of those who sing in the choir is my brother. (Here, the main clause is *One of those . . . is my brother;* the subject is *One* and its verb is *is.* The phrase *of those* modifies the subject pronoun *One.* The relative pronoun *who* is the subject of the clause *who sing in the choir,* which modifies the plural pronoun *those.* Thus, the verb *sing* agrees with its plural subject *who,* while the verb *is* agrees with its singular subject *one.*)

Many of the *volumes* in the Tenth Avenue branch of the public library, *which have been moved* recently from the main branch, *have* been shelved upside down. (The relative pronoun *which,* the subject of the non-restrictive clause enclosed in commas, refers to the noun *volumes* and thus it and its verb, *have been moved,* are plural.)

Most important of the numerous historical events that are of interest to Nicole is the entry of Newfoundland into Confederation. (Until we reach the verb *is*, we do not know whether what is ''most important'' is singular or plural.)

4 *There is, there are. There* is not usually a subject. That's the trouble. Whether you use *is* or *are* depends on what follows the word *there*.

There is something I want to discuss with you. (The subject here is *something*, which agrees with the singular *is*.)

There are reasons that I can't see you tonight. (*Reasons* is the plural subject here—agreeing with the plural verb *are*.)

5 *A number of, the number of. The number of* always takes a singular verb; *a number of* always takes a plural verb.

A number of dogs are playing in the garden.

The number of dogs playing in the garden *is* small.

6 Quantities. When the subject of a verb is a plural quantity or a fraction, determine whether the emphasis is on the number of items (plural) or on a single unit (singular).

Five hundred kilometres *is* a long journey on foot.

Twelve pancakes *are* more than I can eat.

Two-fifths of my life *is* behind me.

He guessed that 2.5 *was* the average number of children per family in his home town.

Two-thirds of the union members *are* satisfied with the contract offer; one-third *are* prepared to strike.

7 *Part* and *portion*. These words, though they indicate a quantity, always take a singular verb, because each signifies a single unit or fraction.

Part of my time *is* spent loafing

Part of my work *is* boring.

A *portion* of my salary *goes* into savings bonds.

A *portion of cherries is* fine for dessert.

8 Expressions such as *together with, as well as, in addition to,*

S

including. A parenthetical expression introduced by phrases such as these does not affect the agreement of the subject and the verb.

> The *truck cab* and the *trailer are* barrelling down the highway. (The compound subject—*truck cab and trailer*—requires the plural verb *are*.)

> The *truck cab*, together with the trailer, is barrelling down the highway. (The subject is now *truck cab*—the parenthetical expression introduced by *together with* doesn't count—and the verb is therefore the singular *is*.)

TEST YOURSELF ON
Subject-Verb Agreement in Special Cases

For each of the sentences below, cross out the verb in the parentheses that does not agree with the italicized subject.

1. *Billiards* (is, are) a difficult game to learn.

2. *Economics* (involve, involves) a lot of statistics.

3. Joanna noticed that René's *trousers* (was, were) dirty.

4. *Gymnastics* (require, requires) a high degree of agility.

5. The *news* these days (depress, depresses) me.

6. Now that I have graduated, a *part* of my life's tasks (is, are) over.

7. A *portion* of these marbles (is, are) yours.

8. A *portion* of blueberry pancakes (is, are) served with butter and syrup.

TEST YOURSELF ON
Proofreading to Catch Subject-Verb Agreement Errors

Each of the following paragraphs contains five errors in subject-verb agreement. See if, by careful proofreading, you can catch them all.

1. Paris is a city that has something for everyone. There is gardens, the Louvre, restaurants, and—ah, yes!—cafés. These are the very centre of outdoor life in this beautiful city. Rising up from the tables at cafés are talk of politics, art, love, the very stuff of sophisticated European life. One of those who sings the praises of Paris most loudly is my brother Lazare. Neither Lazare nor I are stinting in our praise, but he is a fanatic. Although I never fail to be charmed by a visit to the Louvre or a walk along the beautiful Seine, I manage a quiet joy. Lazare, on the other hand, think that Paris not only has something for everyone but that all these "somethings" are for him.

2. Either my mother or my father are always pestering me about progress in my school work. Their attitude is that I need to report improvement every semester. I tell them that living alone in dormitories have deepened my maturity and that I don't need their pressure. But neither of them will listen. The music of my grade reports are beautiful to them, and they never forget to ask for those reports. Economics, my major, are a difficult subject for me, but even though I'm running a B + in economics, you should hear my parents bellow when I report a B in advanced statistics. Neither my father nor my mother and her sisters (who also get into the act) understands that sometimes progress isn't measurable by grades alone and that I need to be left alone to make more progress as a human being.

Subjunctive Mood

S

See **Verbs** and Part 1, Verbs.

Subordination

Subordination is the technique of indicating that one idea is not as important as another. Consider these two ideas.

1. The rate of inflation in Canada is growing at a steady pace.
2. Prices and wages continue to rise slowly.

Both ideas are interesting, but though we can be sure the two are related, there is nothing to indicate their *relative* importance. In a piece of writing whose thesis was that sentence 1 was more important than 2, we should rewrite the sentences like this:

Because prices and wages continue to rise slowly, the rate of inflation in Canada is growing at a steady pace.

Of course, your thesis might be that the reverse is true and that sentence 2 is more important than 1. Then the two ideas would be expressed like this:

Because the rate of inflation in Canada is growing at a steady pace, prices and wages continue to rise slowly.

In either case, however, it is important that you learn the technique of subordination and then go on to use it habitually in your writing.

Subordinate ideas may be expressed, as above, by putting them in the form of a dependent (subordinate) clause. They may also be put in the form of phrases or even single words.

Included in my wardrobe is a summer suit, *which is made of cotton.* (subordinate idea cast in the form of a dependent subordinate clause)

Included in my wardrobe is a summer suit *made of cotton.* (subordinate idea cast in the form of a participial phrase)

Included in my wardrobe is a *cotton* summer suit. (subordinate idea made into an adjective)

Probably the most important technique of subordination is casting subordinate ideas into the form of subordinate clauses. Otherwise your prose can sound like the following childish and monotonous passage:

I went to the movies. I ran into my friend Aaron. The film ran two hours. I hated it. Aaron wanted to sit in the front. I wanted to sit in the balcony. We ended up in the third row.

Because these seven ideas are presented as seven separate sentences, they appear to be of equal importance. But of course they are not. Nor would it be much help to string them together with *and* or *but* or other co-ordinating conjunctions. In fact, you should avoid such strings at all costs. What is needed is subordination—reducing the less important ideas and highlighting the more important ones. One possible way of revising the passage is this:

> I went to the movies, where I ran into my friend Aaron. The film, which I hated, ran for two hours. Although I wanted to sit in the balcony, Aaron wanted to sit in the front and we ended up in the third row.

You might disagree over whether this is the best way to revise the passage, but you would surely agree that this change is for the better.

In practicing subordination, you should be wary of two errors that are likely to crop up.

1 Don't subordinate the more important idea. Where you have two ideas and want to subordinate one of them, do not haphazardly make your choice. That is, do not subordinate one of the ideas without thinking through the problem and deciding what you want to stress. What you want to stress will, of course, go into the main clause.

> Dewitt won the fight
> Dewitt was tiring at the end.
> Although Dewitt won the fight, he was tiring at the end. (Are you just subordinating the first of the two ideas because it is the first one your eye fell on, or do you really want to stress the fact that Dewitt was tiring rather than that he won the fight?)

> I break out in hives.
> I eat strawberries.
> Whenever I break out in hives, I eat strawberries. (In this case, subordinating the first of the two ideas because your eye fell on it first results in an absurdity.)
> Whenever I eat strawberries, I break out in hives. (Of course, this is in keeping with the more probable sequence of events.)

2 Don't use the wrong subordinating conjunctions. Be sure to use the correct subordinating conjunction whenever you *do* subordinate.

> ***Poor***   *While* my English professor is not Martin Short, he does have a good sense of humour.

Better *Although* my English professor is not Martin Short, he does have a good sense of humour.

Poor I read in the paper *where* the Beatles' music is making a comeback.

Better I read in the paper *that* the Beatles' music is making a comeback.

Poor My final exams, *what* I have to take next week, have me scared.

Better My final exams, *which* I have to take next week, have me scared.

TEST YOURSELF ON

Subordination

A Combine each of the following groups of sentences into one or two effective ones by using the techniques of subordination.

Example: 1. I ran into the water.
It was cold.

When I ran into the water, it was cold.

2. James Joyce was an Irish novelist.
He did all his writing in exile in Europe.
He wrote five books.
Dubliners was a book of short stories he wrote.

James Joyce, an Irish novelist who did all his writing in exile in Europe, wrote five books including *Dubliners*, a book of short stories.

Note: Not every student will combine the groups in exactly the same way. Several ways are possible.

1. Mila has a lovely blue shirt.
The shirt is cotton.
She likes to take it to the beach.
She likes to walk around with it.

2. My television set is broken again.

I paid four hundred dollars for it.
It happens.
I get furious.

3. Air pollution is a problem.
   The problem affects us all.
   The problem affects us if we live in the country.
   The problem affects us if we live in the city.

4. We left Kingston.
   It was raining there.
   We arrived in Niagara Falls.
   Niagara Falls surprised us with its sunlit beauty.

5. My friend's name is Colin.
   He is English.
   He loves Toronto.
   He occasionally longs to return to Manchester.

6. Some crimes are against the person.
   These crimes are increasing.
   These crimes must be dealt with.
   These crimes must be dealt with firmly.

7. It was early.
   It was a Sunday.
   It was morning.
   The streets were deadly quiet.

8. Promises are made.
   These promises are sincere.
   Promises can be broken.
   The breaking is easy.

S

9. It rains.
   My roof leaks.
   The roof tiles are loose.
   They were never repaired by the former owner.

10. Paul Klee was a painter.
    He was Swiss.
    His paintings look like drawings.
    The drawings are made by children.

B Revise the following sentences through the effective use of subordination.

1. My hair is drying. I'll read a book.

2. I eat too much pastry and I gain a lot of weight.

3. A whole set of encyclopedias came in the mail and I didn't order it.

4. You see a rainbow across the meadow and you know there's been a recent rainstorm.

5. Julie was unpacking but Peter was cooking supper.

6. She was frightened of air travel and she got on the plane for Paris.

7. Her exams were over, so she could afford to relax.

8. She had enough money and she had enough time and she needed a change of scenery, so she went out to Victoria to visit Craig.

9. The car is a symbol of his virility, so he spends a lot of time polishing it to a high lustre.

10. He likes working in the darkroom, so he does his own printing.

Thesis Statement

Thesis statement is the name given to a central idea when it is written out as a sentence. A thesis is simply the stand you take on an issue or the main point you want to make about a subject.

Cocaine in the Suburbs, for example, is not a thesis statement but a title. In fact, it isn't a sentence, and a thesis statement must be a complete sentence. "My subject is the increasing use of cocaine in the suburbs" is not a thesis statement, either, but an announcement to the reader of what your subject will be—a job done better by a title. (Notice that it is not an improvement to write "My *thesis* is the increased use of cocaine in the suburbs.") "The increased use of cocaine in the suburbs is deplorable" is also not a thesis statement, because it needs no essay to support it; it is a fairly obvious statement of fact. A reader would be as interested in reading an essay about it as he would be in reading one that supports the statement, "Wayne Gretzky holds the record for goals scored in a season."

You need an effective thesis statement in order to control your writing. A poorly worded thesis statement guarantees a poorly constructed, badly focused, and uninteresting piece of writing. In order to be sure that you have a thesis statement that will help control your writing, you should pay attention to the following criteria of a good thesis statement:

1 An effective thesis statement is limited or narrowed down from a larger statement. The idea is to give yourself a manageable, *limited* piece of territory to cover. "College teachers go too fast for the average college student" is a very broad statement that would take you into too large a territory. For example, you would have to talk about more than one college teacher and would also have to deal with whatever is an "average college student." The territory can be scaled down considerably if this topic is changed to "Dr. Frankel goes too fast for her mathematics students." You can see how this limits the territory to one professor in just one class and how it provides real material in the form of actual students. Here are two more examples of large and narrower statements:

> *Large*   Our tax burdens are too great.
> *Narrower*   Revenue Canada penalizes people for being single.
>
> *Large*   Baseball is fun.
> *Narrower*   Nothing matches the excitement of a low-scoring baseball game between evenly matched teams.

2 An effective thesis statement is singular. More than one major idea in an essay is too many. If you have too many major ideas, you will write diffusely, your essay will wander all over the territory, and the reader will lose track of what he or she is supposed to be following. "The United Nations has not fulfilled its original purpose of keeping world peace; it is used for narrow political purposes instead, and many countries neglect to pay their share of its upkeep—which is quite expensive." This is a mouthful—enough for at least two and probably three essays. Better would be either "The United Nations has not fulfilled its original peace-keeping purpose" or "The United Nations is used for narrow political purposes." Here are two more examples:

T

Multiple   The social life of a new student at this college is very limited; the place is so big that you can get lost looking for a classroom, and besides, the instructors are an unfriendly bunch.

Singular   A new student at this college has a number of difficult adjustments to make.

The social life of a new student at this college is very limited.

The instructors at this college are an unfriendly bunch.

Multiple   Contributions to our mounting ecological problems will be made by the energy crisis, rapid increases in world population, and the plans for modern industrial development by the third-world countries.

Singular   The energy crisis is contributing to our mounting ecological problems.

Plans for industrial development by third-world countries will contribute to our ecological problems.

Rapid increases in world population will contribute to our ecological problems.

3 An effective thesis statement is concrete. A thesis statement that is limited and singular must also be concrete. An abstract or vague expression can ruin it.

Vague   The Winnipeg Blue Bombers are a great football team. (What does *great* mean?)

Concrete   The Winnipeg Blue Bombers are solid at every position. (that is, at quarterback, tackle, end, etc.)

Vague   Those who stop smoking care about their health. (What *aspect* of health?)

Concrete   Giving up smoking reduces the smoker's chances of contracting lung cancer. (Lung cancer is a concrete item to work with.)

TEST YOURSELF ON

Recognizing an Appropriate Thesis Statement

T

Place a check next to any of the following sentences that seem to be strong and effective thesis statements. Rework the others.

1. Diabetes is a leading killer of Canadians.

2. American films are obsessed with nostalgia for the sixties.

3. My Aunt Ruth is a stylish dresser.

4. Punk rock is for punks.

5. Mathematics is an engineering student's most useful basic subject.

6. The difference between newspaper coverage and television coverage of the fire on 29th Street illustrates an important media principle.

7. *Hamlet* is a better play than *Macbeth*.

8. The rules for getting a candidate on the ballot for mayor in this town are unfair to those without funds.

9. Utilities in this country make a fortune in profit.

10. The life of a professional athlete is a poor model for youth.

11. Science and art have nothing to say to one another.

12. A person's hobby is the key to that person's character.

Topic Sentence

See **Unity**.

Transitions

Transition is the relating of one idea to the next as your essay proceeds from start to finish. Smooth transition contributes to the coherence of sentences, paragraphs, and essays. A tight organizational pattern is usually the best guarantee that you will achieve coherence. (For more on **Coherence**, see pages 68–80.)

The necessity for coherence is based on your readers' need to be guided from beginning to end in the writing by some familiar principle of order. In other words, readers need bridges to step from sentence to sentence, paragraph to paragraph, idea to idea. When such bridges are absent, readers lose confidence in the writing and, distracted, wander away from what they are reading.

Unless the organizational pattern is so obvious that the writing flows with exceptional ease from part to part, it is a good idea to use what are called *transitional devices* to establish points of reference. These devices are also useful because they establish exact relationships between succeeding parts. In that sense they are useful in *saying* more, and saying is the essential function of expository writing.

The major transitional devices, sometimes used in combination, are the following:

Repetition

Repeating a word or a phrase is a most common device. Sometimes a pronoun, referring back to a subject, will also do the trick, as will repeating a reference to an idea. For example, "Farley Mowat, in *People of the Deer*, shows us clearly what life was like on the arctic barrens. His description of the 'People' using their parkas to withstand the cold demonstrates how survival depends on ingenuity as well as on courage."

Whole Sentence or Brief Paragraph

A sentence can be used as a transition between different ideas following and preceding it. A brief paragraph can also serve as a transition between two longer paragraphs.

Transitional Words or Phrases

Standard transitional words and phrases are good bridges, and most are also useful in indicating relationships. The following are a few of the large number available:

soon	likewise
later	in the same way
at the same time	on the other hand
afterward	however
meanwhile	but
simultaneously	nevertheless
in a little while	still
subsequently	yet
nearby	by contrast
close by	moreover
there	furthermore
here	finally
at the other end	also
therefore	in addition
thus	indeed
hence	in fact
consequently	in other words
similarly	

TEST YOURSELF ON
Making Effective Transitions

Each of the groups of sentences below could be made more coherent by the use of one or more transitional devices. Use either repetition (which will require a little rewriting) or standard transitional words and phrases.

1. She had given Mario a handsome wedding gift. She had offered him a well-paying job with the firm.

2. He stood in a small ravine. There was a running brook.

3. The world is running out of fossil fuels. Our oil supply is diminishing. Research and development for new energy sources are at a standstill.

4. She received a receipt for her tuition. She was able to register.

5. She wanted to go to the seashore. He preferred the mountains.

T

6. Reading stimulated his taste for mulling over in his mind the writer's great ideas. The notions gave him a sense of participating in some great enterprise. He was always reading.

7. Among his possessions were a sports car, a motorcycle, a boat, and a bicycle. He had no need to use public transportation.

8. Jason made his way through his classes by impressing on his teacher what a bright, personable young man he was. He made contact with girls and impressed them, too.

9. After walking around downtown for an hour, she stopped and had dinner. She went to the movies.

10. She graduated with first-class honours. She was able to pick and choose from a number of high-paying jobs.

11. She treated him shabbily, never letting him know from one minute to the next how she felt about him, breaking appointments, speaking rudely to him in public. He could find things about her to love.

12. She said she had known him in Sudbury. He had never been to Sudbury.

Underlining

See **Italics**.

Unity

U

Effective paragraphs possess a quality called *unity*. All the sentences in a unified paragraph are directed toward a single purpose: they supply specific details to illustrate, explain, or define a single generalization made somewhere in—often near the beginning of—that paragraph. This generalization is called the *topic sentence*, and it states what the paragraph is *about*.

Thus every unified paragraph is about one thing and pursues the one thing by organizing itself about its topic sentence. The three ways of placing the topic sentence are illustrated by the following sample paragraphs:

1 The topic sentence can be the opening sentence of the paragraph. Such a paragraph follows the deductive method of stating the generalization and then adding illustrative or supporting details.

> In the folklore of the country, numerous superstitions relate to winter weather. Back-country farmers examine their corn husks—the thicker the husk, the colder the winter. They watch the acorn crop—the more acorns, the more severe the season. They obseve where white-faced hornets place their paper nests—the higher they are, the deeper will be the snow. They examine the size and shape and color of the spleens of butchered hogs for clues to the severity of the season. They keep track of the blooming of dogwood in the spring—the more abundant the blooms, the more bitter the cold in January. When chipmunks carry their tails high and squirrels have heavier fur and mice come into country houses early in the fall, the superstitious gird themselves for a long, hard winter. Without any scientific basis, a wider-than-usual black band on a woolly-bear caterpillar is accepted as a sign that winter will arrive early and stay late. Even the way a cat sits beside the stove carries its message to the credulous. According to a belief once widely held in the Ozarks, a cat sitting with its tail to the fire indicates very cold weather is on the way.
> Edwin Way Teale, *Wandering Through Winter*

> Observations indicate that the different clusters of galaxies are constantly moving apart from each other. To illustrate by a homely analogy, think of a raisin cake baking in an oven. Suppose the cake swells uniformly as it cooks, but the raisins themselves remain of the same size. Let each raisin represent a cluster of galaxies, and imagine yourself inside one of them. As the cake swells, you will observe that all the other raisins move away from you. Moreover, the further away the raisin, the faster it will seem to move. When the cake has swollen to twice its initial dimensions, the distance between all the raisins will have doubled itself—two raisins that were initially a foot apart will have moved two feet apart. Since the entire action takes place within the same time interval, obviously the

more distant raisins must move apart faster than those close at hand.
So it happens with the clusters of galaxies.
Fred Hoyle, "When Time Began"

2 The topic sentence can be the final sentence of the paragraph.
Such a paragraph follows the inductive method by giving details
first and allowing these details to lead up to the concluding general
statement.

Television sells cars as if they were sex objects. It tells one-hour
stories that wind up with all the pieces in the right places, the hero-
ines and heroes clearly marked. It pictures the news only in pictures—
as if there were nothing else newsworthy. It relegates "educational"
programs to a special channel—as if educational material did not
belong with the other material. And it's right to do so, because
commercial television does everything it can to sell us illusions.

The sports pages have columns telling us how to hit a tennis ball
and how to flog a golf ball. The slick magazines give us expert
advice on how to sew, build furniture, repair cars, use tools, and
redecorate our houses. Stirring books are printed every day with
titles bearing the words "How To . . ." and television talk shows
consistently feature people who are *experts*, people who have
accomplished something. Thus it is easy to see that Canadians value
nothing so much as competence.

3 The topic sentence can be unstated but implied. This is a frequent
tactic of narrative and descriptive paragraphs. In the example given
below, the implied topic is *a contrast of animals (and by extension,
people) living full, rounded lives with animals treated as objects,
alive for one purpose only.*

I wished for the days when I was little, before we had the turkeys.
We had cows, and sold milk to the cheese factory. A turkey farm is
nothing like as pretty as a dairy farm or a sheep farm. You can see
that the turkeys are on a straight path to becoming frozen carcasses
and table meat. They don't have the pretense of a life of their own,
a browsing idyll, that cattle have, or pigs in the dappled orchard.
Turkey barns are long, efficient buildings—tin sheds. No beams or
hay or warm stables. Even the smell of guano seems thinner and
more offensive than the usual smell of stable manure. No hints there
of hay coils and rail fences and songbirds and the flowering haw-

U

thorn. The turkeys were all let out into one long field, which they picked clean. They didn't look like great birds there but like fluttering laundry.

Alice Munro, "Miles City, Montana," *The Progress of Love* (Toronto: McClelland, 1986) 93.

TEST YOURSELF ON
Identifying Topic Sentences

What are the topic sentences in the paragraphs below? If you cannot find one expressed directly, consider the possibility that it may be implied.

1. Listening . . . is active and involves making an effort to decode incoming sounds and interpret them. Although we can hear numerous sounds simultaneously, we find it difficult to pay attention to more than one at a time. You almost certainly have had the experience of being in the middle of a telephone conversation when someone comes to your desk urgently signalling to attract your attention. While you try to decipher what he or she wants, you realize that you have missed what was being said on the telephone even though you were still aware of the voice in the receiver.

   It doesn't have to be an external distraction to prevent us from listening. It can equally well be, and in fact more often is, caused by some internal factor. Suppose you are sitting in a meeting paying careful attention to what is going on; suddenly you think you've left your keys in the ignition of your car. A quick check of your pockets is fruitless, and you mentally retrace your steps to see where else you might have left them. While this is going on, your attention to the meeting has dropped and your recollection of what has been said is close to zero.

   Most impediments to listening are not random distractions like the ones just mentioned but are habits and attitudes that people adopt and which greatly impair their ability to listen. A number of cases of poor listening will help to diagnose the problem. Then, with these diagnoses, we can move on to look for solutions.

   Michael A. Nisbet, "Listen—Who Said It Was Easy?" *Canadian Banker* 95.2 (1988): 38.

U

2. The gallows stood in a small yard, separate from the main grounds of the prison, and overgrown with tall prickly weeds. It was a brick erection like three sides of a shed, with planking on top, and above that two beams and a crossbar with the rope dangling. The hangman, a greyhaired convict in the white uniform of the prison, was waiting beside his machine. He greeted us with a servile crouch as we entered. At a word from Francis the two warders, gripping the prisoner more closely than ever, half led, half pushed him to the gallows and helped him clumsily up the ladder. Then the hangman climbed up and fixed the rope round the prisoner's neck.

George Orwell, "A Hanging," *Shooting an Elephant and Other Essays*

3. According to Dr. Jim Leake, an associate professor with the University of Toronto's community dentistry department, "Most orthodontic needs are culturally defined." That is, beauty is in the eye of the beholder. Anthropologists have studied several tribes whose notions of dental glamor differ from ours: tribes in which women filed their teeth to vampirish points, chiefs embedded their teeth with precious stones, or youngsters had their incisors knocked out in puberty rituals. In our culture, we revere a full set of teeth in neat, even rows, unadorned but glistening, looking healthily natural but machine-made perfect.

Ian Allaby, "That Certain Smile," *Successful Executive* 2.1 (1987): 40.

4. The wars and famine of the world have driven more people to seek refuge. The jet age has increased the mobility of people, giving them access to new countries. But the fact that fewer people can successfully apply as immigrants to this country is another factor explaining the increased number of refugee claimants at Canada's doors. In 1980, 2,000 people applied for refugee status in Canada. In 1986, that number had increased ninefold. In a shrinking world, we can only expect that more people each year will want to come here to live. We must recognize that we cannot stand by while people in the rest of the world starve to death, or are destroyed by war and revolution, nor can we isolate ourselves from the rest of the world. Nor should Canadians look for scapegoats to blame for our economic woes. Because of their backgrounds, immigrants have learned to make do with less and work more. Canadians must learn to do the same.

U

Emilia Kolcon-Lach, ''Immigration Doors to Canada: Too Narrow or Too Wide?'' *Perception* 11.1 (Ottawa: The Canadian Council on Social Development, 1987): 9.

5. Hackers are the mutant offspring of the eggheads who once prowled through engineering buildings with slide rules attached to their belts. The computer's power has made the hackers a subculture to be reckoned with. Their fellow students may consider them creepy, but among themselves they are risk takers, explorers, artists. They communicate with one another by intricate computer networks, speak in their own jargon and qualify for lucrative jobs in which they will create the complex programs essential for the everyday functioning of our nation, our world. They have the potential to be supercriminals, to use digital skeleton keys to electronic vaults holding money, confidential personal data and national security secrets. But the power is not without a price: an addiction to computing, a compulsion to program. And they think it's fun.

Stephen Levy, ''Hackers in Paradise''

TEST YOURSELF ON
Achieving Unity in Paragraphs

Each of the three topic sentences printed below is accompanied by a set of statements. Each topic sentence together with its accompanying statements could be made into an effective paragraph were it not for one problem: some of the statements in each set are irrelevant to the topic sentence. In each set, eliminate the potential hurdles to unity and organize the rest into an effective paragraph. Slight alterations in the statements are permissible.

A Basketball is the game requiring great physical skills and co-ordination.

1. Basketball players must be able to run backward as well as forward.

2. They must have good peripheral vision in order to see their team-mates and their opponents.

3. In order to leap for the ball off the backboard, players must have excellent timing.

U

4. Timing is also important in passing and shooting—the exact moment counts in basketball.

5. In football, such skills and co-ordination are not necessary; there you need brute strength.

6. Basketball can be played anywhere.

7. The speed at which the game is played seems to be the factor that requires these skills.

B Your chances of getting a summer job are best if you make a systematic search and present yourself as a useful worker.

1. Explore all the relevant sources for jobs: want ads, school placement agency, friends and relatives, and signs hanging in the windows of businesses in your home town.

2. Begin your campaign early.

3. If you get the right summer job, you can earn thousands of dollars over the summer.

4. If you are applying to a large corporation, show your professionalism by presenting a résumé.

5. The résumé should not be modest; it should list all the skills you possess.

6. Then decide on what kind of job you want and go after it.

7. In appearing for an interview, be on time and present a neat and businesslike appearance.

8. The vigorous job seeker will appear vigorous to an employer.

9. A summer job is not so tiring that you will not be able to have fun and work at the same time.

C There are a number of reasons why it is difficult for most high school graduates to adjust to university life.

1. For one thing, they usually come to a large campus from a much smaller high school setting, and this change alone is unsettling.

2. University administrators should be forced to go to first-year registration and see what's involved.

3. Not only a big school but big classes contribute to the first-year student's unease.

4. Crowded together in a large lecture hall with hundreds of students, they miss the intimacy they enjoyed in high school.

5. Where they were once friendly with a small number of teachers, they are now subject to the alienating presence of the "professor."

6. Moreover, going to university often involves a change of residence—from home with the family to a university residence in another town—and this factor requires some adjustment.

7. Universities should try to make this transition easier.

Verbs

A verb is a part of speech that expresses either action or some state of existence or condition of being.

> Dr. J. *sank* a jumper.
> The Rolling Stones *played* a concert.
> My Uncle Gene *eats* like a whole football team.
> The typewriter *sits* waiting.

> After a while, I *felt* better.
> Nick *seemed* depressed today.
> She *is* a princess.
> They *were* startled.

The verbs italicized in the second set of examples above are called *linking verbs*. (See Part 1, Verbs, for more information about them.) The verbs italicized in the first set of examples above denote some kind of action. (See Part 1, Verbs, under the headings *transitive* and *intransitive* for information about them.)

What all these verbs have in common is the fact that each one not only carries a meaning but also indicates *time*.

1. I *begin* work at eight o'clock. (present tense)
2. I *am beginning* work at eight o'clock. (continuous or progressive present tense)
3. I *was beginning* work at eight o'clock. (continuous past tense)
4. Yesterday, I *began* work at nine o'clock. (past tense)
5. Every day this week, I *have begun* work before ten o'clock. (perfect tense)
6. Before that, I *had begun* work at eleven o'clock. (past perfect tense)
7. Tomorrow, I *will begin* work at twelve o'clock. (future tense)
8. I *will have begun* work by twelve noon. (future perfect tense)

Sentence 1 indicates action taking place in the present or action that is typical and ongoing (something like "I *always* begin work at eight o'clock—I have done so and I will do so in the future"). Sentence 2 says much the same, perhaps with a bit more urgency— the statement could be read as a kind of warning, that is, "You'd better say what you have to say to me now because I'll be too busy after eight: I am beginning work at eight o'clock." Sentence 3 might answer the question "What time were you beginning work last week?" Sentence 4, the simple past tense, indicates that the action took place in the past and was completed then. Sentence 5 suggests that the action was begun in the past and has continued on up to the present. Sentence 6 tells us that the action specified took place and was completed *prior* to some other time in the past, perhaps prior to the week spoken of in sentence 5. Sentence 7 indicates future time, and sentence 8 indicates an action that *will be* completed at or by some specific time in the future.

There are other important things to notice about these examples. First, you should notice that a verb can consist of more than one word. Second, you should notice that in all the examples there appear only four forms of the verb *begin*:

begin (stem, or present tense form)
began (past tense)
begun (past participle)
beginning (present participle)

These are called the *principal parts* of the verb. Knowing the principal parts of a verb and knowing the forms of the auxiliary (helping) verbs *be* and *have* will enable you to form any tense or form of that verb.

Conjugation of Be and Have

The *conjugation* of a verb is a listing of its forms:

Be		**Have**	
present tense		*present tense*	
I am	we are	I have	we have
you are	you are	you have	you have
he, she, it is	they are	he, she, it has	they have
past tense		*past tense*	
I was	we were	I had	we had
you were	you were	you had	you had
he, she, it was	they were	he, she, it had	they had

perfect tense: have been   *perfect tense:* have had
past perfect tense: had been   *past perfect tense:* had had
future tense: will be   *future tense:* will have
future perfect tense: will have been   *future perfect tense:* will have had

Regular and Irregular Verbs: Principal Parts

Notice these principal parts:

Present (stem)	**Past**	**Present Participle**	**Past Participle**
talk	talked	talking	talked
play	played	playing	played
freeze	froze	freezing	frozen
catch	caught	catching	caught

Notice that in the case of the first two verbs, the past and the past participle simply add -*ed* (the two forms are the same). These are called regular verbs. The last two are *irregular*.

Irregular verbs in English do not form the past and past participle with -*ed*. The irregularities of these verbs must be studied and memorized; the following is a list of some of the main irregular verbs, together with their principal parts.

V

Present (stem)	Past	Present Participle	Past Participle
arise	arose	arising	arisen
bear	bore	bearing	borne
begin	began	beginning	begun
bind	bound	binding	bound
blow	blew	blowing	blown
break	broke	breaking	broken
bring	brought	bringing	brought
buy	bought	buying	bought
catch	caught	catching	caught
choose	chose	choosing	chosen
come	came	coming	come
creep	crept	creeping	crept
deal	dealt	dealing	dealt
do	did	doing	done
draw	drew	drawing	drawn
drink	drank	drinking	drunk
drive	drove	driving	driven
eat	ate	eating	eaten
fall	fell	falling	fallen
flee	fled	fleeing	fled
fly	flew	flying	flown
forbid	forbade	forbidding	forbidden
forget	forgot	forgetting	forgotten
freeze	froze	freezing	frozen
get	got	getting	gotten
give	gave	giving	given
go	went	going	gone
grind	ground	grinding	ground
grow	grew	growing	grown
hang	hung*	hanging	hung*
hold	held	holding	held
hurt	hurt	hurting	hurt
know	knew	knowing	known

V

*The past and past participle forms are *hanged* when the word is used in the sense of *executed*.

Present (stem)	Past	Present Participle	Past Participle
lay	laid	laying	laid
lead	led	leading	led
lend	lent	lending	lent
lie	lay	lying	lain
lose	lost	losing	lost
mean	meant	meaning	meant
mistake	mistook	mistaking	mistaken
ride	rode	riding	ridden
ring	rang	ringing	rung
rise	rose	rising	risen
run	run	running	run
see	saw	seeing	seen
seek	sought	seeking	sought
send	sent	sending	sent
shake	shook	shaking	shaken
shine	shone/ shined	shining	shone/shined
sing	sang	singing	sung
sleep	slept	sleeping	slept
slide	slid	sliding	slid
speak	spoke	speaking	spoken
spin	spun	spinning	spun
spill	spilt/ spilled	spilling	spilled
spit	spat	spitting	spat
spread	spread	spreading	spread
spring	sprang	springing	sprung
steal	stole	stealing	stolen
sting	stung	stinging	stung
stink	stank	stinking	stunk
strike	struck	striking	stricken/struck
swear	swore	swearing	sworn
swim	swam	swimming	swum
swing	swung	swinging	swung
take	took	taking	taken
teach	taught	teaching	taught
tear	tore	tearing	torn

V

Present (stem)	Past	Present Participle	Past Participle
thrive	throve/ thrived	thriving	thrived/thriven
throw	threw	throwing	thrown
wear	wore	wearing	worn
weep	wept	weeping	wept
win	won	winning	won
write	wrote	writing	written

TEST YOURSELF ON

Forming the Tenses of Irregular Verbs

A Construct five sentences using the perfect tense of the following irregular verbs: *blow*, *drink*, *forbid*, *hang* (what is done to a picture on the wall), and *strike*.

B Fill in the blanks in the following sentences with the correct form of the verb that is given in parentheses:

1. For almost twenty years, he had (arise)_____

   early every Sunday because he had (sing)_____

   in the church choir.

2. Every day he (drink)_____coffee for break-

   fast, but on Saturday, out of deference to his wife, he (choose)

   tea and then (lie)_____around reading his

   paper before doing the grocery shopping.

3. On some of her birthdays, her children (bring)_____

   her the same gifts she had (bring)_____

   them on their birthdays. It was a family joke and whenever it

   happened she was always (shake)_____with

   laughter and tears.

V

4. She (lay)_____the package down on the table
   and, after she had (take)_____off her hat,
   she (lend)_____Susan a hand with her
   packages.

5. Every night after supper, Grandpa (spin)_____
   a yarn about the old days in Manitoba while the children's faces
   (shine)_____with pleasure.

6. Suddenly, the dog (spring)_____at him, but
   he (freeze)_____for just a moment and the
   animal (flee)_____through the bushes.

7. He had always (sleep)_____on his side, but
   now with his leg injury he was (drive)_____
   to flip over onto his back.

8. She had (teach)_____for a number of years,
   but the whole experience had just about (grind)_____
   her down and now she wanted to be (bear)_____
   away into retirement.

9. The stories the newspapers had (write)_____
   about their marriage and divorce were (forget)_____
   but the whole unpleasant experience still (sting)_____
   him.

V

10. She had (seek)_____peace by buying a little

    cottage on the lake, but there new and vexing problems had (arise)

    _____.

TEST YOURSELF ON
Forming Principal Parts

In the boxes below, some principal parts are given; others are not. Fill in the blank spaces with the appropriate principal part. Find the part you need by looking at the forms already filled in.

	Stem	Past	Present Participle	Past Participle
1		kept		kept
2	lose			
3		played		
4	tell			told
5	pursue			
6	love	loved		
7			growing	grown
8	answer			
9		dreamt/dreamed	dreaming	
10		tried	trying	
11			asking	asked
12		wanted		
13	shave		shaving	

	Stem	Past	Present Participle	Past Participle
14	walk	walked		
15		sewed		
16			smoking	
17		went		
18		hit		
19			having	
20	build			
21			breaking	
22				seen
23				become
24		rode		
25	prove			

TEST YOURSELF ON

Forming Tenses

Circle the form or forms appropriate to complete each of the phrases given.

Example: I will have *went,* (*played,*) *doing,* (*grown,*) *build*

   I will have played and *I will have grown* are correct.

1. I will have   *went, played, doing, grown, build*

2. She was   *giving, lose, wrote, prepared, saw*

V

3. They could have   *became, run, saw, operated, driven*

4. We had   *travel, happened, dreaming, walk, wish*

5. They will   *going, believed, decided, grown, punish*

6. We are not   *became, laughed, dance, jumping, buying*

7. They could be   *want, follow, requested, teach, guess*

8. This property might have been   *change, appraise, divide, rent, sold*

9. Complications could not have been   *rule, testing, know, avoided, saw*

10. Many men should have   *telephone, speaking, singing, talked, known*

11. The ordinary problem is   *say, use, suggested, going, called*

12. My son Jacob might have been   *named, charge, singing, swearing, known*

Using Verb Tenses Correctly

Present Tense
The present tense indicates action taking place at the present moment:

> I *suggest* you go later.
> He *suggests** we take a walk.
> They *suggest* dinner and a film.

*Note the *-s* ending on this verb. See **Subject-Verb Agreement** for information about this ending.

The present tense is also used to indicate an action that is habitual or ongoing:

This dog *bites* people.

My mother *hates* bananas.

Lucia *loves* beautiful plates.

Another form of the present tense is called the progressive present tense. Used with forms of the verb *to be*, it denotes action that is *continuing*:

I *am suggesting Reading, Writing, and Rhetoric* for my first-year students.

He *is draining* the water out of the boat.

Note: Substitute *suggest* for the first verb and *drains* for the second in these sentences. Can you see what is gained or lost by the changes?

Past Tense

The past tense consists of a single form—the simple past:

I *suggested* the book.

I *wrote* my paper.

You should be careful to use the proper form of the past. This is not a problem with regular verbs (which end in *-ed* in both the past and the past participle) but it *is* a problem with irregular verbs:

Wrong   I *rung* the bell.
Right   I *rang* the bell.

Wrong   He *torn* his pants.
Right   He *tore* his pants.

Perfect Tense

The perfect tense uses the past participle with a form of the auxiliary verb *have*. This tense denotes action begun some time in the past and continuing up to and including the present moment:

I *have written* a letter.

He *has played* basketball every day this week.

The problem in using this tense is that writers frequently use the auxiliary with the *past tense* instead of the auxiliary with the *past participle*. Again, there is no problem when the verb involved is a regular verb; there *is* a problem where the verb is irregular:

> ***Wrong***   She *has wrote* her term paper.
> ***Right***   She *has written* her term paper.
>
> ***Wrong***   He *has rode* horses since he was a boy.
> ***Right***   He *has ridden* horses since he was a boy.

Past Perfect Tense
The past perfect tense is used to denote the earlier of two actions, both of which have taken place in the past:

> Domenic *discovered* [simple past tense] that he *had taken* the wrong road. (past perfect tense for earlier action)
>
> René *saw* that Joanna *had rearranged* the furniture. (The *seeing* is later than the *rearranging*.)

Future Tense
Few problems are presented by the future tense. It is formed by using the words *will* or *shall* with the present stem of the main verb:

> I *will go* tomorrow.
>
> We *shall begin* Wednesday.

Note: In formal English, *shall* in the first person and *will* in the second and third person are used to express simple future:

> I shall go to the library tomorrow.
>
> Mary will go with me.

For more on this verb, see the ''Glossary of Usage,'' **shall, will, should, would.**

Future Perfect Tense
The future perfect tense is used to express the *earlier* of two actions, both of which will be completed in the future:

> By the time I *arrive* in Sherbrooke, she *will have risen*. (*Arrive* here is used to denote the *future; will have risen* denotes the earlier of the two actions.)

Before I *leave* for the airport, he *will have packed* my bag. (The *leaving* must take place *after* the packing.)

TEST YOURSELF ON
The Correct Use of Tenses

Underline the verbs in parentheses that make the sentences correct.

1. The tournament will end soon and our team (will lose, will have lost) its chance for the championship.

2. By the time the police get here, the burglar (will be, will have been) gone for half an hour.

3. When Jean (entered, had entered) the room, she saw that Jorge (rearranged, had rearranged) the furniture.

4. I (learned, have learned) quite a lot about Shakespeare this year, and I am hoping to learn even more next year.

5. Sotos was terrified that his dog (bit, had bitten) the policeman.

6. By my next birthday, I (will live, will have lived) for half a century.

7. Once I (finished, had finished) writing Volume 1, I (began, had begun) to worry about Volume 2.

8. The people we saw in the restaurant (acted, had acted) like clowns.

9. Fettucini (was, had been) my favorite pasta before I discovered linguini.

V

10. When the game (ended, had ended), the stadium (closed, had closed).

11. The chairperson (left, had left) the meeting before it (adjourned, had adjourned).

12. He (was brought up, had been brought up) on charges after we (discovered, had discovered) his misconduct.

Some Problems with Verbs

1 Final *-d* or *-ed*

Some writers make the error of omitting a final *-d* or *-ed* from past tense or past participle verb forms. It is especially important that you beware of the problem in one-syllable words, where the *-ed* ending is not likely to be sounded (as in *blamed, dreamed, missed,* and so forth). The *-ed* ending is not so frequently forgotten in words of more than one syllable, such as *completed* or *departed*, but the error is occasionally made in two-syllable words. *Supposed* and *used* (as in *I used to go to church regularly* and *I was supposed to see my analyst today*) are especially likely to be pronounced or written incorrectly.

TEST YOURSELF ON

The Final -d Sound

A Pronounce the following italicized words so that the sound of the final *-d* is clearly heard by other students in the room:

1. I am *tired*.
2. He is *prejudiced*.
3. After she *arrived*
4. The store he *owned*
5. The lesson she *learned*

6. He *blamed* me.
7. The meat is *weighed*.
8. Vegetables are *preferred*.
9. The defendant is *judged*.
10. Students are *graded*.

11. The army *surrendered*.

12. My song was *played*.

13. The crowd *cheered*.

14. Drowning man *saved*

15. My pay *increased*.

16. Food is *provided*.

17. Choice is *offered*.

18. Package is *received*

19. My heart was *deceived*.

20. I am *relieved*.

B In the passage below, some words have had -*d* endings removed and some are spelled correctly. Read the passage aloud and notice how the fact that you pronounce some endings (the ones that are there) influences your pronunciation of others (ones that are *not* there). Write in endings wherever they are needed.

Something was needed to cheer me up. I was tire and hadn't been to bed in two days. I thought I would never be rescue and I was worried that even my best friends would not have notice me gone. My foot hurt a lot from when I had slip down the side of the gully and I would have given anything for a little sip of water.

A bird start to chirp. I wish I was as happy as he was. I wish I had his wings!

The accident must have happen because I wasn't as young as I use to be. Still, I was only twenty-three! Are people suppose to lose all their agility after the age of nineteen? It all weighed on my heart. Suddenly, I notice that the sky was getting very dark. If anybody look for me now, they would have a hard time seeing me. I try to move a little, to see if I could climb to the crest of the hill and make myself more visible. But it was no use. I wish I had climbed up there earlier, when I had more strength.

2 Sequence of Tenses

If you are using two or more verbs in a sequence, either within a single sentence or in sentences that follow each other, it is important that you indicate precise time to the reader.

A *Finite verbs* (forms expressing tense, person, number, and mood):

> When the judge *banged* her gavel, the courtroom *grew* silent. (Both verbs in the past—both actions took place at the same time in the past.)

> Although I *have complained*, I *have received* no satisfaction. (Two perfect tenses—the actions started in the past and are continuing up to the present, in both cases.)

> He *said* that he *was* a Martian. (Indirect discourse; both tenses should match—here, the past.)

> By the time I *hand in* my papers, I *will have finished* the term's work. (Correct sequence for use of future perfect.)

B *Infinitives* (*to* forms): use the present infinitive to indicate action that happens at the same time as or later than the main verb, and use the present perfect infinitive (*to* + *have* + past participle) for action prior to that of the main verb.

> Bill *needed* [past tense] *to forget* [present infinitive]. Bill *needs* [present tense] *to forget* [present infinitive].

> He *would love to have charged* his purchase. (Present perfect infinitive used for time prior to main verb.)

C *Participles:* to denote action happening at the same time as the action of the main verb, use the present participle. To denote action that happened prior to that of the main verb, use the present perfect participle (present participle of *have* + past participle of verb).

> *Jogging* along the main road, he *noticed* many other joggers. (The *noticing* and the *jogging* take place at the same time.)

> *Having mastered* geometry, he *knew* he could tackle calculus. (First came the *mastering*, then the *knowing; having mastered* is the present perfect participle.)

TEST YOURSELF ON

Sequence of Tenses

Underline the correct verb form in the parentheses for the sequence of tenses in each of the sentences below.

1. Because the patient's heart has begun beating, the doctors believe that the danger to his life (diminished, has diminished).

2. (Having finished, Finishing) the painting, Edward walked away from the easel.

3. They had not expected (to go, to have gone) to California last winter.

4. Ursula plans (to publish, to have published) her novel next year.

5. Arthur thought Guido missed the point, that he (neglected, had neglected) important issues.

6. (Having been taught, Being taught) good manners by my parents, I did not yawn when he began to speak.

7. (Reaching, Having reached) Calgary, she knew she could drive to Edmonton.

8. When they (visited, have visited) Italy, they never ate a poor meal.

9. Paranjit regretted (being born, having been born) handsome instead of rich.

10. Antonia wanted (to read, to have read) the books in sequence.

11. Dan insisted that he (once saw, had once seen) a drunken Irishman.

V

12. (Teaching English, Having taught English), she thought she

knew grammar.

___

3 Could of, being that, would have

Never use the expression *could of*. It is an approximation of what some writers hear when they say *could have* or *could've*.

> ***Wrong***   He *could of* gone with me to the movies.
> ***Right***   He *could have* gone with me to the movies.

The same holds true for the forms *would of* and *should of* and any other *of*.

> Never use the expression *being that* for *since* or *because*.

> ***Wrong***   *Being that* he was just a child, I helped him across the street.
> ***Right***   *Because* he was just a child, I helped him across the street.

> Never use the expression *would have* in place of *had*.

> ***Wrong***   If he *would have* done well on his finals, he would have been admitted to graduate school.
> ***Right***   If he *had* done well on his finals, he would have been admitted to graduate school.

4 The Subjunctive Mood

The subjunctive mood expresses actions or states of being that are contrary to fact, are wishful, imaginary, or not yet actualities. It is not commonly used in ordinary speech. Current English usage has found substitute expressions for virtually all uses of the subjunctive:

If she *were* to leave	If she *leaves*
Had he *taken* the course	If he *took* the course
I wish I *were* finished.	I wish I *was* finished.

Nevertheless, there are a few circumstances in which the subjunctive is required usage.

A In contrary-to-fact, wishful, or imaginary propositions:

> Rather than *be* thought callous, Margaret took care to explain her motives.

I wish you *were* here.

Alexander is eating the pizza as if there *were* nothing else on his mind.

Had Maria *taken* an earlier bus, she would have been on time.

B In certain *that* clauses making recommendations or requirements for possible action:

I insist that the barn *be* painted red. (Substituting *is* for *be* makes the sentence say something entirely different, i.e., that the speaker insists the colour of the barn is *already* red.)

The member moved that Parliament *be* adjourned.

Is it right that a woman *suffer* just because she is a woman?

It is not enough that justice *be* done; justice must *be* seen to be done.

The student demanded that the teacher *respect* her intelligence.

C In certain conventional expressions:

Peace *be* with you.

Come what may, . . .

Long *live* the Queen.

Heaven *forbid* . . .

For nearly all verbs, subjunctive forms remain the same as indicative forms, except that the *s* (*es*) is dropped from the third-person singular form. For example,

I know that she *respects* my intelligence. I insist that he *respect* my intelligence as well.

The forms of the verb *to be* are the exception. For all present conditions, use *were* or *be*. For all past conditions, use *had been*. For example,

Present I wish you *were* here. They also wish you *were* here. But if we *were* all to be there, that would be an equally satisfying solution. *Be* that as it may, we cannot get together for now.

Past If we *had been* together, we would all have been satisfied.

TEST YOURSELF ON

The Correct Use of Verb Forms

A In each of the sentences below, some form of *could*, *should*, *would*, or *being* is misused. Correct the errors.

1. If he would have gone earlier, he would have seen the pre-game show.

2. Being that it had the best forestry program she could find, she went to the University of British Columbia.

3. I could of been a star.

4. She wasn't as alert as she should of been.

5. If he had gone earlier, he would of seen the pre-game show.

B For each italicized verb form in the sentences that follow, supply the correct subjunctive form.

1. It is necessary that justice *is* done.

2. He was eating as if there *was* no tomorrow.

3. She suggested that their lunch date *is* postponed until the following week.

4. Is it right that a man *suffers* for someone else's crime?

5. My brother asked that he *is* given the car tomorrow.

V | *Voice*

Most verbs can be used in either the active or the passive voice.

> *Active Voice*   John *saw* his son yesterday.
>
> *Passive Voice*   John *was seen* by his son yesterday.

The subject of both sentences is *John*. In the first (active voice) sentence, *John* is performing the action; in the second sentence, *John* is undergoing the action.

In English, the active voice is more vigorous and more emphatic than the passive voice. Beginning writers frequently find their sentences slipping into the passive voice because they are not quite sure what they want to emphasize.

> ***Passive*** These fancy jeans *were bought* by me at the Clothes Barn.
>
> ***Active*** I *bought* these fancy jeans at the Clothes Barn.

These sentences convey the same information, but each emphasizes a different thing. The passive emphasizes the *fancy jeans* (because *jeans* is in the subject position in the sentence) and the active emphasizes *I*. The passive sentence also requires two more words to say the same thing that the active sentence says. The passive sentence is also made awkward because of the *by me* phrase.

We emphasize that the active voice is the stronger and therefore the preferred choice because beginning writers, as well as more experienced ones, are frequently evasive in their use of the passive voice. The use of the active voice corrects this tendency.

Evasion by a Beginning Writer
Tutoring help in algebra *is needed* by Nick. (The sentence reads as if the writer were a little reluctant to mention Nick's name, so he has delayed saying that name as long as possible.)

Evasiveness Corrected by Using the Active Voice
Nick *needs* tutoring in algebra.

Evasion by a More Experienced Writer
It *has been decided* that your application *will not be considered* at this time. (The evasion here is that no decision maker is named.)

Evasiveness Corrected by Using the Active Voice
We *have decided* not to consider your application.

Of course, there are circumstances where the use of the passive voice is appropriate.

V

1 Use of the passive voice when the doer of the action is not known.

The making of bronze *was begun* in Southwest Asia around 2500 BC.

A fire *was set* in an abandoned warehouse on Pier 88 this morning.

It is easy to see why the specific doer in the first of these examples—the person who began to make bronze—is not known. In the second, the opening sentence of a newspaper story, it is clear that the person who set the fire is unknown. Nor would this sentence be improved if the author had written something like, ''Somebody set a fire . . .'' or ''A person or persons unknown set a fire . . .''

2 Use the passive voice when it is more important to emphasize the receiver than the doer of the action.

> The vote on the Capital Punishment Bill *was* not *taken* until after midnight.

> My vegetable garden *was ruined* by the heavy rainstorm in April, but it *was replanted* in time to give us enough vegetables to last the summer.

In the first sentence, the vote on the bill is much more important than those who voted. In the second, the rainstorm is unimportant compared to the garden (in the first clause), and the people who replanted it less important than the garden itself (referred to by the pronoun *it* in the second clause).

Nevertheless, you should beware of using weakly or evasively passive sentences in a consistent pattern in your work. Sentences such as ''This class *was taken* by me last semester'' and ''My car *was smashed into* by a truck'' can only make your writing weak and uninteresting.

TEST YOURSELF ON

The Appropriate Use of the Active Voice

A Change each of the following passive sentences into an active one.

1. I was bored by the book.

2. Dr. Waldhorn is respected by his patients.

3. Everyone on my block is annoyed by Joe's dog.

4. The rich and the famous are admired by most people.

V

5. The police are angered by disrespect.

6. Financial aid is hoped for by all students.

7. Milk cows are given special care by dairy farmers.

8. Paying bills in an inflationary economy is disliked by everybody.

9. Help is urgently needed by the earthquake victims.

10. Subway riders are exhausted by rush hour traffic.

B Some of the sentences below use the passive voice appropriately. Next to these, write C. Where the passive voice is either weak or evasive, recast the sentence into the active voice.

1. _____ It is thought by my mother that I'm too young to drive.

2. _____ The Boston Bruins were badly beaten by the Montreal Canadiens at the Montreal Forum last night.

3. _____ Freedom was sought by slaves.

4. _____ The ring was given to me for Christmas by my brother.

5. _____ Television is watched by more and more people in this country.

6. _____ Crime is feared more by people in the cities than by people in the country.

7. _____ The labels on canned foods are not read by shoppers in supermarkets.

8. _____ While the children were being filled with Cokes at the fountain, the car was being filled with gas.

9. _____ It is forbidden to feed the animals.

10. _____ The victims of the two-car crash were taken to the hospital by ambulance.

11. _____ The fuse was ignited.

12. _____ Hot cereal was eaten for breakfast by Lina.

Wordiness

Direct expression is best. Wordiness, the use of more words than necessary, defeats directness. A good rule is to use as few words as possible but as many as necessary to say what you mean. Below are listed some of the writing faults that cause wordiness; discussed under each heading are ways of making your writing more economical.

Redundancy: The Elimination of Deadwood

Redundancy means ''needless repetition.'' Examine your writing carefully to make sure you are not being redundant.

1 Transform your clauses into phrases and your phrases into single words wherever possible. What you eliminate is called *deadwood*.

Unnecessary Clause   The professor, *who teaches mathematics*, was angry.
Revised   The professor *of mathematics* was angry.
Revised   The *mathematics* professor was angry.

Unnecessary Phrase   She was lovely *in appearance*.
Revised   She was lovely.

Deadwood   After the concert had come to a close, we went to dinner.
Revised   After the concert, we went to dinner.

Deadwood   I am learning the skill of how to do the work of the job.
Revised   I am learning how to do the job.

Deadwood   The driver of the truck was angry.
Revised   The truck driver was angry.

W

2 Avoid the use of two words that mean virtually the same imprecise thing where a single more accurate word, or one of the pair, will do.

Redundant He was a *real* and *true* friend.
Revised He was a *genuine* friend.

Redundant The *light* and the *brightness* were dazzling.
Revised The *sun* was dazzling.

Redundant I had a lot of *love* and *regard* for her.
Revised I *cared* for her very much.

Redundant She gave me a *warm* and *friendly* smile.
Revised She gave me a *friendly* smile.

3 Eliminate words that needlessly repeat what you have already said. *He made revised changes in his book* has a needless repetition. The sentence should read either *He made changes in his book* or *He revised his book*.

Repetitious A hermit is someone who is isolated by himself.
Revised A hermit is someone who is isolated.

Repetitious The animals' roars were audible to the ear.
Revised The animals' roars were audible.

Repetitious Her shawl was a deep red in colour.
Revised Her shawl was deep red.

Repetitious The assignments he gave were several in number.
Revised He gave several assignments.

4 Do not use several words where one will do. Eliminate from your writing any long-winded expressions you have acquired.

Long-winded *In this day and age* [or, *in this modern world*], people have increased expectations of prosperity.
Better *Today*, people have increased expectations of prosperity.

Long-winded *It should be noticed* that few cocktail party conversations manage to avoid the subject of computers.
Better *Notice* that few cocktail party conversations manage to avoid the subject of the computer.

Long-winded *As far as* Cameron *is concerned*, he drinks too much.
Better Cameron drinks too much.

W

TEST YOURSELF ON

Eliminating Redundancies

The following sentences all contain some kind of redundancy. Correct each one by eliminating the redundancy.

1. Paul is an expert in the field of urban government.

2. Professor de Groot referred back to the War of 1812.

3. The snow which fell yesterday is melting into water today.

4. At 9 a.m. in the morning, the driver started to drive toward Moncton.

5. As soon as he started to look for a job, he connected up with a large corporation.

6. I'm going to repeat again what I said a moment ago.

7. As far as reading is concerned, I would say that it is a difficult thing for me to do.

8. Most students spend the majority of the hours in each school day attending classes for which they are registered.

9. Although he seemed to be a warm and friendly man, I didn't care for him or like him for some reason.

10. It was not exactly a meaningful or worthwhile experience.

Awkward Repetition

Effective repetition of words can make for emphasis. Awkward repetition is merely wordy: it makes for dullness.

> **Awkward**   The *driver drove* steadily; his *driving* made us feel safe.

Revised   The driver was steady; his skill made us feel safe.

Awkward   My *membership* application was accepted by the club and I was made a *member*.

Revised   The club accepted my membership application.

Awkward   If *one examines* the *case*, *one can* see that it is *one* of the *cases* that *cannot* stand close *examination*.

Revised   The case cannot stand close examination.

Effective Repetition   The average politician has a *sinister* past, a *sinister* attitude, and a *sinister* plan for the future.

Effective Repetition   *New* mouthwash, *new* deodorant, *new* toothpaste, *new* teeth—television sells them all with equal enthusiasm.

Wordy Formulas

Eliminate from your writing phrases such as *to be*, *there is*, *it is*, *the type of*, *the fact that*, *the use of*. These can just as well be left out of most sentences.

Wordy   She seems *to be* sad this morning. (Read the sentence without the italicized portion and notice that nothing is lost.)

Wordy   Higher mathematics appears *to be* difficult.

Wordy   The pilot was considered *to be* a hero.

Wordy   *There is* something I have to say.

Revised   I have something to say.

Wordy   *It is* the truth that is important.

Revised   The truth is important.

Wordy   I got *the type* of job I wanted.

Revised   I got the job I wanted.

Wordy   Because of *the fact that* it was raining, we couldn't play the game.

Revised   Because it was raining, we couldn't play the game.

Wordy   His *use of* English is bad.

Revised   His English is bad.

Passive Voice

By using the active instead of the passive voice, you can eliminate words and create a more vigorous style.

W

Passive   Anxiety about examinations *is felt* by some students.
Active   Some students *feel* anxious about examinations.

Passive   The holiday *was enjoyed* by everybody.
Active   Everybody *enjoyed* the holiday.

Pompous Diction

Eliminate pompous diction from your writing. Invariably, the fancy way to say something requires more words than the plain way and is less effective.

Fancy   It is my intention to make a careful scrutiny of the record.
Plain   I plan to look closely at the record.

Fancy   I observed that his behavior was somewhat less than intelligent.
Plain   I saw that he was acting the fool.

TEST YOURSELF ON
Eliminating Wordiness

Each of the following sentences contains awkward repetitions, wordy formulas, wordy passive voice constructions, or complicated diction. Correct each by using straightforward, active language.

1. The important subject of my speech will be a subject important to students, educators, and others to whom the subject is of professional interest.

2. It should be made clear to everyone that the utmost silence is necessary while working in a library.

3. Whenever he's in trouble, he makes use of rationalization.

4. There is a special beach I'd like to take you to.

5. It is a terrible thing to be chronically sick.

6. That point was made by Darwin.

7. He is the type of person unaware of the fact that people in this modern day and age are unhappy.

8. Because of the fact that we used logic, we solved the problem and came up with the solution.

9. Karen is known to be moody.

10. Some of the best times we had were when we were on vacation.

W

Part 3
The Research Paper

The Nature of the Research Paper

If you were assigned to write a paper on your life, you would simply reach into your memory for the necessary information. If an assignment asked you to describe the physical landscape of your town or neighbourhood, again you would have no difficulty: you'd simply wake up your perceptions, take a good long look, and start making notes. In both these writing assignments, you would of course be asked to come to some conclusion, to develop a point of view about your information. Essays not under the control of a central idea or thesis statement—facts without a conclusion—are dull stuff.

The research paper differs from these assignments in that you are asked to gather the information you need not from your own perceptions or memory but—by means of an active and systematic search—either from library resources or through a direct investigation of some aspect of experience. The research paper is similar to the others in that here, too, you are asked to come to a conclusion about your facts—to develop a thesis statement.

You'll be able to do this because after completing your research you should be something of an expert in your field—more of one than your instructor or anyone in your class.

Finding and Narrowing a Topic

If your instructor hands you a ready-made topic, you may skip this section. In general, however, instructors are likely to ask you to participate in the search for one. It's an invigorating exercise, for one thing, but more important is that your participation will lead you to a topic that excites your interest and that will produce a more interesting paper.

Limiting the Range of Topics

To begin the search, you should understand the limitations that govern the selection of a topic.

1 Certain subjective topics are not good choices. For example, it is futile to look for facts that will determine whether Corey Hart is a better musician than Bryan Adams, or Leonard Cohen a better poet than Irving Layton. Such judgements depend not on research but on taste.

2 Topics that are too recent should be avoided. It takes time to develop the good evidence and careful thought that produce useful writing on a subject. If your topic is too recent, you won't find much on it in the library.

3 Topics that rely on a single source should be eliminated. You can gather all you need to know about photosynthesis or steel manufacturing from a single source. Therefore, these are not good topics because one object of the research paper is to offer the writer practice in using and synthesizing many sources.

4 Topics that call for the direct investigation of some private aspect of your experience are also poor choices. To interview all your relatives for their impressions of you at various stages in your development so that you can research how your character was formed—that may be fun, but its appeal to a reader is doubtful.

5 The length of the usual college research paper—1,500 to 2,000 words—will also limit your choice of a topic. You cannot, for example, fit a biography of Pierre Trudeau into a paper of that length. Nor can you do an adequate job in that space on the conflicts causing so much turmoil in the Middle East. The size of your topic must be appropriate to the space limits set by your instructor.

6 You will also be limited by your choice of a purpose. That is, do you wish to write a paper that is informative, analytic, or argumentative? Although a paper on Trudeau's travels in China would have a point of view or thesis statement, it would argue nothing —only inform. A paper on the slang used by teenagers in your home town or neighbourhood would naturally analyze—that is, it would dissect the meanings of words and come to some conclusions about patterns of speech and dialect. Finally, an argumentative research paper might undertake to show that its position was correct—for example, that capital punishment does not deter potential murderers.

Informative purposes also generate papers that qualify as market research, that is, those papers that, relying on questionnaires, interviews, sampling, and testing, develop information useful for the production of new consumer products. Allied to market research are technical studies that produce information for industry and business—for example, a study that gives information on traffic flow in and around two adjacent towns for the purpose of deciding where a shopping mall might be best situated. A computer-generated research paper also qualifies as informative. It asks you to generate and organize data in the most useful ways for a variety of purposes.

Exploring Your Interests

Now that you understand these limitations, how should you proceed? There are two ways, both based on exploring your own interests.

1 If you have a question about something—Why are they fighting in Northern Ireland? Why did President Truman drop the atomic bomb on Hiroshima *and* Nagasaki?—you are very far along toward a topic *and* a thesis statement. The answers to those questions will be thesis statements for the paper; simply research the answers.

2 If you have an interest in a large subject area, such as John Diefenbaker or China or language, you're not quite so far along but are at least ready to start narrowing your subject down.

Narrowing the Topic

Here are some ways that subjects might get narrowed down:

> *China*—education in China—grammar school education in China—
> the kindergarten curriculum in China—kindergarten reading texts in
> China—the content of kindergarten reading texts in China—*the
> political content of kindergarten reading texts in China*

> *John Diefenbaker*—the government of John Diefenbaker—defence
> policy during the government of John Diefenbaker—defence policy
> and nuclear weapons during the government of John Diefenbaker—
> *Diefenbaker's decision not to allow nuclear warheads on Canada's
> Bomarc missiles*

> *Language*—the English language—the English language in Canada
> —the language of British Columbia—the language of Vancouver,
> B.C.—the language of teenagers in Vancouver—the vocabulary of
> teenagers living on Renfrew Street in Vancouver—*the slang vocab-
> ulary of teenagers living on Renfrew Street in Vancouver*

The last (italicized) strings of words in each example are suitable
topics. But how do we get there? Is it as easy as it looks? Not quite.
But the following suggestions may make the job easier:

1 Notice that each successive term in an example *qualifies* the preceding term, makes it more precise, focuses it. Try doing free-
writing on your subject with the aim of adding qualifications to
the successive terms, as in the examples.

2 Consult somebody you think is an expert in the field. Ask that
person about narrower topics within the subject area you're thinking of. For example, if you're interested in art, ask an artist or an
art teacher what you can learn about the subject through research.

3 Do some preliminary reading in your broad subject area. See what
details you find that stir your interest in some specific corner of
the subject or that suggest specific questions whose answers you'd
like to know.

4 Ask yourself some questions about the subject area. Any sort of

question will do; it's not easy to get to *the* question, the one your paper will answer, but even odd questions will keep your mind running toward possible pay dirt.

5 Do this preliminary work with a pencil or pen in hand. Simply sitting in a chair thinking is not conducive to bringing together ideas that will set off sparks. Writing things down *is*.

The topic-selection stage does not necessarily go smoothly, so persistence here is crucial. This stage more or less comes to a close when you have finally whittled your large subject area down to a manageable one and can formulate a good research question for yourself.

Formulating a Research Question

A good research question for the paper on China might be, How do the Chinese begin to inform their citizens about their political system? The Diefenbaker paper might answer the question, What major considerations went into Diefenbaker's decision not to allow nuclear warheads on the Bomarc missiles? The primary research undertaken for the language paper would probably answer a question such as, What linguistic operations and dialectical considerations govern the kinds of slang used by teenagers on Renfrew Street in Vancouver?

Additional Sources for Ideas

If after exploring your interest in a large subject area and trying the narrowing process, you are still not satisfied that you've found a topic, you must work harder at the search. You need to be continually *active* in your search by making such inquiries as these:

1 Go over notes for other courses. What issues, people, or events puzzle you or excite your interest? Are there problems in anthropology, history, sociology that stick in your memory?

2 Look at your neighbourhood or community. What aspects of these

places are you curious about? Is there a problem on the streets or on the farm or in the town that you notice and care about?

3 Read a newspaper from first page to last every day for as long as it takes you to uncover some group, person, or event that excites or interests you. Begin to work with one of these.

4 Ask for an appointment with one of your instructors. Explain your problem and see if the instructor can suggest a broad area of interest.

Finally, let us repeat, only your *active* search can find you a topic and the sooner the better.

TEST YOURSELF ON

Identifying or Narrowing Down to a Suitable Topic

Listed below are a number of possible topics. If you think one is suitable, mark it with a check. If not, mark it with an X. In either case, be prepared to explain your judgement. Decide which unsuitable topics could be successfully narrowed down to make good ones. Do some preliminary reading on the topics; consult both your instructor and the library for reading suggestions. Then narrow down the broad subjects until they are appropriate research paper topics.

1. How bees make honey.

2. The development of communications technology in Canada.

3. Canada's diplomatic recognition of China.

4. Reviewers' comments on a film you have seen recently.

5. The voting habits of people in your town or city.

6. Crime melodramas on prime time television: what they have in common.

7. Mohammed and Jesus.

8. Symbolism in dreams.

9. The rationing of food and gasoline during World War II.

10. The significance of agribusiness to Canadian farming.

11. The job market in Canada for people graduating in the year you plan to graduate.

12. The vitality of Canadian theatre.

Research Tools

Direct Investigations

Some instructors will permit you to do direct research on some aspect of experience.* A variety of interesting papers can be written reporting on the results of research into such features of the public landscape as advertising (both television and print); television programming; the opinions, values, ideas, politics, and future plans of various campus groups—instructors, administrators, art majors, or technical students—or off-campus populations.

The principal research instruments used in projects like these are the *interview*, the *survey*, and the *questionnaire*.

The Interview

The advantage of the interview is that you can ask follow-up questions. The difficulty is that you must think on your feet and be ready to respond to what your subject says. So a careful plan is necessary: you must prepare a good set of questions keyed to what you want to know, along with several follow-up questions based on anticipated responses. For interviews, it is best to use a tape recorder, but ask permission first. For neat record keeping, identify the interview by name of subject and date of interview.

The Survey

A survey is a measurement, and you can make measurements with

*In a course like this, you will probably not be permitted to do scientific research.

various kinds of rulers. For example, you can survey the kind and quality of television programming on a particular station or during specific viewing hours. You could also survey ads that appear in the print media. By analyzing a specific number of, say, full-page ads from a single source, you could measure the kinds of appeals that are being made to sell particular items to particular age groups. The survey can be presented in tabular form; the research paper can first justify the procedure of the survey and then go on to explain the results depicted in the table.

The Questionnaire

The advantages of the questionnaire are that (1) it permits anonymity for the subject and perhaps therefore a greater willingness to respond, and (2) it accommodates the kind of answer that can be treated numerically; a number of questionnaires can be handed out and the results tabulated. A questionnaire is a kind of interview; the possibilities for answers are limited, but some researchers think materials from questionnaires are easier to obtain and work with than materials from interviews. Using shrewdly worded questionnaires, you could do projects to analyze the plans, opinions, tastes, and professional objectives of the members of various groups on campus or elsewhere.

Primary and Secondary Sources

Materials such as interviews, survey results, and questionnaire answers are called *primary sources*. Also falling into this category are plays, novels, and poems; letters, diaries, journals, and speeches; eyewitness accounts; certain official documents; scientific findings, market research, and other kinds of informational research. Primary sources are the first-hand documents of experience.

Secondary sources are those which comment upon and analyze primary sources. Secondary sources include books, magazine and newspaper articles, encyclopedia entries, and any other works that inquire into, analyze, or argue about your topic.

Whenever possible, you should use a primary source. The use of primary sources enlivens and enriches your paper by bringing the reader closer to the experience you're writing about; secondary sources are one step removed from that experience.

Preparing a Bibliography

Once you have narrowed your topic and have found your way to the library, you will want to begin searching for appropriate materials in the library's catalogues and other resources. As you collect material, you will create a *working bibliography*, a record of books, articles, pamphlets, and other reference materials that you are using for your research. It is kept on a series of index cards according to a system explained below. As your essay develops, you may add some items or drop some, so the list you actually use for your essay—the list of *works cited* or your *final bibliography*—may not be identical with your working list. (For information on organizing a Works Cited list, see "Bibliographic Form: Sample Entries," pages 346–49 and "Setting up a List of Works Cited," pages 349–50.)

Using the Library to Locate Sources

Before you begin using the library catalogues, you can make your task simpler by first looking at two important reference books, the *Library of Congress List of Subject Headings* and *Canadian Subject Headings*. Select a specific term that applies to the topic you are researching, e.g., PAINTING rather than ART, PERU rather than SOUTH AMERICA. Look in the lists to see if the term you have selected is listed; if it appears in **boldface** type, it is a certified heading. Under some certified terms, you may find references to other certified terms. Make note of these, as they may help you to find additional material. When you have noted all the relevant subject headings, you are prepared to use the SUBJECT section of the library's catalogues and, later, the periodical indexes and other resources.

Two other useful books are Eugene P. Sheehy's *Guide to Reference Books* and Claire England's *Guide to Basic Reference Material for Canadian Libraries*. Keep in mind that subject headings certified for materials listed in the catalogues may differ from those used in other resources such as these guides and the periodical indexes. For example, if you are looking for information on the disease AIDS, you will find it in the microfiche catalogue under the heading ACQUIRED IMMUNE DEFICIENCY SYNDROME, in the *Social Science Index* under IMMUNOLOGICAL DEFICIENCY SYN-

DROME, and in *The Reader's Guide* under AIDS. Also, topics on current issues may not be well covered in either these guides or the library catalogues. If you are writing on a current topic, extend your subject search to *current* periodical and newspaper indexes.

Sources

Once you have settled on the appropriate subject headings, you are ready to use the sources. The following are the principal sources for your working bibliography:

Card and Microfiche Catalogues

Probably your most important sources will be your library's catalogues. Older catalogues consist of boxed index cards which list alphabetically every piece of printed or recorded material the library owns. Newer catalogues record listings on microfiches, pieces of positive film that are used with a mechanical reader that shines light through the film. In either case, for each book there are usually three cards or three fiches, one organized by author, one by title, and one by subject (see pages 333–34 for samples). The author card or fiche is the basic one; the others duplicate it with title or subject heading typed across the top.

The different kinds of cards or fiches provide different pathways to the information you are seeking. You may, for instance, remember that a particular author writes well on the subject that interests you. Finding that author's name in the catalogue will lead you to the books you want. Or you may remember a title but not the author; the title card will be most useful to you in this case. Finally, if you know neither author nor title but have only a subject in mind, the card or microfiche catalogue lists books under the subject headings you have identified using the *Library of Congress Subject Headings* or *Canadian Subject Headings* lists.

It is useful to read the explanatory key printed with the sample microfiche entries shown below. Knowing the meaning of the data on a fiche or card can help you select books on your topic that are of specific rather than just general use. For example, the data may include information on the book's contents: whether or not it contains an index or a bibliography, illustrations, maps, graphs, and so on. When you can quickly assimilate this information, you can make a much shrewder choice of books to add to your working bibliography than can a researcher who lacks this skill. For another example, it may be useful to pay attention to dates of publication and information on the edition of the book (how many times it has been revised and reissued). As a researcher, you may be making a good choice by consulting a recently published book on your topic, but you may also find that a book first published, say, ten years ago, is now marked ''4th ed.'' This information suggests that the book may be on its way to achieving status close to that of a standard in its field, by virtue of its having been reissued so often in such a relatively short period of time.

Sample Microfiche Entries

①→ **CANADA—HISTORY—1945–**
②→ 1986
③→ Granatstein, J. L. , 1939–
④→ Canada 1957–1967 : the years of uncertainty and innovation /
    J.L. Granatstein.—Toronto : McClelland and Stewart, c1986.
⑤→   xv, 375 p. ; 24 cm.
    1. Canada—History—1945–   . 2. Canada—Politics and ←⑥
    government—1957–1963. 3. Canada—Politics and government
    —1963–1968.
   ● FC 620 G72 1986 KEC C.1-2 ←⑦
   ● FC 620 G72 1986 Langara C.1   56379039 ←⑧

1. Subject Heading

2. Year of Publication

3. Author's Name: following name, author's dates are often given.

4. Title of book, repetition of author's name, place of publication, name of publisher, date of publication or copyright.

5. Number of pages (roman numerals indicate pages of introductory matter); illustrations, if present; height of book in centimetres. (This book is small enough to be found in its regular shelf place; large books are often shelved on a separate large-size shelf.)

6. Other subject headings under which this book may be found.

7. Call number under the Library of Congress system. (This listing comes from the catalogue of Vancouver Community College Library. The College has three campuses, and each campus has its own branch of the Library. "KEC C.1-2" indicates there are two copies of the book at King Edward Campus; "Langara C.1" indicates one copy is held at Langara Campus.)

8. The eight-numeral number in the lower right corner presents no useful information to a researcher; it is of interest only to the cataloguer.

> **CANADA—POLITICS AND GOVERNMENT—**
> **CARICATURES AND CARTOONS**
> 1980
> Macpherson, Duncan Ian, 1924–
> Daily smile : a travelling exhibition of original Duncan ←①
>   Macpherson cartoons, donated to the Public Archives of Canada
>   by the Toronto Star = Sourire quotidien : une exposition ←②
>   itinérante de caricatures originales signées Duncan Macpherson
>   et données aux Archives publiques du Canada par le Toronto
>   Star / organized by Denis Castonguay, Deborah McNeill and
>   Douglas Schoenherr.—Hull, Quebec : Minister of Supply and
>   Services, 1980. 227 p. : ill. ←③
>   1. Includes indexes. 2. Caricatures and cartoons—Canada. 3.
>   government—Politics and government—Caricatures and cartoons.
> ● NC 1449 M26 Langara C.1   56349255

1. The description following the title contains useful information: "a travelling exhibition . . ." tells you that before appearing in book form, the cartoons and accompanying text toured the country as an art exhibit; "donated . . ." means that although the cartoons are in the possession of the Public Archives of Canada, *The Toronto Star* owns the copyright.

2. The title and description appear in both English and French, indicating that the text is printed in both languages.

3. The text is illustrated. (The cartoons are illustrations.)

One problem presented by both card and microfiche catalogues is that they are often not as current as they could be. Libraries are continually receiving new materials, and much time and energy are required from library staff to enter each new title into the catalogue. Paper cards require the most time to update. Microfiches require less, but even so, they are updated only twice each year. If you want to look over the most recently acquired books to see if they include a book you can use, you had best check your library's "New Arrivals" list or speak to a librarian.

However, thanks to recent technological developments, the problem of slow updating of catalogues will gradually fade into history. If your university or college library is among the most technogically advanced, it may have begun introducing a computerized on-line catalogue.

The Public Access Catalogue

Many institutional libraries are converting to computerized catalogues, generally called the Public Access Catalogue. Where this is occurring, libraries are dispensing altogether with the listing of new acquisitions in traditional card and microfiche catalogues (typically, any of the library's holdings acquired since the late 1970s). A researcher using an on-line catalogue, instead of hunting through boxes of paper cards or scanning a microfiche by optical reader, views the listing on a computer terminal display screen. Because the information in each entry is organized in the same way it is in the traditional catalogues, you, the researcher, do not need to learn a new way of reading the entries. All you need to learn are the few simple commands to be typed at the computer terminal. When the majority of institutional and other major libraries have adopted the Public Access Catalogue and have integrated the *PAC* with the major database services, most of the information in the civilized world may become available for research from a single computer terminal. Of course, such database services can already be tapped from most libraries (see "Computer Databases," following the next section on using Periodical Literature).

Lists of Periodicals

Other than books, a major source of information is periodicals: journals, magazines, newspapers, and other serials. Researchers who want to locate a periodical may begin by consulting the following:

Canadian Serials Directory/Répertoire des publications sériées canadiennes: this lists periodicals and serials currently being published in both French and English in Canada.

Gale Directory of Publications (formerly *Ayer Directory of Publications*): this annual guide is a standard source of information about newspapers and magazines published in Canada, the United States, and Puerto Rico.

The Serials Directory: An International Reference Book: this lists periodicals around the world; it first appeared in 1986.

Ulrich's International Periodicals Directory: this also lists periodicals around the world; it and *The Serials Directory* are competitors.

Indexes to Periodical Literature
Articles in newspapers and magazines are an important source for research material, but they are not listed in the library's catalogue and must be sought in the various indexes to periodical literature. The major indexes for articles on a wide variety of subjects published in non-specialized magazines are the *Canadian Periodical Index/ Index de périodiques canadiens*, the *Canadian Magazine Index*, and the *Reader's Guide to Periodical Literature* (the last especially for U.S. periodicals). These are published each month and then accumulated in annual volumes. Articles are indexed by subject and author and by titles of certain creative works.

The *Canadian Periodical Index/Index de périodiques canadiens* lists French and English language journals having significant Canadian or regional content, including seventeen relevant American journals. General subjects covered are art/culture, business, Canadian perspectives, computer science, consumers, education, environment, health sciences, humanities, information/media, international perspectives, literature, sciences/technology, and social sciences. As well as appearing in book form, the *CPI* list is also available on-line as part of the Info Globe News package (see "On-line Retrieval Systems," page 341). Here is a sample listing from the printed index:

CAMBODIAN conflict
               Atrocities
   Journey to Angkor Wat 3: Komar's story. Kathleen
      Gough. il. *Can Dimension* 21 no 8 (Ja '88):
      p39-41
CAMCO Inc
   Camco: the appliance industry leader. Better than
      30% of the market [stock analysis]. Roland Jones.
      tab. *Investor's Digest* 20 no 1 (Ja 5 '88): p7
CAMERON, Duncan, editor
   Free trade papers; book review. Duncan Cameron,
      ed. *Studies in Political Economy* no 24 (autumn
      '87): p151-7
CAMERON, Elspeth
   Home is where the heart is. *Chatelaine* 60 no 12
      (D '87): p57,105-6
   Vicki Miller: angel of mercy or fanatic? In her
      passionate crusade for animal rights, no act is too
      flamboyant, no strategy too outrageous. port.
      Chatelaine 60 no 11 (N '87): p69,97 +
CAMERON, Silver Donald
   First cruise: would you want to go to sea in a vessel
      built by a novelist? il. *Can Yachting* 13 no 1 (Ja
      '88): p48-50,52 +
CAMERON, Stevie
   Like magic: Frank Moores's Ottawa lobbying firm
      can pull contracts out of government like rabbits
      out of hats. port. *Report on Business Mag* 4 no 8
      (F '88): p49-56,58

(*Canadian Periodical Index/Index de périodiques canadiens* 41.1 [Toronto: 1988]
23.)

In many ways similar to the *CPI*, the *Canadian Magazine Index*
provides a guide to popular, special interest, and academic magazines, including eighteen relevant American magazines. Its coverage
includes arts, business, children's literature, computers, cookery,
education, geography, health, history, hobbies, nature, recreation,
regional interest, science, and social sciences. Like the *CPI*, the *CMI*
is available on-line. Unlike the *CPI*, which blends authors and subjects in a single list, the *CMI* lists subjects and personal names
separately, as you can see in the following sample listings:

Cambodia
Journey to Angkor Wat: III. Komar's Story
● *CDN DIMENSION* 21(8) Ja'88
p39-41
Camco Inc.
Camco: the appliance industry leader ▼
INVESTORS DIGEST 20(1) Ja 5'88 p7
Camcorders
See Camera recorders

Cameron, Duncan
Editor: [The Free Trade Papers]
BOOK REVIEW *CDN PUBLIC
POLICY* 13(4) D'87 p538-539
Cameron, Peter A
[Chromalox Inc appointment]
● *FINANCIAL POST*
82(1) Ja 4'88 p4
[Chromalox Inc appointment
● *FINANCIAL TIMES*
76(29) Ja 4'88 p29
Cameron, Roy
Author: Behavioral intervention for
health promotion: developing a
partnership between research
producers and research
consumers **Bibl.** *CDN JNL
PUBLIC HEALTH* 78(6) N/D'87
pS15-S20
Cameron, Silver D
Author: First cruise: would you
want to go to sea in a vessel
built by a novelist? ●
CDN YACHTING 13(1) Ja'88
p48-53 +
Cameron, Stevie
Author: Like magic ●
REPORT ON BUSINESS MAG
4(8) F'88 p49-56 +

Specialized Indexes
In addition to the periodical indexes, you can consult a large number of specialized indexes by subject area. The following partial list includes some of the major ones, listed according to Library of Congress Call Number. The title appears on the left and the Call Number on the right:

Essay and General Literature Index	REF AI 3 .E752
Humanities Index	REF AI 3 .H855
Social Sciences Index	REF AI 3 .R49
Psychological Abstracts	REF BF 1 .P72
Biography Index	REF CT 104 .B5
Sports and Recreation Index	REF GV 182 .Z976
Public Affairs Information Service	REF H 41 .Z963
Business Periodicals Index	REF HF 1 .Z928
Canadian Business Index	REF HF 1 .Z933
Sociological Abstracts	REF HM 1 .S67
Index to Canadian Legal Periodical Literature	REF KE 8 .Z943
Education Index	REF L 1 .Z944
Resources in Education	REF L 1 .Z974
Art Index	REF N 1 .Z937
General Science Index	REF Q 1 .Z944
Microcomputer Index	REF QA 76.5 .M527
Cumulative Abridged Index Medicus	REF R 5 .Z938
Biological and Agricultural Index	REF S 1 .Z925
Engineering Index	REF TA 9 .Z945
Consumers' Index	REF TX 335 .C676

As well as these, numerous other, even more specialized indexes are available and listed in your library's catalogue. Look in the catalogue for the listings that follow a subject or author entry and that have the word **BIBLIOGRAPHY** or **INDEX** printed across the top.

Note: all indexes, including the *Reader's Guide*, the *Canadian Periodical Index*, and the *Canadian Magazine Index*, supply the reader with keys to their abbreviations. The ''key'' pages usually appear at the front of the volume. Looking over these pages before you begin to search the volume can usually save you a great deal of time.

Indexes to Current Issues
Very useful for topics of current interest as well as for topics that require day-to-day information are The *New York Times Index* and the *Canadian News Index*. The latter lists selected articles from major daily newspapers in six Canadian cities: Calgary, Halifax, Montreal, Toronto, Vancouver, and Winnipeg. The *CNI* is also available on-line. Here is a sample listing from the printed version of the *CNI*:

> **Cambodia**
> *See also* Kampuchea
> Sihanouk ready to stand alone on Cambodia
>   deal ● *G&M* Ja 9'88 pA9
> Troops could pull out of Cambodia this year,
>   Vietnamese sources say *G&M* Ja 13'88
>   pA1,A2
> **Camcorders**   *See* Camera recorders

(*Canadian News Index* 12.1 [Toronto: Micromedia, 1988] 16.)

Government Documents
Federal governments publish an enormous amount of material on numerous subjects. Guides to this literature are the *Government of Canada Publications Catalogue* and, for U.S. government materials, the *Monthly Catalog of United States Government Publications*.

Computer Databases
With the help of your librarian, you may be able to add to your working bibliography by searching on-line information retrieval systems, the electronic equivalent of printed references. If your library provides such a service—and most do—it has computer terminals capable of logging on to an international network of database files by means of telephone. Some databases are also available on compact disks (CD-ROM) that can be searched at the library on its own

microcomputers. The librarian will ask you to co-operate by providing such information as the topic or possible title of your essay, at least three words (keywords) that the computer can use in the search, and specific ways in which you want to narrow the search. .When the search is complete, you may be rewarded with citations of various printed materials appropriate to your topic, along with summaries of their contents. One drawback is that you will be charged money for making such searches. The cost may not equal the benefit for your specific research project. The librarian you consult will be able to help you determine whether or not a search is worthwhile.

Databases come in two major forms: bibliographic databases, which closely resemble traditional printed indexes, and full text databases, which more often than not provide—as the label suggests—the complete text of an article or book. Typically, a database is tapped through an information service company (a kind of information bank) such as Info Globe News, which provides access to a number of different databases. Some of the major service companies are listed below, including a sampling of their databases.

On-line Retrieval Systems

CAN/OLE (maintained and operated by CISTI, the Canada Institute for Scientific and Technical Information) allows a user to access information on a large variety of subjects from agriculture and aquatic sciences for example, through fisheries, geology, metallurgy, and physics, to the social sciences/humanities and transportation. A sampling of databases includes BOREAL (all aspects of polar and cold regions), ELIAS (from archaeology to wildlife), STATCAN (references to Statistics Canada publications), MICROLOG (literature from government and institutional publications), and OONL (all subjects about Canada or written by Canadians).

DIALOG (American based) provides access to nearly 300 databases in business, chemistry, current events, economics, engineering, general science, law, medicine, social sciences, technology, and more. It also provides indexes to book reviews and biographies; directories of companies, people, and associations; and full text of many newspapers and journals. Some of its specific databases are *The Academic American Encyclopedia*, the Architecture Database, British Official Publications, Canadian Business and Current Affairs (including the *Canadian Business Index*, *Canadian Foreign Relations*, the *Canadian Magazine Index*, and *Canadian News Index*), the Educational Resources Information Centre (ERIC), Japan Technology, MEDLINE (index to biomedical literature), Soviet Science and Technology, and *Ulrich's International Periodicals Directory*. *DIALOG* also makes some of its databases (such as ERIC and MEDLINE) available on compact disk.

IAC (the American based Information Access Company) provides its ACADEMIC INDEX on compact disk, indexing 375 scholarly and general interest journals on current events, general science, and the humanities and social sciences.

Info Globe News (Canadian based) specializes in information about Canadian business and current affairs. For instance, it provides the *Canadian Periodical Index* (bibliographic list), full text of *The Globe and Mail*, full text of selected Federal and Provincial budget speeches and other papers, and full text of press releases from the Federal Department of Finance, Revenue Canada, and Statistics Canada (all since 1977).

Infomart Online (Canadian based) provides access to the full text of major Canadian newspapers such as the Ottawa *Citizen*, the *Financial Times*, *The Vancouver Sun*, and *The Windsor Star*. Through the DATATIMES database, it provides a gateway to literally millions of American newspaper stories, and through the DOW JONES NEWS/RETRIEVAL database, access to *The Wall Street Journal* and many other business and investment databases.

ScholarNET (American based) consists of two systems: PoliNET specializes in political science, criminal justice, and public administration; HumaNET specializes in history, philosophy, religion, and English. Also, through ScholarNET, a researcher can access *DIALOG*.

Wilsonline (American based) makes over 25 databases available, most of them bibliographic, e.g., *Business Periodicals Index* (since 1982), *General Science Index* (since 1984), *Humanities Index* (since 1984), *Reader's Guide to Periodical Literature* (since 1983), and *Social Sciences Index* (since 1983).

Note: One limitation of on-line databases is that they provide information for recent years only, as the description of Wilsonline indicates. The oldest of the retrieval services goes back only to the late 1970s. For earlier information, a researcher must still consult the traditional printed sources.

The Library's Serial List
Once you have identified the magazines, journals, newspapers, and any other serials that you think you may find useful, your final step before beginning to read them is to ascertain whether or not your library actually holds the material. Find this out by checking your library's Serial List, usually available on microfiche or in printed form.

TEST YOURSELF ON
Sources of Information

Using your research paper topic or a sample topic provided by one of your instructors, make a list of subject headings under which you may find sources of information. Take the list to the library and look up each subject heading in the following sources:

1. The *Canadian Periodical Index/Index de périodiques canadiens*

2. The microfiche or card catalogue

3. The *Canadian News Index*

Add to your list of subject headings as you discover new ones. Which source was best for your topic? Why?

Setting Up the Working Bibliography

The mechanics of setting up your working bibliography are simple, even though they may appear tedious. No matter how mechanical the job may seem, if you establish good work habits at this stage, your life while you work on developing the essay will be relatively free from stress. Ignoring the meticulousness required at this point will probably cause you grief later, a fact attested to by the experience of millions of researchers.

As was mentioned earlier, you record your working bibliography on a series of index cards. Use one card for each book, article, pamphlet, film, or whatever other source you are referring to. Look over the sample cards that follow, one for a book and the other for a journal article. Note the information recorded on them, and consider carefully the reasons given for including each piece of information.

PS
8585
Y4
E3

Ryga, George

The Ecstasy of Rita Joe and Other Plays. Intro. by Brian Parker. Toronto: New Press, 1971.

- Copy of play plus good intro.

1. In the upper left corner of the first card is the Call Number of the book; once you have noted it here, you need not return to consult the catalogue every time you want the book. The second card lacks a Call Number because the journal was available on the current periodical shelves.
2. In the upper right corner of both cards is a number supplied by the researcher. These items were the eighth and ninth recorded.

> 9
>
> Boire, Gary. "Wheels on Fire:
> The Train of Thought in George
> Rygaʼs _The Ecstasy of Rita Joe._"
> _Canadian Literature_ 113–114 (Summer-
> Fall, 1987): 62–74.
> –Rygaʼs use of train imagery compared
> to Alex Colvilleʼs painting "Horse and Train"

To save time while working on your rough draft of the essay, you can use this item number instead of formal documentation. You can also use this number when making notes.

3. The chief information is the name of author, the title, and the facts of publication, including page numbers if the item is an article or is part of an anthology. It is important to record these details exactly; you will use this card for your final list of Works Cited.

4. Finally, you can make a note to remind yourself of an especially important feature of the item.

When you transfer the bibliographic information from these index cards to the Works Cited page at the end of your essay, it is essential to use the correct form for each kind of entry. What follows is a series of sample entries for various kinds of books, articles, and other materials. You may use these samples as models for your own bibliography. Note carefully the order in which information is presented and the exact punctuation and spacing used to separate the items. For examples of complete Works Cited lists, refer to those that conclude the sample research papers.

Bibliographic Form: Sample Entries

Book

Munro, Alice. The Progress of Love. Toronto: McClelland,
   1986.

Note: It is acceptable to abbreviate the names of publishers. In this item, for example, ''McClelland and Stewart'' has been shortened to ''McClelland.'' (See page 373.)

Book by More Than One Author

Artibise, A. F. J., and Gilbert A. Stelter. Canada's Urban Past:
   A Bibliography and Guide to Urban Studies. Vancouver:
   U of British Columbia P, 1981.

Article from a Book in Several Volumes

Fraser, Allan M. "The Newfoundland Archives." The Book of
   Newfoundland. Ed. Joseph R. Smallwood. 6 vols. St.
   John's: Newfoundland, 1937–1975. 4: 187–9.

Later or Revised Edition

Moss, John. A Reader's Guide to the Canadian Novel.
   2nd ed. Toronto: McClelland, 1987.

Article from an Edited Collection

Pacey, Desmond. "The Course of Canadian Criticism." A
   Literary History of Canada: Canadian Literature in
   English. Ed. Karl F. Klinck. 2nd ed. 3 vols. Toronto:
   U of Toronto P, 1976. 3: 16–31.

Article from a General Reference Work

"Page, Patricia Kathleen (Mrs. William Arthur
   Irwin)." Canadian Who's Who. 1987 ed.

"Nahanni National Park." <u>The Canadian Encyclopedia.</u>

    3 vols. Edmonton: Hurtig, 1985.

Article from a Weekly or Monthly Magazine

Cameron, Duncan. "The Dealers." <u>This Magazine</u>. Feb. 1988:

    18–23.

Shortell, Ann. "Policing the Stock Market." <u>Maclean's</u> 3 Aug.

    1987: 32–33.

Note: Observe that all months except May, June, and July are abbreviated. Where you are citing an unsigned article, simply begin with the title.

Article from a Learned Journal

Barnes, Gordon E. "Canadian Indian Health: A Needs Assess-

    ment Project." <u>The Canadian Journal of Native Studies</u>

    5.1 (1985): 11–25.

Article from a Newspaper

Kohut, John. "Banks Showing More Caution Regarding Third

    World Loans." <u>The Globe and Mail</u> 7 Aug. 1987: B6.

Note: Observe that August is abbreviated and that the notation ''B6'' means the story appears on page 6 of section B. If the article is unsigned, simply begin with the title.

Public Document

Canada. Parliament. House of Commons. <u>Debates, Official</u>

    <u>Report</u>, 32nd Parl., 1st sess., vol. 5. Ottawa: Supply and

    Services Canada, 1980.

Interview—Personal

Taylor, Carole. Personal Interview. 12 Feb. 1988.

Interview—Printed

Galdikas, Birute.   Interview.   Omni July 1987: 76–85+.

Interview—Radio or Television

Roberts, James.   Interview.   The Gary Bannerman
　　Show.   CKNW, New Westminster.   11 Mar. 1988.

Film, Radio or Television Program

Bayo.   Dir. Mort Ransen.   Jape, NFB, CBC, 1984.   98 min.

"Puffins and Their Prey."   The Nature of Things.   Dir. and
　　Prod. Richard Donovan and James Murray.   With David
　　Suzuki.   CBC, 1987.

Note: If you are concentrating on the contribution of a particular
person, begin with the person's name instead of the title of the film
or program.

Recording

Peacock, Kenneth.   Songs of the Newfoundland Out-
　　ports.   Pigeon Inlet, PIP-7319, 1984.

Computer Software

WordPerfect.   Version 4.1.   Satellite Software International,
　　1985.

Material from an On-Line Computer Service

Schomer, Howard.   "South Africa: Beyond Fair Employ-
　　ment."   Harvard Business Review May-June 1983: 145+.
　　DIALOG file 122, item 119425 833160.

This last example is drawn from the *MLA Handbook for Writers of
Research Papers* (1984). Refer to this book for examples of entries
encountered more rarely than those listed here.

　　Other styles than the MLA style are used by certain publications.

Anthropological and psychological journals, for example, follow the standards of procedure described in the *Publication Manual of the American Psychological Association* (1983). Specific examples will best demonstrate the differences between APA style for items in a "Reference List" and MLA style for items in "Works Cited":

APA Style

Schell, Jonathan. (1982). The Fate of the Earth. New York:

Knopf.

Smith, John Maynard. (1978, September). The evolution of

human behavior. Scientific American, pp. 176–192.

MLA Style

Schell, Jonathan.   The Fate of the Earth.   New York: Knopf,

1982.

Smith, John Maynard.   "The Evolution of Human Behav-

ior."   Scientific American Sept. 1978: 176–92.

Papers written for journals specializing in the physical sciences may require yet other styles: e.g., the Council of Biology Editors has published a manual for papers printed in biological journals. Other manuals exist for chemistry, geology, linguistics, mathematics, medicine, and physics. For additional information, see Robert A. Day's *How to Write and Publish a Scientific Paper*, the resource referred to in the section on "Documenting Scientific Papers" (see page 372).

Setting Up a List of Works Cited

In order to document quotations, summaries, or paraphrases of the works of others, you need a page in your research essay called "Works Cited." On this page, you give full information on every source that you use in your essay. To do this job, simply take those working bibliography cards you collected while you did your research and put them in alphabetical order according to the authors' last names. For unsigned material, alphabetize the first word of the title that is not *The* or *A*. Then simply type the information on the cards in a list that looks exactly like the Works Cited page of the sample research paper (see page 413). Be sure to follow the same spacing and indentation that the sample uses: each entry begins flush with the left margin, subsequent lines are indented five spaces, and the whole page is double spaced. Be careful to follow the punctuation of the sample (or the sample entries above), and notice that none of the items is numbered.

The method you use to refer to individual Works Cited entries in the body of your essay is considered under Documentation (see page 363).

TEST YOURSELF ON

Bibliographic Form

Using the sample entries as models, set up working bibliography cards for each of the following items and then organize them in a Works Cited list:

1. A book by Claude Levi-Strauss called Structural Anthropology, translated by Claire Jacobson and Brooke G. Scoepf and published in New York City in 1963 by Basic Books, Inc.

2. A review (called Lost in the City of Light) of the film Frantic, appearing in the issue of *Maclean's* magazine that was published on March 14, 1988. It was written by Lawrence O'Toole.

3. A book in fourteen volumes edited by G. R. Potter called The New Cambridge Modern History, published in Cambridge by the Cambridge University Press in 1957.

4. A newspaper article by Jamie Lamb called Plainly Guilty, Canada Bows to Fish Ruling, published on the third page of the B section of The Vancouver Sun for March 22, 1988.

5. A book edited by Gordon Ripley and Anne Mercer called Who's Who in Canadian Literature 1987–88. It was published in 1987 by Reference Press in Toronto.

Reading and Taking Notes

You are now ready to begin a period of intensive reading of the material in your working bibliography. How do you go about it and how do you take notes on what you read?

First, avoid overloading yourself. That is, avoid all emergency schedules—such as all-night sessions or forty-eight hour squeezes. Instead, plan on a reading period of two weeks, during which you read in the library or your room for two to three hours every working day.

Second, read the whole of each article on your list but not the whole of each book. When using books, you should learn to look carefully at the indexes and tables of contents so that you can select chapters or shorter passages that relate directly to your topic. If you're working on the ecology of Western Red Cedar, you can limit your reading of *Trees and Shrubs of British Columbia* to just a few pages. It's important that you learn to pick your way selectively through the jungle of data to find precisely what you need.

Two things will guide your note-taking. One will be a rough outline. You will object at this point that you can hardly have any kind of outline since you have not yet begun to read. However, at this time, you *will* have a research question, and most research questions lead to a very rough outline:

TOPIC: Mandatory retirement
QUESTION: Should it be abolished?
ROUGH OUTLINE: **I. Advantages of retirement at ages 65–70**
    A. Advantages to individual
    B. Advantages to society
    II. Disadvantages of retirement at a prescribed age
    A. Disadvantages to individual
    B. Disadvantages to society

As you can see, your note-taking should aim to fill in these divisions.

Your good instincts will guide you in note-taking. They will help you to decide what needs noting. These instincts, sharpened by general reading and some acquaintance with your field, will also enable you to write the *personal observation note*, which may make an important contribution to your paper. Here is a sample of such a note:

> Why is 65 the usual mandatory retirement age? Many people have many good years left and like to work.

As you can see, the note does not cite facts or quotations or ideas from the source. Rather, it makes a tentative evaluation of the field of research and nudges the researcher's mind along toward his or her eventual thesis statement.

In addition to the personal observation note, it is possible to make three other kinds of notes: the *summary*, the *paraphrase* and the *direct quotation*.

The summary can condense information or a narrative. In summarizing, you give the essential details in your own concise words. You must be careful not to distort the meaning of the original. You may, however, omit a certain level of unimportant detail. Such omissions are not distortions.

Original

Alice Anne Munro was born on 10 July 1931, in Wingham, Ontario, the eldest of three children of Robert Eric and Anne Chamney Laidlaw. Her father was a marginal farmer, raising silver foxes during the depression years, switching to turkey farming during the 1940s, and augmenting the fluctuating family income by working as a night watchman in the local foundry. At a fairly advanced age, he began writing articles and sketches about his own life, and just before his death in 1976 he completed a novel about a pioneer southwestern Ontario family, which was edited and published after his death as *The McGregors: A Novel of an Ontario Pioneer Family* (1979). Alice's mother had been an elementary-school teacher in Alberta and Ontario before her marriage, an occupation she was not permitted to pursue in the unemployment-ridden Ontario of the depression. Like many of the unfulfilled and despairing mothers of Munro's fiction, she expended her energies during the formative years of the three Laidlaw children in the nurturing of a family

under conditions of deprivation and hardship. She fought a long and painful battle with Parkinson's disease, to which she succumbed in 1959, a situation poignantly evoked in such stories as "The Peace of Utrecht" and "The Ottawa Valley."
(Hallvard Dahlie, "Alice Munro," *Canadian Writers and Their Works*, ed. R. Lecker, J. David, E. Quigley, 7 vols. [Toronto: ECW, 1985] 7: 215.)

Poor Summary

Alice Anne Munro was born on 10 July 1931, in Wingham, Ontario, to Robert Eric and Anne Chamney Laidlaw. Robert Laidlaw was a farmer who raised foxes during the depression and moved over to raising turkeys during World War II. He added to his income by working as a night watchman. As an old man, he wrote about his own life and finished a novel called *The MacGregors: A Novel of an Ontario Pioneer Family* (published in 1979) just before his death in 1976. Anne Laidlaw had worked as a school teacher in Alberta and Ontario before she was married but could not do this work during the depression in Ontario. Instead, she devoted herself to nurturing her children until she died in 1959. Munro wrote about this in a number of stories, e.g., "The Ottawa Valley."

Better Summary

Alice Anne Munro was born on 10 July 1931, in Wingham, Ontario, the eldest child of Robert and Anne Laidlaw. Her father worked at various jobs, breeding foxes during the depression and farming turkeys during the 1940s. In his later years, he wrote sketches of his own life and completed a novel, edited and published in 1979—three years after his death. Although Alice's mother had been a school teacher prior to her marriage, she could not find a teaching job during the depression. Professionally unfulfilled and personally unhappy, she gave her life to raising her family, dying in 1959 of Parkinson's disease. Munro has touchingly pictured her mother's pain and frustration in some of her short stories.

The poor summary is wordy and sometimes awkward, as in the choppy final sentence. While including inessential facts such as the title of Robert Laidlaw's novel, the poor summary omits the detail that Munro's mother died of Parkinson's disease, which in the original and in the better summary, allows a reader to appreciate the frustration of her last years.

The *paraphrase* is also a condensation, but of an idea or an opinion or a train of reasoning, rather than of information or of a story. The paraphrase tries to stay close to the gist of the original but uses the language of the note-taker.

Original

Feminism is an ideology that seeks equal rights for women and while there are few who would publicly espouse an opposing view ("I'm sorry, dear, but I believe in chauvinism") there are all too many who prefer to believe that the game is over, the battle won, the struggle no longer necessary. There are those who think the struggle tasteless, who call feminist thought and writing "strident" and "humourless" when it touches them at all or suggests the world might change in any way.

There are those who'd like to believe that feminism is unnecessary. "Do you want to be considered a *woman* director/writer/actor?" one is asked. It's a question that seems to imply that to be a woman, to write of a woman's experience from a woman's perspective, is to aspire to something less than the "real" world where "real" men write of "real" concerns like how they fought with their fathers and what Daddy did in the war or the boardroom. (Carol Bolt, "Female Leads: Search for Feminism in the Theatre," *The Canadian Forum* June/July 1987: 37.)

Poor Paraphrase

Feminism seeks equal rights for women. While not many would profess an opposing view in public, too many prefer to think that the struggle is no longer necessary and that to continue it is tasteless, describing feminist writing as strident and lacking humour. Some people even believe that feminism is out of date, that wanting to be considered a *woman* director/writer/actor is wrong-headed. They imply that writing from a woman's perspective is aspiring to less than writing about the "real" world of "real" men and their "real" concerns, such as what Daddy did in the war.

Better Paraphrase

While few people would deny equal rights for women, too many take the position that this goal has been achieved. Some think that feminists who continue the struggle are too forceful and lack a sense of humour. Others believe the feminist stand unnecessary, that women who write, direct, and perform plays as *women* are less in touch with the real world than are similarly occupied men.

The better paraphrase avoids the language of the original wherever possible, while the poor paraphrase does not. Notice ''struggle is no longer necessary'' and ''a woman's perspective.'' The better paraphrase is briefer and more to the point.

In direct quotation, the note-taker must be careful to quote exactly. However, judgement can be used in omitting parts of the original as long as you do not distort the original by the way in which you've made your cuts.

Original

The issue of women's rights was not dealt with at the time because too many men felt uncomfortable about having to confront their own established attitudes.

Distorted Quotation

The issue of women's rights was not dealt with at the time because too many men felt uncomfortable . . . (The three dots signal a cut has been made, but this cut is distorting because it omits an essential point made in the original—that is, *why* the men felt uncomfortable.)

Acceptable Quotation

The issue of women's rights was not dealt with at the time because too many men felt uncomfortable about . . . their own established attitudes.

In general, a reader will be looking at what you have written in order to find out what *you* have to say. If what you've written consists of a series of quotations from sources, the reader is likely to be put off. Therefore, it is usually better to be sparing in your use of quotations.

Direct quotation should be used only when (1) you need to prove something, and only the actual words you have read will do that job; (2) you intend to criticize or to praise the actual words an author has used; or (3) the words are so appropriate, dramatic, emphatic, or witty that no paraphrase can do them justice. For example, if you were writing a paper on what distinguishes a great hockey player from a merely good player, you may choose to draw information from Ken Dryden's excellent analysis in *The Game*, particularly his use—as his theme's focus—of the Italian phrase *inventa la partita* (invent the game).

A great player's body is conditioned to respond to new situations without conscious thought. As Ken Dryden has written, when the player meets with an unusual challenge that poses a new question, his body "finds an answer he didn't know was there. He *invents the game*" (136).

For an example using a long quotation, see page 366.

As you read and take notes, you will become more expert at making wise decisions. You can always go back—after gaining some experience—and check to see what you can do to improve your notes.

After each reading session, you are likely to have several pages of notes. Whatever the number, you must now perform an important task. Read each note carefully and see what its essence is: that is, see if you can summarize each note in one or two words. Take a large felt-tip marker and write this term near the top. After your two-week reading period, you will have a large number of notes, ready to be organized by the subject headings you've written on each. These subject headings should correspond—or with slight revision can correspond—to the rough outline you had in mind before you started the period of intensive reading. In any case, they are needed for the next step: preparing an outline.

Preparing an Outline

An outline is an instrument for controlling the writing of a paper. It details the order in which you present your material. A *topic outline* is useful for the preliminary stages of a research paper because it assists you in ordering your reading and your notes. Here is a typical—and simple—topic outline for a paper on the issue of refugees in Canada:

    I. The refugee situation in Canada before 1987
    II. Public response to events of 1987
    III. Proposed legislation in 1987

This is an efficient way to order a chronological set of materials. But notice that while this kind of outline orders the material, it *says* nothing about that which it orders; it expresses no point of view, so that we have no idea of the writer's viewpoint on the material. A point of view can be provided by a *sentence outline*.

I. **The arrival of refugees in Canada before 1987 attracted little public interest.**

II. **Incidents occurring during 1987 caused many people to object to supposed "loopholes" in the law.**

III. **Proposed legislation was discussed during late 1987, intended to make the entry of undocumented immigrants more difficult.**

What makes this outline more useful than the topic outline is the fact that each of the roman numerals precedes a sentence—a statement which *says* something, which articulates a point of view, and which gives you direction as you write the paper.

What is most essential for the sentence outline is a thesis—a controlling, central point of view, the conclusion you have come to after all your reading and thinking about your topic. The thesis can emerge in one of two ways. (1) You have been, as you were engaged in intensive reading and note-taking, an avid reader of your own notes; each day, after you finished, you thought about the notes you had taken, the subject headings you had written across them, and the implications of all this. Now you read your notes one last time and suddenly your thesis appears full-blown in your mind. (2) You work on your notes in an organized way until your thesis emerges from your subject headings.

Writing the Thesis Statement

As you have been collecting information, you have kept in mind your topic and a question, or series of questions, relating to it. To devise a suitable thesis statement that will govern the direction of the whole essay, you will answer the major question about your topic in such a way that you make a value judgement. For instance, if your topic is "Mandatory Retirement" and your question is "Should it be abolished?" your thesis statement could read as follows: "In the light of the Charter of Rights, justice prescribes that mandatory retirement should be abolished." You have taken a position. You have a point of view to defend, and your essay will provide the argument defending it. (For more information on thesis statements, see the entry in Part 2.)

Writing the Outline

Now that you have a thesis, you are ready to "divide" your main point into subsidiary points. You do this by creating an outline. Each of the points in your sentence outline can be further developed. Your notes will provide some guidelines. The rest is up to you.

The following few rules may be useful if you want to check your outline against some standard before committing yourself to writing the essay.

1 No outline should be written unless you are sure the thesis is a satisfactory one. Here is an example of an unsatisfactory thesis:

> There are many advantages and disadvantages to mandatory retirement.

This is unsatisfactory because it is too vague—and would remain so even if it named some of the advantages and disadvantages it speaks of. It is also a failure in not saying specifically what the writer thinks *after* doing the research; a statement like this one could have been made *before* reading about the subject. Compare it to the thesis statement on page 357.

2 The outline should always divide its material logically. For example, consider this section of an outline:

> **II. Evidence of a disaster at the Chernobyl nuclear reactor grew day by day.**
> A. High atmospheric radio-activity was measured in Sweden.
> B. The Swiss reported increased radio-activity in their air.
> **III. Satellite photographs revealed a fire in the reactor buildings.**

Notice that roman numeral III should be capital C. It clearly refers back to roman numeral II and is in parallel form with A and B.

3 The outline should present its material in logical order. Consider this preliminary outline:

    I. Modern methods of early diagnosis cut down on heart disease fatalities.

   II. Treatment of heart disease was hampered before 1950 by inadequate diagnostic understanding.

  III. Treatment of heart disease cases used to consist of rest and only rest.

  IV. Modern treatment of heart attack is based on the theory of prevention by physical and psychological conditioning.

Can you rearrange these into a more logical order? If you changed I to III, kept IV, and changed II and III to I and II, respectively, you have a good eye for logical order.

Writing the Paper

If you have done your work efficiently to this point, you now have an outline in hand and batches of notes in the same order as the divisions in that outline. You are ready to write the essay.

The Mechanics

You should be prepared to write at least two drafts. It is not inappropriate to suggest, in fact, that you write as many drafts as you need to write; it is hard to imagine extra attention spoiling your work. Depending on your preference in work habits, you may either write your drafts in longhand or type them; either way, be sure to keep careful track of your notes and documentation from draft to draft. (See Documentation, below, for detailed information.)

When you are ready for a final draft, it should be typed on good white bond, 21.5 × 28 cm, on one side of the page only. You should supply a title page (see Sample Research Paper) and a final bibliography (Works Cited list). All of these should be proofread carefully.

Finally, you should know that there are a variety of words and phrases available to use in introducing quoted material. It is useful rhetorical strategy, for example, to introduce a quote with an expression like ''as the noted astronomer and cosmologist Carl Sagan has observed . . .'' In this way, you let the reader know that an authority's words are about to be spoken, and the reader might be appropriately impressed. In any case, there are many ways to introduce quotations and you should think about the values inherent in each. For your convenience, here is a small list (there are many others):

As Prof. X *declared*   Margaret Thatcher *asserted that*
Dr. Falk *notes*   Mulroney *summarized it as*
Winston Churchill *observed*   In Kennedy's *analysis*
As Pablo Picasso *put it*   By Freud's *definition*
Nietzsche *has written that*

The Rhetoric

Everything you know about writing should, of course, be applied to the writing of the research paper. But this paper presents a special problem that you have not encountered before: the necessity to weave into your paper materials taken from a number of sources. The way to deal with this problem is to take the approach that these materials are *not* in and of themselves the heart of your paper; the heart of your paper is *your* purpose in writing, the thesis that you have set out to present. Once you have made the decision to take this approach, the materials you have been collecting will fall into their proper place. That is, you will see that they are to be used for your purposes, *woven* into the texture of your paper to support and illustrate your thesis and *not* haphazardly strung together like numerous odd beads because they are all you have to show.

Documentation

What to Document

In a research paper, you must tell the reader where you found your material. The telling is known as documentation. It takes the form

of a parenthetical reference* in the body of your text to the source
of any of the following:

1. A direct quotation, the actual words someone has used.
2. Statistics, including graphs, tables, charts, maps, or diagrams
   taken from someone else's work.
3. A summary or condensation of someone else's narrative or array
   of facts.
4. Your paraphrase of someone else's ideas or opinions.

   You need not document details you did not know before you
began work on the paper *provided those details are considered common
knowledge in the field of your topic*. For example, if you're
writing on some aspect of the history of Canada from 1960 through
1963, you need not document the names of Prime Ministers or other
members of the cabinet. Such facts are considered common knowledge
in the history of that period.

Plagiarism and the Ethics of Authorship

In working with other people's material—an invariable part of writing
a research paper—you are faced with two ethical considerations.
The first is the necessity to acknowledge the debt you owe to a source
for words, ideas, or facts. The failure to make such acknowledgments
is a serious breach of ethics known as plagiarism. For plagiarism,
published writers are subject to court action and student writers to
disciplinary action by the schools they attend. The second consideration
is the duty you have to present with absolute fairness the
essential meaning of what you are quoting. Failure to make such a
presentation is at best carelessness and at worst deception.

   To ensure that you are not guilty of plagiarism, you should be
scrupulous in acknowledging your sources, whether you paraphrase
or quote directly. Moreover, you should transcribe quoted material
exactly as you find it in your source, being sure to include every
punctuation mark, because even a misplaced comma can alter the
meaning of a passage.

---

*It may also take the form of a superscript number referring a reader to an endnote.
The superscript system, often called the footnote system, is discussed on pages 368–73.

To avoid deceiving a reader, you should quote a passage without distorting its essential meaning. For example, suppose you had in your notes a quoted passage such as this one:

> The Canadian father seems solidly behind his teenage child, though numerous research studies and cultural articles like novels and television shows indicate that he is greatly troubled by his child's participation in the drug culture or his early involvement with sex. He is proud of his teenager's accomplishments and is likely to support teenage pursuits in sports, hobbies, or socializing, but he admits to little awareness of how to provide discipline or vocational guidance.

Since you have at your disposal an ellipsis (. . .) to indicate an omission, you might quote in your paper a shortened version of the passage:

> The Canadian father seems solidly behind his teenage child. . . . He is proud of his accomplishments and is likely to support teenage pursuits. . . .

This, however, would be a deceptive distortion, since the original passage clearly shows the parent to be much more uncertain than the abbreviated quotation would suggest.

To be sure that your work follows the highest ethical standard, the best guidelines are these: quote with accuracy, convey the essential meaning of what you are quoting, and acknowledge the source of the quotation. To acknowledge the source, use either a parenthetical reference to a list of works cited or a superscript numeral referring to an end note.

Parenthetical References

The list of works cited at the end of your paper will be one part of your documentation of sources. The other part will be a brief parenthetical reference in the body of your text giving the last name of the author or shortened title of a book or article together with a page number.

The following samples of various kinds of parenthetical references have been adapted from the *MLA Handbook for Writers of Research Papers* (1984). Take careful note of the placement of the various punctuation marks in each example.

References to Authors

Parenthetical Reference to Author and Page Number

To a dedicated jogger, the pain of shin splints is not so much

an adequate reason to stop running as it is a joyous signal

that he is doing his duty by his body (Rovit 319).

 Note: In the parenthetical reference there is no comma after
Rovit and neither *p.* nor *page* before the number.
 To find the full details on this source, the reader looks under *R*
in Works Cited.

Entry in Works Cited

Rovit, Earl H.   Fitness and the Music of Pain.   Boston: Little,

1985.

 If the author's name appears within the text itself, only the page
number is needed in parentheses.

Author's Name in the Text

Rovit insists that to a dedicated jogger the pain of shin splints

is not so much an adequate reason to stop running as it is a

joyous signal that he is doing his duty by his body (319).

Rovit (319) insists that to a dedicated jogger the pain of shin

splints is not so much an adequate reason to stop running as

it is a joyous signal that he is doing his duty by his body.

Note: The placement of the parentheses should interfere as little as
possible with the reader's concentration on the flow of your words.
Therefore, parentheses should go where there is a natural pause in
the sentence, that is, before a comma, or at the end, before a period.
Of course, they should go as near as possible to the borrowed material. By this rule, then, the placement of *(319)* after *Rovit* in the
preceding example is permissible—but not wise. However, a cir-
cumstance *could* arise where you would place page numbers in parentheses after authors' names:

Two Authors' Names in the Text

Rovit (234) and Sherwin (10) come to exactly opposite conclusions.

The overriding concern of the writer should be clarity. The writer should supply information in the parentheses in such a way that the reader has no difficulty finding the source or determining whose ideas are being expressed. Two authors of a single book would, of course, be treated differently.

Dual Authors' Names in the Text

Brooks and Warren regard poetry as a kind of sovereign speech (23–24).

Dual Authors' Names in the Reference

They regard poetry as a kind of sovereign speech (Brooks and Warren 23–24).

If several authors are listed in Works Cited as ''et al.,'' they are referred to that way in the text.

Multiple Authors' and Editors' Names in the Reference

Their descriptions of the various historical periods of English literature are concise yet very informative (Thomas et al.).

Entry in Works Cited

Thomas, Gillian, et al., eds.   Introduction to Literature: British, American, Canadian.   2nd ed.   Toronto: Holt, 1989.

References to Books and Articles

Reference to a Work in More Than One Volume

Jaeger underscores the educational value to Hellenic Greeks of all the Homeric Texts (2:13).

Note: The "2" in parenthesis refers to the second of three volumes. The "13" is the page number.

Reference to a Work Listed by Title

Inhabitants of a large area of the province were outraged at their inability to communicate when their telephones stopped working ("One Million").

In Works Cited, the entry, an unsigned newspaper article, would be found under *O*.

Entry in Works Cited

"One Million Albertans Hit by Major Fault in Telephone Service," The Globe and Mail 23 Mar. 1988: A11.

Reference When There Are Two or More Works by a Single Author

Lustig writes that "students of modern physics have no trouble eating math for breakfast, lunch and dinner" (Scientists 29).

In Works Cited, Lustig is listed as the author of two books, *Problems in Higher Education* and *Educating Modern Scientists.* The parenthetical reference *Scientists* obviously refers to the latter. Note that in this example, the parentheses come after the quotation marks and before the period.

Two or More Works in a Single Reference

Prominent musicians report that from an early age they could distinguish sharply between conflicting sounds (Copeland 379; Thomson 244).

Two references in parentheses should be a limit. More than that tends to disrupt the reader's concentration and should be left for a content note. (See pages 367–68.)

Reference at the End of a Long, Indented Quotation

Clara Thomas' erudition and critical sensitivity are clear to a reader of any of her books. Her summary description of Ethel Wilson's female characters provides a short but excellent example of both and deserves to be quoted in full:

> Mrs. Wilson's women do not affect one with the power or the pathos of a Mrs. Bentley or a Hagar. This does not mean, however, that they are superficial characters. They are ... written out of a novelistic tradition which explores the nuances of morality rather than its great absolutes. They relate to Mrs. Ramsay of Virginia Woolf's To The Lighthouse [sic] or to Mrs. Moore and Adela of A Passage to India and their power lies in the subtlety of their presentation and not in its passion.
> (Our Nature 104)

Note: Long quotations are indented ten spaces, and the references are placed outside the quoted material. Because the author's name is mentioned in the text, it does not appear in the reference; the appearance of the shortened title indicates that other books by Thomas are referred to in the essay. (The presence of ''[sic]'' in the quotation indicates that the erroneous capitalization of *the* in the title of Woolf's novel is in the source quoted and has not been introduced by the writer of the essay.)

Reference to Indirect Source

Fisher said he always suspected that Capablanca was a "timid player" at heart (qtd. in Bell 57).

The *qtd. in* stands for *quoted in*. Whenever you can, you should use first-hand sources, but there are occasions when this is impossible—either because someone like Bell (above) is the *only* source or because the first-hand source is impossible to get to, being available only in manuscript or other documentary form.

Referring to an Entire Work in General Terms

Literature and Psychology covers the field thoroughly (Kauvar).

or, better:

Kauvar covers the field thoroughly.

In comments like this one, where you refer to a book as an entity, you can do so *without* the use of a parenthetical reference since you need not refer a reader to a specific location.

Content Notes

Along with parenthetical documentation, it is sometimes useful to offer a reader information that cannot be included in the body of your text. Such information would include explanations of methods (interviewing, surveying, and the like), conflicts in the evidence you've been dealing with, and multiple citations that seem too long to include in a single parenthetical reference.

Place the content note reference numeral in your text about half a space above the line of text. The notes should be placed on a separate page, labeled "Notes," at the back of your text before Works Cited. Here is a sample piece of text followed by a sample content note:

Text

Victims of abusive husbands are in many cases the middle child in the family and, when growing up, were subjected to certain additional stresses that weakened their potential resistance to being abused by violent males.[4]

Content Note

[4] For a complete review of the suggestive evidence on the

family position of abuse victims and the childhood stresses
that would make them vulnerable, see Baker 23–26, Charles
127–129, and Eamon 345–348.

The purpose of this content note is to refer a reader to research
materials. Other purposes of such notes would be to explain conflicts
in evidence you are presenting, to explain research methods and
tools, or to provide certain supporting materials that would impede
the reader's progress if they were included in the text.

Endnotes or Footnotes

Another form of documentation consists of a superscript numeral in
the body of the text to mark the passage to be documented and a
corresponding note identifying the source. Once, this was normal
practice, and because these notes always appeared at the foot of the
page, they were given the name *footnote*. Your instructor will probably ask you to use parenthetical references. However, if you are
required to use the superscript method, placement of the notes on a
separate page at the end of the essay is the preferred method; these
notes are called *endnotes*.

Number the separate page in sequence after the last page of
your text. Call it ''Notes'' in a title centred two centimetres (one
inch) from the top. To begin your notes, indent five spaces from the
left margin, record the superscript numeral of the note, move one
space to the right, and begin to write the information on the reference.
Number the notes consecutively and double space throughout. If
more than one line is needed for the reference, the second line and
any subsequent lines should begin at the left margin. (See Notes at
the end of the Sample Research Papers.)

If you are using this system, your instructor may or may not
require a bibliography (Works Cited). If one is required, follow the
instructions for setting up a list of works cited (see page 349). Note
the difference between a bibliographic and a footnote/endnote citation.

Works Cited or Bibliography Entry

Moss, John. Sex and Violence in the Canadian Novel.

Toronto: McClelland, 1977.

Footnote/Endnote First Citation

¹ John Moss, Sex and Violence in the Canadian Novel

(Toronto: McClelland, 1977) 31.

As you can see, the Works Cited entry has the author's name inverted, and each section of information (author's name, title, publication data) ends with a period. The footnote or endnote entry does not invert the author's name, separates it from the title with a comma, and then gives the publication data in parentheses. The parentheses are followed by the page number.

After the first citation, references to the same book are shortened.

Subsequent Reference

¹³ Moss 38–9.

Note: if two or more works by the same author are cited, abbreviated forms of the titles should be included between the author's name and the page number:

¹³ Moss, Sex and Violence 38–9.

¹⁴ Moss, Reader's Guide 72.

Notice the details of punctuation and spacing in the following samples of first footnote/endnote citations:

Reference to a Book by More Than One Author

² A. F. J. Artibise, and Gilbert A. Stelter, Canada's Urban

Past: A Bibliography and Guide to Urban Studies (Vancouver:

U of British Columbia P, 1981) 26.

Reference to a Book in Several Volumes

³ Allan M. Fraser, "The Newfoundland Archives," The Book

of Newfoundland, ed. Joseph R. Smallwood, 6 vols. (St. John's:

Newfoundland, 1961) 4: 187.

Reference to a Later or Revised Edition

[4] John Moss, A Reader's Guide to the Canadian Novel, 2nd ed. (Toronto: McClelland, 1987) 72.

Reference to an Article from an Edited Collection

[5] Desmond Pacey, "The Course of Canadian Criticism," A Literary History of Canada: Canadian Literature in English, ed. Karl F. Klinck, 2nd ed., 3 vols. (Toronto: U of Toronto P, 1976) 3: 18.

Reference to an Article from a General Reference Work

[6] "Page, Patricia Kathleen (Mrs. William Arthur Irwin)," Canadian Who's Who (1987): 1074.

[7] "Nahanni National Park," The Canadian Encyclopedia, 3 vols. (Edmonton: Hurtig, 1985) 2: 1191.

Reference to an Article from a Weekly or Monthly Magazine

[8] Duncan Cameron, "The Dealers," This Magazine Feb. 1988: 20.

[9] Ann Shortell, "Policing the Stock Market," Maclean's 3 Aug. 1987: 32.

Reference to an Article from a Learned Journal

[10] Gordon E. Barnes, "Canadian Indian Health: A Needs Assessment Project," The Canadian Journal of Native Studies 5.1 (1985): 24.

Reference to a Newspaper Article

[11] John Kohut, "Banks Showing More Caution Regarding Third World Loans," The Globe and Mail 7 Aug. 1987: B6.

Reference to a Public Document

[12] Canada. Parliament. House of Commons. Debates, Official Report, 32nd Parl., 1st sess., vol. 5 (Ottawa: Supply and Services Canada, 1980) 3.

Reference to Interviews

[13] Carole Taylor, personal interview, 12 Feb. 1988.

[14] Birute Galdikas, interview, Omni July 1987: 76.

[15] James Roberts, interview, The Gary Bannerman Show, CKNW, New Westminster, 11 Mar. 1988.

Reference to a Film, Radio or Television Program

[16] Bayo, dir. Mort Ransen, Jape, NFB, CBC, 1984.

[17] "Puffins and Their Prey," The Nature of Things, dir. and prod. Richard Donovan and James Murray, with David Suzuki, CBC, 1987.

Reference to a Recording

[18] Kenneth Peacock, Songs of the Newfoundland Outports, Pigeon Inlet, PIP–7319, 1984.

Reference to Computer Software

[19] WordPerfect, 4.1, computer software, Satellite Software, 1985.

Reference to Material from an On-Line Computer Service

[20] Howard Schomer, "South Africa: Beyond Fair Employment," Harvard Business Review May–June 1983: 145+ (DIALOG file 122, item 119425 833160).

Subsequent references to these first entries use shortened forms.

As in parenthetical references, include only the author's last name followed by the page number, but end the reference with a period. If you are using two or more books by the same author, add a shortened form of the title between author's name and page number, placing a comma after the author's name. Use these shortened forms even when two consecutive notes refer to the same work.

Documenting Scientific Papers

General practice when preparing to document references in scientific papers is the same as for other papers: record the bibliographic information for each reference on an index card, make clear copies of the information you draw on (see "Reading and Taking Notes," p. 351) and avoid cluttering your Works Cited (or Literature Cited) pages with insignificant or unpublished materials. Include all the usual details of author's name, title of book or article, date of publication, and the numbers of the pages on which the article appears.

When you cite references within the text, however, different practices prevail, depending on the policy of the journal to which you submit your manuscript. Generally, one of three styles will be asked for, as described in Robert A. Day's *How to Write and Publish a Scientific Paper*, 2nd ed. (Philadelphia: ISI, 1983) 42–7.

Name and Year System (the Harvard System)
The author's name and the year of publication appear in the text immediately following the quotation or paraphrase, e.g., "Sagan (1985)."

Alphabet-Number System
This system closely resembles that used for Endnotes. A number in parentheses immediately following the quotation or paraphrase corresponds with a numbered note in the alphabetized Works Cited list at the end of the paper. For example, if a writer were to paraphrase a comment from J.B.S. Haldane's essay, "On Being the Right Size" from *Possible Worlds*, the paraphrase could appear as follows: The eye's rods and cones have diameters about the length of an average

light wave (3). A reader will find the source's bibliographic data following the numeral 3 in the Works Cited list, beginning with the name, Haldane, J.B.S.

Citation Order System
This system is the *same* as that used for Endnotes. A number (either superscripted or in parentheses) immediately following the citation refers the reader to a list of numbered notes at the end of the paper. The materials referred to are listed by number in order of appearance, not alphabetically. The list is titled "Notes."

Acknowledgements
In addition to listing literature referred to, it is common courtesy to acknowledge (on a separate page titled "Acknowledgements") any significant help you have been given by individuals in the laboratory or elsewhere. It is also good practice to give credit to sources of special equipment and other materials, along with any financial assistance you may have received from agencies outside the institution for which you work.

Abbreviations

Abbreviations of Publishers' Names
It is preferred practice to use shortened forms of publishers' names in your documentation. Usually, a single word in the publisher's full name is enough, as in *McClelland* for *McClelland and Stewart* or *Holt* for *Holt, Rinehart and Winston*. Where appropriate, you may simply use *UP* for *University Press*, along with the name of the university, as in *McGill-Queen's UP*; otherwise, the form *U of [name of university] P* is usual, as in *U of Toronto P*. Initials are permissible for such entities as the Canadian Association of University Teachers (CAUT), the Association of Canadian Community Colleges (ACCC), and the Modern Language Association of America (MLA). What is important is that whatever abbreviation you use, your reader can easily identify the publisher's name.

Other Abbreviations

The following abbreviations may be helpful in your documentation:

Abbreviation	Term Abbreviated
anon.	anonymous (the author is unknown)
c., ca.	Latin word *circa*, meaning ''about,'' as in *Mohammed was born c. AD 570.*
cf.	Latin word *confer*, meaning ''compare''
ch., chs., chap., chaps.	chapters
diss.	dissertation
ed., eds.	edition, edited by, editor(s)
e.g.	Latin *exempli gratia*, meaning ''for example''
et al.	Latin *et alii*, meaning ''and others'' (used when citing a book with numerous editors)
ibid.	Latin *ibidem*, meaning ''in the same place'' (once used in footnotes but no longer accepted style)
i.e.	Latin *id est*, meaning ''that is''
illus.	illustration
intro.	introduction
l., ll.	line, lines (now used rarely; the complete words are preferred, or simply numbers, if clear)
loc. cit.	Latin *loco citato*, meaning ''in the place cited'' (once used in footnotes but no longer accepted style)
MS., ms., MSS., mss.	manuscript(s), e.g., the mss. of Chaucer
narr.	narrator, narrated by
no.	number, usually referring to the issue of a periodical, as in ''vol. 6, no. 4.''
op. cit.	Latin *opere citato*, meaning ''in the work cited'' (once used in footnotes but no longer accepted style)
p., pp.	page, pages

passim	Latin *passim*, meaning "here and there, in various places" (often used in indexes)
pref.	preface, preface by
qtd.	quoted in (used in parenthetical notes to indicate a second-hand source)
rev.	revised
sic.	Latin *sic*, meaning "thus, so" (most often used within square brackets within quotations to indicate that an error in grammar, spelling, or punctuation is in the original)
syn.	synonym
trans., tr.	translated by, translator, translation
var.	variant
vol., vols.	volume, volumes

Sample Research Paper

The sample research papers that follow are shown in final typed form. Commentary on the text appears facing each page.

1 A title page is not necessary for a research paper. However, Robert included one at the request of his teacher. Had the teacher not made this request, Robert could have included the relevant information at the top of the first page, beginning at the left margin (see Shorter Sample Paper, page 419).

1   WORD PROCESSING AND THE WRITING PROCESS

Robert Keats

English 250

Section 1

Ms. Claire Griswold

February 23, 1989

Robert's instructor required that this thesis statement and outline accompany the draft he submitted.

THESIS: Computerized word processing provides writers with significant technological advantages as they work through the process of composing and polishing a piece of writing.

I.   The Problem: what is the value of word processing programs and other writing aids to writers?
      A. Computer enthusiasts' claims
      B. The more complex reality

II.   Defining the writing process
      A. The cognitive processes
      B. The creative composing processes
         1. Motivation and generation of first draft
         2. Reformulation
         3. Editing

III. Traditional tools compared to the computer
      A. The attachment of writers to traditional tools
      B. The ease of learning to use the computer

IV.   The effects on writing of using a word processor
      A. Improved attitudes toward the composing process
      B. Improved performance at various stages of the composing process
         1. Generation of first draft
         2. Reformulation
         3. Editing

V.   The Problem Solved: word processing programs are of great value to writers, and although text editing programs are still of limited use, they do offer some benefits.

2 Since Robert is aware that most readers would welcome the idea of making their writing tasks easier, he catches their attention with an imaginary ''ideal'' scene, using examples that cover a variety of practical writing tasks.

3 His introductory remarks complete, Robert states his thesis.

In the near future, a writer may sit down at a computer to compose a piece of writing—a memo, a magazine article, a report on the feasibility of marketing a new line of shoes—fully expecting the computer to assist with many of the tasks that once were the writer's alone. Instead of simply recording what is typed at the keyboard, the computer may someday prompt the writer to inform it of his or her initial problem and then, by asking questions and suggesting alternatives, lead the writer through a process of expanding and organizing his ideas into a reasonable first draft. Later, another program may scan the first draft or other early drafts, correcting any errors of spelling, punctuation, grammar, usage, and tone until—the whole process complete—the writer can print out a copy ready for public consumption, perfect in every detail. This is a dream that many computer enthusiasts repeatedly predict is just around the corner.

This dream, however, is not as close to reality as those enthusiasts would like the writing public to believe. In the first place, writing is a far more subtle and complex activity than any computer can master. What goes on in a writer's mind while a topic takes shape can be imitated in only the crudest way by any of the prewriting, word processing, and text editing programs currently on the market. Nevertheless, progress is being made, and the programs currently available hold much promise for writers

4 Robert digresses from the focus on computers to define a concept (*the writing process*) central to the development of his argument.

5 Notice here that since Robert has used Coe's name in his text, he doesn't use the name in the parenthetical reference—only the page numbers.

at all levels. As they work their way through the process of composing and polishing, both experienced and inexperienced writers can benefit greatly from computerized word processing.

First, it is important to establish in some detail what we mean when we refer to the process of writing. The jotting, elaborating, organizing, and editing already mentioned roughly sum up the activities involved in what most teachers of writing and other specialists in the field call
4 "the writing process." Elizabeth A. Sommers identifies four cognitive processes that writers employ—"planning, translating, reviewing, and monitoring" (6). At first glance, these may appear to describe an orderly progression from first thoughts to final consideration; however, the process is not so simple. Real writers work more haphazardly. "Reviewing" may lead to changed plans, "translating" to changed ideas. "Monitoring" means the writer is aware that with each change of direction, the meaning of what he or she is writing is changed, so further review becomes necessary. Still, while it is granted that the ways in which real writers create meaning do not fit neatly into one fixed
5 sequence, it is still possible to describe them. Richard M. Coe, for one, has divided the writing process (or as he calls it, "the creative composing process") into six phases (297–8).

The first of these is <u>motivation</u>, the desire or necessity

6 In bringing in these specific examples of prewriting techniques, Robert is looking ahead to the comments he will make later about the availability of such techniques for computer users.

that impels a writer to write. Responding to this desire, the writer passes on to the generation phase, a time of
6 planning or prewriting, which resembles the typical pattern of creative activity: first comes a period during which information is gathered and the mind is focused; then comes inspiration of some kind, leading to another period of hard work in which the inspiration is developed. Considered more closely, inspiration can be encouraged by using specific focusing techniques such as "talk then write, freewriting, brainstorming, keeping a journal, and various types of primary and secondary research (interviewing, experimenting, reading, etc.)" (299). The next phase is characterized by the selection and composition of the researched material into a unified and sensible draft, based on the structures of an appropriate genre.

Once the draft is complete, Coe explains, the writer moves on to reformulation of that draft to make it more effective, an activity that may include reorganization and additions as well as deletions and substitutions. Coe's research reveals that the habits of experienced and inexperienced writers often differ markedly when they come to reconsidering drafts. Although reviewing is an important aspect of revision, it is one that inexperienced writers frequently do not practise. Where inexperienced writers often limit revision to polishing or editing—changing a word here, a comma there—experienced writers will do

7 The superscript number following the parenthesis corresponds to a note at the end of the paper just before the Works Cited page. This bibliographic note indicates that the authors Robert has just cited acknowledge other researchers in their remark; this note records their citation.

8 By using quotation marks around the word *good*, Robert implies that he disagrees with its use to characterize writers, preferring the more neutral term *experienced*.

9 Robert uses the contrast between traditional writing tools and the new technology to create a transition to his focus on computers.

much more. In reformulating, "They make significant changes in the substance of what they have written. They qualify propositions, add new arguments ... They make strategic changes designed to make the writing more effective in a given communicative context" (301). By stepping back, they can see where they need to unify the piece of writing by co-ordinating their own purposes with the concerns of their audience and with the occasion. Research into writers' cognitive processes shows that "good writers revise their work continuously—and at several levels—as they compose. Poor writers do not. ... Good writers plan and revise as they go along, while poor writers write without self-monitoring feedback" (Von Blum and Cohen
7 155)[1]. What experienced (so-called "good") writers seem
8 to keep more in the forefront of their minds is the meaning their words are creating for a reader.

Following the reformulation phase—which, depending on the length and complexity of the piece of writing, may require many drafts—the writer enters the editing phase, concentrating on details of the prose style and conformity with appropriate conventions of genre, usage, grammar, punctuation, and spelling. When the editing is finished, the piece of writing is ready for the final phase, publication: delivery of the coherent body of meaning to its audience.

9   In creating meaning, a writer's choice of tools may

10 This paragraph is written in a less formal style, setting a more casual tone to help ease the fears some readers may have about computers.

seem irrelevant, so why use a computer? A pen and paper can record thoughts and feelings just as readily as the most sophisticated word processing system. To a writer who has not used a computer, pen and paper may seem easier to use. After all, writers have been using them since the primary grades, and, as one study has indicated, simply transferring handwritten text directly into a computer does not improve the writing (Sommers 7)[2]. Further, learning to use the computer may itself seem to present a problem; to write by typing at a computer keyboard requires additional skills—first, typing itself, then those skills called "computer literacy," and finally a knowledge of how to use the word processing program (and each one works differently). However, these apparent difficulties diminish when a writer actually sits down at a computer keyboard.

10   To begin with, the new skills one needs are not demanding. In fact, a writer whose typing skills are somewhat deficient can afford to be less skilled at a computer keyboard than at a typewriter; corrections are much easier to make. Second, a writer does not need to acquire much "computer literacy." To write well, one doesn't need to know all about RAM and ROM and bits and bytes, any more than one must know about f/stops and focal lengths to take a well-composed and interesting photograph with an automatic camera. Third, most word processing systems

11 Robert now begins to make use of his earlier definition and description of the writing process (his pages 2–4), working through the process from the generation to editing.

are fairly easy to learn. Although the manuals that accompany them have a reputation for being written in dense and murky prose, the most popular systems provide sufficiently clear operating instructions, and if a writer still experiences difficulty, they can be supplemented by easy-to-read "how-to" books available in many book stores.

Many writers discover that when they use the computer, their attitudes toward writing change, a change of special importance to inexperienced writers who have 11 doubted their ability. Where such writers tended before to ignore the process and worry too much about the product, they now "realize the latter is merely a printed copy they can get in a matter of seconds from the printer. Therefore, the major concern ... is composing the draft, not the final copy" (Lindemann and Willert 53). As one of the students who participated in Cynthia Selfe's study said, "I don't think of separate drafts on the computer. It just seems like a continuous flow of changes and hard copy. Writing a draft is like a re-write of the entire paper and that's what the computer saves you from" (61). In another study, a student called Adam said, "if I had to rewrite an entire page just to make one or two corrections, I would just leave them there" (Womble 78). Experienced writers studied in yet another research project discovered a similar advantage. The one benefit that seemed obvious to them all in the early stages was "they didn't have to retype if

they changed something" (Bridwell and Durin 119).

In other respects, the experienced writers demonstrated significant differences both from the inexperienced and from each other: those

> who planned initially and then executed a draft were most satisfied with what the computer could do for them, probably because their style of composing meant that large-scale problems were solved in advance ... [whereas] those who used the forward progress of their words appearing on paper as "discovery drafts" were least pleased. (Bridwell and Durin 118)

These researchers concluded that the degree to which the experienced writers they studied "found the computer helpful seemed to depend on how they composed, rather than on any specific effects of the technology alone" (118).

As an aid to writing, the computer seems to foster different effects at different stages of the process. Also, writers at different levels of expertise find different programs useful. For instance, experienced writers who have already devised their own idea-generation strategies find prewriting aids of little or no help, even an irritation. Inexperienced writers, however, may welcome such assistance, because a computer program can imitate what writing teachers do in conferences with their students: help them to find inspiration and overcome writer's block, suggest strategies, and provide an audience. A typical problem encountered by inexperienced writers is their

12 Notice the use of "qtd. in" in the parenthetical note. This indicates that Burns' remark was quoted in Strickland's article. The superscript refers the reader to a bibliographic note recording the origin of the quotation.

inability to "transform prose for an audience outside the self. Instead, they create what [one analyst] calls 'writer-based' prose" (Sommers 8)[3]. James Strickland expands this point, asserting that a "writer needs to learn to use language in the absence of context, to learn reader-based prose . . . ," and adding that prewriting programs "can act as an audience of sorts by asking follow-up questions or for an elaboration of an answer" (69). According to Hugh Burns, a pioneer in the development of prewriting programs, such interaction "raises to the conscious level what writers already know about their subjects and makes them write down their ideas. Also the programs have an uncanny ability to ask questions that writers don't know the answers to yet" (qtd. in Strickland 69)[4]. Computer programs that offer assistance at the stage of brainstorming, free-writing, and audience analysis appear to be of most value to novice writers; standard word processing programs are useful to writers at many levels, for both writing and revising.

The individual effort required to revise a piece of writing—that is, to analyze, reformulate, and reorganize it—remains constant no matter how expert the writer or what tool the writer uses. No machine has been built to substitute for human effort and intelligence, nor is one likely. As Elizabeth Sommers points out, computers "alone cannot teach writers why revision is important, or how

13 Robert here is taking care to consider both sides of the matter, providing a balanced argument.

to bring a first draft to full meaning" (9). Balajthy, McKeveny, and Lacitignola concur, stating that using "a word processor will not suddenly confer linguistic or con-

13 ceptual knowledge upon students" (29). However, as Sommers concludes, "The micro-computer is most valuable as a writing tool enhancing our writers' abilities to explore, to articulate, and to reshape" (9), an opinion supported by Cynthia Selfe's study, which revealed that writers tended to produce "more drafts using the computer (an average of four) than they did using traditional methods (an average of two) because they could work with clean copy each time" (61).

Appealing though the uncluttered page may be, one danger produced by the presence of clean copy is the tendency of some inexperienced writers to make "smoke-screen revision," the tendency "to equate attractive copy with a well-written paper"(Womble 79)[5]. Again, the difference seems to reside in the writers themselves. As Bridwell and Durin concluded from their research,

> some students felt that word processing interfered with their creative processes because the quickness of editing didn't allow them enough time to 'mull things over.' For some students, the quick look of a 'polished' text lured them into thinking they were further along in their writing processes than they actually were; for others, the polished look of their texts ... provided a strong incentive to continue revising their papers. (120)

14 Notice the use of ''et al.'' in the parenthetical note. It is an abbreviation of the Latin term *et alii* meaning ''and others.'' Using it, Robert avoids having to repeat all three authors' names.

15 Moving the focus onto the adoption of computers by various institutions allows Robert to show how important word processing is perceived to be, even where a reader may not expect it to have such value.

Despite the drawbacks, most experts conclude that writing with a word processor is likely to improve the quality of inexperienced writers' efforts: "students using word processors are often motivated to deal with higher level aspects of writing such as coherence and idea content"

14 (Balajthy, et al. 28). In short, for a significant number of novices, writing at a computer seems to encourage revision and make it easier to accomplish, helping them to develop more positive attitudes toward the act of writing.

15   Some educational institutions are taking such developments seriously, to the extent that they are investing heavily in microcomputers. In the United States, Reed College and Brown, Drexel, Carnegie Mellon, and Stanford Universities all demonstrate commitment "to the idea that putting powerful tools in the hands of students and faculty can make a difference . . ." (Osgood 165). In Canada, Queen's University, for example, asks all engineering students to use personal computers and makes them available on campus. Roughly ninety percent of all the first-year students take advantage of the purchase plan made available through the Faculty of Applied Science. At Clarkson University, an American institution, all students are given microcomputers at the time they enrol (the cost covered by tuition). Because this institution is primarily an engineering school, one may assume the computers are used

mostly for scientific and engineering calculations, but data gathered by the University dispel this assumption:

> At Clarkson, where a humanities degree is con-
> ferred only once in a great while, budding engi-
> neers, scientists, and business managers are
> using their computers principally for writing,
> rather than for programming, calculating, or
> designing integrated circuits and bridges.
> (Turner 30)

One Clarkson professor interviewed by Judith Turner, while cautioning that "the level of thinking may have not gotten better," was impressed that students were turning in papers which were "pretty much error free" (30). He believed the reduction of errors resulted from writers' using software that helped them correct their grammar and spelling.

The final stage of the writing process, the work of detailed editing and polishing, can be assisted by programs that check the spelling and certain aspects of the style. Spelling and style checkers are not "intelligent," but are essentially search-and-replace routines, entailing "little linguistic knowledge or sophistication. And, of course, they are insensitive to the content and quality of what has been written" (Ross 106). Spelling checkers do present some problems, a major one being that writers often use words that are not in the checker's dictionary; thus, words that have been correctly spelled may be flagged and appear to be errors. This can be confusing for an inexperienced writer. As John Thiesmeyer has warned, if writers "are forced to

16 It is common practice to render titles of computer programs or systems in upper-case letters; compare the similar practice used for names of informational retrieval services or databases (such as CAN/OLE, DIALOG, and ERIC).

look up a fair number of correctly spelled words, they will
soon become cynical ... and prone to guess that some of
their incorrect spellings are correct and need not be looked
up" (qtd. in O'Donnell 363)[6]. This problem lessens as the
size of the word processor's dictionary increases. The best
may include 100,000 words or more; IBM's EPISTLE, for
instance, contains a 130,000 item dictionary.

16   EPISTLE provides a good example of those programs
which, in addition to checking spelling, check style. Like
most of the better so-called text editors, the program

> notices jargon, identifies words with connota-
> tive values ("he hates his job"), and critiques
> clumsy or overqualified phrases ("a very, very
> good idea"). At the sentence and paragraph level,
> EPISTLE comments on fragments and sentences
> that are too long, too short, or overly complex.
> (O'Donnell 364)

Style checkers can be useful at improving what is called
the "readability" of prose, the effort needed to read it, as
measured by standard indexes such as Robert Gunning's
Fog Index and Rudolph Flesch's READ scale (Weiss 154–55).
However, their usefulness is limited. Michael E. Cohen,
who devised a style checker called HOMER, admits that
"No one yet has successfully quantified irony or lyricism,
and what we haven't quantified, computers can't calcu-
late" (Cohen and Lanham 83). On the other hand, these
authors also point out that defining readability by "cir-
cling prepositions and be verbs and graphing sentence

17 When a program or system has been published for general use, its title may appear in the same form as a book title—italicized.

18 Because the information used from Michael Rogers' article begins on one page and finishes on the next, both page numbers are placed in parentheses.

lengths manually takes time and patience," and they go on to say that "HOMER does the bean counting, leaving the ... writer free for the big job" of revising and editing (85). Another checker, called The Writer's Workbench, analyzes such features as spelling, diction, vagueness, punctuation, sentence structure, and readability, among others. A majority of student writers who participated in a test of the system's effectiveness responded positively: "63 percent felt that they were learning more about style and diction than if they had no computer assistance; ... 65 percent agreed that 'if the next composition course I take uses computers, I will look forward to it'" (Kiefer and Smith 76). Another program, called WANDAH (since

17 published under the title HBJ Writer), integrates the whole process—prewriting, word processing, and reviewing and revising aids—into one system (Von Blum and Cohen 158). In future, more such integrated packages are likely to appear, and as the technology moves further into what is called the "third generation," systems may eliminate the need to type. A writer will be able to dictate directly to the computer and, using desktop publishing programs and a laser printer, produce documents that appear typeset: "Old-fashioned typing will soon go the way of the purple mimeo-

18 graph" (Rogers 61–62).

Whatever the future promises, one danger of on-line text editors is that they may replace a writer's creation

19 In his concluding sentence, Robert returns to his thesis question, now including a value judgement, one given substance by the essay's main argument.

Keats   14

of lively, original prose with a narrowly standardized "official" style lacking any individual stamp. Thus, from the perspective of a writer seeking to develop a distinctive style, a "program which teaches students to make corrections is better than a program which makes corrections for students.... We are interested in programs which teach a skill rather than create a dependency" (Hull and Smith

19 100). Heeding this warning, writers can still appreciate the value of a device which reduces the drudgery of "counting beans," and considering current developments, one can predict with some certainty that word processing will eliminate much of the drudgery involved in the writing process and make the process more enjoyable as well.

20 The title "Notes" is centred. These notes are not "content notes" providing explanatory comments but rather what the *MLA Handbook* describes as "bibliographic notes" identifying original sources cited in the secondary sources that Robert used. Three of the original sources were papers read at educational conferences (notes 1, 4, and 6). The notes are formatted as endnotes (see **Endnotes** and **Footnotes**).

20   Notes

[1] L. Flower and J.R. Hayes, "Protocol Analysis of the Writing Process," AERA Conference, San Francisco, 1979.

[2] L. Flower and J.R. Hayes, "A Cognitive Process Theory of Writing," College Composition and Communication 32 (1981): 365–387.

[3] L. Flower, "Writer-Based Prose: A Cognitive Basis for Problems in Writing," College English 41 (1979): 19–37.

[4] Hugh Burns, "A Writer's Tool: Computing as a Way of Inventing," NYCEA Conference, Saratoga Springs, 1980.

[5] Helen J. Schwartz, "Monsters and Mentors: Applications for Humanistic Education," College English 44 (1982): 141–152.

[6] John Thiesmeyer, "Some Boundary Considerations for Writing Software," U of Minnesota Conference on "Computers and Writing: Research and Applications," Minneapolis, Minn., April, 1984.

21 Notice that ''Works Cited'' is centred. The entire page is double-spaced. The first line of each entry is flush with the left margin, and subsequent lines are indented five spaces. This makes it easy for a reader to look up a reference.

21   Works Cited

Balajthy, Ernest, Robert McKeveny, and Lori Lacitig-
    nola. "Microcomputers and the Improvement of
    Revision Skills." Computing Teacher 14.4 (1986–87):
    28–31.

Bridwell, Lillian, and Anne Durin. "Looking In-Depth at
    Writers: Computers as Writing Medium and Research
    Tool." Writing On-Line. Ed. James L. Collins and
    Elizabeth A. Sommers. Upper Montclair, N.J.: Boyn-
    ton, 1985. 115–21.

Coe, Richard M. "Teaching Writing: the Process Approach,
    Humanism, and the Context of 'Crisis.'" Literacy,
    Society, and Schooling: A Reader. Ed. Suzanne de Cas-
    tell, Allan Luke, and Keiran Egan. New York: Cam-
    bridge UP, 1986. 270–312.

Cohen, Michael E., and Richard A. Lanham. "HOMER:
    Teaching Style with a Microcomputer." The Com-
    puter in Composition Instruction. Ed. William
    Wresch. Urbana, Ill.: NCTE, 1984. 83–90.

Hull, Glynda A., and William L. Smith. "Error Correction
    and Computing." Writing On-Line. Ed. James L. Col-
    lins and Elizabeth A. Sommers. Upper Montclair, N.J.:
    Boynton, 1985. 89–101.

Kiefer, Kathleen, and Charles R. Smith. "Improving Stu-
    dents' Revising and Editing: The Writer's Workbench

Keats   17

System." The Computer in Composition Instruction. Ed. William Wresch. Urbana, Ill.: NCTE, 1984. 69–74.

Lindemann, Shirlee, and Jeanette Willert. "Word Processing in High School Writing Classes." Writing On-Line. Ed. James L. Collins and Elizabeth A. Sommers. Upper Montclair, N.J.: Boynton, 1985. 47–53.

O'Donnell, Holly. "Computerized Spelling Checkers and Text Editors—Their Potential in the Classroom." Journal of Reading 30.4 (Jan. 87): 362–365.

Osgood, Donna. "The Difference in Higher Education." Byte Feb. 1987: 165–178.

Rogers, Michael. "The Next Computers." Newsweek 6 Apr. 1987: 60–62.

Ross, Donald. "Realities of Computer Analysis of Compositions." Writing On-Line. Ed. James L. Collins and Elizabeth A. Sommers. Upper Montclair, N.J.: Boynton, 1985. 105–113.

Selfe, Cynthia. "The Electronic Pen: Computers and the Composing Process." Writing On-Line. Ed. James L. Collins and Elizabeth A. Sommers. Upper Montclair, N.J.: Boynton, 1985. 55–66.

Sommers, Elizabeth A. "Integrating Composing and Computing." Writing On-Line. Ed. James L. Collins and Elizabeth A. Sommers. Upper Montclair, N.J.: Boynton, 1985. 1–9.

Strickland, James. "Prewriting and Computing." Writing On-Line. Ed. James L. Collins and Elizabeth A. Sommers. Upper Montclair, N.J.: Boynton, 1985. 67–74.

Turner, Judith Axler. "At Clarkson U., Every Student Has a 'Z,' but Computer 'Geeks' Are Few." The Chronicle of Higher Education 33.15 (1986) 1+.

Von Blum, Ruth, and Michael Cohen. "The WANDAH Programs." The Computer in Composition Instruction. Ed. William Wresch. Urbana, Ill.: NCTE, 1984. 154–73.

Weiss, Edmond H. How to Write a Usable User Manual. Philadelphia: ISI, 1985.

Womble, Gail G. "Revising and Computing." Writing On-Line. Ed. James L. Collins and Elizabeth A. Sommers. Upper Montclair, N.J.: Boynton, 1985. 75–82.

Shorter Sample Research Paper

Robert Keats worked very hard to produce the lengthy paper preceding this page, the major project for his second year course. Had the course been part of his first year rather than his second, and had the project been a smaller component of the course, he probably would have been required to write a much shorter paper.

Assume that this was the case—that Robert had been asked to write a paper of about 1000 words—and consider the following sample paper as an example of how he could have handled a similar subject, using some of the same sources. You will notice that in the shorter version he has concentrated on pages 6–9 of the longer paper.

1 A title page is not necessary for a research paper. Instead, Robert has typed the relevant information at the top of the first page, beginning at the left margin. Notice also that Robert has typed his last name beside the page number in the upper right corner; he identifies each page of the essay as his, in case a page comes loose.

2 The introductory paragraph is short and to the point, beginning with a general statement about the subject and moving directly to the essay's thesis statement.

3 In each documented reference in this paragraph, the author's name or authors' names are included in the parenthetical note because Robert has not mentioned them in the text of the essay. Notice the absence of punctuation between the names and page numbers.

1 Robert Keats   1
  Ms. Claire Griswold
  English 250, Section 1
  February 23, 1989

                Learning to Write at a Computer

2   Many writers discover that when they use the computer instead of traditional pen and paper or typewriter,
  their attitudes toward writing change, a change of special
  importance to inexperienced writers. Some student writers are finding that with the computer's help, the task is
  made easier and they are learning faster at various stages
  of the writing process: prewriting, drafting, revising, and
  editing.
         In the past, novice writers have often given insuffi-
  cient attention to the process of writing, either worrying
  too much about the final product or neglecting to polish
  it as well as they could. As one student reported, "if I had
  to re-write an entire page just to make one or two cor-
3 rections, I would just leave them there" (Womble 78). Now,
  using the computer as their writing tool, many such writers come to realize that the product "is merely a printed
  copy they can get in a matter of seconds from the printer.
  Therefore, the major concern ... is composing the draft,
  not the final copy" (Lindemann and Willert 53). As another
  student said, "I don't think of separate drafts on the com-

4 The name *L. Flower* is placed within square brackets because, although it is the name of the person who used the words ''writer-based,'' it was not used in the sentence Robert is quoting from. The bracketed name replaces the pronoun *she*.

5 Notice here that since Robert has used Strickland's name in his text, he doesn't use the name in the parenthetical reference—only the page numbers.

6 Notice the use of ''qtd. in'' in the parenthetical note. This indicates that Burns' remark was quoted in Strickland's article. The superscript numeral refers the reader to a bibliographic note recording the origin of the quotation.

puter. It seems like a continuous flow of changes and hard copy. Writing a draft is like a re-write of the entire paper and that's what the computer saves you from" (Selfe 61).

As an aid to writing, the computer seems to foster different benefits at different stages of the process. For instance, some computer programs serve as prewriting aids, imitating what writing teachers do in conferences with their students: help them to find inspiration and to overcome writer's block, suggest strategies, provide an audience. A typical problem encountered by novice writers is their inability to "transform prose for an audience out-
4 side the self. Instead, they create what [L. Flower] calls 'writer-based' prose" (Sommers 8). James Strickland expands this point, asserting that a "writer needs to learn to use language in the absence of context, to learn reader-
5 based prose ..." (69). He adds that prewriting programs are useful because they can serve as an audience by asking follow-up questions or requesting an elaboration of an answer. Hugh Burns, a pioneer in the development of pre-writing programs, has stated that such interaction not only "raises to the conscious level what writers already know about their subjects and makes them write down their ideas," but prods their imaginations by asking "ques-
6 tions that writers don't know the answers to yet" (qtd. in Strickland 69)[1]. While computer programs that assist with prewriting techniques appear to be of value chiefly to nov-

7 Notice the use of "et al." in the parenthetical note. It is an abbreviation of the Latin term *et alii* meaning "and others." Using it, Robert avoids having to repeat all three authors' names.

ice writers, standard word processing programs are useful to writers at many levels, for both writing and revising.

The individual effort required to revise a piece of writing—that is, to analyze, reformulate, and reorganize it—remains constant no matter how expert the writer is or what tool the writer uses. No machine has been built to substitute for human effort and intelligence, nor is one likely. As Elizabeth Sommers puts it, computers "alone cannot teach writers why revision is so important, or how to bring a first draft to full meaning" (9), a point reinforced by others: "a word processor will not suddenly confer linguistic or conceptual knowledge upon students"
7 (Balajthy et al. 29). However, as Sommers concludes, the microcomputer works best as a tool to enhance "our writers' abilities to explore, to articulate, and to reshape" (9), an opinion supported by Cynthia Selfe's study, which revealed that writers tended to produce "more drafts using the computer (an average of four) than they did using traditional methods (an average of two) because they could work with clean copy each time" (61). One student found a "sloppy paper (one with arrows and crossouts) confused her and slowed her down. The computer provided her with the uncluttered copy she needed in order to revise effectively" (Womble 80).

Appealing though the uncluttered page may be, one danger produced by the presence of clean copy is the ten-

8 A quotation longer than four lines is set off from normal text as Robert has done here, indented ten spaces from the left margin.

dency of some inexperienced writers to make "smoke-screen revision," the tendency "to equate attractive copy with a well-written paper" (Womble 79)[2]. Again the difference resides not in the technology, but in the writers themselves. As Bridwell and Durin concluded from their research,

8   some students felt that word processing interfered with their creative processes because the quickness of editing didn't allow them enough time to "mull things over." For some students, the quick look of a "polished" text lured them into thinking they were further along in their writing processes than they actually were; for others, the polished look of their texts … provided a strong incentive to continue revising their papers. (120)

Despite the drawbacks, most experts conclude that writing with a word processor is likely to improve the quality of inexperienced writers' efforts: "students using word processors are often motivated to deal with higher level aspects of writing such as coherence and idea content" (Balajthy et al. 28). For a significant number of novices, using a word processor seems to encourage revision and to make it easier to accomplish, helping them to develop more positive attitudes toward the act of writing.

Revision is encouraged even more if the word processor is accompanied by a program that assists the editing process by checking spelling and certain aspects of style

9 In his concluding sentence, Robert summarizes by returning to the details introduced in his thesis statement. He avoids repeating them word for word; instead, he expands on them in ways supported by the main body of the essay.

(e.g., diction, punctuation, readability). M. E. Cohen and R. A. Lanham grant that some factors of style resist computer analysis because they cannot be quantified; however, these authors go on to say that in dealing with factors that can be quantified (e.g., number of prepositions used or average number of words per sentence), the computer "does the bean counting, leaving the ... writer free for the big job" of revising and editing (85). A majority of student writers who participated in a test of the effectiveness of such a program felt they learned more about style and diction than if they had not been assisted by the computer (Kiefer and Smith 76).

9   Considering the progress made to date and the speed with which developments occur, one can predict with some certainty that the computer will continue to make the writing process more enjoyable by stimulating the writer's imagination in interesting ways, by making revision simpler, and by eliminating unnecessary retyping and much of the drudgery involved in editing.

10 The title ''Notes'' is centred. These notes are not ''content notes'' providing explanatory comments but rather what the *MLA Handbook* describes as ''bibliographic notes'' identifying original sources cited in the secondary sources Robert used. One of the original sources was a paper read at an educational conference (note 1). The notes are formatted as endnotes (see **Endnotes** and **Footnotes**).

10   Notes

[1] Hugh Burns, "A Writer's Tool: Computing as a Way of Inventing," NYCEA Conference, Saratoga Springs, 1980.

[2] Helen J. Schwartz, "Monsters and Mentors: Applications for Humanistic Education," College English 44 (1982): 141–52.

11 The title ''Works Cited'' is centred. The entire page is double spaced. The first line of each entry is flush with the left margin, and subsequent lines are indented five spaces. This makes it easy for a reader to look up a reference.

11   Works Cited

Balajthy, Ernest, Robert McKeveny, and Lori Lacitig-
    nola. "Microcomputers and the Improvement of
    Revision Skills." Computing Teacher 14.4 (1986–87):
    28–31.

Bridwell, Lillian, and Anne Durin. "Looking In-Depth at
    Writers: Computers as Writing Medium and Research
    Tool." Writing On-Line. Ed. James L. Collins and
    Elizabeth A. Sommers. Upper Montclair, N.J.: Boyn-
    ton, 1985. 115–21.

Cohen, Michael E., and Richard A. Lanham. "HOMER:
    Teaching Style with a Microcomputer." The Com-
    puter in Composition Instruction. Ed. William
    Wresch. Urbana, Ill.: NCTE, 1984. 83–90.

Kiefer, Kathleen, and Charles R. Smith. "Improving Stu-
    dents' Revising and Editing: The Writer's Workbench
    System." The Computer in Composition Instruc-
    tion. Ed. William Wresch. Urbana, Ill.: NCTE,
    1984. 69–74.

Lindemann, Shirlee, and Jeanette Willert. "Word Pro-
    cessing in High School Writing Classes." Writing On-
    Line. Ed. James L. Collins and Elizabeth A. Som-
    mers. Upper Montclair, N.J.: Boynton, 1985. 47–53.

Selfe, Cynthia. "The Electronic Pen: Computers and the
    Composing Process." Writing On-Line. Ed. James L.

Keats   8

Collins and Elizabeth A. Sommers.   Upper Montclair, N.J.: Boynton, 1985.   55–66.

Sommers, Elizabeth A.   "Integrating Composing and Computing."   Writing On-Line.   Ed. James L. Collins and Elizabeth A. Sommers.   Upper Montclair, N.J.: Boynton, 1985.   1–9.

Strickland, James.   "Prewriting and Computing." Writing On-Line.   Ed. James L. Collins and Elizabeth A. Sommers.   Upper Montclair, N.J.: Boynton, 1985.   67–74.

Womble, Gail G.   "Revising and Computing."   Writing On-Line.   Ed. James L. Collins and Elizabeth A. Sommers.   Upper Montclair, N.J.: Boynton, 1985.   72–82.

Glossary of Usage

Each of the entries in this section discusses words or phrases that are frequently usage problems for student writers—as well as for more experienced ones. Suggestions for correct usage given in the entries describe current usage among educated writers and are based on the best dictionaries and recent studies in usage. Naturally, not every problem is treated here. Elsewhere in the book, you will find a brief list of troublesome idiomatic combinations (pages 110–112) and a list of homonyms (pages 242–246). However, if you are unable to find the word, expression, or rule you are interested in, you should consult either a good dictionary or your instructor.

The following labels are used in the glossary:

Formal: words or expressions of standard educated usage; appropriate to a high level of serious writing. Students are expected to produce this kind of writing in most colleges and in most courses.

Informal: the language of the everyday world. Informal words and expressions occur widely, but are also widely avoided in formal writing.

Colloquial: the language used in conversation, mainly informal. Colloquialisms are used by writers and speakers both educated and uneducated but should, in most cases, be avoided in all but the most informal writing.

Standard: the language used in most printed matter; includes formal and informal, but is understood to stand closer to formal.

Non-standard: applies to words or expressions that good dictionaries label as *illiterate, non-standard, obsolete, slang, dialect* or *substandard*. These are to be avoided in all kinds of writing.

Idiomatic: words and expressions peculiar to a language or dialect. Their use is determined by convention (custom) rather than by logic or grammar.

A, an Use *a* before a word beginning with a consonant *sound*—even when the word begins with a letter classified as a vowel, as in *a university*. Use *an* before a word beginning with a vowel *sound* (*an egg, an orange*) including words with a silent *h* (*an hour, an honour*).

Accept, except *Accept* is a verb, meaning "to receive" or "to agree to," and *except* is a preposition, meaning "other than" or "but."

I *accept* your invitation.
I have invited everyone *except* Kelley.

Adapt, adopt To *adapt* is to be able to adjust to a situation or set of circumstances; to *adopt* is to take in or to agree to a course of action.

Enzo was not able to *adapt* to college life.
We would like to *adopt* a child.

Advice, advise *Advice* is the noun, *advise* the verb.

I can give you good *advice*.
Let me *advise* you.

Affect, effect Usually, *affect* is a verb, meaning "to influence." The verb *effect* means "to bring or achieve"; the noun *effect* means "the result."

The music *affected* me deeply.
We can, through political action, *effect* a change in government.
The *effect* of a shave is to open little cuts on the face.

Aggravate Means "to make worse" or "to intensify." Used colloquially to mean "annoy" or "provoke."

Formal The argument *aggravated* my headache.
Colloquial I was *aggravated* by his attitude.

Agree to, agree with To *agree to* is to consent; to *agree with* is to concur.

I *agree to* the contract, but I do not *agree with* his estimate of how much money I will make under its terms.

Ain't Contraction of *am not*. Extended frequently to *is not, are* *not, has not,* and *have not.* Not only non-standard, but also strongly disapproved by most educated speakers and writers.

All, all of   Use *all of* before proper nouns or pronouns, as in *all of Africa, all of these.* The *of* may be omitted to make expression more concise in constructions like *all of his energy* (better: *all his energy*) or *all of her strength* (better: *all her strength*).

All ready, already   *Already:* "before" or "by a certain time"; *all ready:* "completely prepared."

When I arrived, she was *already* in the shower.
The Cosmos are *all ready* for the big game.

All that   Colloquial when used in constructions like "I didn't like the course *all that* much." How much is *all that*?

Allusion   See **illusion, allusion**.

Almost   See **most, almost**.

Alot   Should be two words: *a lot.*

Among, between   *Among* is usually reserved for more than two persons or things. *Between* is commonly used only for two. However, it is possible to use *between* for three or more items when they are regarded as having a reciprocal relationship or to express the relationship of one to the others.

Among those at the meeting, there wasn't a single New Democrat.
The choice *between* ice cream and pie is easy to make.
There's much competition *between* the three major car companies.
We sailed directly *between* the three big rocks.

Amount, number   *Amount* refers to quantities, like water and air, that cannot be counted individually; *number* refers to things, like trees, that can be counted individually.

The *amount of traffic* on the road is staggering.
The *number of cars* going through the tunnel is staggering.

An, a   See **a, an**.

And/or   A construction found in legal documents. Some find it objectionable in formal writing.

Anyone, any one   Not interchangeable. *Anyone* means "any person at all"; *any one* refers to a specific individual or thing in a group.

Anyone can learn to drive a car.

Any one of those drivers can teach you to drive a car.

Note: This distinction also applies to *everyone* and *someone*.

Anyways   Non-standard for *anyway*.

Apt, likely, liable   *Apt* refers to a habitual tendency or a natural talent; *likely* means "probable" or "to be expected"; and *liable* means "legally responsible" or "susceptible to."

Correct   She is *apt* at solving equations.
Correct   She is not *likely* to go to college this fall.
Correct   He is *liable* to prosecution for assault.

Informal usage sometimes confuses these meanings.

Informal   She is *apt* to go to college this fall.
Informal   She is *liable* to go to college this fall.

As, as if, like   See **like, as, as if**.

Bad   Sometimes confused with the adverb *badly*. But *bad* is an adjective.

She felt *bad* about breaking up with her boyfriend.
She was hurt *badly* in the accident.

Be sure and, try and   Colloquial for *be sure to, try to*.

Between   See **among, between**.

Breakdown   Standard when used to mean "collapse," but colloquial when used instead of "itemization" or "analysis."

Standard   She suffered a nervous *breakdown*.
Colloquial   He made a *breakdown* of our receipts from the dance.

Bunch   Colloquial when used to mean a *group* or a *gathering* of people, as in a *bunch of people*, but standard when appropriately applied to, for example, *grapes*, as in a *bunch of grapes*.

But, hardly, scarcely   Each alone is negative; thus they should not be used with other negatives. See Part 2, **Double Negative**.

Can, may   In informal usage, *can* is used to signify both ability (I *can* play basketball) and permission (*Can* I get you a drink?). In formal writing, many reserve *may* for permission (*May* I get you a drink?). *May* also expresses possibility (I *may* not vote this year.).

Case, in the case of   Cases of wordiness. See that entry in Part 2.

Centre about, centre around Colloquial for *centre on*.

Commence Pretentious. Use *begin* or *start*.

Compare with, compare to Similar items are compared *with* one another; dissimilar ones are compared *to* each other.

> *Compared with* Florence, New York City is ugly.
> *Compared to* an airplane, a bird is a model of flight efficiency.

Compliment, complement A *compliment* is an expression of praise; a *complement* is something that makes up or completes something else.

> The remark was a *compliment*.
> The remarks were a *complement* to the previous speaker's.

Contact There are those who believe the use of *contact* as a verb meaning "to meet with" or "to talk to" is non-standard, but it is in wide use just the same. The trouble with the word is that it is too general, and it is better replaced in writing by more specific terms such as *meet, consult, talk to*.

Continual, continuous That which is *continuous* proceeds without interruption in time or space; the *continual* proceeds with some interruption.

> The Alaska pipeline provides a *continuous* flow of oil.
> We had a *continual* debate over the energy crisis.

Could of Non-standard (illiterate) for *could have* (*could've*). Based on a perception by users who hear *of* instead of *have*.

Couple Should be followed by *of*, whether used to mean *a few* (in colloquial use) or *two* (in formal use).

Data, phenomena Plural forms of *datum*, "a fact used to draw a conclusion," and *phenomenon*, "a fact or event perceptible to the senses." Informally, *data* is used as a collective noun and agrees with a singular verb.

> *Formal* These *data are* invaluable.
> *Informal* This *data is* invaluable.

Definite, definitely Vague intensifiers, used colloquially, as in "He has a *definite* talent," or "I will *definitely* come tonight."

Different from, different than *Different from* is idiomatic. *Different than* is becoming widely used, but should be restricted to introducing a clause.

Rugby is *different from* football.
Rome was *different than* I had expected.

See also Idioms under **Diction**, Part 2.

Differ from, differ with   To differ *from* someone or something is to be unlike that person or thing; to differ *with* someone is to have a dispute with that person or hold an opposite opinion.

Disinterested, uninterested   *Disinterested* means "without bias"; *uninterested* means "without interest." Disinterested is often used to mean "without interest." The distinction is worth preserving.

Due to   Opinion is divided on this. Some authorities criticize the construction used in the sense of *owing to* or *because of*. The criticism objects to its use as a preposition at the head of an adverbial phrase, but this use is becoming widespread and is acceptable in all but the most formal circumstances.

> ***Formal***   Our picnic was cancelled *because of* rain.
> ***Informal***   Our picnic was cancelled *due to* rain.

Each other, one another   *Each other* refers to two people, *one another* to more than two people.

> Bob and Doug congratulated *each other*.
> The Blue Jays congratulated *one another* after the victory.

Effect   See **affect, effect**.

Eminent, imminent, immanent   *Eminent* means "distinguished"; *imminent* means "about to happen"; *immanent* means "within a realm of reality or discourse."

> Ichbal is an *eminent* sociologist.
> Amanda's arrival is *imminent*.
> David's book is on history as *immanent*.

Etc.   Latin abbreviation for *and so forth*. Use it in formal writing only when its meaning is perfectly clear. Since etc. already includes *and*, never write *and etc*. See **Abbreviations** in Part 2.

Everyone   See **anyone, any one**.

Except   See **accept, except**.

Expect   "I *expect* he'll be here soon" or "I *expect* I should be going now" are colloquial. Use *suppose* and *believe* instead.

Fact, the fact that, due to the fact that   Wordy ways to say *that*. See **Wordiness**, Part 2.

> *Wordy*   Are you aware of *the fact that* she's leaving?
> *Better*   Are you aware *that* she's leaving?

Fantastic, fabulous   Avoid these terms of exaggerated astonishment.

Farther, further   *Farther* is the correct word to express physical distance; *further*, the correct term for all other distance.

> His house is *farther* down the road than mine.
> In politics, he is *further* to the left than I am.

> In informal usage, *further* is widely used in both senses.

Fewer, less   *Fewer* is used when countable units are discussed; *less* is proper when an uncountable amount is discussed.

> There are *fewer* calories in diet soft drinks than in regular.
> If the pollution stories are true, we'll soon have *less* water to drink.

Fine   Vague when used as a general term of approval (as in "We had a *fine* meal") and colloquial when substituted for *well* in a construction like "The car works *fine*."

Former, latter   *Former* is applied to the first of two items, *latter* to the second. Use *first* and *last* when there are more than two items.

Gentleman   See **lady, gentleman**.

Get   There are many colloquial and slang expressions of which the verb *get* is part. These are not appropriate in formal writing. Among them are the following: *get with it, get smart, get wise, get lost, get going*.

Good   A good adjective that should not be used as an adverb.

> *Good*   The weather is *good* today.
> *Not Good*   She dances *good*. (Should be *well*.)

Guess   In a construction like "I *guess* you'll be happy with your motorcycle," formal usage would prefer *think* or *suppose* to *guess*.

Guy   Colloquial for *man, boy*, or *fellow*.

Half a   *Half a* is good usage; *a half a* should be avoided.

> *Half a* loaf is better than none.

Hanged, hung In formal writing, use *hanged* to refer to executed people, *hung* to refer to pictures or other objects.

Hardly See **but, hardly, scarcely**.

He or she This is a construction used to compensate for the exclusive use of *he* to refer to both males and females. It is also possible, of course, to rephrase the sentence in some appropriate way:

> *Correct* When a student is well motivated, *he* or *she* earns good grades.
> *Rephrased* When students are well motivated, they earn good grades.
> *Rephrased* A student who is well motivated earns good grades.

Hopefully Used to mean "It is to be hoped" or "Let us hope," as in the sentence, "Hopefully, it won't rain while we're on vacation," *hopefully* is strongly disapproved of by most educated speakers and writers. Colloquially, it is in general use in those senses. Used as an adverb meaning "in a hopeful manner," it is correct.

> The gambler placed his bet *hopefully*.

If, whether Either *if* or *whether* may be used after such words as *say, ask, doubt, know, wonder*, or *understand*.

> She asked if [whether] she could join us.
> I wonder if [whether] you have a pencil to lend me.

In standard usage, choose *whether* when your sentence expresses alternatives.

> I don't understand *whether* you're going or not.

Ignorant, stupid An *ignorant* person has not been taught very much; a *stupid* one is not capable of learning.

Illusion, allusion *Illusion* means a "false image or impression"; *allusion* means an "indirect reference to" something or someone.

> It is an *illusion* to think you'll get a job this summer.
> She made an *allusion* to the fact that she needed the money.

Immanent, imminent See **eminent, imminent, immanent**.

Imply See **infer, imply**.

In, into, in to *In* denotes "within the confines of" or "inside." *Into* is the better word to mean "toward, to the inside of," but *in* is widely used in both senses. *In to* are separate words.

> My shirt is *in* the closet.
> Go back *into* the room and get it.
> You may go *in to* see her now.

In behind, in between Wordy formulas for *behind, between.*

Infer, imply *Infer* means "to draw conclusions from evidence"; *imply* means "to suggest obliquely without actually saying" something.

> He *implied* he wouldn't go on the trip with us.
> Therefore, we *inferred* that he didn't like the people who were going.

In regards to Non-standard when substituted for *as regards* or *in regard to.*

In terms of A vague and wordy expression; to be avoided.

> *Wordy* *In terms of* power, Bell can hit home runs.
> *Better* Bell has the power to hit home runs.

In the case of A vague and wordy expression; to be avoided.

> *Wordy* *In the case of* my Shakespeare class, it's boring.
> *Better* My Shakespeare class is boring.

Irregardless Non-standard. It may have originated because it resembles the standard word *irrespective*. Use plain old *regardless*.

Is because See **reason is because**.

Is when, is where Clumsy and illogical expressions when *where* and *when* are used to introduce noun clauses as the complement of *is*.

> *Clumsy* Capitalism *is where* there is private ownership of capital.
> *Better* Capitalism is a form of economic development with private ownership of capital.

> *Clumsy* A neurosis *is when* there is a disturbance of ego function.
> *Better* A neurosis is a disturbance of ego function.

It is me, it is I The latter is very (almost too) formal; the former is in general use in English as is its equivalent in French (*C'est moi*). See **Case** in Part 2.

It's, its *It's* is the contraction of *it is*. *Its* is a possessive pronoun.

-ize, -wise The former suffix is frequently used to make a verb out of a noun or an adjective (*revolutionize, ionize*), the latter to make an adverb out of a noun or an adjective (*clockwise, otherwise, likewise*), but both are overworked, especially in bureaucratic jargon. Avoid their use except in established words.

> Not "The agreement was *finalized*," but "The agreement was *made final*."
> Not, "*Moneywise*, it was a good decision," but "From a *financial* viewpoint, it was a good decision."

Lack, need, want As nouns, a *lack* is a shortage; a *need* is a condition brought on by a *lack*; and a *want* is a lack of things that are necessary combined with an awareness of that lack.

> The drought produced a *lack* of drinking water.
> He had a *need* for friendship and affection.
> The people feel a *want* of responsiveness to their problems.

Lady, gentleman *Man* and *woman* are plainer and therefore preferred to *lady* and *gentleman*—unless you are using the terms to make real distinctions in refinement. *Ladies and Gentlemen* is a conventional phrase used in addressing various gatherings.

Latter See **former, latter**.

Lay, lie This pair of verbs continues to give trouble. *To lie* is to "rest in or place oneself into a horizontal position." *To lay* something is "to set it or place it somewhere." The only way to correct the trouble is to memorize the forms of this pair.

Infinitive	Past Tense	Past Participle	Present Participle
to lie	lay	lain	lying
to lay	laid	laid	laying

Here are correct examples of the use of each form:

Lie
I want to *lie* down.
After I *lay* there awhile, I had an idea.
After I *had lain* there for an hour, I made my decision.
After *lying* down past lunch hour, I got up and made myself a snack.

Lay

Please *lay* the package on the table.
She *laid* the package on the table.
She *had laid* the package on the table.
I *was laying* the package on the table.

Note: *Lay*, unlike *lie*, has a passive voice:

The package *had been laid* neatly inside the drawer.
The body *has been laid* to rest.

Less   see **fewer, less**.
Liable, likely   See **apt, likely, liable**.
Lie   see **lay, lie**.
Like, as, as if   In formal use, *like is* usually an adjective indicating similarity; *as* and *as if* are usually adverbs or conjunctions indicating equality or that an action occurs to the same degree, in the same way, or at the same time. *Like* is much used in conversation as a conjunction, but in writing this usage should be avoided.

Correct   My daughter looks *like* me. (adjective)
Avoid   My daughter speaks *like* I do. (conjunction)
Correct   My daughter speaks *as* I do. (conjunction)

Avoid   He spends money *like* he's rich. (conjunction)
Correct   He spends money *as if* he were rich. (conjunction)

Likely, liable   See **apt, likely, liable**.
Lose, loose   *Lose* means "misplace; no longer having," or in better terminology, the opposite of *win*. *Loose* is an adjective meaning "free or unattached."

If I don't make an A average, I'll *lose* my scholarship.
My notes are on some *loose* sheets of paper.

Mad   Colloquial for "angry."
May   see **can, may**.
Maybe, may be   *Maybe* means "perhaps"; *may be* is a two-part verb form.

It *may be* necessary to take Vitamin C in large amounts.
Maybe he hasn't got the money.

Moral, morale　*Moral* as a noun is "a lesson" or "a conclusion to be drawn from a story"; the adjective *moral* means "pertaining to right or ethical conduct." *Morale*, a noun, refers to "the enthusiastic state of mind of an individual or a group."

> Does this story have a *moral*?
> Her action was considered to be *moral* behaviour.
> The *morale* among the workers was high.

Ms.　A recently adopted abbreviation to identify women, married or unmarried. Ms. is in widespread use. It can be used when you are uncertain of a woman's marital status. In other cases, the individual's preference should be respected.

Must of　Illiterate for *must have*.

Myself (himself, etc.)　Do not use *myself* where you would normally use *I* or *me*. *Myself* is used (1) reflexively, (2) for emphasis, (3) in absolute constructions, or (4) to indicate the normal, healthy state of the self. All other uses should be regarded as informal.

> 1. I'm going to buy *myself* a new car.
> 2. I *myself* will go to the station.
> 3. A professor *myself*, I nevertheless avoided other professors.
> 4. I'm not *myself* today.

> ***Non-standard***　Darlene and *myself* went to visit her parents. (Formal: *I*.)
> ***Informal***　The property was left to my sister and *myself*. (Formal: *me*.)

Need　See **lack, need, want**.

Number　See **amount, number**.

Off of　No need for the *of*.

Okay　This or abbreviations like O.K. or OK are all okay—standard—but use a more specific word in formal writing.

One and the same　Stale and wordy for *the same*.

One another　See **each other, one another**.

Per　Appropriate only in business or technical writing (*per diem, per capita, kilometres per hour*) but stuffy in formal writing where *a* and *an* are preferable (six dollars *an* hour, four kilometres *a* day).

Percent, percentage　Both mean "rate per hundred"; *percent* may be written as two words or as one, but *percentage* is always written as one. In formal writing, use *percent* to follow a numeral (seventy-five *percent*). Do not use either word when you simply mean *part*.

Formal A small *part* of my home is used as an office.
Formal A small *percentage* of the team lacks spirit.
Informal A small *percent* of government officials are corrupt.

Phenomena   See **data, phenomena**.
Plus   As a preposition, means "increased by." It is informal when used in place of *and*.

Informal Solomon had a high fever *plus* he was breaking out in red spots.

Prejudice   A noun, not to be used as a substitute for the adjective *prejudiced*.

Incorrect The racist was a *prejudice* man.
Correct The racist was a *prejudiced* man.

Principal, principle   *Principal*, a noun meaning "person in controlling authority" or an adjective meaning "main" or "chief," should be distinguished from *principle*, a noun meaning "fundamental law" or "concept."

The *principal* idea was to begin our vacation in January instead of June.
The *principal* of the high school came to dinner.
With her, it was a matter of *principle*.

Prior to   Overblown usage for *before*; avoid it.
Provided, provided that, providing   All three are now considered correct conjunctions.

I will go on the trip *provided that* you take your camera.
He will invite you to lunch *providing* you apologize.

Quite a few, quite a bit, quite a little   Colloquial and wordy when used to substitute for *many*, *a substantial amount*, or *more than a little*.
Raise, rise   Two different verbs. *Raise* (*raised, raised, raising*) is a transitive verb meaning "to cause or help to rise to a standing

position." *Rise* (*rose, risen, rising*) is an intransitive verb meaning "to assume an upright position" or "to wake up from sleep."

He had *risen* at five and gone straight to work.
She *raises* chickens and sells eggs.

Real   This adjective is formally used to mean *actual, true, genuine*. It is not an acceptable substitute for the adverb *really*.

Incorrect   We had a *real* good time at the party.
Correct   We had a *really* good time at the party.

Reason is because   *Because* in this construction is superfluous and should be replaced by *that*.

Informal   The *reason* he can't see you tonight *is because* he has to make up a chemistry lab.
Formal   The *reason* he can't see you tonight *is that* he has to make up a chemistry lab.
He can't see you tonight *because* he has to make up a chemistry lab.

Reason why   The *why* is usually superfluous.

The *reason* she left him is obvious.

Relate to   Abstract and vague when used as a substitute for more specific verbs describing a sense of identity with someone or something.

Vague   I can *relate to* Paul's dissatisfaction.
Specific   I can *understand* Paul's dissatisfaction.
Specific   I can *empathize with* Paul's dissatisfaction.

Said   Adapted from legal language (*said* party, *said* action), it should be avoided in ordinary writing.
Scarcely   See **but, hardly, scarcely.**
Seeing as how, seeing that   Colloquial for *since* or *because*.
Shall, will, should, would   *Will* is now generally accepted for all persons (*I will, you will, he will*) except for questions in the first person requesting an opinion or consent. (*Shall I* order dinner? *Shall* we dance?) or in formal contexts (I *shall* hope to see you on Thursday in my chambers). Ordinary questions about the future still employ *will* (When *will* I see you again?) *Should*

expresses obligation or condition for all three persons (*I should* go swimming; *you should* take a nap; *Paul should* write a letter). *Would* is used for all three persons for a wish or a hypothetical or a customary action (*Would* that he had taken the job! *You would* do it if you could. Every morning, *they would* drink coffee on the verandah.).

Should   See **shall, will, should, would.**

Situation   Unnecessary addition in such phrases as "a *crisis* situation" (a *crisis* will do) and "The *situation* is that we need money" (where the last three words will do).

So   In clauses describing purposes, *so* used in place of *so that* is colloquial.

> *Formal*   We met in a hotel room *so that* we could discuss our plans in private.
> *Colloquial*   We met in a hotel room *so* we could discuss our plans in private.

So used instead of *very* is colloquial and inappropriate in any formal context.

> *Formal*   She seems *very* sad.
> *Colloquial*   She seems *so* sad.

Someone   See **anyone, any one**.

Sometime, some time   The former is used when an occasion or time not specified is meant and the latter when a period of time (of unspecified duration) is meant.

> *Sometime* I must visit the Gaspé Peninsula.
> I must spend *some time* walking up Sherbrooke Street.

Stationary, stationery   *Stationary* means "at rest" or "in a fixed posture or position." *Stationery* is "paper, envelopes," and other such materials.

Stupid   See **ignorant, stupid**.

Such   Colloquial when used as an intensifier.

> *Formal*   He owned a *very* handsome dog.
> *Colloquial*   He owned *such* a handsome dog.

Supposed to, used to   Remember to include the final *-d* in the words *supposed* and *used*.

Sure   Colloquial when used to mean *certainly*.

Than, then   Two different words. *Than* is a conjunction; *then* is an adverb or adverbial conjunction.

> His grades are better *than* mine.
> He had a long, cool drink; *then* he plunged into a cold shower.

That, which   *That* always introduces restrictive clauses; *which* can introduce both restrictive and non-restrictive clauses, but in formal speech and writing some prefer to limit *which* to introducing non-restrictive clauses.

> *Restrictive*   The fruit *that I bought yesterday* is delicious.
> *Non-restrictive*   The fruit, *which I bought yesterday*, is delicious.

Their, there, they're   Frequently confused. *Their* is the possessive pronoun; *there* is an adverb or expletive; *they're* is a contraction of *they are*.

> *Their* eyes stared straight at the flag.
> *There* is no reason to be afraid.
> *They're* going off on a holiday in July.

Thing   Too often used for everything. Where possible, a more specific word should be used.

To, too, two   Distinguish between the preposition *to*, the adverb *too*, and the number *two*.

> If it isn't *too* much trouble, I'd like *two* pounds of candy to give *to* my mother.

Try and   See **be sure and, try and**.
Uninterested   See **disinterested, uninterested**.
Used to   See **supposed to, used to**.
Want   See **lack, need, want**.
Ways   When referring to distance, *ways* is non-standard, *way* standard.

> *Informal*   Davenport is a long *ways* from here.
> *Formal*   Davenport is a long *way* from here.

Where, were   Pronounced differently, these are two different words. *Were* is the plural verb; *where* is an adverb, a conjunction, and a noun. Do not substitute *where* for *that*.

Informal   He could see *where* she was getting ready to leave.
Formal   He could see *that* she was getting ready to leave.

Whether, if   See **if, whether**.

Which, who, that   Use *who* to refer to persons, *which* or *that* to refer to all other things. See **that, which**.

Who, whom   See **case** in Glossary of Grammatical Terms or **Case** in Part 2.

Will   See **shall, will, should, would**.

-wise   Characteristic of governmental, business, or advertising jargon is the practice of converting a noun to an adverb by tacking on *-wise*. In formal writing, this is unacceptable practice.

Jargon   *Moneywise*, it's not a good deal.
Better   *Financially* it's not a good deal.

Jargon   *Defencewise*, we need an organization like NATO.
Better   For *defence purposes*, we need an organization like NATO.

Would   See **shall, will, should, would**.

Would of   Non-standard (illiterate) for *would have* (*would've*) based on a perception by users who hear *of* instead of *have*.

Answer Key to Exercise Questions

Answers to the first five questions of each exercise, except those that ask you to write clauses, sentences, or paragraphs, are given here.

Part 1   A Basic Grammar

Test Yourself on Identifying Nouns (p. 5)
1. elephant   2. notebook   3. light   4. cheese, New Brunswick   5. Blue Jays, team

Test Yourself on Identifying Verbs (p. 7)
1. plays   2. earns   3. is jumping   4. waited   5. trusted

Test Yourself on Identifying Verbs by Changing Tenses (p. 8)
1. plays; *played*   2. will pass; *passes*   3. are; *were*   4. has made; *makes*   5. seems; *seemed*

Test Yourself on Identifying Types of Verbs (p. 10)
1. feel—L   2. smokes—I   3. is riding—T   4. plays—T
5. exploded—I

Test Yourself on Identifying Auxiliaries (p. 11)
1. will, can, may, must, should, ought to, etc.   2. will, do, etc.   3. is, was, should be, must be, ought to be, etc.   4. are, were, have been, should have been, etc.   5. did, will, etc.

Test Yourself on Identifying Adjectives (p. 13)
1. better   2. courageous   3. kind   4. happier   5. childish, greedy

Test Yourself on Identifying Adverbs (p. 16)
1. quickly; slowly   2. up; in   3. out; up   4. there; here   5. sourly; sweetly

Test Yourself on Identifying Verbals (p. 18)
1. *sailing* (present participle: verb)
2. *performing* (participle: true verbal)
3. *prejudiced* (participle: true verbal), *singing* (gerund)
4. *to become* (infinitive), *old-fashioned* (participle: true verbal), *puzzled* (participle: true verbal)
5. *Thinking* (participle: true verbal), *decided* (past participle: verb), *proposed* (participle: true verbal)

Test Yourself on Using Prepositions (p. 21)
Typical Phrases
1. on the farm   2. behind the apple   3. about the newspaper   4. against the automobile   5. away from the ferry

Test Yourself on Using Pronouns (p. 27)
B.
1. She needs false teeth.
2. My grandmother needs something.
3. He or she complained to me.
4. They are funny.
5. All are politicians.
C.
1. his   2. mine   3. everybody, something   4. you, yourself   5. my, him, everyone

Test Yourself on Locating Subjects of Sentences (p. 30)
A.
1. whisky   2. she   3. father   4. hot dogs   5. parents
B.
1. *the charming English teacher* (teacher)

2. *the man in the blue suit* (man)
3. *the beautiful old woman* (woman)
4. *sensible young people* (people)
5. *my mother's old college roommate* (roommate)

Test Yourself on Identifying Basic Sentence Parts: Subjects, Predicates, Predicate Nouns, Predicate Adjectives, Direct Objects, Indirect Objects, Object Complements, Nouns, and Adjectives (p. 32)

A. & B.

               VL   PN
1. My mother is a good cook.

        VT   DO   OCN
2. We elected Anne our spokesperson.

     VT   DO
3. He had an idea.

               VT   DO
4. Everybody likes ice cream.

        VI
5. Some do not.

Test Yourself on Clauses (p. 36)

C.
1. What I want for supper—N
2. Until you come home—ADV
3. that pleases me most—ADJ
4. whatever you do—N
5. whom I pointed out—ADJ

D.
1. (I) The man was Judy's father; (D) who was here yesterday.
2. (I) I can write well. (D) Although I never went past the tenth grade.

3. (I) You're in danger. (D) Whenever you cross the yellow line at the centre of the road.
4. (D) Whoever asks (I) the whole sentence.
5. (D) What you're thinking (I) the whole sentence.

Test Yourself on Phrases (p. 39)
A.
1. in the afternoons—ADV
2. carried in stock—ADJ
3. after a few minutes—ADV; over the trees—ADV
4. Known for his pure tenor voice—ADJ; in the park—ADV
5. To love deeply—N; in life—ADJ
B.
1. The man *walking fast* looked sinister.
2. Karen travelled in *an old car.*
3. *Swimming today* should be a pleasure.
4. She looked like a student *needing sympathy.*
5. He talked *for a long time.*

Part 2   An Index to Usage and the Principles of Effective Writing

Test Yourself on Abbreviations (p. 48)
1. Mr. Tuten; 8 a.m.; 55 km/h
2. 100 cc
3. C
4. South America
5. second sentence: When asked, a spokesperson for CIDA said that last year's budget had been in excess of $2,000,000 and that this year's budget figures would be available by St. Patrick's Day.

Test Yourself on Changing from One Form of Possession to the Other (p. 52)
1. the game's outcome   2. Jenny's tirade   3. the mayor's argument   4. the girl's future   5. my father's impatience

Test Yourself on the Correct Use of the Apostrophe (p. 55)
1. women's; its
2. '60s; wouldn't; society's; theirs
3. Charles' (or Charles's); races
4. Provincial Attorney General's; crimes
5. 90's; 100's

Test Yourself on Appositives (p. 57)
1. , an old piece of canvas with a dozen holes in it
2. , Thomas Jones,
3. , a pickpocket and a burglar
4. , Rebecca Rose,
5. , a book by someone named Tolstoy

Test Yourself on Capitalization (p. 61)
1. Friday; Venus   2. Parliament; member   3. C   4. I; Federal
Government   5. Arabian

Test Yourself on Using the Correct Case of Pronouns (p. 67)
1. me   2. his   3. I   4. she   5. me

Test Yourself on Revising Incoherent Sentences (p. 72)
1. The basket is where I put the apples
2. Cheating the consumer is so widespread that we need a
   permanent Ministry of Consumer and Corporate Affairs.
3. After the heat, the crowds, and the excitement, Jack fainted.
4. Because he suspected a kidney problem and wanted to be sure,
   the doctor wanted a urine sample.
5. The invitation said I was to reply only if I couldn't make it.

Test Yourself on Making Coherent Paragraphs (p. 75)
A. Robertson Davies, the distinguished Canadian writer, was born
in Thamesville, Ontario in 1913. His broad experience as a
dramatist, journalist, critic, and teacher has provided him with a
wealth of literary material. Fourteen plays have been published by
this prolific author. From 1942 until 1962, he was editor of the
Peterborough Examiner. Davies published his first book, called

Shakespeare's Boy Actors, in 1939, but it wasn't until he had transformed his Peterborough experiences into the "Marchbanks" novels during the 1950s that he began to acquire major distinction. He received the prestigious Stephen Leacock medal for humour in 1955. As a novelist, he may be best remembered for the "Deptford Trilogy" of novels, including the much admired *Fifth Business*, which he published in the 1970s. In the "Deptford Trilogy," Davies' fascination with psychology, myth, magic, and theatre combine.

B.
1. Order of sentences: 1, 5, 3, 6, 2, 7.
2. Order of sentences: 1, 7, 4, 3, 2, 6, 5.

Test Yourself on Revising Incoherent Paragraphs (p. 79)

1. My parents always argue with me about my wanting a moped. They say the machines are dangerous, but I believe they are not, because mopeds go only thirty kilometres an hour. Besides, they run cheaply and they're not very expensive to insure. Moreover, the initial purchase price is relatively cheap, too.
2. Cooking is both easy and fun if you observe certain basic rules. First, you should have the right utensils. As the saying goes, "a cook is only as good as his pots." You should buy and use only fresh ingredients. Moreover, you should learn how much heat to apply to particular foods, and, finally, you should save good recipes.
3. A professor I know who is older than I am says that rock and roll is terrible music. But I say it's just a form of what he used to think was popular music when he was young. He says that rock lyrics can't be heard because the music is too loud and that the lyrics are foolish anyway. It may be true that the lyrics are foolish but they are not more foolish than the ones that go with his pop music. Besides, the degree of loudness is a matter of taste.

Test Yourself on the Use of the Colon (p. 82)

1. It is now 2:45 p.m.
2. Whatever he wanted from Suzanne, he got the following: love, affection, kindness, money, or food.

3. The things that need repairing around the house are the following: the eavestroughs, the front steps, the upstairs storm windows, and the leaks in the attic.
4. What do I spend my money on? I spend my money on the following: food, clothing, shelter, movies, medicine, skateboards, lobsters—a lot of things!
5. You need only one thing for a perfect golf swing: control.

Test Yourself on the Use of the Comma (p. 89)

B.
1. Placement of these commas depends on where *all* the boys are sitting. If they are all in the back of the room, then the phrase is non-restrictive and needs to be enclosed in commas; if the boys are scattered throughout, then the phrase is restrictive and does not require commas.
2. eliminate the comma
3. summer,
4. all,
5. no comma if *pretty* is construed as an adverb modifying *slim*; comma after *pretty* if it's construed as an adjective.

Test Yourself on Recognizing and Correcting Dangling Modifiers (p. 95)

1. Before leaving for Winnipeg, we must make hotel reservations.
2. Being a Canadian, he had limited knowledge of Mauritius.
3. Arriving in Charlottetown, he discovered that his suitcase was in Vancouver.
4. To understand one's spouse, one should establish good communications with him or her.
5. C

Test Yourself on the Use of the Dash (p. 98)

1. thing—loyalty
2. we—who have paid our rent—will be evicted, etc.
3. —Catholicism's holy city
4. —a crying shame
5. life—divorce, separation from his children, the loss of his job, the attack of pneumonia—these, etc.

Test Yourself on Identifying Slang and Colloquial or Informal Language (p. 107)
Labels are those applied by the *Gage Canadian Dictionary* (1983).
1. slang   2. slang   3. informal   4. slang, when it means "to embellish" as in "don't jazz up the story"   5. slang

Test Yourself on Selecting the Proper Level of Usage for a Specific Piece of Writing (p. 107)
1. formal
2. informal, inclined to slang
3. informal
4. somewhat more formal
5. formal

Test Yourself on Using Exact Expressions (p. 109)
1. revealed   2. executed   3. understood   4. scarce   5. factor

Test Yourself on Using Correct Idiomatic Expressions (p. 112)
1. to   2. to tell   3. on   4. about   5. to; from

Test Yourself on Identifying Clichés (p. 114)
1. financially embarrassed; fatter than a pig; do justice to; the bigger the better; eating like there was no tomorrow; last but not least; topped the whole thing off; the last straw; eaten myself sick; believe it or not; sadder but wiser
2. in this day and age; life in the fast lane; get on the ball; well-rounded personality; straight from the shoulder; hitting the books; get what you pay for; pass the acid test; beyond a shadow of a doubt; if you want to get more out of life, you have to put more into it

Test Yourself on Using Specific, Concrete Language (p. 117)
A.
1. napped; dozed   2. wolfed; gobbled   3. admit; confess   4. cried; screamed   5. reveal; display

Test Yourself on Eliminating Unacceptable Double or Triple Negatives (p. 119)

1. I don't want anything to do with you.
2. There was never anybody like him.
3. She never had a reason to give anybody a present.
4. He had hardly any friends.
5. There was scarcely a soul in the library when I was there on Saturday night.

Test Yourself on Using the Exclamation Mark Appropriately (p. 122)

1. eliminate   2. C   3. eliminate   4. C   5. C

Test Yourself on Correcting Sentence Fragments (p. 124)

1. . . . basketball court because she wasn't wearing sneakers.
2. I'm worried about my final exams, which come in about three weeks.
3. Professor Urban took me out for an expensive dinner, although he had mentioned to me that he was short of money.
4. Unless I'm given the salary I want, I won't take the job.
5. Whenever he hears the Beatles sing ''Yesterday,'' he's reminded of the sixties.

Test Yourself on Recognizing and Correcting Sentence Fragments (p. 126)

A. Cross out:
1. until   2. although   3. whenever   4. unless   5. because
C.
1. Horses racing together through the surf make a beautiful sight.
2. C
3. convert the period after *goal* to a colon; small *t* in *to*
4. eliminate the period after *dinner*; make the next letter small
5. change the period to a comma and make the *w* in *which* small

Test Yourself on Correcting Fragments by Proofreading (p. 128)

My father was a farmer, (1) although he'd gone to college where he studied technology. Life on the farm was hard, but my

father was ingenious, probably because of his training as a
technician, and he took delight in solving mechanical problems,
(2) problems that would come up with the tractors or the milking
machines or even the plumbing in the house. He never had time
for long vacations, (3) which doesn't mean he ever in any way
felt ''burnt out,'' (4) the way so many of us feel today when we
work long hours without appropriate rest. My father's secrets were
two: he was a champion at resting whenever rest periods came, at
night, for example, (5) when he'd settle down with the weekly
paper by the fire after a good supper. The other secret was the
real sense of joy he took in his work. No aspect of the work on
the land or with the livestock ever seemed to bore him,
(6) although some of the tasks required constant repetition. In
fact, whenever he needed to leave the farm to be present at
ceremonial occasions, a wedding, a funeral, a party, (7) he'd be
nervous and irritable for all the time he was away. It would be
fine if all of us could live a work life like my father's, (8) loving
the labour we performed.

Test Yourself on the Appropriate Use of the Hyphen (p. 133)
1. well-trained; well-paid
2. re-sort
3. C
4. do-it-yourself
5. C

Test Yourself on the Use of Italics (p. 136)
1. no italics for nostalgia
2. *freaked out*
3. *The Vancouver Sun*
4. *Moby Dick; Anna Karenina*
5. C

Test Yourself on Judging the Fairness of Generalizations (p. 139)
1. *Argumentum ad verecundiam.* The prestige of the great book is
   being used instead of an argument.

2. Pure prejudice. The speaker obviously doesn't like rock music.
3. Pure prejudice, fuelled by the malice of envy.
4. Again, pure prejudice—a prejudgement not based upon evidence.
5. *Argumentum ad hominem* and begs the question, too.

Test Yourself on Recognizing Biased, Insufficient, and Statistically Unreliable Evidence (p. 141)
1. Statistically unreliable. The twelve percent cannot be applied to any subgroup of a whole population.
2. Insufficient evidence. "Everybody" the speaker knows may not be a sufficient number on which to base the conclusion.
3. Insufficient evidence. Some Whitehorse residents feel the cold continually.
4. Biased evidence. Those interested in ecology in British Columbia might be the whole population of the province—minus the number of lumberjacks.
5. Insufficient evidence. The sister is just one woman.

Test Yourself on Applying Induction and Deduction (p. 147)
A.
1. A reasonable conclusion. The facts seem to hold up. By analogy we can be reasonably sure that Richard's government experience will fit him for the business job.
2. Not reasonable because other factors are not considered: for example, the condition of the U.S. dollar on the world market and other international economic influences beyond the direct control of the Canadian government.
3. A poor conclusion because it is based on too few facts—one marriage is not a convincing case upon which to base the conclusion.
4. What the speaker "heard" is a weak fact upon which to base a course of action. Besides, if he *did* study, he'd be more likely to be prepared, even for a "springer" like Brodsky.
5. Reasonable. Many temperature readings over many years have gone into making the average. It seems reliable.

B.
1.

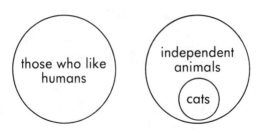

Valid but not true.

2.

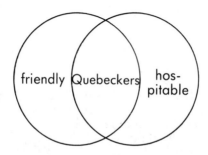

Valid and probably true.

3.

Invalid.

4.

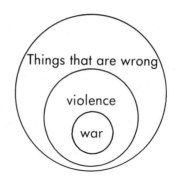

Valid and true.

5.

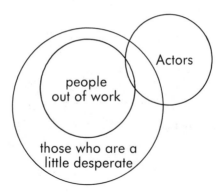

Valid and probably true.

Test Yourself on Recognizing Logical Fallacies (p. 151)
1. post hoc
2. begs the question
3. begs the question
4. faulty analogy
5. hasty generalization

Test Yourself on Revising Misplaced and Squinting Modifiers (p. 154)

1. With this calculator, I can show you in twenty seconds how to make a million dollars.
2. Happily, the sick patient wanted to live.
3. The sunset that we loved stunned us completely.
4. C if the plans were to *depart* either on Friday, Saturday, or Sunday; not correct if the plans to leave—on an unspecified date—were formulated over the weekend.
5. Professors who teach get rich rarely.

Test Yourself on Recognizing Modifiers: Adjectivals and Adverbials (p. 157)

1. adjectival   2. adverbial   3. adverbial   4. adverbial
5. adjectival

Test Yourself on Using Numerals Correctly (p. 159)

1. Two thousand years ago, an important event took place in Palestine.
2. $10,638
3. 908 Queen Street East; 3E
4. thirty-six
5. forty; thirty-seven; twelve

Test Yourself on Developing Fragmentary Paragraphs (p. 170)

1. The more money you make, the more money you spend. When your income is low, you yearn for more—but learn to be restrained. Your low income will only go so far, and you know it. You make a budget and strive to live within the limits set for each category. You are careful to see to it that you do not overspend because you realize that there are limits to what you may spend. As soon as your salary rises, however, you begin to give in to your desires. You imagine that if your salary has risen once, it can rise again. Therefore, the idea of limits no longer has validity for you and you begin to spend more.
2. Television tends to make us passive. The reason for this is that

we have nothing to *do* as television viewers. It's all done for us. Heroes chase and capture villains; family troubles are quickly solved; games are won and lost. Television shows never ask us to think—which is a form of action even if it is internal. Television shows are simple-minded; therefore, they can't ask us to think. All they can do, finally, is ask us to be manipulated. We give in and become passive.

3. Woodworking is not as difficult as it appears. The first thing you need is a reliable set of tools. Once you have the tools, you need to learn the precise action of each tool on the particular type of wood you wish to work with. Knowing the characteristics of the various kinds of wood is also essential. And, of course, a good deal of practice is essential before mastery comes. There are many good manuals that show the best methods of joining wood and there are equally good manuals on wood finishing. Woodworking is not difficult; it merely requires the correct and patient approach.

Test Yourself on Understanding Methods of Paragraph Development (p. 182)

A.
1. Comparison and contrast. There is an argumentative purpose here and the writer intends to argue against the parents' position by making marijuana appear less harmful than alcohol.
2. Spatial development for this description of a place
3. Illustrative details and examples
4. Causal analysis. The writer intends to pursue the reasons why the commercials are dedicated to selling.
5. Definition

Test Yourself on Filling in the Other Side of *and, but, or* Constructions (p. 184)

1. tiger's milk
2. whose father came from Yugoslavia
3. that hasn't been heard of
4. who dresses like a derelict
5. tall

Test Yourself on Making Constructions Parallel (p. 185)
1. eliminate the words *so that we can*
2. . . . philosophy, biology, and term-paper writing (*or* term-paper technique).
3. neat, patient, and proud.
4. falling in love and writing poetry.
5. C

Test Yourself on Using Parentheses Correctly (p. 188)
1. C
2. C
3. C
4. C
5. The author (authors?) of Genesis spoke the stories with reverence.

Test Yourself on Pronoun Agreement (p. 195)
1. Anybody who knows *his or her* music would know Bob Marley
2. The committee did its work in private.
3. Neither the new professor nor the first-year students knew *their* way around the campus.
4. Anybody who likes *his or her* coffee cold is peculiar.
5. When the team scored a touchdown, the band raised *their* instruments to play.

Test Yourself on Pronoun References (p. 198)
1. . . . on the Canadiens' [or Bruins'] home ice last night.
2. C
3. . . . the Federal government and the Métis struggled over the question of native land rights.
4. . . . was one that Peter [or Marc] had thought of some years earlier.
5. . . . it was a wonderful weekend.

Test Yourself on Proofreading Technique (p. 201)
A. Line 2: period after "live"; capital "T"
   Line 3: "They're" for "their"

Line 5: "unprocessed" (sp.); "foods"
Line 6: "plague" (sp.); period after this word. Capital "all"
Line 7: an extra letter in "buttout"
Line 8: "effects" instead of "affects"; an extra letter in "the"

B. Line 1: apostrophe "what's" or "what is"
Line 2: extra letter in "therapy," period after the word; capital "It"; "it's" needs an apostrophe
Line 3: "toward" should be "to"; leave off the -s on the end of "associates"
Line 7: "opposite" (sp.)
Line 8: Here "the pits" really is and must go.
Lines 10: "associate" for "experience"; "his or her" for "their"
Last line: good lesson in this business of "he or she" and "they"

Test Yourself on the Use of the Question Mark (p. 203)
A.
1. Marcia ran the school?
2. Give you my pen?
3. Take off my coat?
4. Jorge likes apples?
5. Susannah likes parties?
B.
1. C
2. . . . ball game?"
3. . . . seriously? . . . paper? . . . session? . . . fairly?
4. . . . correctly?—
5. . . . (?) . . . (?)

Test Yourself on the Use of Quotation Marks (p. 208)
A.
1. The student said, "I consider you one of the best professors in the English Department."
2. Mark said that Ling's ceramics are elegant.
3. Matt said that in his opinion Sabina is a talented actress.
4. Jim said, "The policeman asked me why I was speeding."

5. Maria said to Jean, "I want to see you over Easter."
B.
1. C
2. . . . "Sailing to Byzantium" . . . "The salmon-falls, the mackerel-crowded seas"?
3. . . . "wet" . . .
4. . . . "Elephants . . . cage."
5. That song "Snowbird" was a winner.
C.
1. "You made a fool of me," Margaret said, "and I won't forgive you for it. The name of my article is not 'Childhood Reams' but 'Childhood Dreams.' "
2. She had written: "I don't care for the climate in the tropics," but when I saw her in Edmonton she said, "I'm looking forward to visiting Cuba for the second time."
3. "Can you lend me a hundred dollars?" she asked timidly. Slapping his hand down hard on the table, he replied, "I think not, madam. I never saw you before in my life."
4. "Imagine," he said, "that you are in a strange environment and surrounded by alien creatures. What thoughts go through your mind as you try to integrate yourself into this scene?" he went on.
5. She said to me, "He smirked, 'you're a loser,' and I was startled, to say the least."

Test Yourself on Linking Independent Clauses with a Co-ordinating Conjunction (p. 214)
1. . . . Committee, and he . . .
2. . . . car, for a motorcycle policeman was . . .
3. . . . type, but the paper . . .
4. . . . issue, and the Prime Minister knew . . .
5. . . . Montreal, or she could . . .

Test Yourself on Linking Independent Clauses with a Semicolon and a Conjunctive Adverb (p. 215)
1. . . . write; therefore, he sat down . . .
2. . . . mass; consequently, they paint pictures . . .
3. . . . heritage; moreover, we have a tradition . . .

4. . . . points; thus the car was . . .
5. . . . July 25; therefore, on August 1, he began . .

Test Yourself on Recognizing and Correcting Run-On Sentences (p. 216)

1. . . . swim; there is no better exercise.
2. . . . on the 18th; therefore . . .
3. C
4. . . . fish; therefore . . .
5. C

Test Yourself on Proofreading to Catch Run-On Sentences (p. 217)

Hospitals can really be depressing. It's depressing seeing all those sick people in beds. Of course, some of them get well and go home to their families, but it's depressing knowing that some of them will die in those beds. It doesn't matter. Hospitals are still depressing places.

The white walls are gloomy. The beds are small and narrow. Some nurses are snobbish and make your stay impossible with their aloofness, but some of them are so nice you hate to leave. But doctors are so busy that they have no time for you personally, and they treat you like an experiment most of the time. As for the food, it too is depressing. It's supposed to make you healthy but it really makes you sick just to look at it; even the way it's prepared, the way it looks, causes that depressed feeling.

Some people enter the hospital with a minor illness, but by the time they have been there a few days, they have a major problem. Remember the movie *Hospital?* They had it right.

Of course, it's not all bad. The candy and fruit your family and friends bring can lighten your day, and you may finally be able to read the novel you were given for your birthday.

Test Yourself on the Correct Use of the Semicolon (p. 219)

1. . . . lazy; therefore,
2. . . . bad; consequently,
3. . . . hotel; . . . trains;

4. . . . up; nevertheless,
5. . . . away; however

Test Yourself on Revising Sentences of Monotonous Length (p. 222)

A.
1. Because TV commercials annoyingly insult the intelligence and waste one's time, they should be banned from the airwaves.
2. President Reagan, an actor in California and former governor of that state, brought many business leaders to Washington.
3. Because she wanted to be a doctor, she studied chemistry and biology, putting in long hours in order to get good grades. Then when her final year arrived, she applied to medical school and was accepted.
4. When the doctor came, he took my temperature, checked my heart and blood pressure, and prescribed some medicine. Then he said I'd probably recover in a few days.
5. Since I needed a job, I looked at want ads, went to employment agencies, and even visited a number of factories and offices. I got very tired, but I finally landed a job.

B.
1. As the train entered the station, I got ready to board, but when I found I'd left my bag in the checkroom, I ran back inside the waiting room to get it.
2. The *Star Wars* trilogy was a very successful series and broke many box office records, showing that science fiction adventure films appeal greatly to the movie-going public.
3. There are thousands of Canadian university students, most of whom believe that they need this education to get better jobs, but the job market is not encouraging the hopes of these students, some of whom might do better in vocational training.
4. Dedicated members of the volunteer fire department, who give much of their time in public service, are not appreciated enough and often feel bitter because of this.
5. For a while, soccer was the fastest growing sport in America, having as many as 70,000 fans turn out for a single game, but even Pelé's giving the sport a boost failed to save the NASL from decline and eventual collapse.

Test Yourself on Achieving Sentence Variety (p. 225)
1. Because the car had broken down the night before, they had to take the bus to school.
2. Holding a fund-raiser at the Château Laurier, the Liberal Party attracted a surprising number of young people.
3. Because his grades were poor and his scholarship money almost gone, he knew he had to do something.
4. Working all night at the site of the cave-in, the rescue team was unable to stop for dinner.
5. When readers with lively imaginations read *The Hobbit*, they project themselves into its adventurous moments.

Test Yourself on Correcting Shifts (p. 230)
1. People need to be praised when *they* work hard and accomplish *their* goals.
2. . . . argued . . . asked . . .
3. . . . went . . . asked; or . . . goes . . . asks . . .
4. . . . him—or herself (not themselves)
5. My wife said she was thirsty and asked me to please get her a glass of water.

Test Yourself on *ie* and *ei* (p. 235)
1. friend   2. conceive   3. belief   4. achievement
5. experience

Test Yourself on Final Silent *-e* (p. 237)
1. moving   2. proving   3. movement   4. peaceable
5. changeable

Test Yourself on Final *-y* (p. 238)
1. occupying   2. loneliness   3. annoying   4. piles   5. turkeys

Test Yourself on Spelling Rules 1–4 (p. 241)
1. occasionally   2. Sheik   3. sensible
commitment   4. proceed   5. perceived

Test Yourself on Catching Spelling Errors by Proofreading (p. 252)
1. stud*y*ing, activit*y*, le*i*sure, con*f*erences
2. calend*a*r, panic*k*ed, shop*p*ing, fee*l*ing, inte*l*ligent, begi*n*ning, paral*l*el

Test Yourself on Limiting a Topic (p. 262)
A.
1. Clothing fashions (volumes)—Clothing Fashions in Canada (volumes)—Clothing Fashions in Nova Scotia (volumes)—Informal Clothing Fashions in Nova Scotia (still volumes)—Informal Clothing Fashions on Campus (20 pp.)—The Role of Designer Jeans on Campus (750 words)
2. Education—Education in Canada—Higher Education in Canada—Higher Education in My Province—Education on My Campus—My Education on Campus—My Education in Biology—My Troubles at the Beginning of Biology 101 (750 words)
3. Television—Prime-Time Television—Science Series on Prime-Time Television—The Science Series Hosted by David Suzuki—The Values David Suzuki Professes as Host of his Science Series—What David Suzuki Likes Most (750 words)
4. Student self-government—Student Self-Government in Universities and Colleges in Canada—Student Self-Government in My School—The Student Union at My School—The Duties of the Student President at My School (750 words)

B.
1. The Prospects of the Boston Celtics in NBA Basketball This Year
2. A Day on Vacation in Quebec City
3. Testing the Quality of Water from Your Kitchen Tap
4. David Peterson's Resistance to the Free Trade Agreement
5. How Brewing Companies Link Popularity and Beer Drinking

Test Yourself on Subject-Verb Agreement (p. 263)
A.
1. Cars are his main interest.

2. My only hobby is rock and roll records.
3. Dollars are our greatest need.
4. The cause of his breakdown was many days of non-stop studying.
5. The cause of his drunkenness was too many drinks on an empty stomach.

B.
1. He amuses himself when he has no toys to play with.
2. These turn me off.
3. They seem to like being fed by the children.
4. Those force the argument in another direction.
5. It happens a lot more often than you think.

Test Yourself on Subject-Verb Agreement with Compound Subjects and *either/or, neither/nor* Subjects (p. 265)

1. *father* or *mother* (singular); *are* (plural), should be changed to *is*.
2. C
3. *Professional* and *rich man* (plural subject); *decides* (singular verb) should be changed to *decide*.
4. *Coffee and croissants* (plural subject); *is* (singular verb) should be changed to *are*.
5. Were the sofa and chair on sale?

Test Yourself on Subject-Verb Agreement with Collective Nouns as Subjects (p. 267)

Following are the correct verbs.
1. decides   2. renders   3. is   4. are   5. votes

Test Yourself on Choosing the Correct Verb for Subjects Modified by Phrases and Clauses (p. 268)

Following are the correct verbs.
1. looks   2. want   3. is   4. lies   5. punches

Test Yourself on Subject-Verb Agreement in Special Cases (p. 272)

1. is   2. involves   3. were   4. requires   5. depresses

Test Yourself on Proofreading to Catch Subject-Verb Agreement Errors (p. 272)

1. . . . There *are*. . . Rising up from the tables at cafés *is* . . . One of those who *sing* . . . Neither Lazare nor I *am* . . . Lazare *thinks*
2. . . . mother or my father *is* . . . living . . . *has* . . . music . . . *is* . . . Economics . . . *is* . . . sisters *understand*

Test Yourself on Subordination (p. 276)

A.
1. Mila has a lovely, blue cotton shirt which she likes to take to the beach and walk around in.
2. The television set I paid four hundred dollars for is broken again. Whenever it happens, I get furious.
3. Air pollution is a problem that affects us all, whether we live in the city or the country.
4. It was raining in Kingston when we left, but when we arrived in Niagara Falls, that city surprised us with its sunlit beauty.
5. My English friend's name is Colin. Although he loves Toronto, he occasionally longs to return to Manchester.

B.
1. While my hair is drying, I'll read a book.
2. When I eat too much pastry, I gain a lot of weight.
3. A whole set of encyclopedias came in the mail, although I didn't order them.
4. Whenever you see a rainbow across the meadow, you know there's been a recent rainstorm.
5. Although Julie was unpacking, Peter was cooking supper.

Test Yourself on Recognizing an Appropriate Thesis Statement (p. 280)

1. Effective
2. Effective
3. This one might be effective, but the writer would need to launch immediately into a definition of ''stylish'' and follow up with very striking details of Aunt Ruth's dress. The problem with the statement is the vagueness of the phrase ''stylish dresser.''

4. Not effective. Too general. Should be limited by making more precise the audience it describes as ''punks.''
5. Effective

Test Yourself on Making Effective Transitions (p. 283)
1. She had given Mario a handsome wedding gift; moreover, she had offered him a well-paying job with the firm.
2. He stood in a small ravine; close by was a running brook.
3. Although the world is running out of fossil fuels and our oil supply is diminishing, research and development for new energy sources are at a standstill.
4. She received a receipt for her tuition; consequently, she was able to register.
5. She wanted to go to the seashore. He, on the other hand, preferred the mountains.

Test Yourself on Identifying Topic Sentences (p. 287)
1. First paragraph: the second sentence. Second paragraph: the first sentence. Third paragraph: the first sentence.
2. Implied: a description of preparing a prisoner to be hanged.
3. The first sentence
4. Implied: an argument for allowing more refugees into Canada.
5. The first sentence

Test Yourself on Achieving Unity in Paragraphs (p. 289)
A. Basketball is a game requiring great physical skills and co-ordination. Players must be able to run backward as well as forward. They must have good peripheral vision in order to see their teammates and their opponents. In order to leap for the ball off the backboards, players must have excellent timing. Timing is also important in passing and shooting—the exact moment counts in basketball. The speed at which the game is played necessitates the players acquiring these skills.

Test Yourself on Forming the Tenses of Irregular Verbs (p. 296)
1. arisen, to sing
2. drank, chose, lay
3. brought, brought, shaken

4. laid, taken, lent
5. spun, shone

Test Yourself on Forming Principal Parts (p. 298)

1. keep, keeping
2. lost, losing, lost
3. play, playing, played
4. told, telling
5. pursued, pursuing, pursued

Test Yourself on Forming Tenses (p. 299)

1. played, grown
2. giving, prepared
3. run, operated, driven
4. happened
5. punish

Test Yourself on the Correct Use of Tenses (p. 303)

1. will lose
2. will have been
3. entered, had rearranged
4. have learned
5. had bitten

Test Yourself on the Final -*d* Sound (p. 304)
B.

Something was needed to cheer me up. I was tired and
hadn't been to bed in two days. I thought I would never be
rescued and I was worried that even my best friends would not
have noticed me gone. My foot hurt a lot from when I had slipped
down the side of the gully, and I would have given anything for a
little sip of water.

A bird started to chirp. I wished I were as happy as he was. I
wished I were as happy as he was. I wished I had his wings!

The accident must have happened because I wasn't as young
as I used to be. Still, I was only twenty-three! Are people
supposed to lose all their agility after the age of nineteen? It all
weighed on my heart. Suddenly, I noticed that the sky was getting

very dark. If anybody looked for me now, they would have a hard time seeing me. I tried to move a little, to see if I could climb to the crest of the hill and make myself more visible. But it was no use. I wished I had climbed up there earlier, when I had more strength.

Test Yourself on Sequence of Tenses (p. 307)
1. has diminished
2. having finished
3. to go
4. to publish
5. had neglected

Test Yourself on the Correct Use of Verb Forms (p. 310)
A.
1. If he had gone earlier, he would have seen the pre-game show.
2. Because it had the best forestry program she could find, she went to the University of British Columbia.
3. I could have been a star.
4. She wasn't as alert as she should have been.
5. If he had gone earlier, he would have seen the pre-game show.
B.
1. be   2. were   3. be   4. suffer   5. be

Test Yourself on the Appropriate Use of the Active Voice (p. 312)
A.
1. The book bored me.
2. Dr. Waldhorn's patients respected him. *Or* His patients respected Dr. Waldhorn.
3. Joe's dog annoys everyone on my block.
4. Most people admire the rich and the famous.
5. Disrespect angers the police.
B.
1. My mother thinks I'm too young to drive.
2. C—if the writer is focusing on the Bruins
3. Slaves sought freedom.

4. My brother gave me the ring for Christmas.
5. More and more people in this country watch television.

Test Yourself on Eliminating Redundancies (p. 316)
1. Paul is an expert in urban government.
2. Professor De Groot referred to the War of 1812.
3. Yesterday's snow is melting today.
4. At 9 a.m., the driver started toward Moncton.
5. As soon as he started to look for a job, he connected with a large corporation.

Test Yourself on Eliminating Wordiness (p. 318)
1. My speech will interest students and professional educators.
2. Be quiet in the library.
3. Whenever he's in trouble, he rationalizes.
4. I'd like to take you to a special beach.
5. To be chronically sick is terrible.

Test Yourself on Identifying or Narrowing Down to a Suitable Topic (p. 328)
1. This is not suitable because it can be written from a single source. Narrowing it will not help much either.
2. This is much too large for a student research paper. It can be narrowed to something like "The Effects of Communication Satellites on the Northwest Territories."
3. Though it would benefit from narrowing, this is a suitable topic. Both books and government documents should provide sufficient details.
4. This is a good topic. Current periodicals will provide the sources for research.
5. This is a good topic for both direct investigation and research into periodicals, particularly newspapers that appeared at election times.

Index

To the owner of this book:

We are interested in your reaction to *The Portable Canadian Handbook* by Keith Gilley and William Herman.

1. What was your reason for using this book?

_____ university course   _____ continuing education course
_____ college course   _____ personal interest
                               _____ other (specify)

2. In which school are you enrolled?_____

3. Approximately how much of the book did you use?

_____ $1/4$ _____ $1/2$ _____ $3/4$ _____ all

4. What is the best aspect of the book?

5. Have you any suggestions for improvement?

6. Is there anything that should be added?

Fold here
- -